# STUDY GUIDE

# Principles of Microeconomics

## FOURTH EDITION

Taylor

## David H. Papell
*University of Houston*

## Wm. Stewart Mounts, Jr.
*Mercer University*

## John Solow
*University of Iowa*

HOUGHTON MIFFLIN COMPANY   BOSTON   NEW YORK

Sponsoring Editor: Ann West
Editorial Associate: Tonya Lobato
Senior Manufacturing Coordinator: Priscilla J. Bailey
Executive Marketing Managers: Andy Fisher

Printed in the U.S.A.

ISBN: 0–618–23004–1

123456789 -POO - 07 06 05 04 03

# Contents

# PREFACE

The chapters of this study guide follow those of John B. Taylor's *Principles of Microeconomics*, Fourth Edition. Why use this study guide? The best reason is to help you learn the course content more efficiently. For each chapter of the book, this study guide highlights the major concepts, defines the most important terms, shows you how to work problems, and provides you numerous opportunities to test your understanding of the material.

## WHAT YOU'LL FIND HERE

Each chapter begins with a *Chapter Overview*, which introduces the major topics covered in the text. This is followed by a *Chapter Review*, which defines and explains the key terms and concepts. Next comes a section called *Zeroing In*, which provides a more in-depth look at several of the chapter's most important topics. In this section, figures are often used to illustrate concepts.

The focus of the study guide chapter changes with the next section, called *Active Review*, which consists of a total of 40 to 50 fill-in, true-false, and short-answer questions. You will find answers to all review questions, including explanations for the true-false and short-answer questions, at the end of each chapter.

An important part of studying economics is learning how to solve problems, and the study guide provides you with extensive assistance in this area. The section called *Working It Out* begins by explaining how to use the techniques covered in the chapter. These may be analytical, graphical, numerical, or algebraic. Next comes several *Worked Problems*, for which complete answers are provided. These are followed by *Practice Problems*, for which the answers can be found at the end of each chapter.

Each chapter ends with a twenty-question multiple-choice *Chapter Test*. This test covers material from throughout the chapter and contains several graph-based and table-based questions. The answers to the chapter test can also be found at the end of the chapter.

This study guide also contains a multiple-choice *Sample Test* at the end of each text part—covering material from all the chapters in that part. There are four of these *Sample Tests* (and answers) in this volume.

## HOW TO MAKE THE BEST USE OF THIS BOOK

Every student studies differently, and we do not presume to tell you how to study most effectively. Nevertheless, here are some suggestions. First, read the chapter in the text but don't worry too much about understanding everything. Second, read the *Chapter Overview, Chapter Review*, and *Zeroing In* sections in the study guide. When you find a concept that you do not understand, look it up in the text. Third, answer the *Active Review* questions. Write down your answers and provide explanations for the true-false questions. When you miss a question, refer back to the text or study guide. Fourth, learn how to solve the problems in the *Working It Out* section. Study the *Worked Problems*, and answer the *Practice Problems*. Fifth, carefully read the chapter in the text to make sure that you understand it completely. Sixth, take the *Chapter Test* as if you were taking an exam. If you miss any questions, don't just find the correct answer at the end of the chapter, but go back to the appropriate sections of the text and study guide to make sure that you learn the material. Finally, when you reach the end of a part, take the multiple-choice *Sample Test*, again under exam conditions. You will be well prepared for the midterm and final. Good luck!

# PART 1

# Introduction to Economics

Scarcity exists because people's wants exceed their resources (or means). This forces them to make choices concerning the wants they will fill and the way they will use their resources. Economists investigate this behavior in order to explain facts and observations about the economy. Economists establish patterns by carefully organizing data and present this information in tables and graphs. They develop models of behavior and test them with data that have been collected. Chapters 1 through 4 address the fundamental questions of economics and the basics of "economic thinking."

Within a market economy, basic economic questions are answered by buyers (demand) and sellers (supply) interacting in markets and guided by prices. Demand and supply curves are graphical representations of the actions of individuals. Changes in demand and supply (seen as shifts in the demand and supply curves) introduce surpluses or shortages into the market and thereby change the market price. An actual market price moves toward the equilibrium price. In addition, the price elasticity of demand and supply quantifies the responsiveness of market participants to changes in prices. While governments can affect market processes by instituting price ceilings and price floors, free competition between buyers and sellers promotes economic efficiency, maximizes social welfare, and minimizes the deadweight loss.

*Scarcity - people's wants exceed resources*
*buyers - demand ; sellers - supply*
*Demand & supply curves - graphical representations*
*of the actions of the individuals*
*+ changes in these curves = surplus or shortages →*
*market price*

# CHAPTER 1

# The Central Idea

## CHAPTER OVERVIEW

Economic interactions involve scarcity and choice. Time and income are limited, and people choose among alternatives every day. In this chapter, we study the choices people make when faced with a scarcity of resources and the economic interactions among people when they make their choices. We begin by looking at scarcity, choice, and interaction for individuals. We study consumer and producer decisions, learn about the gains from trade, and see how the same principles that guide interactions between individuals can be used to study interactions between countries. We then look at scarcity and choice for the economy as a whole, and introduce the production possibilities curve. We conclude by studying two alternative economic systems, the market economy and the command economy, and by focusing on the role of prices.

## CHAPTER REVIEW

1.  **Scarcity** is a situation in which people's wants exceed their resources. Scarcity is a fact of life; wants are unlimited, but resources are not. Because of scarcity, people must make a **choice**—to forgo, or give up, one thing in favor of another. **Economics** is the study of how people deal with scarcity. They make *purposeful choices* with *scarce resources* and *interact* with other people when they make their choices.

2.  **Economic interaction** between people occurs when they trade or exchange goods and services with each other. Economic interactions occur in **markets**, arrangements where buyers and sellers can interact with each other, and within *organizations* such as families, firms, universities, and governments.

3.  The **opportunity cost** of a choice is the value of the forgone alternative that was not chosen. The opportunity cost of football tickets is dinner, and the opportunity cost of studying economics is not doing as well in the physics test.

4.  Economic interactions often involve **gains from trade**. Suppose that you can afford season tickets for either football or basketball, but not both, and that you would prefer attending half of the football games and half of the basketball games to attending all of either. If you could find someone with similar preferences to trade tickets with, you would both be better off. Gains from trade can occur in markets, such as a ticket agency, or in organizations, such as a family or a college dormitory.

5.  Individual producers also face scarcity and choice; you cannot produce unlimited goods with limited time and resources. Gains from trade allow people to **specialize** in what they are good at. If a guitarist and a drummer form a rock group, **division of labor** allows each to concentrate on playing one instrument.

6.  One person or group of people has a **comparative advantage** in producing one good relative to another good if they can produce with comparatively less time, effort, or resources than another person can produce that good. In the above example, production can be increased if the guitarist plays the guitar and the drummer plays the drums, rather than both trying to play both

instruments. (There is one subtle aspect of the idea of comparative advantage: Even if the guitarist plays both the guitar and the drums better than the drummer, the guitarist will be able to play one instrument, presumably the guitar, and the drummer will be able to play the other instrument, presumably the drums, *comparatively* better than the other musician.)

7.  **International trade** occurs when individuals who live in different countries trade with each other. There are gains from international trade for the same reasons that there are gains from trade within a country: By trading, people can either better satisfy their preferences for goods or better utilize their comparative advantage.

8.  **Production possibilities** represent the alternative choices of goods that the economy can produce. Consider an economy that produces two goods, steel and food. If it produces more of one, it must produce less of the other. The opportunity cost of producing more steel is the value of the forgone food. The idea of **increasing opportunity costs** is that as steel production rises, the value of the forgone food increases. The rate of decline in food production increases as we produce more steel.

## ZEROING IN

1.  The **production possibilities curve** is a graphical representation of the idea of production possibilities. We will see how to construct the production possibilities curve, what causes a movement along the curve, and what causes the curve to shift.

    a.  Figure 1.1 depicts the production possibilities curve for steel and food. Steel is on the vertical axis, and food is on the horizontal axis. Both are measured in tons. If the economy devotes all of its resources to either steel or food production, it can produce the maximum amount of one and none of the other. The production possibilities curve slopes downward and is bowed out from the origin. The curve is bowed out because the opportunity cost of producing food increases as more food is produced. As more resources are shifted from steel to food production, each additional ton of food means a greater loss of steel produced.

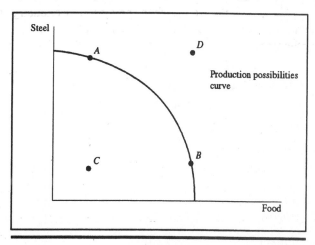

**Figure 1.1**

    b.  The production possibilities curve shows three situations. Points on the curve are *efficient* because they represent the maximum amount that can be produced with available resources. Production of food can be raised only by lowering production of steel, such as by moving from point *A* to point *B*. Points inside the production possibilities curve, such as point *C*, are *inefficient*. Using the same resources, the economy could produce more steel, more food, or both. Points outside the production possibilities curve, such as point *D*, are *impossible*. The economy does not have the resources to produce those quantities of steel and food.

c.    It is important to understand the distinction between movements along a curve and shifts of the curve. A change in the production of one of the variables on the axes causes a movement along the production possibilities curve. For example, an increase in steel production is a movement from point *B* to point *A* in Figure 1.1. Economic growth causes an outward shift in the production possibilities curve. When there is economic growth, more resources are available, and more goods and services can be produced. The effects of economic growth are illustrated in Figure 1.2. The production possibilities curve shifts out from the curve labeled "Original" to the curve labeled "Growth."

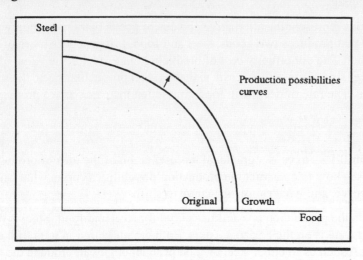

**Figure 1.2**

2.    Every economy focuses on three essential questions: *What* goods and services are to be produced? *How* are these goods and services to be produced? and *For whom* are the goods and services to be produced? In a **market economy**, these decisions are made by consumers, firms, governments, and other organizations interacting in markets. In a **command economy**, these decisions are made through a central plan by those who control the government. A command economy is also called a centrally planned economy. One of the most important economic events of recent years has been the attempt by the countries of Eastern Europe, the former Soviet Union, and China to make the transition from command economies to market economies.

3.    There are a number of important characteristics that distinguish market economies from command economies, and we consider some of these differences.

a.    **Freely determined prices**, set by individuals and firms, are an essential characteristic of a market economy. In a command economy, most prices are set by the government. **Property rights**, the legal authority to keep or sell property, provide **incentives** for invention and specialization and are another key element of a market economy. Competitive markets and freedom to trade at home and abroad also characterize market, but not command, economies.

b.    The role of government in a market economy is a subject of much debate among economists. It is generally agreed that the government should provide for defense, help establish property rights, and keep the overall price level stable, but modern governments do much more. **Market failure** is a situation in which the market economy does not provide good enough answers to the three questions posed above—what, how, and for whom—and in which there is a role for government in improving the market outcome. However, when the government, even in the case of market failure, does worse than the market would have done if left on its own, there is **government failure**.

c.   Many of the economic interactions in market economies take place within organizations, such as firms, households, and universities, instead of in markets. One important reason why organizations are created is that they reduce market *transaction costs*, the costs of buying and selling. These costs include the cost of finding a buyer or a seller and the cost of reaching agreement on a price.

d.   Prices play three important roles in a market economy. They serve as *signals* about what should be produced and consumed when there are changes in tastes or technology, they provide *incentives* to people to alter their production or consumption, and they affect the *distribution of* income.

## ACTIVE REVIEW

## Fill-In Questions

1.   _____Scarcity_____ is a situation in which people's wants exceed their resources.

2.   _____Economics_____ is the study of how people deal with scarcity.

3.   People make _____ with scarce resources.

4.   Economic interactions occur in _____ and within _____.

5.   The _____ of a choice is the value of the forgone alternative that was not chosen.

6.   When both participants are made better off by an economic interaction, there are _____.

7.   Specialization in production results in _____.

8.   One person or group of people has a(n) _____ in producing one good relative to another good when they can produce that good with comparatively less time, effort, or resources than another person can produce that good.

9.   _____ occurs when individuals who live in different countries trade with each other.

10.   _____ represent the alternative choices of goods that the economy can produce.

11.   The graphical depiction of production possibilities is called the _____.

12.   _____ causes an outward shift in the production possibilities curve.

13.   The two major types of economies are _____ economies and _____ economies.

14.   _____ are the legal authority to keep or sell property.

15.   In a market economy, prices serve as _____, provide _____, and affect the _____.

## True-False Questions

1.   T   F   Economics is the study of how people can get anything they want.

2.   T   F   Scarcity is a characteristic of a command economy, but not of a market economy.

3.   T   F   An opportunity cost occurs every time there is a choice.

4.    T   F      Gains from trade occur only in markets.

5.    T   F      If Canada produces two goods with less resources than the United States, there can be no comparative advantage in those two goods.

6.    T   F      Trade takes place both within and between countries.

7.    T   F      Production possibilities represent the best choice of goods for the economy to produce.

8.    T   F      The production possibilities curve slopes downward.

9.    T   F      The production possibilities curve is linear.

10.   T   F      Points on the production possibilities curve are efficient.

11.   T   F      Points inside the production possibilities curve are inefficient.

12.   T   F      A market economy is also called a centrally planned economy.

13.   T   F      In recent years, Eastern Europe, the former Soviet Union, and China have moved away from central planning.

14.   T   F      Freely determined prices and property rights are characteristics of centrally planned economies.

15.   T   F      One reason why organizations are created is that they eliminate market failure.

## Short-Answer Questions

1.    What must people do because of scarcity?

2.    When do economic interactions between people occur?

3.    Where do economic interactions occur?

4.    What are opportunity costs?

5.    What is comparative advantage?

6.    Why are there gains from international trade?

7.    Why are there increasing opportunity costs?

8.    Why is the production possibilities curve bowed out?

9.    What are the three situations defined by the production possibilities curve?

10.   Why are points outside the production possibilities curve characterized as impossible?

11.   How does economic growth affect the production possibilities curve?

12.   What are the three essential questions faced by every economy?

13.   Name four characteristics of market, but not command, economies.

14.   What is the difference between market failure and government failure?

15.   What are the three roles of prices in a market economy?

## WORKING IT OUT

1.    We have studied the idea of production possibilities and the production possibilities curve by using graphs. We will first consider the same two concepts using numerical examples and then see how we can combine graphs and numbers.

a.    Suppose that the production possibilities for steel and food are as follows:

| Choice | Steel | Food |
|--------|-------|------|
| A | 0 | 100 |
| B | 25 | 95 |
| C | 50 | 85 |
| D | 75 | 50 |
| E | 100 | 0 |

Both steel and food are measured in tons. Increasing opportunity costs are illustrated by moving down the table. As we move from row to row, steel production increases by the same amount, 25 tons. The decline in food production, in contrast, gets larger, going from 5 tons between the first and second rows to 50 tons between the fourth and fifth rows. Each extra 25 tons of steel requires a loss of more and more food.

b.    The production possibilities curve for these numbers is depicted in Figure 1.3, with steel on the vertical axis and food on the horizontal axis. Both axes are measured in tons. The production possibilities curve is constructed by plotting pairs of points, labeled points *A* through *E*, for steel and food, and then connecting the dots. Since we do not know exactly how much food can be produced in between the 25-ton intervals for steel, we use straight lines to connect the dots.

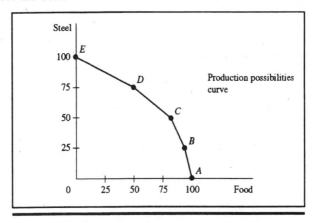

**Figure 1.3**

2.    We have learned that economic growth shifts out the production possibilities curve. We will illustrate this with a numerical example. Suppose that economic growth allows us to produce more goods, so that the new production possibilities for steel and food are as follows:

| Choice | Steel | Food |
|--------|-------|------|
| A | 0 | 125 |
| B | 25 | 120 |
| C | 50 | 110 |
| D | 75 | 90 |
| E | 100 | 50 |
| F | 125 | 0 |

The new production possibilities curve, labeled "Growth," is drawn with the original production possibilities curve in Figure 1.4. The new curve is farther away from the origin than the original curve at all points, indicating that more can be produced. For example, food production of 90 tons and steel production of 75 tons was impossible with the original production possibilities curve. After growth, that point is on the new production possibilities curve, and is therefore efficient.

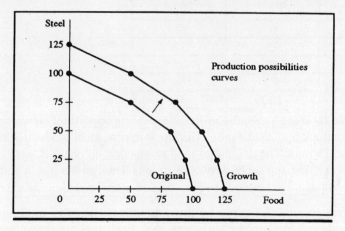

**Figure 1.4**

## Worked Problems

1. Suppose that you must allocate your time between studying economics and studying physics. The percentage of time you spend studying economics and the grades you will get on the two exams are as follows:

| Percent of Time Studying Economics | Economics Grade | Physics Grade |
|:---:|:---:|:---:|
| 100 | 80 | 0 |
| 80 | 75 | 30 |
| 60 | 65 | 50 |
| 40 | 50 | 65 |
| 20 | 30 | 75 |
| 0 | 0 | 80 |

Draw the production possibilities curve. How does this example illustrate increasing opportunity costs?

**Answer**

*The production possibilities curve is drawn in Figure 1.5. The example illustrates increasing opportunity costs because, as you move down the table or the curve, each additional point on your physics grade comes at a cost of more and more points on your economics grade.*

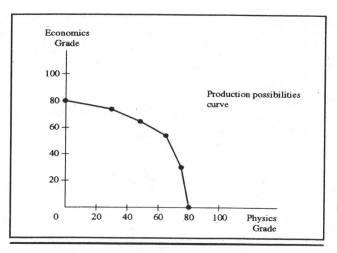

**Figure 1.5**

2. Now suppose that, by using the study guide for economics, you are able to improve your choices as follows:

| Percent of Time Studying Economics | Economics Grade | Physics Grade |
|:---:|:---:|:---:|
| 100 | 100 | 0 |
| 80 | 95 | 30 |
| 60 | 85 | 50 |
| 40 | 70 | 65 |
| 20 | 40 | 75 |
| 0 | 0 | 80 |

    a.    Draw the new production possibilities curve, and describe how the new curve is related to the old curve.

    b.    Characterize an economics grade of 70 and a physics grade of 65 under the original and the new production possibilities curves.

**Answers**

    a.    *The new production possibilities curve, labeled "Study Guide," and the original curve are depicted in Figure 1.6. Using this study guide raises your economics grade at each percent of time, above zero, spent studying economics, but it does not help your physics grade. Although the new curve is above the original curve, it tilts out rather than shifting out.*

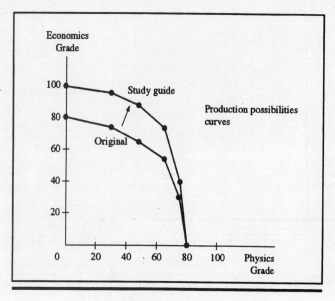

**Figure 1.6**

b.   *An economics grade of 70 and a physics grade of 65 were impossible to attain with the original production possibilities curve, but this combination is now efficient.*

## PRACTICE PROBLEMS

1.   Suppose that the production possibilities for steel and food are as follows:

| Choice | Steel | Food |
|--------|-------|------|
| A | 0 | 100 |
| B | 25 | 90 |
| C | 50 | 70 |
| D | 75 | 40 |
| E | 100 | 0 |

Both steel and food are measured in tons. Draw the production possibilities curve. How does this example illustrate increasing opportunity costs?

2.   Suppose that economic growth allows us to produce more goods, so that the new production possibilities for steel and food are as follows:

| Choice | Steel | Food |
|--------|-------|------|
| A | 0 | 120 |
| B | 25 | 115 |
| C | 50 | 105 |
| D | 75 | 90 |
| E | 100 | 60 |
| F | 125 | 0 |

a.   Draw the new production possibilities curve, and describe how the new curve is related to the old curve.

b.   Characterize the production of 75 tons of steel and 40 tons of food under the original and the new production possibilities curves.

3.  Suppose that you must allocate your time between studying economics and studying physics. The percentage of time you spend studying economics and the grades you will get on the two exams are as follows:

| Percent of Time Studying Economics | Economics Grade | Physics Grade |
|---|---|---|
| 100 | 90 | 0 |
| 80 | 88 | 40 |
| 60 | 80 | 70 |
| 40 | 70 | 80 |
| 20 | 40 | 88 |
| 0 | 0 | 90 |

Draw the production possibilities curve. How does this example illustrate increasing opportunity costs?

4.  Now suppose that, by using the study guide for economics, you are able to improve your choices as follows:

| Percent of Time Studying Economics | Economics Grade | Physics Grade |
|---|---|---|
| 100 | 100 | 0 |
| 80 | 96 | 40 |
| 60 | 90 | 70 |
| 40 | 80 | 80 |
| 20 | 50 | 88 |
| 0 | 0 | 90 |

a.  Draw the new production possibilities curve, and describe how the new curve is related to the old curve.

b.  Characterize an economics grade of 80 and a physics grade of 70 under the original and the new production possibilities curves.

## CHAPTER TEST

1.  A situation in which people's wants exceed their resources is called

    a.  abundance.
    b.  choice.
    c.  scarcity.
    d.  allocation.

2.  Economists study how

    a.  people make purposeful choices with scarce resources.
    b.  people make purposeful choices with abundant resources.
    c.  people make random choices with scarce resources.
    d.  people make random choices with abundant resources.

3.  An arrangement by which economic exchanges between people takes place is called

    a.  a choice.
    b.  a market.
    c.  scarcity.

      d.    gains from trade.

4.   Which of the following represents the alternative choices of goods that the economy can produce?

      a.    Opportunity costs
      b.    Economic interactions
      c.    Budget constraints
      d.    Production possibilities

5.   The value of the alternative that was not chosen is called the

      a.    marginal cost of the choice.
      b.    average cost of the choice.
      c.    opportunity cost of the choice.
      d.    gain from the choice.

6.   Exchange of goods and services between people or firms in different nations is called

      a.    intranational trade.
      b.    international trade.
      c.    gains from trade.
      d.    comparative advantage.

7.   When one person or group of people can produce one good relative to another good with comparatively less time, effort, or resources than another person can produce that good, this is called

      a.    comparative advantage.
      b.    specialization.
      c.    opportunity cost.
      d.    division of labor.

8.   The production possibilities curve slopes

      a.    downward and is bowed out from the origin.
      b.    upward and is bowed out from the origin.
      c.    downward and is bowed in toward the origin.
      d.    upward and is bowed in toward the origin.

9.   Points outside the production possibilities curve are

      a.    efficient.
      b.    inefficient.
      c.    impossible.
      d.    possible.

10.   Economic growth causes a(n)

      a.    inward shift in the production possibilities curve.
      b.    outward shift in the production possibilities curve.
      c.    upward movement on the production possibilities curve.
      d.    downward movement on the production possibilities curve.

11.   Which of the following is *not* one of the essential questions that an economy focuses on?

      a.    What are the goods and services to be produced?
      b.    When are the goods and services to be produced?
      c.    How are the goods and services to be produced?
      d.    For whom are the goods and services to be produced?

12. Which of the following is *not* one of the characteristics of a market economy?

   a.   Freely determined prices
   b.   Property rights
   c.   Competitive markets
   d.   Centrally planned production

13. The costs of buying and selling are called

   a.   transaction costs.
   b.   market costs.
   c.   opportunity costs.
   d.   incentive costs.

14. Which of the following is *not* one of the important roles of prices in a market economy?

   a.   They serve as signals.
   b.   They provide incentives.
   c.   They form preferences.
   d.   They affect the distribution of income.

Use the following table for questions 15 and 16.

Suppose that the production possibilities for guns and flowers are as follows:

| Choice | Guns | Flowers |
|--------|------|---------|
| A | 0 | 100 |
| B | 25 | 90 |
| C | 50 | 70 |
| D | 75 | 40 |
| E | 100 | 0 |

15. If all of the economy's resources were devoted to the production of flowers, the amount of guns that would be produced is

   a.   100.
   b.   75.
   c.   0.
   d.   50.

16. If the economy is currently producing 50 guns and 60 flowers, then

   a.   it is at an efficient level of production.
   b.   an efficient level of production can be achieved by producing 20 more flowers.
   c.   an efficient level of production can be achieved by producing less flowers and more guns.
   d.   an efficient level of production can be achieved by producing 10 more flowers.

Use Figure 1.7 for questions 17, 18, and 19.

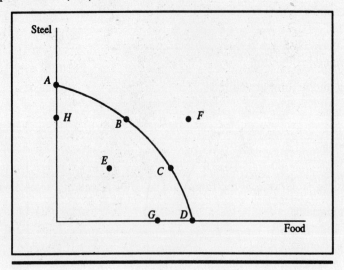

**Figure 1.7**

17. If the economy devotes all of its resources to steel production, it will be producing at point

    a.   *A.*
    b.   *B.*
    c.   *H.*
    d.   *G.*

18. Point *F* in Figure 1.7 represents

    a.   an efficient production level.
    b.   an inefficient production level.
    c.   an impossible production level.
    d.   a possible production level.

19. If the economy is currently producing at point *E*, then

    a.   it is utilizing its resources efficiently.
    b.   it is utilizing its resources inefficiently.
    c.   it is on its production possibilities curve.
    d.   it is beyond its production possibilities curve.

Use Figure 1.8 for question 20.

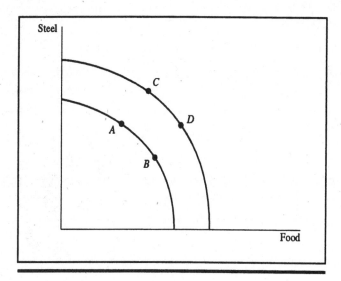

**Figure 1.8**

20.  An economy experiences economic growth when it moves

    a.    from point *A* to point *B*.
    b.    from point *A* to point *C*.
    c.    from point *D* to point *C*.
    d.    from point *D* to point *B*.

# ANSWERS TO THE REVIEW QUESTIONS

## Fill-In Questions

1.  Scarcity

2.  Economics

3.  purposeful choices

4.  markets; organizations

5.  opportunity cost

6.  gains from trade

7.  division of labor

8.  comparative advantage

9.  International trade

10.  Production possibilities

11.  production possibilities curve

12.  Economic growth

13.  market; command

14.  Property rights

15.   signals; incentives; distribution of income

## True-False Questions

1.   **False.**   Economics is the study of how people deal with scarcity.

2.   **False.**   Because wants are unlimited but resources are not, scarcity is a characteristic of all economies.

3.   **True.**   The opportunity cost of a choice is the value of the forgone alternative that was not chosen.

4.   **False.**   Gains from trade can also occur within organizations.

5.   **False.**   The United States will still produce one of the goods with relatively less resources than Canada, leading to a comparative advantage in that good.

6.   **True.**   International trade occurs when individuals who live in different countries trade with each other.

7.   **False.**   Production possibilities represent the alternative choices of goods that the economy can produce.

8.   **True.**   As more of one good is produced, less of the other can be produced.

9.   **False.**   The production possibilities curve is bowed out.

10.   **True.**   They represent the maximum amount that can be produced with available resources.

11.   **True.**   Using the same resources, the economy could produce more of both goods.

12.   **False.**   A command economy is also called a centrally planned economy.

13.   **True.**   They are making the transition from command economies to market economies.

14.   **False.**   Freely determined prices and property rights are characteristics of market, not centrally planned, economies.

15.   **False**.   One reason why organizations are created is to reduce market transaction costs.

## Short-Answer Questions

1.   Because of scarcity, people must make choices to forgo one thing in favor of another.

2.   Economic interactions between people occur when they trade or exchange goods or services with each other.

3.   Economic interactions occur in markets and within organizations.

4.   The opportunity cost of a choice is the value of the forgone alternative that was not chosen.

5.   One person or group of people has a comparative advantage in producing one good relative to another good if they can produce that good with comparatively less time, effort, or resources than another person can produce that good.

6.   There are gains from international trade because by trading, people can either better satisfy their preferences for goods or better utilize their comparative advantage.

7.   There are increasing opportunity costs because as the production of one good increases, the value of the forgone good increases.

8.   The production possibilities curve is bowed out because of increasing opportunity costs.

9.  Points on the production possibility curve are efficient, those inside the curve are inefficient, and those outside the curve are impossible.

10. They are called impossible because the economy does not have the resources to produce outside the production possibilities curve.

11. Economic growth shifts out the production possibilities curve.

12. Every economy must determine what are the goods and services to be produced, how are these goods and services to be produced, and for whom are the goods and services to be produced.

13. Freely determined prices, property rights, competitive markets, and freedom to trade at home and abroad characterize market, but not command, economies.

14. Market failure is a situation in which there is a role for the government in improving the market outcome. Government failure occurs when the government, even in the case of market failure, does worse than the market would have done if left on its own.

15. Prices serve as signals about what should be produced and consumed when there are changes in tastes or technology, provide incentives to people to alter their production or consumption, and affect the distribution of income.

## SOLUTIONS TO THE PRACTICE PROBLEMS

1.  The production possibilities curve is drawn in Figure 1.9. The example illustrates increasing opportunity costs because, as you move down the table or up the curve, each additional 25 tons of steel comes at a higher cost in food production.

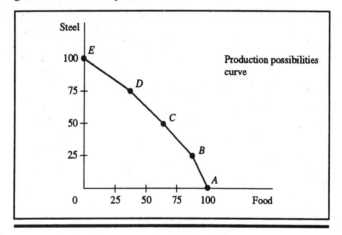

Figure 1.9

2.  a.   The new production possibilities curve, labeled "Growth," is drawn with the original production possibilities curve in Figure 1.10. The new curve shifts out from the old curve.

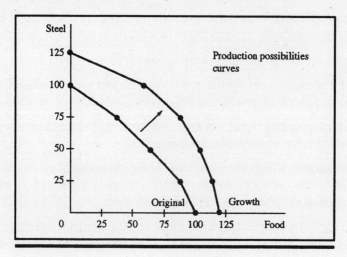

**Figure 1.10**

   b.   Production of 75 tons of steel and 40 tons of food was efficient under the original production possibilities curve. It is inefficient under the new curve.

3.   The production possibilities curve is drawn in Figure 1.11. Each additional point on your physics grade comes at a cost of more and more points on your economics grade.

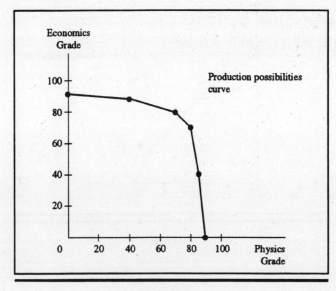

**Figure 1.11**

4.    a.    The new production possibilities curve, labeled "Study Guide," and the original curve are depicted in Figure 1.12. The new curve is above the original curve, but it tilts out rather than shifting out.

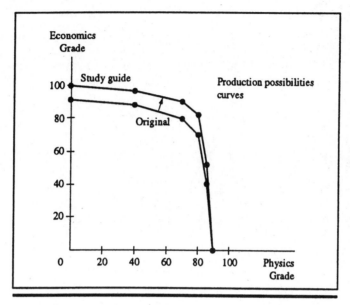

**Figure 1.12**

b.    An economics grade of 80 and a physics grade of 70 were efficient with the original production possibilities curve, but this combination is now inefficient.

## ANSWERS TO THE CHAPTER TEST

1.    c

2.    a

3.    b

4.    d

5.    c

6.    b

7.    a

8.    a

9.    c

10.    b

11.    b

12.    d

13.    a

14.    c

15.    c

16.    d

17.  a
18.  c
19.  b
20.  b

# CHAPTER 2

# Observing and Explaining the Economy

## CHAPTER OVERVIEW

What is economics? If you are tempted to answer "everything," you are at least partly correct. Economics is a way of thinking. It entails *describing* economic events, *explaining* why they occur, *predicting* whether they might occur in the future, and *recommending* appropriate courses of action to policymakers. When you listen to your professor in class, read the text, or work through the study guide, you should be learning to actively analyze economic events. This chapter introduces some of the tools of analysis. We consider the timely issue of health-care spending and see what economists attempt to explain and how to interpret what they find. We look at economic models and learn how economists abstract reality in order to make it manageable. We see how economics is used for public policy and consider some of its limitations. Finally, we introduce some tools that economists use in their analysis. Using both graphs and algebra, we begin to learn how to document and quantify observations about the economy.

## CHAPTER REVIEW

1.  Economists divide people into broad categories. *Households* are either individuals or groups of individuals who share the same living quarters. *Organizations,* which include firms and governments, are producers of goods and services. *Firms* are private organizations that produce goods and services. *Governments* also produce goods and services, such as national defense and education. **A circular flow diagram** shows how funds flow through the economy from households to firms and back again.

2.  A *market* is an arrangement through which exchanges of goods or services between people take place. Households supply their *labor* to the firms that employ them. The resources used by firms to produce goods and services are called *capital*.

3.  An **economic model** is an explanation of how the economy or a part of the economy works. Economic models, like models in other sciences, are always simplifications of reality. Economic models can be described with words, with numbers, with graphs, or with algebra, and you will use all four as you work through the text and study guide.

4.  An **economic variable** is any economic measure that can vary over a range of values. *Correlation* means that two variables move together, either in the same direction or in opposite directions. There is a positive correlation, and the two variables are **positively related**, if the two variables move in the same direction: One increases when the other increases. There is a negative correlation, and the two variables are **negatively related**, if the two variables move in opposite directions: One decreases when the other increases. *Causation* means that the movements in one variable bring about, or cause, the movements in another variable. Correlation does not imply causation. Just because two variables move together does not mean that the movements of one caused the movements of the other.

5.  The assumption of *ceteris paribus*, which means "all other things equal," is often used by economists for prediction. The idea of *ceteris paribus* is easiest to explain through an example.

Suppose that you wanted to predict the effect of cold weather on football attendance. In making your prediction, you would want to hold other things, such as the team's won-lost record, equal.

6.    Keeping other things equal is not easy in economics. In many sciences, such as physics, researchers perform **controlled experiments** to determine whether one event causes another. In economics, as in astronomy, controlled experiments are rare. If you want to study the causes of the Great Depression of the 1930s, you cannot ask the government to go back and change policy. In **experimental economics**, a new and growing area of economics, researchers have begun to conduct economic experiments in laboratory settings.

7.    The two main branches of economics are microeconomics and macroeconomics. **Microeconomics** studies the behavior of individual firms, households, and markets. Questions such as how much milk consumption will fall if the price of milk rises or how much a college education increases an individual's lifetime earnings are part of microeconomics. **Macroeconomics** focuses on the whole national, or even world, economy. Questions such as what were the effects of lowering inflation in the early 1980s in the United States or what are the prospects for economic reform in the former Soviet Union are part of macroeconomics.

8.    There are two basic types of economic systems: *market economies*, where the vast majority of prices are free to vary, and *command economies*, where the vast majority of prices are determined by the government. Command economies are also called *centrally planned* economies. In modern market economies, the government plays a large role, and such economies are sometimes called **mixed economies**.

9.    Economics is an important part of public policy making. **Positive economics** describes or explains what happens in the economy. **Normative economics** makes recommendations about what the government should do. For example, interest rates in the United States were increased in the spring and summer of 1994. Positive economics describes the effects of the higher interest rates and explains why interest rates were raised. Normative economics is concerned with recommending whether they should be raised further. The work of the **Council of Economic Advisers**, which gives policy advice to the president, is an example of normative economics.

## ZEROING IN

1.    Health-care reform has been a major economic and political issue since the early 1990s.  Health care provides a good introduction to thinking about economics.

    a.    Two facts about health-care spending stand out. First, health-care spending grew more rapidly than the rest of the U.S. economy in the early 1990s and then slowed down beginning in the mid-1990s. Second, the price of health care has increased faster than most other prices. It is the task of economics to quantify, document, and explain these observations.

    b.    Let's look at the first observation, that health-care spending has grown more rapidly than the rest of the U.S. economy. In order to evaluate this assertion, we need to measure both health-care spending and the economy as a whole. **Gross domestic product (GDP)** is the most comprehensive measure of the size of an economy. GDP for the United States is the total value of all goods and services made in the United States during a specified period of time, usually one year. In 2000, GDP for the United States was $9,873 billion.

    c.    We can measure health-care spending the same way we measure GDP, by adding up what we spend on all categories of health care. That number was $997 billion in 2000. Health care is the largest industry in America, about three times as large as the entire automobile industry.

d.  Health-care spending as a *share* of GDP (in percentage terms) can be calculated by dividing health-care spending by GDP and multiplying by 100:

$$\text{Health-care spending as a share of GDP} = \frac{\text{Health-care spending}}{\text{GDP}} \times 100$$

In 2000, health-care spending as a share of GDP was (997/9,873) x 100 = 10.1 percent. [If we did not multiply by 100, the share would have been .101 (out of 1) instead of 10.1 (out of 100). While we will usually represent shares in percentage terms, you should understand that the two numbers represent the same thing.]

e.  Now let's turn to prices. The health-care price is a measure of the price of all the items included in the measure of health-care spending. The relative price of health care can be calculated by dividing the health-care price by the average price of all goods and services:

$$\text{Relative price of health care} = \frac{\text{Health-care price}}{\text{Average price}}$$

f.  Health-care spending and GDP for all years from 1990 to 2001 are reported in the text. Although both health-care spending and GDP have been rising, health-care spending has been increasing more quickly. The share of health-care spending as a percent of GDP has therefore been rising. The relative price of health care for the same years is also reported in the text. The relative price of health care has increased since 1990 because the price of health care has risen more rapidly than the average price level.

## ACTIVE REVIEW

## Fill-In Questions

1.  _____ are individuals or groups of individuals who share the same living quarters.

2.  Private organizations that produce goods and services are called _____.

3.  A(n) _____ is an arrangement through which exchanges of goods or services between people take place.

4.  Two factors of production are _____ and _____.

5.  A(n) _____ is an explanation of how the economy or a part of the economy works.

6.  Two variables are _____ if they move in the same direction.

7.  The assumption of _____ means "all other things equal."

8.  _____ is the branch of economics that studies the behavior of individual firms, households, and markets.

9.  _____ is the branch of economics that focuses on the whole economy.

10.  _____ economics is economic analysis that explains what happens in the economy.

11.  _____ economics is economic analysis that makes recommendations about economic policy.

12.  The most comprehensive measure of the size of an economy is _____.

13.  The _____ is the price of a particular good compared to the average price level.

14. An _____ is any economic measure that can vary over a range of values.
15. The _____ gives policy advice to the president.

## True-False Questions

1. T  F   Governments produce goods and services.
2. T  F   Money and capital are called factors of production.
3. T  F   It is desirable to make economic models as realistic as possible.
4. T  F   If two economic variables have a positive correlation, one must cause the other.
5. T  F   The question of by how much a college education increases an individual's lifetime earnings is part of microeconomics.
6. T  F   The question of what were the effects of lowering inflation in the early 1980s in the United States is part of macroeconomics.
7. T  F   Gross domestic product (GDP) is measured for a specified time period.
8. T  F   Health-care spending is over 10 percent of GDP in the United States.
9. T  F.  In the United States, we spend more for automobiles than for health care.
10. T  F   Health-care spending as a share of GDP has been rising during the last 20 years.
11. T  F   The relative price of health care has increased since 1970.
12. T  F   In experimental economics, researchers conduct economic experiments in uncontrolled environments.
13. T  F   Normative economics explains why interest rates were raised in 1994.
14. T  F   The two basic types of economic systems are market and planned economies.
15. T  F   A circular flow diagram shows how funds flow through the economy from households to the government.

## Short-Answer Questions

1. What is a market?
2. What is the difference between labor and capital?
3. What is the difference between correlation and causation?
4. What does it mean for two variables to be negatively correlated?
5. What is the assumption of *ceteris paribus*?
6. What is experimental economics?
7. In the context of public policy making, what is the difference between positive and normative economics?
8. What are two important facts about health-care spending during the last 20 years?
9. How do economists calculate health-care spending as a share of GDP?
10. What is the average price level?
11. What is the difference between inflation and the inflation rate?

12. How do economists calculate the relative price of health care?

13. What is a circular flow diagram?

14. Define the four categories in which economists divide people.

15. How do economists study the economy?

## WORKING IT OUT

1. We have studied how to calculate health-care spending as a share of GDP and how to compute the relative price of health care. These techniques are applicable to any category of spending. Let's consider housing spending for a fictional economy, starting in the year 2000.

   a. Suppose you are given the following data on GDP and housing spending:

   | Year | GDP | Housing Spending |
   | --- | --- | --- |
   | 2000 | 1,000 | 50 |
   | 2010 | 2,000 | 20 |
   | 2020 | 4,000 | 280 |
   | 2030 | 8,000 | 640 |

   GDP and housing spending are in billions of dollars. You can calculate housing spending as a share of GDP (in percentage terms) by dividing housing spending by GDP and multiplying by 100.

   | Year | Housing Spending/GDP | Housing Spending Share |
   | --- | --- | --- |
   | 2000 | 0.05 | 5 percent |
   | 2010 | 0.06 | 6 percent |
   | 2020 | 0.07 | 7 percent |
   | 2030 | 0.08 | 8 percent |

   Housing spending as a share of GDP has increased from 5 percent to 8 percent over this 30-year period.

   b. Now suppose you are given the following data for the same time period on the average price level and the price of housing:

   | Year | Average Price | Housing Price |
   | --- | --- | --- |
   | 2000 | 1.00 | 0.80 |
   | 2010 | 1.10 | 0.99 |
   | 2020 | 1.21 | 1.21 |
   | 2030 | 1.33 | 1.46 |

You can calculate the relative price of housing by dividing the price of housing by the average price level.

| Year | Relative Price of Housing |
|------|---------------------------|
| 2000 | 0.80 |
| 2010 | 0.90 |
| 2020 | 1.00 |
| 2030 | 1.10 |

The relative price of housing has increased over this period.

2.  We can also use graphs to understand the relationship between housing spending as a share of GDP and the relative price of housing in the fictional economy described above.

    a.  The movements in housing spending as a share of GDP and the relative price of housing can be shown by using time-series plots. In the first panel of Figure 2.1, the housing spending share is on the vertical axis and time (the year) is on the horizontal axis. The curve is upward sloping, indicating that housing spending as a share of GDP has increased over this period. The second panel of Figure 2.1 depicts the relative price of housing on the vertical axis and the year on the horizontal axis. This curve is also upward sloping, indicating that the relative price of housing has also increased over this period.

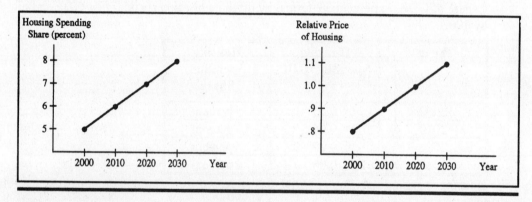

**Figure 2.1**

    b.  The relationship between the housing spending share and the relative price of housing can be illustrated by using a scatter plot. In Figure 2.2, the relative price of housing is on the vertical axis and the housing spending share is on the horizontal axis. Each dot represents a different year, and the curve, which has a positive slope, is drawn by connecting the dots. The housing spending share and the relative price of housing are positively related; one increases when the other increases.

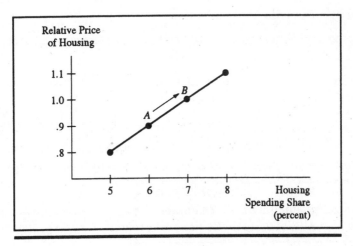

**Figure 2.2**

c.     Changes in the value of one of the variables on the axes cause movement along a curve. In this example, if the relative price of housing increases from 0.9 to 1.0, the housing spending share increases from 6 percent to 7 percent. This is shown as a movement from point *A* to point *B* in Figure 2.2.

d.     Changes in the value of variables not depicted on the axes cause shifts in the curve. In this example, suppose that something causes the housing spending share to increase by 1 percent at each relative price of housing. This is illustrated in Figure 2.3 as a shift of the curve marked "Original" to the right, to the curve marked "New."

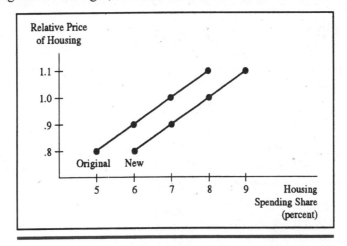

**Figure 2.3**

# Worked Problems

1.     Consider the following data for a fictional economy, starting in the year 2000:

| Year | GDP | Food Spending | Average Price | Food Price |
|------|-----|---------------|---------------|------------|
| 2000 | 1,000 | 100 | 1.00 | 1.00 |
| 2010 | 2,000 | 180 | 1.20 | 1.32 |
| 2020 | 4,000 | 320 | 1.40 | 1.68 |
| 2030 | 8,000 | 560 | 1.60 | 2.08 |

GDP and food spending are in billions of dollars.

a.   Calculate food spending as a share of GDP (in percentage terms) and the relative price of food.

b.   What has happened to the food-spending share and the relative price of food over this period?

**Answers**

a.   *Food spending as a share of GDP equals food spending divided by GDP multiplied by 100. The relative price of food equals the price of food divided by the average price level.*

| Year | Food-Spending Share | Relative Price of Food |
|------|---------------------|------------------------|
| 2000 | 10 percent | 1.00 |
| 2010 | 9 percent | 1.10 |
| 2020 | 8 percent | 1.20 |
| 2030 | 7 percent | 1.30 |

b.   *The food-spending share has decreased, and the relative price of food has increased during this period.*

2.   Using the data for the economy in Worked Problem 1:

a.   Draw a scatter plot to illustrate the relationship between food spending as a share of GDP and the relative price of food. Are the two variables positively or negatively related?

b.   Suppose that the relative price of food rises from 1.1 to 1.2. Is this a movement along the curve or a shift of the curve? Illustrate your answer.

c.   Suppose that something causes the food-spending share to decrease by 1 percent at each relative price of food. Is this a movement along the curve or a shift of the curve? Illustrate your answer.

**Answers**

a.   *The scatter plot, with the relative price of food on the vertical axis and the food-spending share on the horizontal axis, is shown in Figure 2.4. The curve is downward sloping, indicating that the two variables are negatively related.*

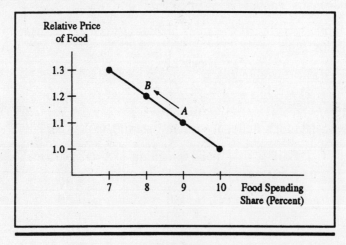

**Figure 2.4**

b.   *The increase in the relative price of food is a movement along the curve; it is depicted by a movement from point A to point B in Figure 2.4. The food-spending share falls from 9 percent to 8 percent.*

c.   *The decrease in the food-spending share by 1 percent at each relative price of food is a shift of the curve; it is depicted in Figure 2.5 by a shift of the curve marked "Original" to the left, to the curve marked "New."*

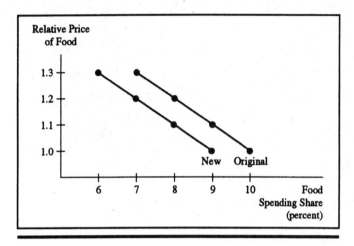

Figure 2.5

## PRACTICE PROBLEMS

1.   Consider the following data for a fictional economy, starting in the year 2000:

| Year | GDP | Automobile Spending | Average Price | Automobile Price |
|------|------|------|------|------|
| 2000 | 1,000 | 30 | 1.00 | 1.00 |
| 2010 | 2,000 | 70 | 1.20 | 1.10 |
| 2020 | 4,000 | 160 | 1.44 | 1.21 |
| 2030 | 8,000 | 360 | 1.73 | 1.33 |

GDP and automobile spending are in billions of dollars.

a.   Calculate automobile spending as a share of GDP (in percentage terms) and the relative price of automobiles.

b.   What has happened to the automobile-spending share and the relative price of automobiles over this period?

2.    Consider the following data for a fictional economy, starting in the year 2000:

| Year | GDP | Clothing Spending | Average Price | Clothing Price |
|------|------|-------------------|---------------|----------------|
| 2000 | 1,000 | 30 | 1.00 | 0.900 |
| 2010 | 2,000 | 70 | 1.10 | 1.045 |
| 2020 | 4,000 | 160 | 1.20 | 1.200 |
| 2030 | 8,000 | 360 | 1.30 | 1.365 |

GDP and clothing spending are in billions of dollars.

a.    Calculate clothing spending as a share of GDP (in percentage terms) and the relative price of clothing.

b.    What has happened to the clothing-spending share and the relative price of clothing over this period?

3.    Using the data for the economy in Practice Problem 1:

a.    Draw a scatter plot to illustrate the relationship between automobile spending as a share of GDP and the relative price of automobiles. Are the two variables positively or negatively related?

b.    Suppose the relative price of automobiles falls from 0.92 to 0.84. Is this a movement along the curve or a shift of the curve? Illustrate your answer.

4.    Using the data for the economy in Practice Problem 2:

a.    Draw a scatter plot to illustrate the relationship between clothing spending as a share of GDP and the relative price of clothing. Are the two variables positively or negatively related?

b.    Suppose that something causes the clothing-spending share to increase by 1/2 percent at each relative price of clothing. Is this a movement along the curve or a shift of the curve? Illustrate your answer.

# CHAPTER TEST

1.    Individuals or groups of individuals who share the same living quarters are called

    a.    firms.
    b.    households.
    c.    governments.
    d.    groups.

2.    Private organizations that produce goods and services are called

    a.    firms.
    b.    households.
    c.    governments.
    d.    groups.

3.    An arrangement through which exchanges of goods or services between people take place is called a(n)

    a.    firm.
    b.    industry.

    c.    market.
    d.    economic model.

4.    When the movements in one variable bring about the movements in another variable, this is called

    a.    causation.
    b.    correlation.
    c.    relationship.
    d.    connection.

5.    Two variables have a positive correlation if

    a.    they move in opposite directions.
    b.    they move in the same direction.
    c.    one decreases when the other increases.
    d.    one increases when the other decreases.

6.    An economic model

    a.    is any economic measure that can vary over a range of values.
    b.    shows how funds flow through the economy from households to firms and back again.
    c.    is an explanation of how the economy or a part of the economy works.
    d.    is an arrangement through which exchanges of goods or services between people take place.

7.    The assumption of "all other things equal" is called

    a.    a market.
    b.    a circular flow diagram.
    c.    an economic variable.
    d.    *ceteris paribus*.

8.    Modern market economies in which the government plays a large role are called

    a.    market economies.
    b.    mixed economies.
    c.    command economies.
    d.    centrally planned economies.

9.    Macroeconomics focuses on

    a.    the whole national economy.
    b.    the behavior of individual firms.
    c.    the behavior of households.
    d.    markets.

10.    Which of the following is *most* likely to be studied by a microeconomist?

    a.    Inflation of the general price level
    b.    Unemployment in the economy
    c.    Employment of labor in furniture production
    d.    The growth rate of aggregate output

11.    The work of the Council of Economic Advisers is an example of

    a.    positive economics.
    b.    negative economics.
    c.    experimental economics.
    d.    normative economics.

# 32   Chapter 2: Observing and Explaining the Economy

12. What is the relation between health-care spending and GDP in the 1990s?

   a.   Both health-care spending and GDP have been rising, but GDP has been increasing more quickly.
   b.   Both health-care spending and GDP have been rising, but health-care spending has been increasing more quickly.
   c.   Both health-care spending and GDP have been falling, but GDP has been decreasing more quickly.
   d.   Both health-care spending and GDP have been falling, but health-care spending has been decreasing more quickly.

13. Positive economics

   a.   describes or explains what happens in the economy.
   b.   makes recommendations about what the government should do.
   c.   studies the behavior of individual firms, households, and markets.
   d.   focuses on the whole economy.

14. If a curve has a positive slope, then

   a.   the two variables are negatively related.
   b.   the two variables are positively related.
   c.   one variable increases when the other decreases.
   d.   the curve slopes down from left to right.

15. Health-care spending as a share of GDP is calculated by

   a.   multiplying GDP by health-care spending.
   b.   dividing GDP by health-care spending.
   c.   multiplying health-care spending by GDP.
   d.   dividing health-care spending by GDP.

16. The relative price of health care is calculated by

   a.   multiplying the health-care price by the average price of all goods and services.
   b.   multiplying the average price of all goods and services by the health-care price.
   c.   dividing the health-care price by the average price of all goods and services.
   d.   dividing the average price of all goods and services by the health-care price.

Use the following table for questions 17, 18, and 19.

| Year | GDP | Food Spending | Average Price | Food Price |
|------|------|------|------|------|
| 2000 | 2,000 | 120 | 1.00 | 1.00 |
| 2010 | 4,000 | 200 | 1.20 | 1.44 |
| 2020 | 8,000 | 340 | 1.40 | 1.70 |
| 2030 | 16,000 | 640 | 1.60 | 2.10 |

GDP and food spending are in billions of dollars.

17. What is food spending as a share of GDP (in percentage terms) in the year 2010?

   a.   3 percent
   b.   6 percent
   c.   10 percent
   d.   5 percent

18.   What is food spending as a share of GDP (in percentage terms) in the year 2030?

      a.    4 percent
      b.    5 percent
      c.    10 percent
      d.    8 percent

19.   What is the relative price of food in the year 2010?

      a.    1.00
      b.    1.10
      c.    1.20
      d.    1.30

      Use Figure 2.6 for question 20.

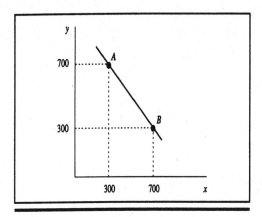

**Figure 2.6**

20.   Movement from point *A* to point *B* is a(n)

      a.    upward movement along the curve.
      b.    downward movement along the curve.
      c.    upward shift of the curve.
      d.    downward shift of the curve.

# ANSWERS TO THE REVIEW QUESTIONS

## Fill-In Questions

1.    Households

2.    firms

3.    market

4.    labor; capital

5.    economic model

6.    positively related

7.    *ceteris paribus*

8.    Microeconomics

9.    Macroeconomics

10. Positive

11. Normative

12. gross domestic product

13. relative price

14. economic variable

15. Council of Economic Advisers

## True-False Questions

1.  **True**.    They produce goods and services such as national defense and education.

2.  **False**.    Labor and capital are called factors of production.

3.  **False**.    Economic models are always simplifications of reality.

4.  **False**.    Correlation does not imply causation.

5.  **False**.    Microeconomics studies the behavior of individual firms, households, and markets.

6.  **True**.    Macroeconomics focuses on the whole national, or even world, economy.

7.  **True**.    GDP is usually specified for one year.

8.  **True**.    Health-care spending was 10.1 percent of the U.S. GDP in 1999.

9.  **False**.    Health-care spending is three times as large as spending on automobiles.

10. **True**.    Although health-care spending and GDP have both been rising, health-care spending has been increasing more quickly than GDP.

11. **True**.    The price of health care has risen more rapidly than the average price level.

12. **False**.    In experimental economics, researchers conduct economic experiments in controlled laboratory settings.

13. **False**.    Positive economics describes the effects of higher interest rates and explains why they were raised.

14. **True**.    There are two basis types of economic systems: market and command economies.

15. **False**.    A circular flow diagram shows how funds flow through the economy from households to firms and back again.

## Short-Answer Questions

1.  A market is an arrangement through which exchange of goods and services between people takes place.

2.  Households supply their labor to the firms that employ them. The resources used by firms to produce goods and services are called capital.

3.  Correlation means that two variables move together, either in the same direction or in opposite directions. Causation means that the movements in one variable bring about, or cause, the movements in another variable.

4.  When two variables are negatively correlated, it means they move in opposite directions.

5.   The *ceteris paribus* assumption is that, when making a prediction of the effect of one variable on another, all other variables are unchanged.

6.   Experimental economics is a new and growing branch of economics in which researchers conduct economic experiments in laboratory settings.

7.   In the context of public policy making, positive economics describes or explains what the government does. Normative economics makes recommendations about what the government should do.

8.   Health-care spending has grown more rapidly than the rest of the U.S. economy, and the price of health care has increased more than most other prices.

9.   Health-care spending as a share of GDP can be calculated by dividing health-care spending by GDP and multiplying by 100.

10.  The average price level is a measure of the average price of all the goods and services in GDP.

11.  Inflation is the general increase in prices over time. The inflation rate is the percentage increase in the average price level from one year to the next.

12.  The relative price of health care is calculated by dividing the price of health care by the average price level.

13.  A circular flow diagram shows how funds flow through the economy from households to firms and back again.

14.  The four categories by which economists divide people are households, organizations, firms, and governments.

15.  Economists study the economy by describing economic events, explaining why they occur, predicting whether they might occur in the future, and recommending appropriate courses of action to policymakers.

## SOLUTIONS TO THE PRACTICE PROBLEMS

1.   a.   The automobile spending share and the relative price of automobiles are as follows:

| Year | Automobile-Spending Share | Relative Price of Automobiles |
|------|---------------------------|-------------------------------|
| 2000 | 3.0 percent | 1.00 |
| 2010 | 3.5 percent | 0.92 |
| 2020 | 4.0 percent | 0.84 |
| 2030 | 4.5 percent | 0.77 |

     b.   The automobile-spending share has increased, and the relative price of automobiles has decreased over this period.

2.   a.   The clothing-spending share and the relative price of clothing are as follows:

| Year | Clothing-Spending Share | Relative Price of Clothing |
|------|-------------------------|----------------------------|
| 2000 | 3.0 percent | 0.90 |
| 2010 | 3.5 percent | 0.95 |
| 2020 | 4.0 percent | 1.00 |
| 2030 | 4.5 percent | 1.05 |

b.    The clothing-spending share and the relative price of clothing have both increased during this period.

3.    a.    The scatter plot is drawn in Figure 2.7. The curve is downward sloping, indicating that the two variables are negatively related.

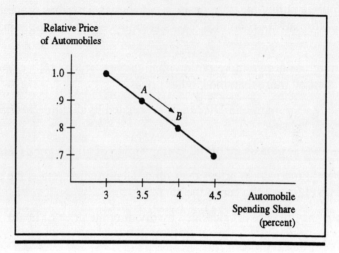

**Figure 2.7**

b.    This is a movement along the curve; it is depicted by a movement from point *A* to point *B* in Figure 2.7.

4.    a.    The scatter plot is drawn in Figure 2.8. The curve is upward sloping, indicating that the two variables are positively related.

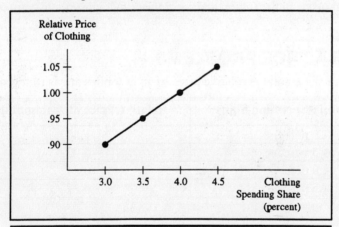

**Figure 2.8**

b.    This is a shift of the curve; it is depicted in Figure 2.9 by a shift of the curve marked "Original" to the right, to the curve marked "New."

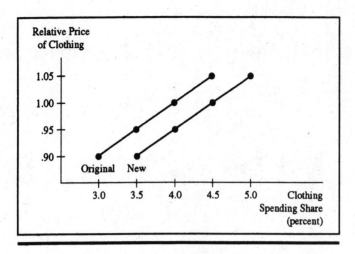

**Figure 2.9**

# ANSWERS TO THE CHAPTER TEST

1.  b
2.  a
3.  c
4.  a
5.  b
6.  c
7.  d
8.  b
9.  a
10. c
11. d
12. b
13. a
14. b
15. d
16. c
17. d
18. a
19. c
20. b

# APPENDIX TO CHAPTER 2

# Reading, Understanding, and Creating Graphs

## OVERVIEW

Graphs and diagrams are used extensively in economics. They are useful both for uncovering correlations in economic variables and for understanding economic models.

## REVIEW

1.

a. In a **Cartesian coordinate system**, pairs of observations on variables can be represented in a plane by designating one axis for one variable and the other axis for the other variable. Each point on the plane corresponds to a pair of observations. In economics, the axes are usually designated the vertical axis and the horizontal axis.

b. A **time-series graph** plots a series—several values of the variable—over time. Figure 2A.1 plots two variables, called $x$ and $y$, over time. The value of the variable is depicted on the vertical axis, and time is on the horizontal axis. More than one variable can be plotted on the same graph. If the scales of measurement of the variables are very different, a **dual scale** can be used.

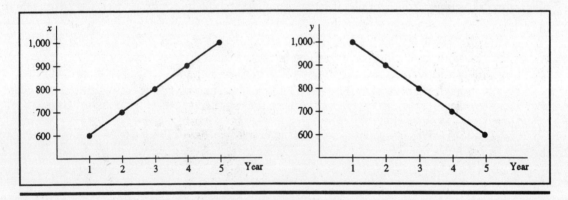

**Figure 2A.1**

c. Two variables can also be depicted with a **scatter plot**, where the vertical axis is used for one variable and the horizontal axis is used for the other variable. Figure 2A.2 shows a scatter plot for the variables $x$ and $y$, with $x$ on the horizontal axis and $y$ on the vertical axis. Connecting the dots in the scatter plot creates a curve. If the curve is a straight line, as in Figure 2A.2, it is called *linear*. Economic relationships do not have to be linear.

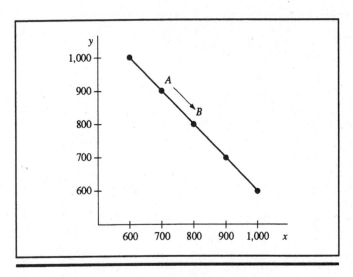

**Figure 2A.2**

d.  The **slope** of the curve is the change in the variable on the vertical axis divided by the change in the variable on the horizontal axis. If the curve slopes up from left to right, it has a **positive slope** and the two variables are positively related. If the curve slopes down from left to right, it has a **negative slope** and the two variables are negatively related. In Figure 2A.2 the slope of the curve is negative because the curve slopes down from left to right and is constant along the curve because the curve is linear. Because $y$ decreases by 100 for every increase of $x$ by 100, the slope is $-100/100 = -1$.

e.  When the value of one of the variables on the two axes changes, it causes a **movement along the curve**. For example, if $x$ rises from 700 to 800 in Figure 2A.2, $y$ falls from 900 to 800. This is a movement along the curve, and is shown by a movement from point $A$ to point $B$. But suppose that the relationship between the variables $x$ and $y$ is affected by the value of a third variable, $z$. In Figure 2A.3, a change in the value of $z$ causes a **shift of the curve**. We will consider movements along and shifts of curves many times in this course. It is important for you to understand that changes in the values of variables that are depicted on the axes cause movements along a curve, whereas changes in the values of other variables cause shifts of the curve.

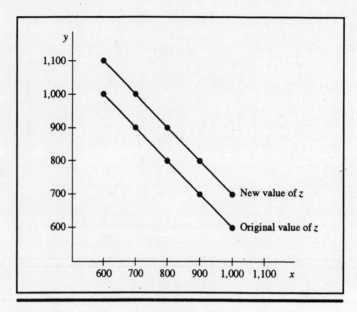

**Figure 2A.3**

# ACTIVE REVIEW

## Fill-In Questions

1.  In a(n) _____, pairs of observations on variables can be represented in a plane by designating one axis for one variable and the other axis for the other variable.

2.  A(n) _____ plots a series over time.

3.  In a(n) _____, the vertical axis is used for one variable and the horizontal axis is used for the other variable.

## True-False Questions

1.  T   F     In a time-series graph, the value of the variable is depicted on the horizontal axis, and time is on the vertical axis.

2.  T   F     If the curve depicting two variables in a scatter plot is linear, the two variables are negatively related.

3.  T   F     When the value of one of the variables on the two axes changes, it causes a shift of the curve.

## Short-Answer Questions

1.  When is a dual scale used?

2.  What is the relation between the slope of the curve in a scatter plot and the correlation between the variables on the axes?

3.  What types of changes cause movements along a curve, and what types cause shifts of the curve?

## ANSWERS TO THE REVIEW QUESTIONS

### Fill-In Questions

1.  Cartesian coordinate system

2.  time-series graph

3.  scatter plot

### True-False Questions

1.  **False**.    The value of the variable is on the vertical axis, and time is on the horizontal axis.

2.  **False**.    Variables depicted by a linear relationship can be either positively or negatively related.

3.  **False**.    Changes in the value of one of the variables on the two axes cause a movement along the curve, not a shift of the curve.

### Short-Answer Questions

1.  A dual scale can be used when more than one variable is plotted on the same graph and the scales of measurement of the variables are very different.

2.  The two variables are positively related if the slope is positive and negatively related if the slope is negative.

3.  Changes in the values of variables that are depicted on the axes cause movements along a curve, whereas changes in the values of other variables cause shifts of the curve.

# CHAPTER 3

# The Supply and Demand Model

## CHAPTER OVERVIEW

If people are left to choose for themselves what to consume and produce, what will society consume and produce? In this chapter, you will be introduced to the most important tool that economists have developed to answer this question. This is the market model of supply and demand. It starts with a description of buyers' behavior and a description of sellers' behavior and shows how their choices respond to changes in the economic environment. We will learn that neither buyers alone nor sellers alone, but both together, determine how much will be bought and sold and what the selling price will be. We will also see that when buyers and sellers respond to changes in the economic environment, the quantity bought and sold and the price are likely to change too. In this way, a price change signals to consumers *and* suppliers that something important has happened in the economy. This provides them with an incentive to make an adjustment to their new circumstances. Finally, we will see that interfering with the interaction of buyers and sellers in the marketplace, even with the best of intentions, can frequently make things worse.

## CHAPTER REVIEW

1.  Economics is concerned with explaining how people behave. To understand how buyers and sellers interact with each other, we need three things: a description of buyers' behavior, a description of sellers' behavior, and a description of how they deal with each other.

2.  The term **demand** describes the relationship between the **price** of a particular good and the amount of that good that consumers want to buy, which is called **quantity demanded**. It is important to distinguish between these two concepts. Quantity demanded is an *amount*; it is measured in pounds, or gallons, or haircuts; and it is determined only by price. Demand is a *relationship* (a function, in mathematical terms); it gives an amount for each possible price, not a single amount for a single price.

3.  The demand relationship can be represented in several ways. One is in the form of a table of numbers that gives the amount that consumers want to buy (quantity demanded) at different prices; this presentation is called a **demand schedule**. Another is in the form of a graph of the amounts that consumers want to buy (quantity demanded) at different prices; this is called a **demand curve**. When graphing a demand curve, it is important to put the quantity demanded on the horizontal axis and the price on the vertical axis.

4.  The **law of demand** says that the demand relationship is a negative relationship; that is, the amount of a good that people wish to buy (the quantity demanded) goes down as the price goes up, all other things being equal. More people will buy, and those who are buying will buy more, at lower prices because at the lower price the good looks more attractive compared to the alternatives than it did before. Remember the *ceteris paribus* condition, however. If other variables are changing at the same time that the price is falling, you can't tell what the relationship is between price and the amount that people want to buy.

5.   Changes in other variables that affect the amount that people want to buy lead to a *shift in demand*. That is, they change the amount that people want to buy (quantity demanded) at each and every price. This is seen in the demand graph as a shift in the curve to the right or to the left and is called a change in demand. Among the most important variables that can shift the demand for a product are *consumers' preferences, consumers' information, consumers' incomes, the number of consumers in the population, consumers' expectations of future prices,* and *the price of related goods.*

6.   Changes in consumers' preferences can clearly change the amount that people want to buy. If consumers decide that a product is more or less desirable, they will obviously want to buy more or less of it at each price. Be careful to distinguish this effect from consumers' desire to buy more when the price falls. In that case, their tastes have not changed (and the demand curve has not shifted); instead, consumers now find it more affordable to indulge their tastes.

7.   When people learn more about a good, they may change the amount that they want to buy at every price. Additional information about the benefits of a good will increase demand for it, and additional information about the harm from consuming a good will reduce demand for it.

8.   When consumers' incomes increase, they can afford to buy more things, and demand for most goods will increase. Those goods are called **normal goods**. However, the demand for some goods will decrease when consumers become richer and can afford better; these are called **inferior goods**. For example, students with low incomes may buy a lot of ramen noodles, because they are a low-cost food. When these students graduate and start full-time jobs, they may buy less ramen and more pizza (or steak if they get a really good job). In that case, ramen is an inferior good, whereas pizza is a normal good.

9.   Since demand is the relationship between the price of a good and the quantity demanded that *all* consumers want to buy, a change in the number of consumers is likely to change the amount that people want to buy at many prices. Therefore, the demand curve shifts when the number of consumers changes.

10.   The demand for a good will shift when the price of a good that is a **substitute** for it changes. If the substitute becomes less expensive, it becomes relatively more attractive, and some consumers will switch. For example, if the price of crab falls and all other things remain equal, consumers as a group (although perhaps not every consumer) will want to buy less lobster. If the price of Corvettes increases and all other things remain equal, then consumers will want to buy more Camaros. Generally, demand for a good increases when the price of a substitute rises, and demand for a good decreases when the price of a substitute falls. The demand for a good is also shifted by changes in the price of a **complement,** a good that tends to be consumed together with another good. For example, if the price of playing a round of golf rises, the demand for golf carts will be reduced. If the price of coffee falls, the demand for coffee creamer increases. Generally, demand for a good decreases when the price of a complement rises, and demand for a good increases when the price of a complement falls.

11.   Finally, demand will also respond to consumers' expectations of changes in the price of that good and of changes in other variables. For example, if consumers think they will be wealthier in the near future, they will start making additional purchases right now. Think about the graduating senior who just got that great job offer; isn't she already driving a new car? Similarly, if people believe that the price of something is going to change, their demand for it may change right away. For example, in December 1973, Johnny Carson's monologue joke on the *Tonight* show about the possibility of a toilet paper shortage led to such a large increase in the demand for toilet paper that in some places it really did become hard to find.

12. Changes in variables other than the price of the good in question *shift* the demand curve for that good. Changes in the price of the good in question, all other things being equal, result in consumers *moving along* the demand curve, but don't shift the demand curve. This is an important distinction to draw; don't confuse the two.

13. The term **supply** describes the relationship between the price of a good and the amount of that good that firms are willing to sell, which is called **quantity supplied**. As with demand, it is important to distinguish between these two concepts. Quantity supplied is an *amount*; it is measured in tons, or barrels, or shirts cleaned. Supply is a *relationship* or function; it gives an amount for each possible price, not a single amount.

14. Like the demand relationship, the supply relationship can be represented in several ways. One is in the form of a table of numbers that gives the amount that firms are willing and able to sell (quantity supplied) at different prices; this presentation is called a **supply schedule**. Another is in the form of a graph of the amount that firms are willing to sell (quantity supplied) at different prices; this is called a **supply curve**. When graphing a supply curve, it is important to put the quantity supplied on the horizontal axis and the price on the vertical axis.

15. The law of supply says that all other things being equal, the higher the price, the more firms will be willing to supply. Thus, the price and the quantity supplied are positively related. More firms will wish to sell and the firms that are selling will wish to sell more when the price rises because producing this product looks more profitable than the alternatives. Again, remember the *ceteris paribus* condition; if other variables that affect the amount that firms wish to sell are changing at the same time that the price is changing, the quantity supplied can either rise or fall.

16. When other variables that affect the amount that producers are willing and able to sell change, this leads to a *shift* in the supply curve. That is, those changes alter the amount that firms are willing to sell (quantity supplied) at each and every price. Among the most important variables that can shift the supply of a product are *technology, the price of goods used in production, the number of firms in the market, expectations of future prices,* and *government taxes, subsidies, and regulations.*

17. Technology refers to the ability to utilize other goods in order to produce the good or service. This can mean being able to utilize a chair, scissors, and someone's time and skill to produce a haircut, or being able to utilize complex equipment, silicon, and many people's time and skills to produce microchips. When knowledge improves in such a way that producers can produce the same amount of a good with fewer inputs, the cost of producing that good falls. Producing it becomes more attractive, all other things being equal, and the quantity supplied will increase at each and every price.

18. Similarly, if the price of the goods used in the production of a good falls, then the cost of producing that good falls. Again, producing that good becomes more profitable, all other things being equal, and firms will wish to sell more of it. This results in a rightward shift of the supply curve. Conversely, if the price of one or more inputs used in producing something rises, then firms will find it less profitable to produce that good and will be willing to sell less at each and every price, shifting the entire supply curve to the left.

19. Since the supply curve shows the amount that *all* of the producers together are willing to supply at different prices, an increase in the number of suppliers will increase that total and shift the supply curve to the right. Conversely, a decline in the number of sellers will reduce the total amount offered for sale at each and every price. This would lead to a leftward shift of the supply curve.

20. If firms expect that the price of their output is going to increase in the future, they will wish to delay selling their output until that price increase occurs. This results in less being offered for sale at any current price and a leftward shift of the supply curve. If the price of the goods that they sell

is expected to fall in the future, sellers will want to sell more now; this increases supply and shifts the supply curve to the right.

21. Taxes imposed by the government raise firms' costs of production and, like increases in input prices, make selling the product less attractive. Subsidies to producers, on the other hand, lower the costs of production and make sales more attractive. Thus, taxes shift the supply curve to the left (decreasing supply), and subsidies shift the supply curve to the right (increasing supply). Government regulations can also increase the costs of production—for example, by requiring the installation of pollution control equipment or additional safety testing of the product. These regulations will have the effect of decreasing supply.

22. As with the demand curve, it is important to distinguish *shifts* of the supply curve from *movements along* the supply curve. Changes in variables other than the price of the good in question shift the supply curve for that good. Changes in the price of the good in question, all other things being equal, result in a movement along the supply curve but do not shift the supply curve.

23. The demand curve describes how much consumers *want* to purchase at different prices, and the supply curve describes how much producers *want* to sell at different prices. In order to determine how much of a good actually gets bought (and sold), we need to understand how these two groups interact with each other. Economists believe that when consumers and producers get together, they will put pressure on the price that brings it to the level at which the amount that consumers want to purchase is just the amount that producers want to sell. This situation is called an *equilibrium*, because the quantity supplied and the quantity demanded are in balance. How much will be traded and the price at which those purchases take place can be determined from the numbers in the supply and demand schedules, or from a diagram that includes both the supply curve and the demand curve.

24. A **shortage** of a good occurs when, at the current price, consumers want to purchase more of the good than producers want to sell; the quantity demanded exceeds the quantity supplied at the current price in the market. In that case, we would expect some producers to take advantage of the situation by trying to get more from those who want to buy, and those consumers who are willing to pay more to try to outbid other consumers. This will cause the price to rise. Some consumers will decide that they are no longer willing to buy at the higher prices, and some producers will decide that they are willing to sell more at the higher prices. Eventually the price increases will bring the quantity supplied and the quantity demanded together, and there will be no further upward pressure on the price.

25. A **surplus** of a good, on the other hand, occurs when producers want to sell more units of the good than consumers want to purchase at the current price; the quantity supplied exceeds the quantity demanded. When there is a surplus, we would expect producers to start lowering the price to get their products sold. The surplus results in a falling price, which will cause some producers to decide that they no longer want to sell as much and some consumers to decide that they want to buy more. When the price falls to a level at which the quantity supplied equals the quantity demanded, there will be no further downward pressure on the price.

26. **Market equilibrium** is a situation with neither upward nor downward pressure on the price. This occurs when the quantity supplied equals the quantity demanded at the current price. We call this price the **equilibrium price**, and the quantity that gets bought and sold at that price the **equilibrium quantity**. If we have the supply and demand schedules for a good, we can find the equilibrium price by finding the price at which the quantity supplied equals the quantity demanded. If we have a supply and demand diagram that graphs the same information, we can find the equilibrium price and equilibrium quantity by finding where the supply curve and the demand curve cross. Look over to the vertical axis from the point at which the curves cross to find

the equilibrium price, and look down to the horizontal axis from that point to find the equilibrium quantity.

27. Suppose a market is in equilibrium, and one or more of the variables that affect supply and demand change. As a result, either the demand curve or the supply curve or both will shift. At the original equilibrium price, there will now be either a shortage or a surplus (depending on which way the curves have shifted and by how much), and pressure on the price will lead to a new equilibrium price and quantity. For example, if an increase in income leads to an increase (rightward shift) in demand, then there will be a shortage at the original equilibrium price, and the price will be forced up to a new equilibrium. A decrease in input prices leading to an increase (rightward shift) in supply will cause a surplus at the original equilibrium price, and the price will fall until a new equilibrium is reached. In this way, the equilibrium price and quantity respond to changes in variables that affect consumers' demand and producers' supply.

28. Governments sometimes put limits on the quantity that can be bought or sold. These limits are called **quotas**. They reduce the supply and raise the equilibrium price.

29. Governments often impose **price controls** in the form of **price ceilings** (maximum prices), to prevent prices from rising to levels that they feel are unfair to consumers, or **price floors** (minimum prices) to prevent prices from falling to levels that are viewed as unfair to suppliers. For example, **rent controls** are laws that put a ceiling on how high the price of rental housing can rise, while the **minimum wage** set by the federal government puts a floor below which wages (the price of labor inputs) cannot fall. When prices are prevented from rising or falling to their equilibrium levels, shortages or surpluses can persist, and other ways must be found to ration the goods. These often have undesirable features: People waste valuable time waiting in lines to make their purchases or take their chances on an illegal black market.

30. The **price elasticity of demand**, sometimes referred to as the elasticity of demand or even just the elasticity when the meaning is clear from the context, measures the responsiveness of quantity demanded to changes in price. It answers the question "By what percentage will quantity demanded change for every one percent that price changes, holding all else equal?" The price elasticity of demand is defined as the percentage change in quantity demanded divided by the percentage change in price, or

$$\text{Price elasticity of demand} = \frac{\text{Percentage change of quantity demanded}}{\text{Percentage change in price}}$$

31. We can also apply the elasticity concept to the responsiveness of quantity supplied to price. The **price elasticity of supply** measures this. It is defined as the percentage change in quantity demanded divided by the percentage change in price, or

$$\text{Price elasticity of supply} = \frac{\text{Percentage change in quantity demanded}}{\text{Percentage change in price}}$$

# ZEROING IN

1.

   a. The key to understanding and being able to use demand and supply diagrams is being able to distinguish between *shifts* of the demand and supply curves and *movements along* them. To see the difference, imagine yourself riding a bicycle on a flat road and think about the relationship between how fast your pedals turn and how fast the bike goes. This is a positive relationship; turning the pedals slowly (say, once every second) makes the bike go slowly, and turning the pedals quickly (say, three times a second) makes the bike go faster. If you were to draw a graph showing how fast the pedals turn on the vertical axis and the speed of the bike on the horizontal axis, the graph would slope upward, something like Figure 3.1.

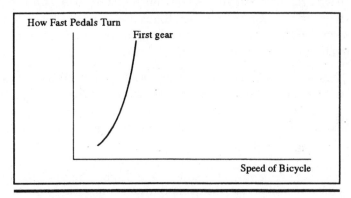

**Figure 3.1**

b.  Now suppose you shift the gears on the bicycle to a higher gear. The relationship between how fast you turn the pedals and how fast the bicycle goes is still a positive one: The faster you turn the pedals, the faster the bike goes. But turning the pedals at the once-per-second low speed now makes the bike go faster than it did in low gear, and turning the pedals at the three-times-per-second high speed also makes the bike go faster than it did in low gear. If you were to graph the relationship between how fast you turn the pedals and how fast the bike goes in the higher gear, you would get a new upward-sloping line to the right of the first line, as in Figure 3.2. For a ten-speed bicycle, there would be ten different lines, one for each gear.

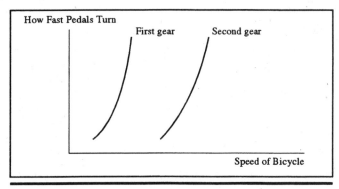

**Figure 3.2**

c.  Whatever gear you are in, you move *along* the line corresponding to that gear by turning the pedals faster or more slowly, or changing the value on the vertical axis. When you shift gears, you *shift* to a different line, and how fast you go on that line depends on how fast you choose to turn the pedals. The same is true of supply and demand curves. For a given set of levels of the other things that affect the supply of or demand for a good, you move *along* the curves when the price of that good (which is on the vertical axis) changes. When one of the other variables that affect supply or demand changes, you *shift* to a new supply or demand curve, and what quantity will be supplied or demanded on that curve depends on what price is chosen.

2.

a.  The next most important issue is being able to separate the things that shift the demand curve from the things that shift the supply curve. Since households demand goods and services, the variables that shift demand curves are generally things that affect households: their income, their preferences or tastes, their beliefs or expectations, and their number. Also remember that a demand curve shows how much of *one particular* product consumers wish to buy at different prices for that product. Since the answer to that question is likely to depend on whatever else consumers are buying, the prices of *other* products affect buyers' decisions and hence shift the demand curve.

b.    Firms supply goods and services, and so the variables that shift supply curves are generally things that affect firms: the prices they pay for inputs, including any taxes they pay or subsidies they receive from the government, their knowledge about how to produce (i.e., technology), their beliefs about profitability, and their number.

3.

a.    It is also important to remember that supply and demand curves shift *left* (decrease) or *right* (increase), not down or up. The reason for this is that quantity is always on the horizontal axis and price is always on the vertical axis. When consumers' income rises, the quantity that consumers wish to buy increases (if the good in question is a normal good) no matter what the price is, and an increase in quantity is shown as a movement to the *right*, as in Figure 3.3.

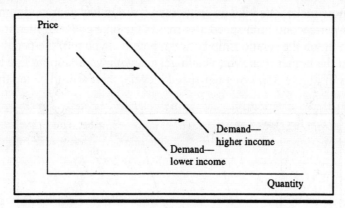

**Figure 3.3**

b.    This point doesn't seem very important when you look at shifts in demand curves, since a leftward shift looks like an upward shift (although the right answer is still that demand curves shift right for increases and left for decreases). But if you don't keep this straight when thinking about increasing or decreasing supply, you will get things wrong. An increase in supply because input prices fall moves the supply curve to the *right*, which looks like a shift downward, as in Figure 3.4. This is still an increase because at each and every price, the amount that firms wish to sell has increased.

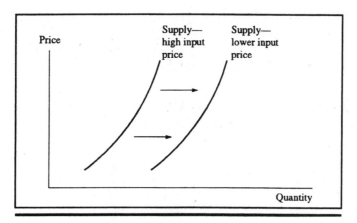

**Figure 3.4**

4.    It is worth remembering how the market adjusts from an initial equilibrium to a new equilibrium when something changes that shifts either supply or demand or both. Recall that an actual price adjusts toward equilibrium as the market responds to surpluses and shortages. It's not merely that one or both of the curves move and there is a new point at which they cross. The supply and demand analysis is intended to capture the behavior of real people. Suppose that the market for small cars is initially in equilibrium and that because of rising gas prices consumers now want to buy more small cars. Car dealers find their inventory of small cars on the lot declining; they also find that they can charge a higher price for small cars without hurting sales. Thus, small car prices start to rise. This means more profits for firms that sell small cars, and they respond by increasing the number of small cars that they produce for sale. Thus, the quantity supplied rises. At the same time, the rising price of small cars deters some buyers who wanted a new small car at the initial price but are not so excited about the prospect at a higher price. The price continues to rise until the dealers find that further price increases hurt business by driving too many customers away. At that point, the new equilibrium has been established; the new equilibrium price is higher, and the quantity bought and sold at that price is higher as well.

## ACTIVE REVIEW

### Fill-In Questions

1.    Demand is the relationship between _____ and the _____ of a good.

2.    A demand schedule is a table of numbers showing _____ and _____. When these numbers are graphed, the resulting line is called a(n) _____.

3.    The law of demand states that as the _____ falls (*ceteris paribus*), the quantity demanded will _____. Therefore, demand curves slope _____.

4.    Changes in the price of a good, all other things being equal, lead to _____ the demand curve for that good.

5.    Shifts in the demand curve for a good are caused by changes in anything that affects the amount consumers want to buy *except* the _____ of that good.

6.    Demand reflects, among other things, consumers' preferences. When consumers' tastes increase, the demand curve _____ to the_____ .

7.    Inferior goods are goods whose demand _____ as consumer _____ rises.

8. When the price of a complement for a good falls, the demand for that good
_____; as a result, the demand curve for that good shifts to the
_____. When the price of a substitute falls, on the other hand, demand for the
good in question _____, and the demand curve shifts to the
_____.

9. If consumers expect that the price of a good will fall in the future, they will wish to buy
_____ of it today. This results in a(n) _____ in demand.

10. The relationship between the _____ of a good and the quantity that producers are
willing to sell is known as _____. The amount that producers wish to sell is
called _____.

11. The _____ is a graph of the _____ of a good and the
_____.

12. The _____ states that as the price of a good rises (all else remaining equal), firms will wish
to sell _____ of that good. As a result, _____ slope upward.

13. Movements along the supply curve are caused by changes in _____, while shifts of the
supply curve are caused by changes in _____.

14. The ability to produce goods and services is known as _____. When
improvements in this ability lead to savings in the amounts of inputs required to produce a given
amount of output, the _____ shifts to the right.

15. When the prices of inputs rise, production becomes more _____. Firms will wish
to sell _____ of the good, and the supply curve will shift to the
_____. The same thing happens when government imposes
_____ or _____ that raise the cost of production.

16. Exit by new firms means that _____ will be offered for sale at every price. This
causes a(n) _____ shift of the _____.

17. A market is said to be in _____ when the amount that _____
want to buy at the current price just equals the amount that _____ wish to
_____.

18. Surpluses occur in a market when the _____ exceeds the _____. At these prices,
_____ is greater than _____.

19. Conversely, if the price is below the _____ price, the quantity
_____ will be less than the quantity _____ and a(n)
_____ will occur. In this case, the price can be expected to
_____.

20. Government restrictions on prices, such as _____, which prevent prices from
rising to their equilibrium levels, or _____, which prevent prices from falling,
lead to _____ or surpluses.

## True-False Questions

1. T   F     Price is determined by the interaction of households and firms.

2. T   F     When beans cost 69 cents a can, consumers in Oskaloosa wish to purchase 357 cans
per month, so we would say that at this price, demand is 357 cans per month.

3. T   F     The law of demand states that, all other things being equal, as price rises, demand falls.

4.   T   F    When T-shirts cost $17.50 apiece, consumers bought 336 T-shirts. After the price rose to $20.00, consumers purchased 286 of them. We would say that quantity demand fell by 50 units.

5.   T   F    The law of demand implies that demand curves slope downward.

6.   T   F    Charcoal and lighter fluid are complementary goods.

7.   T   F    Inferior goods refers to poor-quality, low-cost products.

8.   T   F    When incomes rise, the demand for inferior goods increases.

9.   T   F    Supply shows how much firms wish to sell at different prices.

10.   T   F    As the quantity supplied rises, price rises, according to the law of supply.

11.   T   F    When the price of computer chips falls, lowering the cost of producing computers, the supply of computers can be expected to increase.

12.   T   F    The equilibrium price in a market is the price that equates supply and demand.

13.   T   F    A shortage occurs when supply is greater than demand.

14.   T   F    A rising price will eliminate a shortage by increasing quantity supplied and reducing quantity demanded.

15.   T   F    If supply increases and demand remains unchanged, the equilibrium quantity will increase and the equilibrium price will rise.

16.   T   F    Price ceilings keep prices from falling to equilibrium.

## Short-Answer Questions

1.   Why do consumers wish to buy less when prices increase? How is this reflected in the demand curve?

2.   What is the difference between supply and quantity supplied?

3.   Why does the demand for a good rise when the price of a substitute rises?

4.   List four things that cause demand curves to shift, and explain how changes in them affect demand. What is the only thing that causes movement along the demand curve?

5.   Why do firms wish to supply less at lower prices? How is this reflected in the supply curve?

6.   Why does the supply of a good increase when the expected future price of the good falls?

7.   List four things that cause supply curves to shift, and explain how changes in them affect supply. What is the only thing that causes movement along the supply curve?

8.   Explain how a decrease in price eliminates a surplus.

9.   Explain why people's behavior should cause the price to settle at the equilibrium price.

10.   What happens to the equilibrium price and quantity if demand and supply both increase at the same time? Illustrate your answer with a diagram, and explain.

11.   What is the purpose of a price floor? What does a floor say about the level of the equilibrium price?

## 52  Chapter 3: The Supply and Demand Model

# WORKING IT OUT

1.  Remember that changes in the *price* of a good do not shift its demand or supply curve but represent different points on the supply or demand curve. When price changes, you move *along* the demand or supply curve. Figure 3.5 shows the demand curve for Swiss cheese. When the price falls from $1.50 per pound to $1.25 per pound, and all other things remain the same, the demand curve does not change, but the amount that consumers want to buy increases from 1,250 pounds per day to 1,575 pounds per day. The arrow in Figure 3.5 shows the movement along the demand curve.

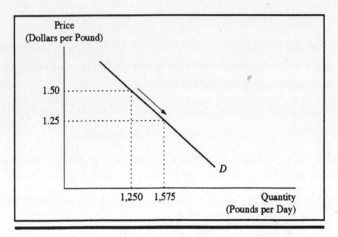

**Figure 3.5**

2.  Changes in *anything else* that affects how much consumers want to buy or firms want to sell shift the demand and supply curves. To know which curve shifts, you need to know what other variable is changing. Is it something that affects consumers' well-being? Then it shifts the demand curve. Is it something that affects producers' profits? Then it shifts the supply curve.

3.  The other thing that is central to understanding the supply and demand model is knowing how to combine supply and demand shifts to predict changes in the equilibrium price and quantity. Remember that supply and demand show the amounts that producers *want* to sell and consumers *want* to buy at different prices. The model also predicts that the price will eventually settle down at the equilibrium level, where the amount consumers want to buy just equals the amount that producers want to sell. When something changes either the supply or the demand, price will adjust to a new equilibrium level.

# Worked Problems

1.  Figure 3.6 shows the demand curve for whitewall tires. Currently the price of tires is $45 per tire. If the price of tires falls to $40 per tire (and all other things remain the same), what happens to the demand for tires and the quantity of tires demanded?

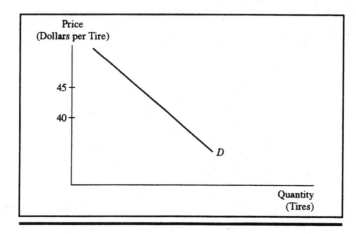

**Figure 3.6**

**Answer**

*Nothing happens to the demand for tires. None of the variables that affect how much consumers want to buy other than the price have changed (remember, "all other things remain the same"). The demand curve remains where it was. Since the price of tires has fallen, however, consumers will wish to purchase more tires. The quantity of tires demanded will increase, and we move downward along the demand curve to the new, higher quantity demanded, as shown in Figure 3.7.*

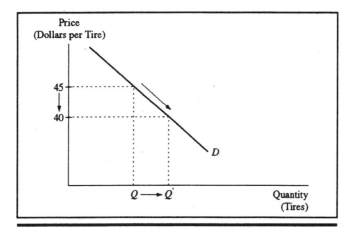

**Figure 3.7**

2.  Suppose the demand curve for whitewall tires is still the one shown in Figure 3.6, but now the price of *blackwall* tires rises from $35 per tire to $40 per tire. What happens to the demand for whitewall tires?

**Answer**

*It seems believable that at least some people who are currently buying blackwall tires view whitewall tires as substitutes. When the price of blackwall tires rises, those consumers will find the blackwall tires a less attractive purchase just because they're more expensive and will switch from blackwalls to whitewalls. This will happen no matter what the price of whitewalls is currently; the demand for whitewalls will increase at each and every possible price. The increase in the price of a substitute (blackwalls) increases the demand for this good (whitewalls), and the demand curve shifts to the right (not up), as in Figure 3.8.*

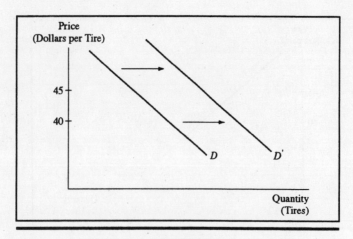

**Figure 3.8**

3.    Figure 3.9 shows the market for peach daiquiris in Greenwich. At first, the market is in equilibrium, with the price of peach daiquiris at $2.50 per drink and 175 drinks being purchased each week. Now suppose that, because of bad weather in Georgia, the price of peaches rises sharply. What happens to the supply and demand for peach daiquiris, and what happens to the equilibrium price and quantity?

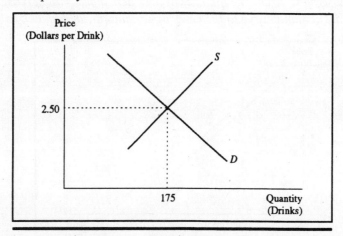

**Figure 3.9**

**Answer**

*First, we need to know what happens to the supply and demand for peach daiquiris. Nothing happens to the demand; none of the variables that affect the amount that consumers want to buy have changed. However, peaches are an important ingredient in peach daiquiris, and an increase in their price increases the cost of making the drink. Producers will find it less profitable to sell peach daiquiris, and some will choose to stop selling them. The increase in the price of an input decreases the supply of the good and shifts the supply curve to the left, as shown in Figure 3.10.*

*At the original equilibrium price of $2.50, consumers still want to purchase 175 drinks each week, but producers now want to sell fewer drinks. There is a shortage of peach daiquiris at this price, and there will be upward pressure on the price. Producers will find that they can still sell all the drinks that they want to sell at $2.50 even if they increase the price; in fact, at the higher price, producers want to sell somewhat more drinks, and they find that they can. At that price, some consumers find that peach daiquiris are not worth the extra outlay, and they switch to strawberry margaritas. Thus, while the demand for peach daiquiris hasn't changed, the quantity demanded* *falls as the price rises. From Figure 3.10, we can see that when the price rises to the new equilibrium (at $2.75), the quantity demanded falls to exactly the amount that producers want to sell at that price on the new supply curve (145).*

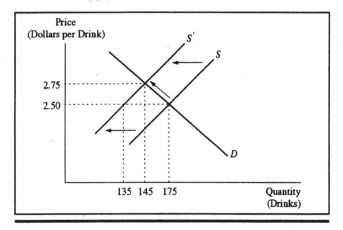

**Figure 3.10**

## PRACTICE PROBLEMS

1.  Figure 3.11 shows the supply curve for jellybeans. Currently the price of jellybeans is $1.00 a pound. If the price of jellybeans rises to $1.25 a pound (and all other things remain the same), what happens to the supply of jellybeans and the quantity of jellybeans supplied?

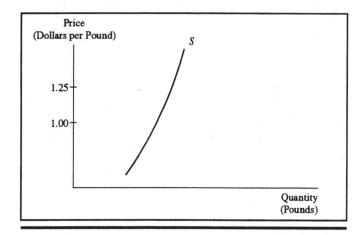

**Figure 3.11**

2.  Figure 3.12 shows the demand for denim skirts. If the price of denim skirts rises from $27 to $32, what happens to the demand for denim skirts and the quantity of denim skirts demanded?

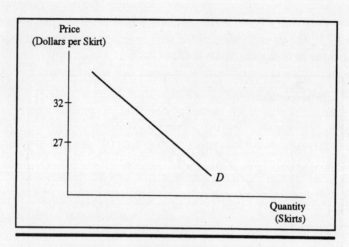

**Figure 3.12**

3.  Suppose the demand for whitewall tires is as shown in Figure 3.6, and suppose that, because of rumors of increasing instability in the Middle East, consumers believe that the price of gasoline is going to increase dramatically and remain at that higher level for a long time. What happens to the demand for whitewall tires?

4.  Suppose the supply of jellybeans is as shown in Figure 3.11, and suppose the price of sugar, which is a major ingredient in jellybeans, rises from $1.50 per pound to $1.78 per pound. What happens to the supply of jellybeans?

5.  Figure 3.13 shows the supply and demand curves for the market for running suits in Portland. The market is initially in equilibrium at a price of $75 and 1,750 suits sold per year. Suppose that, because of an improving local economy, incomes in Portland rise significantly. What happens to the supply and demand for running suits and the equilibrium price and quantity?

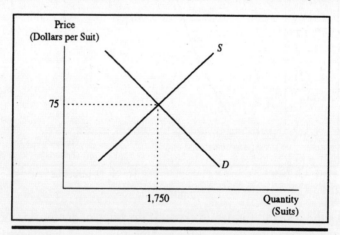

**Figure 3.13**

6.  Figure 3.14 shows the supply and demand curves for the market for tofu in San Leandro, California. The market is initially in equilibrium at a price of $1.50 per container, and 450 containers are consumed per month. Suppose that, simultaneously, consumers become concerned about soybean pesticide residue in tofu and the state government eases regulations on the disposal of soybean wastes, which lowers the cost of producing tofu. What happens to the supply and demand for tofu and the equilibrium price and quantity?

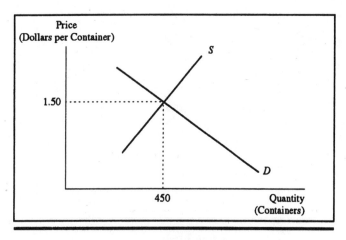

**Figure 3.14**

# CHAPTER TEST

1. Potatoes would be classified as a normal good if

   a.   people at all levels of income consumed them.
   b.   other food was more nutritious.
   c.   more were consumed as incomes rose.
   d.   fewer were consumed when the price of bread fell.

2. The demand curve for pizza is downward-sloping. Suddenly the price of pizza rises from $8 per pizza to $10 per pizza. This will cause

   a.   the demand curve to shift to the left.
   b.   the demand curve to shift to the right.
   c.   quantity demanded to increase.
   d.   quantity demanded to decrease.

3. A leftward shift in the supply of Swiss watches might be due to

   a.   an increase in the wages of Swiss watchmakers.
   b.   an increase in the tax on imported watches.
   c.   the introduction of cost-saving robots in the watch industry.
   d.   increased popularity of foreign watches.

4. The supply curve for children's books is upward-sloping. A decrease in the price of children's books, all other things being equal, will lead to

   a.   an increase in the quantity of children's books supplied.
   b.   an increase in the supply of children's books.
   c.   producers wishing to sell fewer children's books.
   d.   a decrease in the supply of children's books.

Use Figure 3.15 to answer the next three questions. The diagram refers to the demand for and supply of baseball caps. The baseball cap market is initially in equilibrium at point *C*. Assume that baseball caps are a normal good.

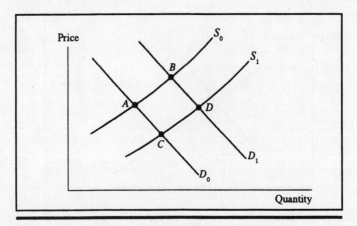

**Figure 3.15**

5.  The baseball cap market moves from point *C* to a new equilibrium at point *A*. There has been a(n)

    a.   decrease in demand and a decrease in supply.
    b.   decrease in demand and a decrease in quantity supplied.
    c.   increase in quantity demanded and an increase in quantity supplied.
    d.   decrease in quantity demanded and a decrease in quantity supplied.

6.  A movement from point *C* to point *D* might have been caused by

    a.   a tightening of worker safety regulations in the production of baseball caps.
    b.   a decrease in the price of cowboy hats (a substitute for baseball caps).
    c.   a decrease in the cost of the cloth used in the baseball cap industry.
    d.   increased income.

7.  The discovery that wearing a hat reduces skin cancer would be likely to move the market from point *A* to

    a.   point *B*.
    b.   point *C*.
    c.   point *D*.
    d.   none of the above.

8.  Which of the following is likely to cause a decrease in the demand for gasoline?

    a.   An increase in the price of cars
    b.   A decrease in the price of gasoline
    c.   An increase in subway and bus fares
    d.   A decrease in the price of crude

9.  You observe that the price of houses and the number of houses purchased both rise over the course of a year. You conclude that

    a.   the demand for houses has increased.
    b.   the demand curve for houses must be upward-sloping.
    c.   the supply of houses has increased.
    d.   housing construction costs must be decreasing.

10. An increase in the quantity supplied is shown by

    a.   shifting the supply curve up.
    b.   shifting the supply curve to the left.
    c.   shifting the supply curve to the right.

    d.    moving upward along the supply curve.

11.    An increase in the price of cars could be explained by all of the following *except*

    a.    stricter auto emission standards.
    b.    a fall in the price of gasoline.
    c.    producers' expectations that car prices will rise in the future.
    d.    an increase in the use of public transportation.

12.    A market is said to be in equilibrium when

    a.    supply equals demand.
    b.    there is downward pressure on the price.
    c.    the amount consumers wish to buy at the current price equals the amount producers wish to sell at that price.
    d.    all buyers are able to find sellers willing to sell to them at the current price.

Use the following supply and demand schedules to answer the next four questions.

| Price | Quantity Supplied | Quantity Demanded |
|---|---|---|
| $3 | 30 | 75 |
| $4 | 40 | 70 |
| $5 | 50 | 65 |
| $6 | 60 | 60 |
| $7 | 70 | 55 |
| $8 | 80 | 50 |

13.    When the price is $4, this market has a

    a.    shortage of 30 units.
    b.    shortage of 10 units.
    c.    surplus of 30 units.
    d.    surplus of 15 units.

14.    There is a surplus of 30 units when the price equals

    a.    $4.
    b.    $5.
    c.    $6.
    d.    $8.

15.    This market is in equilibrium when the price equals

    a.    $5.
    b.    $6.
    c.    $7.
    d.    $8.

16.    Suppose that the demand for this product shifts so that 15 fewer units are demanded at each price. The new equilibrium price will be

    a.    $5.
    b.    $6.
    c.    $7.
    d.    $8.

17. If wine and cheese are complements, then an increase in the price of wine will cause

    a.   an increase in the price of cheese.
    b.   a decrease in the demand for wine.
    c.   less cheese to be demanded at each price.
    d.   a rightward shift in the demand curve.

18. If both supply and demand increase simultaneously, the equilibrium

    a.   price must rise and the equilibrium quantity must fall.
    b.   price must rise and the equilibrium quantity may either rise or fall.
    c.   quantity must rise and the equilibrium price may either rise or fall.
    d.   price must fall and the equilibrium quantity may either rise or fall.

19. Which of the following would *not* eliminate a shortage of a good?

    a.   A fall in the number of consumers
    b.   A fall in the price of a substitute for the good
    c.   A fall in the price of a complement for the good
    d.   An increase in the price of the good

20. Supply for a product could increase for all of the following reasons *except*

    a.   an improvement in technology.
    b.   a rise in the price of the product.
    c.   an expected decrease in the price of the product in the future.
    d.   an increase in the price of an important input.

## ANSWERS TO THE REVIEW QUESTIONS

## Fill-In Questions

1.   price; quantity demanded

2.   price; quantity demanded; demand curve

3.   price; rise; downward

4.   movement along

5.   price

6.   shifts, right

7.   decreases; income

8.   rises; right; falls; left

9.   less; decrease

10.  price; supply; quantity supplied

11.  supply curve; price; quantity supplied

12.  law of supply; more; supply curve

13.  price; technology, input prices, number of firms, expectations or government policies

14.  technology; supply curve

15.  costly; less; left; taxes; regulations

16.  less; left; supply curve

17. equilibrium; consumers; producers; sell

18. price; equilibrium price; quantity supplied; quantity demanded

19. equilibrium; supplied; demanded; shortage; increase

20. price ceilings; price floors; shortages

## True-False Questions

1. **True.**    Household behavior (demand) and producer behavior (supply) determine price.

2. **False.**    Quantity demanded is 357 cans per month. Demand is not an amount.

3. **False.**    When price rises, quantity demanded falls, not demand.

4. **True.**    When the price of a good changes, quantity demanded changes.

5. **True.**    Since the law of demand says that quantity demanded is inversely related to price, it implies that demand curves slope downward.

6. **True.**    When the price of charcoal rises, people will cook outside less often. This reduces the demand for lighter fluid; less lighter fluid will be purchased no matter what its price is.

7. **False.**    Inferior goods are goods that consumers want to buy less of when their incomes rise. They may be perfectly well made products.

8. **True.**    This is the definition of a normal good, not an inferior good. Demand will fall when income rises.

9. **True.**    This is the definition of supply.

10. **False.**    Quantity supply is determined by price, not the other way around.

11. **True.**    Computer chips are an input into the production of computers. When their price falls, producing computers becomes less costly and hence more profitable; firms will increase the amount they wish to sell, no matter what the current price is. Thus, supply increases.

12. **False.**    The equilibrium price equates quantity supplied and quantity demanded.

13. **False.**    A shortage occurs when quantity supplied is less than the quantity demanded.

14. **True.**    A shortage occurs when quantity supplied is less than quantity demanded at the current price. As the price rises, the amount consumers wish to purchase (quantity demanded) will fall, and the amount firms wish to sell (quantity supplied) will rise. This eliminates the shortage.

15. **False.**    If supply increases and demand remains unchanged, the equilibrium quantity will increase, but the price will fall as consumers move downward along the demand curve.

16. **False.**    Price ceilings keep prices from rising to equilibrium.

## Short-Answer Questions

1. When the price of a good rises (all other things being equal), the good becomes a less desirable alternative than other products. More has to be given up in order to consume the product than before, and consumers will generally wish to consume less of it. This inverse relationship between the price and the quantity demanded is reflected in the negative (downward) slope of the demand curve.

2. Quantity supplied is the amount that producers wish to produce. It is measured in units of product (pounds, gallons, haircuts, etc.). The amount that producers wish to sell depends on many things.

Supply is the relationship between one of those things (the price of the good) and the quantity supplied.

3. When the substitute becomes more expensive, people will look for alternatives to buy.

4. Changes in any of the following will cause a shift in the demand curve: consumers' preferences, consumers' information, consumers' income, consumers' expectations of future prices, the number of consumers in the population, and the price of closely related goods. A change in the price of the good is the only thing that leads to movement along the demand curve.

5. Fewer firms will wish to sell, and the firms that are selling will wish to sell less, when the price falls because producing this product looks less profitable than the alternatives. This direct relationship between the price and the quantity supplied is reflected in the positive (upward) slope of the supply curve.

6. If the expected future price of a good falls, firms will want to supply more now while the price is relatively high. This shifts the supply curve to the right.

7. Changes in any of the following will cause a shift in the supply curve: technology, the price of goods used in production, the number of firms in the market, expectations of future prices, and government taxes, subsidies, and regulations. A change in the price of the good is the only thing that leads to movement along the supply curve.

8. When there is a surplus, quantity supplied is greater than quantity demanded at the current price. As the price falls, quantity demanded rises as we move downward along the demand curve, whereas quantity supplied falls as we move back down along the supply curve. If the price continues to falls, eventually quantity demanded and quantity supplied are equal, and the surplus has been eliminated.

9. When there are either shortages or surpluses, there will be pressure on the price to move in the direction that eliminates the shortage or surplus. In the event of a shortage, producers find that they can raise the price and still sell everything they wish to sell. Consumers who are unable to find the product they want to buy will start offering a higher price for it. The increase in price will induce suppliers to offer more and will also reduce the amount that buyers wish to purchase. In the event of a surplus, producers will find themselves unable to sell everything they wish to sell and will lower the price to sell their output. Consumers will find that they can negotiate discounts successfully. The decrease in price will lead buyers to purchase more and will lead suppliers to wish to sell less. In this way, shortages and surpluses are eliminated, and the price moves toward the equilibrium level.

10. When both supply and demand increase (shift rightward) at the same time, the equilibrium quantity will increase. The equilibrium price can either rise or fall, depending on whether the shift of supply or demand is greater. For example, in the first panel of Figure 3.16, while both supply and demand increase, the shift of demand is greater and the new equilibrium price is higher. In the second panel of Figure 3.16, the shift of supply is greater and the new equilibrium price is lower. In both cases, the new equilibrium quantity is larger.

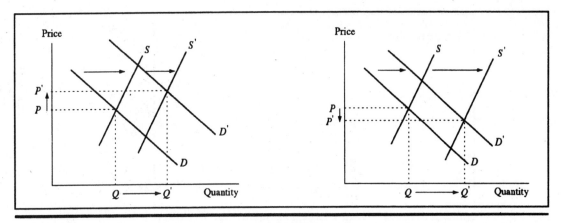

**Figure 3.16**

11. Price floors are attempts to keep prices from falling. They are based on the perspective that the equilibrium price for the product is too low.

## SOLUTIONS TO THE PRACTICE PROBLEMS

1. The *supply* of jellybeans is unchanged. None of the variables that affect how much producers want to sell other than the price have changed (remember, "all other things remain the same"). The supply curve remains where it was. Since the price of jellybeans has risen, however, producers wish to sell more of them. The quantity of jellybeans supplied increases, and we move upward along the supply curve to the new, higher quantity supplied, as shown in Figure 3.17.

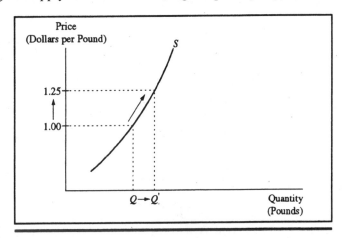

**Figure 3.17**

2. Nothing happens to the *demand* for denim skirts. The price of denim skirts has changed, but none of the other variables that affect how many skirts consumers wish to buy have changed. Since the price has risen, consumers will wish to buy fewer denim skirts, and the quantity demanded falls. We move upward along the demand curve, as shown in Figure 3.18.

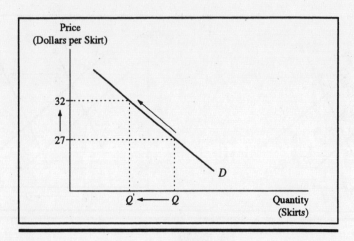

**Figure 3.18**

3.  Tires and gasoline are complements; the more you drive, the more gasoline you purchase and the more tires you purchase. If consumers expect that gasoline is going to be much more expensive in the future, they will probably expect to be doing less driving in the future. In that case, there will be reduced demand for new tires; the old tires will last longer if they aren't going to be driven on as much. The increase in the price of a complement (gasoline) decreases the demand for this good (whitewall tires), and the demand curve shifts to the left (not down), as in Figure 3.19.

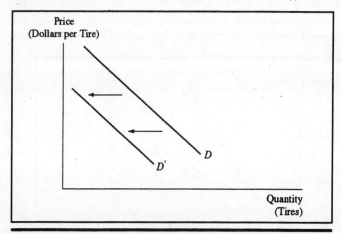

**Figure 3.19**

4.  The increase in the price of sugar raises the cost of producing jellybeans and makes producing them less profitable. Some producers find that they can no longer continue to make a living selling jellybeans, and they stop producing them. This will happen no matter what the price of jellybeans is currently; the supply of jellybeans will decrease at each and every possible price. The increase in the price of an input (sugar) decreases the supply of this good (jellybeans), and the supply curve shifts to the *left* (not down), as in Figure 3.20.

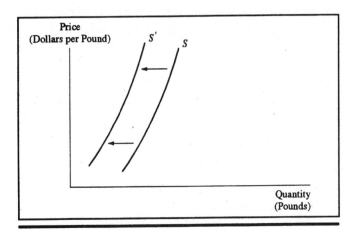

**Figure 3.20**

5.    First, what happens to the supply and demand for running suits? Since none of the (nonprice)
      variables that affect the amount that producers want to sell have changed, nothing happens to the
      supply. It is likely, however, that running suits are a normal good; when people's incomes rise,
      they do more of their running in track suits and less in old sweats. At any price of running suits,
      the increase in income will result in consumers wanting to buy more of them. Demand increases,
      and the demand curve shifts to the right, as shown in Figure 3.21.

      At the original equilibrium price of $75, consumers now want to purchase more running suits per
      year, but producers still want to sell 1,750 per year. There is a shortage of running suits at this
      price, and there will be upward pressure on the price. Producers will find that they can still sell
      1,750 suits per year if they raise the price; in fact, at higher prices, producers want to sell more
      suits, and they find that they can. At that price, some consumers find that running suits are not
      worth the extra outlay, and they stick to their old sweatshirts. Thus, while the supply of running
      suits has not changed, the quantity supplied rises as the price rises. From Figure 3.21, we can see
      that when the price rises to its new equilibrium level, the quantity supplied rises to a level that is
      exactly the amount that consumers want to buy at that price on the new demand curve.

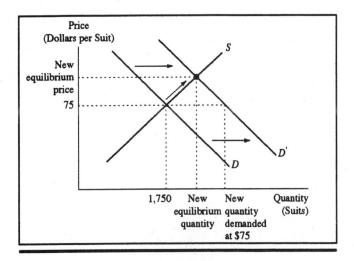

**Figure 3.21**

6.    First, what happens to the supply and demand for tofu? The decreased regulation lowers the cost
      of producing tofu and makes producing it more profitable. Some producers find that they can now
      make a living selling tofu, and they enter production. Others expand their operations. This will

happen no matter what the price of tofu is currently; the supply of tofu will increase at each and every possible price. The supply curve shifts to the right, as in Figure 3.22. At the same time, the change in consumers' tastes decreases the quantity of tofu demanded, no matter what the price; the demand curve shifts to the left, as in Figure 3.22.

At the original price of $1.50, producers now wish to sell more tofu per month, but consumers now wish to buy less tofu per month. There is a surplus of tofu, and there will be downward pressure on the price. Producers will find that they cannot sell all the tofu they wish to, and will start offering discounts to move their stock. As the price falls, some consumers will decide that it is worth taking some health risk when the product is cheaper, and some producers will find that, eased regulation notwithstanding, selling tofu at lower prices is not as profitable as they thought. Thus, the quantity demanded rises as we move along the new demand curve and the quantity supplied falls as we move along the new supply curve, until the two are brought into balance. In Figure 3.22, this occurs at a new equilibrium price of $1.10 per container and a new equilibrium quantity of 500 containers per month. Notice, however, that if the increase in supply had been smaller and the decrease in demand had been larger, the new equilibrium quantity could have been smaller than the initial equilibrium quantity. When demand decreases and supply increases, all you can say for certain is that the equilibrium price will fall.

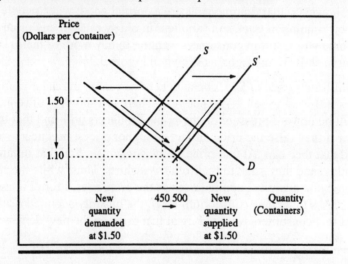

**Figure 3.22**

# ANSWERS TO THE CHAPTER TEST

1.  c

2.  d

3.  a

4.  c

5.  d

6.  d

7.  a

8.  a

9.  a

10. d

11.  d

12.  c

13.  a

14.  d

15.  b

16.  a

17.  c

18.  c

19.  c

20.  b

# CHAPTER 4

# Elasticity and Its Uses

## CHAPTER OVERVIEW

One of the most practical uses of economic analysis is to predict the effects of changes in underlying conditions or policies on the prices and production of different goods and services. In this chapter, you will learn more about the concept of elasticity, a useful way to measure the responsiveness of one economic variable to another. Elasticity can be used in many settings; here, we will use it to explore the sensitivity of quantity demanded to changes in the price of the good, in income, and in the prices of other closely related goods. We will also use elasticity to explore the sensitivity of quantity supplied to price. Finally, we will see how useful the concept is in answering different questions through supply and demand analysis.

## CHAPTER REVIEW

1.  *Elasticity* is a very general concept. It refers to a measure of the sensitivity of one economic variable to changes in another economic variable in percentage terms. There are many different pairs of variables between which we can calculate an elasticity. Here, we will focus on some of the elasticities that are most useful in economics.

2.  Recall from Chapter 3 that the price elasticity of demand is defined as the percentage change in quantity demanded divided by the percentage change in the price, or

    $$\text{Price elasticity of demand} = \frac{\text{Percentage change of quantity demanded}}{\text{Percentage change in price}}$$

    This tells us by what percentage quantity demanded changed for each percentage point change in price.

3.  Remember that to calculate the elasticity of demand, you need to know two points on the *same* demand curve. Price elasticity measures the responsiveness of quantity demanded to a change in price, *holding all else equal*.

4.  To calculate the percentage change in quantity demanded, we take the number of units by which the quantity changed and divide by the initial quantity. Similarly, we take the number of dollars by which the price changed and divide by the initial price to calculate the percentage change in price.

    So, using symbols,

    $$e_d = \frac{\Delta Q_d}{Q_d} \div \frac{\Delta p}{p}$$

    where $e_d$ represents the price elasticity of demand and $\Delta$ means "change in."

5.  Since the demand curve slopes downward, an increase in the price causes a decrease in the quantity demanded. Thus, the elasticity of demand is a negative number; when $\Delta P/P$ is positive,

$\Delta\,Q_d/Q_d$ is negative. It is practice to multiply the number by a negative 1 and then just talk about the absolute value of the price elasticity of demand.

6.  Since elasticities measure changes in percentage terms, you get the same answer no matter what units quantity and price are measured in—elasticity is a **unit-free measure**. The advantage of this is that you can easily compare the responsiveness of quantity demanded to price for different goods. It also means that the elasticity will not change if you use different units of measurement— say, six-packs instead of bottles. A 10-six-pack increase in consumption is not the same as a 10-bottle increase, but a 10 percent increase in the number of six-packs is also a 10 percent increase in the number of bottles.

7.  The elasticity of demand is not the same thing as the *slope* of the demand curve. The slope of the demand curve is the change in price divided by the change in quantity demanded, or $\Delta\,P/Q$, and it depends on the units chosen to measure price and quantity. Changing the units that quantity is measured in, for example, will change the slope of the demand curve. If a 25-cent increase in the price of soft drinks causes a 6,000-bottle reduction in the quantity of soft drink demanded, it causes only a 1,000-six-pack reduction. But if consumption was originally 60,000 bottles (or 10,000 six-packs), the price increase causes a 10 percent reduction either way you measure soft drinks.

8.  Goods for which the price elasticity of demand is greater than 1 are said to have an **elastic demand**. That is, a 1 percent change in the price causes a more than 1 percent change in quantity demanded. Goods for which the price elasticity of demand is less than 1, so that a 1 percent change in the price causes a *less* than 1 percent change in quantity demanded, are said to have an **inelastic demand**. Goods with a price elasticity of demand of exactly 1 are called **unit elastic**.

9.  When the quantity demanded is completely unresponsive to the price, the demand curve is a vertical line, and we say that the demand is **perfectly inelastic**. When the demand curve is a horizontal line, consumers are not willing to buy any of the good if the price rises even a little bit above that price. In this case, even the smallest change in price would cause a total reduction in quantity demanded, and we say that the demand is **perfectly elastic**.

10. When calculating percentage changes in price and quantity, we need to divide the absolute change in price or quantity by the level of price or quantity. However, if the change in price or quantity is big enough, we will get different answers depending on whether we divide by the starting price or quantity, or by the ending price or quantity. For example, when price rises from $1.00 to $1.50, that's a 50 percent increase based on the $1.00 starting price, but only a 33 percent increase based on the $1.50 ending price. Neither of these is "right" or "wrong." What is needed is some standard way of doing things to avoid confusion. The economists' convention is to use the *average*, or *midpoint*, of the starting price (or quantity) and the ending price (or quantity) for calculating percentage changes. Using that convention, the price increase from $1.00 to $1.50 is a 40 percent increase, because 50 cents is 40 percent of $1.25, the average of $1.00 and $1.50.

11. When the price elasticity of demand is calculated using the average of the starting and ending prices and quantities, the *midpoint formula* is used. To calculate elasticity using the midpoint formula, you need to know two points on the demand curve: the old price and quantity ($P_{old}$ and $Q_{old}$) and the new price and quantity ($P_{new}$ and $Q_{new}$). The elasticity of demand is given by

$$\text{Price elasticity of demand} = \frac{\text{Change in burgers demanded}}{\text{Average of old and new quantity}} \div \frac{\text{Change in pizza price}}{\text{Average of old and new price}}$$

$$= \frac{Q_{new} - Q_{old}}{(Q_{new} - Q_{old})/2} \div \frac{P_{new} - P_{old}}{(P_{new} - P_{old})/2}$$

$$\text{Income elasticity of demand} = \frac{\text{Change in quantity demanded}}{\text{Average of old and new quantity}} \div \frac{\text{Change in income}}{\text{Average of old and new income}}$$

$$= \frac{Q_{new} - Q_{old}}{(Q_{new} - Q_{old})/2} \div \frac{Y_{new} - Y_{old}}{(Y_{new} - Y_{old})/2} \quad \text{, where } Y \text{ is income}$$

12. Revenue is the total amount of money that consumers pay and producers receive when some amount of a good is sold at some price. If $Q$ units are sold at a price of $P$ per unit, then revenue is the product of price and quantity, or $P \times Q$.

13. When the price rises, the quantity demanded falls, and so revenue can change as well. But it's not obvious which way revenue will change when the price rises. Two things are occurring at the same time: Each unit that is sold is selling for more, which increases revenue; but fewer units get sold, which decreases revenue. The price elasticity of demand tells us which of these two effects is stronger, and therefore tells us whether revenue will rise or fall when the price rises. When demand is inelastic (elasticity of demand is less than 1), the percentage decrease in quantity will be less than the percentage increase in price, and so revenue will rise as the price rises. When demand is elastic (elasticity of demand is greater than 1), the percentage decrease in quantity will be larger than the percentage increase in price, and so revenue will fall as the price rises. And when demand is unit elastic (elasticity of demand is equal to 1), the percentage decrease in quantity is exactly equal to the percentage increase in price, and revenue will not change when price rises. This explains why grain farmers are worse off when they all share a bumper crop; since the demand for grain is inelastic, the increased quantity sold is more than offset by falling prices.

14. Several variables determine whether the elasticity of demand for a good is large or small. The most important of these is whether there are good substitutes for the product. If there are, changes in price will cause consumers to switch to the substitutes, and the quantity demanded will fall dramatically; in this case, the elasticity of demand will be high. If, on the other hand, good substitutes are not available, consumers will continue to buy as the price rises, and demand will have a lower elasticity.

15. The price elasticity of demand will be higher for goods on which people spend a large fraction of their income. Changes in the price of something that you spend a lot on have big effects on your buying power, necessitating big adjustments. Changes in the price of something that represents only a small part of your income have little effect on what you can buy, and so only small changes in the amount you buy are needed.

16. People will respond more to price changes that are expected to be temporary than to long-lasting price changes, and so the price elasticity of a temporary change will tend to be high. If a price decrease is going to last a long time, there is no hurry to take advantage of the low price. Similarly, if a price increase is expected to persist, you might as well go on buying now, because the good will still be more expensive later on.

17. If a price changes permanently, the price elasticity of demand is likely to be lower immediately after the price change than after some time has passed. In the *short run*, people have only limited opportunities to adjust their consumption, but in the *long run*, more adjustments are possible. For example, when the price of home heating oil rises, in the short run people with oil heat can turn down their thermostats and wear sweaters, but they still have to heat their houses. In the long run, however, more new homes will be built with electric or natural gas heating, and the change in the quantity of oil demanded will be larger.

18. So far, we have been thinking about the price elasticity of demand. Price certainly is an important determinant of quantity demanded, but remember that there are other variables that also affect the

amount that consumers want to buy. When those variables change, the demand curve shifts. We can also use the concept of elasticity to measure the responsiveness of quantity demanded to these changes.

19. One of the most important variables (other than price) that affects consumer demand is consumer income. The **income elasticity of demand** is the percentage change in quantity demanded divided by percentage change in income, holding all else (including the price) constant. That is,

$$\text{Income elasticity of demand} = \frac{\text{Percentage change in quantity demanded}}{\text{Percentage change in income}}$$

Recall that when income rises, consumers wish to buy more of all normal goods and less of all inferior goods. Thus, for normal goods the income elasticity of demand will be positive, whereas inferior goods will have negative income elasticities of demand.

20. We can also apply the elasticity concept to the responsiveness of quantity supplied to price. Recall from Chapter 3 that the **price elasticity of supply** measures this. It is defined as the percentage change in the quantity supplied divided by the percentage change in the price, or

$$\text{Price elasticity of supply} = \frac{\text{Percentage change in quantity supplied}}{\text{Percentage change in price}}$$

21. A vertical supply curve is **perfectly inelastic** because any change in price will lead to no response in the quantity supplied, and the elasticity of supply is therefore zero. A horizontal supply curve is **perfectly elastic**. The slightest decrease in price reduces the supply to zero.

## ZEROING IN

1. From the applications in the chapter, you can see that the elasticity concept is quite general. We can talk about the parking fine elasticity of parking tickets, or the tax rate elasticity of cigarette sales. Remember that elasticity just means responsiveness of one variable to changes in another, in percentage terms.

2. The main formula to learn in this chapter is the midpoint formula. In the section above, this was given for the price elasticity of demand. It also applies when calculating other elasticities, such as the price elasticity of supply. To calculate that elasticity using the midpoint formula, you need to know two points on the supply curve: the old price and quantity ($P_{old}$ and $Q_{old}$) and the new price and quantity ($P_{new}$ and $Q_{new}$). The price elasticity of supply is given by

$$\text{Price elasticity of supply} = \frac{\text{Change in quantity supplied}}{\text{Average of old and new quantity}} \div \frac{\text{Change in price}}{\text{Average of old and new price}}$$

$$= \frac{Q_{new} - Q_{old}}{(Q_{new} + Q_{old}) \div 2} \div \frac{P_{new} - P_{old}}{(P_{new} + P_{old}) \div 2}$$

So, if firms wish to supply 560 units when the price is $13 per unit, and are willing to supply 640 units if the price rises to $17 per unit, then if we call the first price and quantity the old point on the supply curve and the second price and quantity the new point, we have

$$\text{Price elasticity of supply} = \frac{\text{Change in quantity supplied}}{\text{Average of old and new quantity}} \div \frac{\text{Change in price}}{\text{Average of old and new price}}$$

$$= \frac{640-560}{(640+560) \div 2} \div \frac{17-13}{(17+13) \div 2} = \frac{80}{600} \div \frac{4}{15} = \frac{1}{2}$$

3. It's common to think that a demand curve has *a* price elasticity of demand, the way an object has *a* weight. This isn't right, however; the same demand curve can have different elasticities of demand depending on from which prices and quantities you start and finish. To see this, look at the following demand schedule, which is graphed as a demand curve in Figure 4.1.

| Price | Quantity Demanded |
|:-----:|:-----------------:|
| 10 | 0 |
| 8 | 40 |
| 6 | 80 |
| 4 | 120 |
| 2 | 160 |
| 0 | 200 |

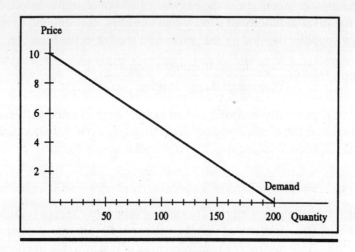

**Figure 4.1**

If we calculate the elasticity of demand using 10 as the starting price (and 0 as the starting quantity) and 8 as the ending price (and 40 as the ending quantity), we get

$$\text{Price elasticity of demand} = \frac{\text{Change in quantity demanded}}{\text{Average of old and new quantity}} \div \frac{\text{Change in price}}{\text{Average of old and new price}}$$

$$= \frac{40-0}{(40+0) \div 2} \div \frac{8-10}{(8+10) \div 2} = \frac{40}{20} \div \frac{(-2)}{9} = 9 \; \textit{(ignoring the minus sign)}$$

But if we calculate the elasticity of demand using 4 as the starting price (and 120 as the starting quantity) and 2 as the ending price (and 160 as the ending quantity), we get

$$\text{Price elasticity of demand} = \frac{\text{Change in quantity demanded}}{\text{Average of old and new quantity}} \div \frac{\text{Change in price}}{\text{Average of old and new price}}$$

$$= \frac{160-120}{(160-120) \div 2} \div \frac{2-4}{(2+4) \div 2} = \frac{40}{140} \div \frac{(-2)}{3} = \frac{3}{7}$$

In each case, the price falls by $2 and the quantity demanded rises by 40 units, so why does the elasticity come out differently? The key is remembering that elasticity uses *percentage* changes. In the first case, the price fell from 10 to 8, which is only a 22 percent change (based on the average price of 9), whereas in the second case, the price fell from 4 to 2, which is a 67 percent change (based on the average price of 3). Similarly, in the first case, quantity demanded rose from 0 to 40, which is a 200 percent increase (based on the average of 20), whereas in the second case, quantity demanded rose from 120 to 160, which is only a 29 percent increase (based on the average of 140). So in the first case, a small percentage change in price led to a large percentage change in quantity demanded, whereas in the second case, a larger percentage change in price led to a smaller percentage change in quantity demanded. In percentage terms, quantity demanded is much more responsive to price in the first case than in the second, and the elasticity of demand shows this.

4.   When you read about how elasticities are used in economic analysis, you will see that often the main issue is whether revenue will rise or fall with an increase in the price, which in turn hinges on whether demand is elastic or inelastic. Remember that revenue is simply $P \times Q$. When $P$ rises, $Q$ falls; the question is, how fast? Elasticity gives you the answer; when demand is elastic, the percentage fall in quantity is greater than the percentage rise in price. When demand is inelastic, the percentage fall in quantity is less than the percentage increase in price. You can remember how this affects revenue by the following:

- Elastic demand: $P\uparrow$ means $Q\downarrow$, so P x Q $\downarrow$

- Inelastic demand: $P\uparrow$ means $Q\downarrow$, so P x Q $\uparrow$

## ACTIVE REVIEW

## Fill-In Questions

1.   _____ is the general concept of measuring the responsiveness of one economic variable to another in _____ terms.

2.   The price elasticity of demand measures how _____ changes in response to a change in _____.

3.   To calculate the price elasticity of demand, you need to know _____ points on a _____ demand curve.

4.   Since the demand curve slopes _____, the elasticity of demand has a(n) _____ sign. Economists, however, multiply elasticity by a_____ to make it_____.

5.   When you calculate elasticities, you will get the same answer no matter what _____ the prices and quantities are measured in; this means that elasticities for different goods can be compared. It is important to remember that elasticity is not the same as the _____ of the demand curve.

6.   Demand is said to be _____ when the elasticity of demand is less than _____.

7.   Since elasticities are _____, we can compare the elasticities of demand for _____ different goods. For example, if the elasticity of demand for peas were 2.5 and the elasticity of demand for carrots were 3.1, we would say that the demand for peas was _____ compared to the demand for carrots. However, we would still say that both of these goods had _____ demands.

8.   When the elasticity of demand is zero, demand is said to be _____. In this case, the demand curve is a _____ line.

9. When the demand curve is horizontal, a tiny price increase will lead to a very large percentage change in quantity demanded. We say that such a demand curve is _____.

10. The midpoint formula uses the _____ of the starting and ending _____ and quantities to calculate the _____ changes used in the elasticity formula.

11. When demand is elastic, price and revenue move in _____ direction(s); that is, an increase in price leads to a(n) _____ in revenue. On the other hand, when demand is inelastic, price and revenue move in _____ direction(s).

12. The elasticity of demand for a product will be larger if many good _____ for that good exist, if consumers spend a(n) _____ of their income on it, or if changes in price are expected to be _____.

13. The _____ elasticity of demand measures the responsiveness of _____ to changes in consumer income, holding all else equal.

14. _____ have positive income elasticities, whereas _____ will have _____ income elasticities.

15. The elasticity of supply measures how _____ changes in response to a change in _____.

## True-False Questions

1.  T  F    The concept of elasticity has only limited applicability, since it refers only to the responsiveness of quantity demanded to price.

2.  T  F    The price elasticity of demand is the same as the slope of the demand curve.

3.  T  F    Elasticity of demand is the change in quantity demanded divided by the change in price.

4.  T  F    The steeper the demand curve, the less elastic the demand.

5.  T  F    Elasticity of demand is generally discussed as a negative number.

6.  T  F    It makes no sense to compare elasticities for different goods, since that is like comparing apples and oranges.

7.  T  F    If the percentage change in quantity demanded is more than the percentage change in price that caused it, demand is inelastic.

8.  T  F    If a 5 percent increase in the price of tea causes a 10 percent decrease in the quantity of tea demanded in Indianapolis, we would say that the demand for tea in Indianapolis is elastic.

9.  T  F    When the demand for a product is perfectly inelastic, its demand curve is a horizontal line.

10. T  F    A rise in the price of a good will always result in a decrease in the amount spent on that good.

11. T  F    If the income elasticity of demand for fast-food cheeseburgers is negative, we know that cheeseburgers must have many close substitutes.

12. T  F    The elasticity of demand will be lower if the change in price is only temporary, since no one pays much attention to temporary things.

13. T  F    If the income elasticity of demand for pizza is 0.75, pizza must be a normal good.

14.  T  F    The elasticity of supply is the ratio of the percentage change in quantity supplied to the percentage change in price, all else being equal.

15.  T  F    Perfectly elastic supply is represented by a vertical supply curve.

## Short-Answer Questions

1.  How would you calculate the rainfall elasticity of umbrella sales? What information would you need to know?

2.  How do you calculate the price elasticity of demand using the midpoint formula?

3.  What is the difference between elastic demand and inelastic demand?

4.  If the demand curve has unit elastic demand, what happens to quantity demanded when price rises 5 percent?

5.  The City Council proposes raising parking fees in order to provide additional funds for the city bus system. What must the council be assuming about the elasticity of demand for parking?

6.  List three things that tend to make the demand for a good more elastic.

7.  Why is the long-run elasticity of demand for gasoline likely to be greater than the short-run elasticity of demand?

8.  Explain the difference between the price elasticity of demand and the income elasticity of demand.

9.  What is the sign of the income elasticity of demand for inferior goods? Explain.

10. Why is the elasticity of supply low if firms' production decisions are based on their expectations of future prices?

11. What is price elasticity of supply?

12. How do you interpret a supply curve that is perfectly inelastic?

13. How does time relate to price elasticity of supply?

## WORKING IT OUT

1.  It is important to be able to use the midpoint formula correctly to calculate elasticities. To calculate an elasticity of demand, you need to know the quantity demanded at two different prices, when all else remains equal. To calculate an income elasticity of demand, you need to know the quantity demanded at two income levels, with all else equal. Then you need to apply the midpoint formula correctly.

2.  It is actually very easy to find the revenue that is collected by sellers of a good (which is also the expenditure on that good by consumers) by looking at the demand curve. For each price, the demand curve tells us how much will be bought—for every $P$, the demand curve gives us a $Q$. Look at Figure 4.2; suppose the price is $P_1$ dollars per unit, and the resulting quantity is therefore $Q_1$ units. Revenue (in dollars) is the number of units sold times the number of dollars for which each one sells, or $P_1 \times Q_1$. This is the area of the rectangle in Figure 4.2 that has $P_1$ as its height and $Q_1$ as its base (since the area of a rectangle is the base times the height).

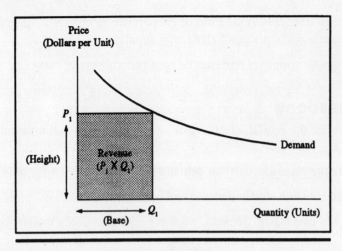

**Figure 4.2**

# Worked Problems

1.  Using the data from Table 4.1 on the demand for burgers and pizzas, calculate the price elasticity of demand for burgers.

| TABLE 4.1 | | | | |
|---|---|---|---|---|
| **Quantity of Burgers** | **Quantity of Pizzas** | **Price of Burgers** | **Price of Pizzas** | **Weekly Income** |
| 750 | 300 | $2.50 | $8.00 | $150 |
| 900 | 150 | $2.00 | $9.00 | $170 |
| 850 | 250 | $2.50 | $10.00 | $150 |
| 800 | 300 | $2.00 | $9.00 | $190 |
| 550 | 200 | $3.00 | $8.00 | $150 |

**Answer**

*First, you need to find two points on the same demand curve for burgers. The first row and the fifth row give you this: The price of pizza (a closely related good) and income are the same in these two rows. The only things that are different are the price and quantity of burgers (and the quantity of pizza, but that's not part of the demand curve for burgers). So if we let $P_{old}$ be $2.50 and $Q_{old}$ be 750, and let $P_{new}$ be $3.00 and $Q_{new}$ be 550, then the midpoint formula says that*

$$\text{Price elasticity of demand} = \frac{\text{Change in quantity demanded}}{\text{Average of old and new quantity}} \div \frac{\text{Change in price}}{\text{Average of old and new price}}$$

$$= \frac{550-750}{(550+750) \div 2} \div \frac{3.00-2.50}{(3.00+2.50) \div 2} = \frac{-200}{650} \div \frac{0.50}{2.75} = \frac{22}{13}$$

2.  Using Figure 4.3, what is the revenue when the price is $6 per unit? What area in Figure 4.3 corresponds to this revenue? What happens to revenue if the price falls to $5 per unit? Is the demand curve elastic or inelastic at $6 per unit?

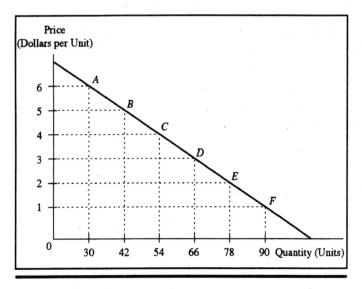

Figure 4.3

## Answer

*At $6 per unit, 30 units are demanded, so the revenue would be $6 per unit × 30 units, or $180. The area that gives this revenue is the area of the rectangle whose corners are $6–A–30–0. If the price falls to $5 per unit, the quantity demanded rises to 42 units, and revenue rises to $210. Since the price decrease leads to a revenue increase, we know that the demand curve must be elastic at this price.*

## PRACTICE PROBLEMS

1. Using the data from Table 4.1, find the price elasticity of demand for pizza.

2. Using the data from Table 4.1, find the income elasticity of demand for burgers.

3. Using the data from Table 4.1, find the cross-price elasticity of demand for burgers with respect to the price of pizza.

4. Using Figure 4.3, what is the revenue when the price is $3 per unit? What area on Figure 4.3 corresponds to this revenue? What happens to revenue if the price rises to $4 per unit? Is the demand curve elastic or inelastic at $3 per unit?

5. Calculate the price elasticity of demand (using the midpoint formula) as the price rises from $3 per unit to $4 per unit in Figure 4.3, and verify your answer to the last part of question 4.

## CHAPTER TEST

1. The price elasticity of demand shows us

    a.  the steepness of the demand curve.
    b.  how fast demand responds to price.
    c.  how much demand shifts when income changes.
    d.  the responsiveness of quantity demanded to price changes.

2. In order to calculate the price elasticity of demand, you need to know

    a.  two prices and two quantities demanded as the demand curve shifts.
    b.  the slope of the demand curve.

  c. the equilibrium price and quantity in the market.
  d. the quantity demanded at two different prices, *ceteris paribus*.

3. Price elasticities are measured in percentage terms because

  a. it makes students' lives more complicated.
  b. the resulting measure is unit-free.
  c. it gives a more accurate answer.
  d. the answer is always negative that way.

4. The price elasticity of demand is given by the formula

  a. $e_d = \dfrac{\Delta Q_d}{Q_d} \div \dfrac{\Delta P}{P}$

  b. $e_d = \dfrac{\Delta Q_d}{Q_d}$

  c. $e_d = \dfrac{\Delta Q_d}{Q_d} \times \dfrac{\Delta P}{P}$

  d. $e_d = \dfrac{\Delta P}{P} \div \dfrac{\Delta Q_d}{Q_d}$

5. Demand is elastic when the elasticity of demand is

  a. greater than 0.
  b. greater than 1.
  c. less than 1.
  d. less than 0.

6. If the price of gasoline rises 10 percent, the quantity of gasoline purchased falls by 10 percent. The demand for gasoline in this case is

  a. perfectly elastic.
  b. unit elastic.
  c. elastic.
  d. inelastic.

7. The quantity demanded of heart transplants does not respond to changes in the price of the operation. This means that the demand for heart transplants is

  a. perfectly elastic.
  b. perfectly inelastic.
  c. inelastic, but not perfectly inelastic.
  d. elastic, but not perfectly elastic.

8. The elasticity of demand for salt is 0.5. We can say that

  a. the demand for salt is inelastic.
  b. the demand for salt is elastic.
  c. the demand for salt is unit elasticity.
  d. the demand for salt is horizontal.

9. Each month, 300 pairs of shoelaces are purchased at a price of $1.30 per pair. When the price rises to $1.50 per pair, the quantity demanded falls to 250 pairs per month. Using the midpoint formula, the elasticity of demand for shoelaces is

  a. 14/11.

    b.    2/77.

    c.    11/14.

    d.    2/11.

10.    The Campus Cinema discovered that when it charged $3 for the afternoon matinee, it took in $360 per showing, but when it lowered the price to $2, it took in $480 per showing. This implies that the elasticity of demand for afternoon matinee movies is

    a.    3/5.

    b.    5/3.

    c.    5/2.

    d.    12/18.

11.    We know that the demand for a product is elastic if

    a.    when price rises, revenue rises.

    b.    when price rises, revenue falls.

    c.    when price rises, quantity demanded rises.

    d.    when price falls, quantity demanded rises.

12.    If a product has an inelastic demand, then

    a.    we are probably thinking about the long-run demand curve.

    b.    it has many close substitutes.

    c.    an increase in the price leads to an increase in revenue.

    d.    it probably represents a large proportion of consumer expenditures.

13.    Which of the following products is likely to have the *most* elastic demand?

    a.    The latest CD for a popular singer

    b.    Compact disks for all singers

    c.    Musical entertainment in general

    d.    The demand for hearing aids

14.    Which of the following goods is likely to have the *least* elastic demand?

    a.    Meals at restaurants

    b.    Vacation travel around the world

    c.    Bubblegum

    d.    College educations

15.    When the price of gasoline rises, people immediately cut back on unnecessary trips. If the price of gasoline stays high, people eventually replace their cars with more fuel-efficient models. As a result,

    a.    the long-run demand for gasoline falls.

    b.    the short-run demand for gasoline is less elastic than the long-run demand.

    c.    the short-run demand for gasoline is more elastic than the long-run demand.

    d.    the price of gasoline is forced down to its original level.

16.    If scissors manufacturers cannot quickly and easily increase their output when the price of scissors rises, it is likely that

    a.    scissors are a normal good.

    b.    the supply of scissors is perfectly elastic.

    c.    the supply of scissors is elastic.

    d.    the supply of scissors is inelastic.

17.  If the income elasticity of demand for boots is 0.4, a 10 percent decrease in consumer income will lead to a

     a.   40 percent increase in the demand for boots.
     b.   40 percent decrease in the demand for boots.
     c.   4 percent decrease in the demand for boots.
     d.   0.4 percent decrease in the demand for boots.

18.  John Taylor, a movie star, makes two movies each year, for which he is paid $1 million each. John tells his agent, Slippery Slim, that if he were paid $2 million per movie, he'd be willing to make an additional movie each year. John's elasticity of movie supply is

     a.   2/3.
     b.   2/5.
     c.   3/5.
     d.   4/15.

19.  Since the fish that are caught each day go bad very quickly, the daily catch will be offered for sale no matter what price it brings. As a result, we know that

     a.   the daily supply curve for fish slopes upward.
     b.   the daily supply curve for fish is perfectly inelastic.
     c.   the daily supply curve for fish is perfectly elastic.
     d.   the daily supply curve for fish is a horizontal line at today's price.

20.  The size of the price elasticity of demand depends on

     a.   the availability of substitutes for the item.
     b.   whether the item represents a large fraction of income.
     c.   whether the price change is permanent or temporary.
     d.   all the above factors.

## ANSWERS TO THE REVIEW QUESTIONS

## Fill-In Questions

1.   Elasticity; percentage

2.   quantity demanded; price

3.   two; nonshifting

4.   downward; negative; 1; positive

5.   units; slope

6.   inelastic; 1

7.   unit-free; relatively; inelastic; elastic

8.   perfectly inelastic; vertical

9.   perfectly elastic

10.  average; prices; percentage

11.  opposite; decrease; the same

12.  substitutes; large fraction; temporary

13.  income; quantity demanded

14. Normal goods; inferior goods; negative

15. quantity supplied; price

## True-False Questions

1. **False.**   Elasticity can be used to measure the responsiveness of the relationship between any two economic variables.

2. **True.**   First, slope is not unit-free while elasticity is not. Second, the formula for calculating elasticity and slope are different.

3. **False.**   The elasticity of demand is the percent change in quantity demanded divided by the percent change in price.

4. **False.**   Slope and elasticity are not the same thing.

5. **False.**   Although price elasticities of demand are technically negative numbers, economists often ignore the minus sign and discuss them in positive terms.

6. **False.**   Since elasticities are unit-free, they can be compared across goods.

7. **False.**   If the percentage change in quantity demanded is more than the percentage change in price, then the former divided by the latter is greater than 1, and demand is elastic.

8. **True.**   Demand is elastic if the percentage change in quantity demanded is greater than the percentage change in price.

9. **False.**   When the demand for something is perfectly inelastic, its demand curve is a vertical line.

10. **False.**   Revenue, which is the amount spent on the good, will rise only when the price rises if the demand is inelastic.

11. **False.**   The income elasticity of demand doesn't tell us about substitutes; it tells us whether goods are normal goods or inferior goods.

12. **False.**   When price changes are expected to be temporary, consumers will respond more quickly in order to take advantage of the limited opportunity to save or to avoid the limited extra cost.

13. **True.**   When income rises 1 percent, demand for pizza rises 0.75 percent. Since demand increases when income increases, this is a normal good.

14. **True.**   This is the definition of the price elasticity of supply.

15. **False.**   The vertical supply curve is inelastic; a higher price cannot bring about a higher quantity supplied.

## Short-Answer Questions

1. To calculate the rainfall elasticity of umbrella sales, you would need to know how many umbrellas were sold on two days when the only thing that was different was the amount of rainfall. You would then calculate the percentage change in the sales of umbrellas (based on the average) and the percentage change in rainfall, and divide the former by the latter to find out what percentage change in umbrella sales you get for each percentage point change in rainfall.

2.  To calculate the price elasticity of demand using the midpoint formula, you need to know two points on the demand curve: the old price and quantity ($P_{old}$ and $Q_{old}$) and the new price and quantity ($P_{new}$ and $Q_{new}$). The elasticity of demand is given by:

$$\text{Price elasticity of demand} = \frac{\text{Change in quantity demanded}}{\text{Average of old and new quantity}} \div \frac{\text{Change in price}}{\text{Average of old and new price}}$$

$$= \frac{Q_{new} - Q_{old}}{(Q_{new} + Q_{old})/2} \div \frac{P_{new} - P_{old}}{(P_{new} + P_{old})/2}$$

3.  Elastic demand refers to a demand curve with an elasticity greater than 1; a 1 percent change in price causes a more than 1 percent change in quantity demanded. Inelastic demand refers to a demand curve with an elasticity less than 1; a 1 percent change in price causes a less than 1 percent change in quantity demanded.

4.  When the demand curve has unit elastic demand (elasticity equal to 1), quantity demanded falls by the same percentage (in this case 5 percent) as the price rises.

5.  The City Council must think that the demand for parking is inelastic; if it is not, the increase in parking fees will lead to such a large decrease in the amount of parking that revenue will fall and there will be less funds for the bus system.

6.  Any three of the following: there are many good substitutes; the good represents a large fraction of consumers' spending; price changes are expected to be temporary; and consumers have lots of time to adjust to the price changes.

7.  In the short run, people can respond to an increase in the price of gasoline by taking fewer trips, carpooling, riding the bus more often, and so forth. In the long run, they can do all those things *plus* buying a more fuel-efficient car the next time they buy a car, moving closer to town to shorten their commute, and so on. In the long run, people have additional opportunities to adjust their consumption, and so the long-run elasticity will be greater than the short-run elasticity.

8.  The price elasticity of demand measures the responsiveness of the quantity of a good that is demanded to a change in that good's price, holding all else equal. The income elasticity of demand measures the responsiveness of the quantity of a good that is demanded to changes in consumer income, holding all else equal.

9.  The sign of the income elasticity of demand for an inferior good is negative. When a good is an inferior good, an increase in consumer incomes will decrease the quantity demanded of that good. Thus, the percent change in quantity demanded that accompanies an increase in consumer income is a negative number.

10. If firms' production decisions are based on their expectations of future prices, they will not want to supply more or less if the current price changes. They will respond only to changes in what they think the future price will be.

11. Price elasticity of supply tells you about the responsiveness of quantity supplied to changes in price, *ceteris paribus*. It is calculated by the percentage change in the quantity supplied divided by the percentage change in price.

12. This would be interpreted as the same quantity supplied regardless of the price. Seats in a movie theater would be an example of this type of supply curve.

13. With time, more and more inputs become variable. As such, producers can change output to a greater degree for a given change in price. Therefore, as the period of time increases, the supply curve will become more elastic.

# SOLUTIONS TO THE PRACTICE PROBLEMS

1.  In this case, you need to find two points on the same demand curve for pizza. The first row and the third row give you this: The price of burgers and income are the same in these two rows. The only things that are different are the price and quantity of pizzas (and the quantity of burgers, but that's not part of the demand curve for pizzas). So if we let $P_{old}$ be \$8.00 and $Q_{old}$ be 300, and let $P_{new}$ be \$10.00 and $Q_{new}$ be 250, then the midpoint formula says that

$$\text{Price elasticity of demand} = \frac{\text{Change in quantity demanded}}{\text{Average of old and new quantity}} \div \frac{\text{Change in price}}{\text{Average of old and new price}}$$

$$= \frac{250\text{-}300}{(250+300)/2} \div \frac{10.00\text{-}8.00}{(10.00+8.00)/2} = \frac{-50}{275} \div \frac{2.00}{9.00} = \frac{9}{11}\text{(ignoring the minus sign)}$$

2.  In this case, you need to find two points where the only things that have changed are income and the quantity of burgers (and possibly the quantity of pizzas). The second row and the fourth row give you this; the prices of burgers and pizzas are the same in these two rows. So if we let $I_{old}$ be \$170 and $Q_{old}$ be 900, and let $I_{new}$ be \$190 and $Q_{new}$ be 800, then the midpoint formula says that

$$\text{Income elasticity of demand} = \frac{\text{Change in quantity demanded}}{\text{Average of old and new quantity}} \div \frac{\text{Change in income}}{\text{Average of old and new income}}$$

$$= \frac{800\text{-}900}{(800+900)/2} \div \frac{190\text{-}170}{(190+170)/2} = \frac{-100}{850} \div \frac{20}{180} = \frac{-18}{17}$$

Here we can't ignore the minus sign; it tells us that burgers are an inferior good. When income rises, the quantity of burgers demanded falls.

3.  In this case, we want to find out how the quantity of burgers responds to a change in the price of pizzas, all else equal, so we return to the first and third rows, where the only things that are different are the price of pizza and the quantities of pizzas and burgers. Let $P_{old}$ be \$8.00 and $Q_{old}$ be 750, and let $P_{new}$ be \$10.00 and $Q_{new}$ be 850; then the midpoint formula says that

$$\text{Cross-price elasticity of demand} = \frac{\text{Change in burgers demanded}}{\text{Average of old and new quantity}} \div \frac{\text{Change in pizza price}}{\text{Average of old and new price}}$$

$$= \frac{850\text{-}750}{(850+750)/2} \div \frac{10.00\text{-}8.00}{(10.00+8.00)/2} = \frac{100}{800} \div \frac{2.00}{9.00} = \frac{9}{16}$$

Here, the sign of the cross-price elasticity is positive, which tells us that burgers and pizzas are substitutes. An increase in the price of pizzas leads to an increase in the demand for burgers.

4.  At \$3 per unit, 66 units are demanded, so the revenue would be \$3 per unit × 66 units, or \$198. The area that gives this revenue is the area of the rectangle whose corners are \$3–D–66–0. If the price rises to \$4 per unit, the quantity demanded falls to 54 units, and revenue rises to \$216. Since the price increase leads to a revenue increase, we know that demand must be inelastic at this price.

5.  Using the midpoint formula,

$$\text{Price elasticity of demand} = \frac{\text{Change in burgers demanded}}{\text{Average of old and new quantity}} \div \frac{\text{Change in pizza price}}{\text{Average of old and new price}}$$

$$= \frac{54\text{-}66}{(54+66)/2} \div \frac{4\text{-}3}{(4+3)/2} = \frac{-12}{60} \div \frac{1}{3.50} = \frac{7}{10}\text{(ignoring the minus sign)}$$

Since the elasticity is less than 1, we have verified that demand is indeed inelastic at \$3 per unit.

# ANSWERS TO THE CHAPTER TEST

1. d
2. d
3. b
4. a
5. b
6. b
7. b
8. a
9. a
10. b
11. b
12. c
13. a
14. c
15. b
16. d
17. c
18. c
19. b
20. d

# PART 1

# Sample Test: (Chapters 1–4) Introduction to Economics

## SAMPLE TEST QUESTIONS

1. The problem of scarcity is

    a. a problem only for poor countries.
    b. faced by all economies.
    c. not faced by free market economies.
    d. eliminated as the economy grows.

2. When an economy is operating on its production possibilities curve, more production of one good means less production of another because

    a. resources are limited.
    b. resources are unlimited.
    c. wants are limited.
    d. wants are unlimited.

3. The value of the alternative that was *not* chosen is called the

    a. marginal cost of the choice.
    b. average cost of the choice.
    c. opportunity cost of the choice.
    d. gain from the choice.

4. An essential characteristic of the market economy is

    a. freely determined prices.
    b. an absence of property rights.
    c. prices set by the government.
    d. lack of competition.

5. In an economic interaction between two people, there are gains from trade if

    a. the two people trade involuntarily.
    b. neither person has any incentive to trade.
    c. reallocation makes at least one of the two people better off.
    d. the trade reallocates goods between the two people in a way that they both prefer.

6. An important reason for international trade is

    a. market failure.
    b. government failure.
    c. comparative advantage.
    d. opportunity costs.

7.    A situation in which the market does *not* lead to an efficient economic outcome and in which there
      is a potential role for government is referred to as

      a.    government failure.
      b.    market failure.
      c.    a competitive market.
      d.    economic growth.

8.    The term *household* refers to

      a.    housing developments.
      b.    private organizations that produce goods and services.
      c.    public organizations that produce goods and services.
      d.    individuals or groups of individuals who share the same living quarters.

9.    Economic analysis that explains what happens in the economy and why and that makes policy
      recommendations is called

      a.    market economics.
      b.    normative economics.
      c.    positive economics.
      d.    subjective economics.

10.   Economic models

      a.    need to be the same as the phenomena they describe.
      b.    require either algebra or graphs.
      c.    are complicated, since human behavior is complicated.
      d.    are simplifications of the phenomena they attempt to explain.

11.   The law of demand states that

      a.    there is a direct relationship between price and quantity supplied.
      b.    as price increases, quantity demanded increases.
      c.    there is an inverse relationship between price and quantity demanded.
      d.    there is an inverse relationship between price and quantity supplied.
      e.    as price decreases, demand increases.

12.   The law of supply states that

      a.    price and quantity supplied are positively related.
      b.    the higher the price, the smaller the quantity that will be sold.
      c.    price and quantity supplied are inversely related.
      d.    price and quantity demanded are inversely related.
      e.    price and supply are positively related.

13.   When both supply and demand shift at the same time,

      a.    the change in equilibrium price cannot be predicted, but the change in equilibrium quantity
            can be predicted.
      b.    the change in equilibrium price can be predicted, but the change in equilibrium quantity
            cannot be predicted.
      c.    neither the change in equilibrium price nor the change in equilibrium quantity can be
            predicted.
      d.    both the change in equilibrium price and the change in equilibrium quantity can be
            predicted.
      e.    if the change in equilibrium quantity cannot be predicted, the change in equilibrium price
            cannot be predicted.

14. A substitute is a good

   a.   that provides some of the same uses or enjoyment as another good.
   b.   for which demand increases when income rises and decreases when income falls.
   c.   that tends to be consumed together with another good.
   d.   for which demand decreases when income rises and increases when income falls.

15. Which of the following is an example of two goods that are complements for each other?

   a.   Bicycles and kayaks
   b.   Rollerblades and knee pads
   c.   Baseball hats and ski caps
   d.   Cobblestones and brick paving

16. What would be the probable effect of the minimum wage if the equilibrium wage were above the minimum wage?

   a.   There would be no effect on employment.
   b.   It could cause increased unemployment.
   c.   It could cause decreased unemployment.
   d.   Unemployment would rise only for workers whose wages were already above the minimum.

17. Elasticity is a measure of

   a.   how quickly a particular market reaches equilibrium.
   b.   the change in income associated with increased education.
   c.   the responsiveness of one variable to a change in another variable.
   d.   the effect of an increase in the number of consumers in a particular market.
   e.   how quickly expansion can take place in an economy.

18. For demand to be *elastic*,

   a.   the percentage change in quantity demanded must be greater than the associated percentage change in price.
   b.   the percentage change in quantity demanded must be less than the associated percentage change in price.
   c.   the percentage change in quantity demanded must be equal to the associated percentage change in price.
   d.   quantity demanded must change with a change in price.
   e.   demand must change with a change in price.

19. If a good represents a small portion of consumers' income, then the price elasticity of demand will be

   a.   low.
   b.   high.
   c.   the same as when it represents a small portion of people's income.
   d.   inelastic.

20. Because the price elasticity of demand for agricultural products is very low,

   a.   increases and decreases in supply result in large price changes.
   b.   increases and decreases in supply result in small price changes.
   c.   increases in supply result in large price changes, whereas decreases in supply result in small price changes.
   d.   increases in supply result in small price changes, whereas decreases in supply result in large price changes.
   e.   increases and decreases in supply do not result in price changes.

# ANSWERS TO THE SAMPLE TEST

1. b

2. a

3. c

4. a

5. d

6. c

7. b

8. d

9. b

10. d

11. c

12. a

13. e

14. a

15. b

16. a

17. c

18. a

19. a

20. a

# PART 2

# Principles of Microeconomics

Chapters 1–4 introduced the important concepts of a competitive market and its pricing process. In Chapters 5–7, the underlying foundations of market supply and demand curves are introduced and examined. The model of consumer behavior (Chapter 5) describes the process of utility maximization, aids in the derivation of a consumer's willingness to pay, allows us to see consumer surplus, and allows us to derive the market demand curve. Sellers (Chapter 6), or firms, are assumed to maximize profits by using the relationship between marginal cost and price as a guide to decision making. Also, producer surplus is introduced into the analysis. Chapter 7 combines the discussions in Chapters 5 and 6 in order to examine the economic efficiency of a competitive market. While these chapters use many abstract concepts and theories to describe the behavior of market participants and their interaction, double-auction market experiments offer confirmation of the predictions of economic models.

# CHAPTER 5

# The Demand Curve and the Behavior of Consumers

## CHAPTER OVERVIEW

We have already seen that the amount consumers want to buy depends on several important economic variables; chief among them is the price of the good in question. In this chapter, we take a closer look at how consumers' choices, constrained by their income, are captured by demand curves. We will take the position that people make choices about what to consume with the goal of making themselves as happy as possible, while recognizing that there are limits to what they can afford. We will see that this model of consumer behavior explains the movements along *and* shifts of demand curves. We will also introduce important concepts that will be used later when we evaluate the performance of the market system.

## CHAPTER REVIEW

1.  Economics starts from the assumption that people act *purposefully*. That is, within the constraints they face, people make choices with the intention of making themselves as well off as possible. What makes people better off is different for each person; some like onions on their pizza while others like spinach. Some people like hiking in the wilderness while others like to watch drag racing (and some like both). But whatever they like, we expect that people will act to satisfy their preferences.

2.  **Utility** is the term economists use to denote people's preferences for particular goods. If someone prefers watching *Survivor* to watching *Law and Order*, we say that that person gets more utility from watching reality TV. This doesn't mean that *Survivor* is better than *Law and Order*, or that watching *Survivor* makes you smarter or more popular. All it means is that this person likes the *Survivor* better than *Law and Order* and, given the choice between the two, would watch the former.

3.  We generally believe that the more people consume of things they like, the happier they are. That is, people prefer more consumption to less, so that *total* utility increases as consumption rises. (Of course, there are some things that people dislike, such as dirty air or moldy bread. In these cases, *less* of the thing is a good, and more consumption of the "good" gives more utility.)

4.  When someone consumes more of a good, his or her utility increases. The amount by which utility increases when one more unit of an item is consumed is called the **marginal utility** of that unit. The word *marginal* means "additional," and it shows up over and over again in economics. In this instance, *marginal utility* means additional utility, and it diminishes as more of a product is consumed.

5.  When consumers have several goods to choose from, different combinations can provide different levels of utility. This is just another way of saying that a consumer can prefer one combination of goods to another. Different combinations can also yield the same level of utility; in that case, the consumer is said to be indifferent between the combinations of goods.

6. You may have wondered what units utility is measured in; after all, we keep talking about how it increases. In fact, there are no units of "happiness" or "well-being" with which to measure utility, but that doesn't really matter. All that matters is the idea of preference. When we say that one amount of a good or combination of goods provides a higher level of utility to an individual, all we mean is that the person prefers that amount or combination.

7. Half of the story of consumer choice involves what makes the consumer happy. The other half involves what the consumer can choose from. Although there are many thousands of goods and services in the world, people have limited incomes and can afford only so much of the things that they prefer. The **budget constraint** tells us which combinations of goods the consumer can afford, given the consumer's income and the prices he or she faces.

8. Changes in either the consumer's income or the prices he or she faces will alter the combinations of goods the consumer can afford. An increase in the amount the consumer can spend (with all else remaining equal) clearly increases the number of units he or she can afford, and a decrease in the price of one or more of the goods the consumer buys will have the same effect. Conversely, a decrease in the amount the consumer can spend or an increase in the price of something he or she buys will make some combinations that were previously affordable become too expensive.

9. The consumer's budget constraint, determined by the consumer's income and the prices he or she faces, determines which combinations of goods are affordable. From these, the consumer has to choose which combination to purchase. Economists assume that when faced with this problem, consumers choose the combination of goods (from those they can afford) that makes them happiest. In more technical language, we assume that consumers engage in **utility maximization**; that is, they choose the combination that gives the highest possible level of utility given their budget constraint. One way to find this combination of goods is to determine the utility level of each affordable combination. The one that gives the highest utility level is the one that makes the consumer happiest, given what he or she can afford.

10. You will generally find that maximizing utility given a budget constraint involves spending all of the money available for the goods in question. Having money left over means not buying some goods that would provide some additional utility, and therefore not being as well off as possible. You may think that it would be better for the consumer not to spend all of his or her available money, and to save some for the future, but saving is just another good. It represents the ability to consume in the future. So when you include goods for consumption today and goods for consumption in the future in the combinations of goods that can be consumed, consumers who are maximizing utility will spend all the money available to them.

11. If the amount that the consumer has to spend increases, he or she can afford to purchase some combinations of goods that he or she couldn't afford previously. From the new set of combinations that are affordable after income has risen, the utility-maximizing consumer will again choose the combination that provides the highest utility. Although the consumer will be able to afford a little bit more of every good, he or she may not choose to spend the additional money that way. The consumer is likely to buy more of some goods, but may buy less of others. For the former, the quantity demanded will increase, even though the price hasn't changed; there is a shift to the right in the demand curve for those goods, which you will recall from Chapter 3 are called **normal goods**. For the latter, the quantity demanded decreases as income rises; these are the **inferior goods**, whose demand curves shift to the left when income rises.

12. Holding all else constant, a change in the price of one of the goods that the consumer purchases changes the budget constraint. In particular, if the price of a good rises, all of the combinations that included some of that good and involved spending all of the available money are no longer affordable. (Think about it—if you fill up your cart at the supermarket with enough things to spend exactly the amount of money you have with you, and then you find out at the checkout

counter that one item in your basket costs more than you thought it did, you don't have enough to cover all your purchases.) The utility-maximizing consumer will have to check the utility level of the combinations that are affordable *after* the price increase and pick the one that provides the highest utility. Generally this involves buying less of the good whose price went up, because other goods that serve as substitutes now look more attractive. The amounts purchased at the two different prices give two points on the consumer's demand curve for that item. As the price went up, the quantity demanded fell. Graphically, this is seen as a movement *along* a demand curve, as we discussed in Chapter 3.

13. There are really two reasons why a change in the price of a good leads to a change in the quantity demanded, and the idea of the budget constraint helps you to understand them. When the price of one good rises, consuming a unit of it means that more of something else must be forgone. Although passing up the alternatives may have been worthwhile before the price increase, at the new, higher price the alternatives that have to be given up may not be worth it. This is the **substitution effect**; when the price of something rises, all else remaining equal (including the prices of other goods and spending power), consumers purchase less of that good and more of other goods that have become relatively cheaper. On the other hand, if the price of something falls (all else remaining equal), that good becomes cheaper relative to other things. Consumers don't have to pass up as much of other things to consume the good whose price fell, and some goods that involved too great a sacrifice of other things before may be worth purchasing now that the sacrifice involved is smaller.

14. The second reason why a change in price of a product leads to a change in quantity demanded relates to the effect of a price change on a person's real income. We have also seen already that when the price of something rises, the spending power of consumers who buy that product falls. They are poorer in terms of the goods and services that they can afford with their income, and being poorer requires adjustments in spending so as not to spend more than you have. This is the **income effect**; when the price of a good rises, spending power falls, and consumers buy less of all normal goods and more of all inferior goods. Of course, when the price of something that you buy falls, your income will now purchase a larger amount of goods and services, and you will buy more of all normal goods and less of all inferior goods.

15. Both the substitution effect and the income effect occur whenever the price of something changes. For normal goods, they work in the same direction on the quantity demanded of the item whose price has changed. When the price of corn flakes rises, consumers buy less corn flakes because other cereals are relatively cheaper (the substitution effect), and they buy less corn flakes because they have to stretch their income farther (the income effect). Both effects cause the quantity demanded to change as the price changes and result in a movement along the demand curve.

16. We have already seen that when a consumer chooses the combination of goods that provides the highest level of utility, he or she is making tradeoffs between a little more of this good and a little less of that. Another way to look at this question is to ask, "Given your income, how much would you be willing to pay for another unit of that product?" (or, more precisely, "Given your income, what is the *most* you would be willing to pay for another unit of that product?"). Assuming that the consumer responds truthfully, his or her response gives his or her **marginal benefit** from that good, or marginal willingness to pay to consume one more unit, which puts a dollar value on the next unit (as opposed to marginal utility, which gives a value in utility terms). You should remember that the dollars represent the other goods that the consumer would buy instead, and so marginal benefit also captures the idea of tradeoffs of one good for others. You should also remember that we are thinking about how much the consumer would be willing to pay *given his or her income*. People who have a high income are willing to pay a lot for many goods (because they have a lot to spend), whereas people with lower incomes are not willing to pay as much (because they have other, more pressing needs).

17. It is pretty easy to see that willingness to pay and marginal benefit are related to the demand curve. In fact, if you plot the marginal benefit of each successive unit of consumption of a product, starting with the unit for which the consumer would be willing to pay the most and going on to the point where the consumer wouldn't be willing to pay anything more for an additional unit in that time period, the curve that you get is the **individual demand curve**. The reason is that at any price you charge, the consumer will want to purchase every unit that provides a marginal benefit greater than the price. After all, if you are willing to pay *more* than the going price, you're getting a pretty good deal *at* the going price.

18. If the consumer wants to buy every unit for which the marginal benefit is greater than the price, and since the marginal benefit of each successive unit falls (as a result of diminishing marginal utility), then the consumer will purchase units up to the point where the marginal benefit of the next unit falls below the price. The utility-maximizing consumer will expand consumption of each and every good to the point at which *price equals marginal benefit* of the last unit consumed.

19. Thinking about consumers' choices in terms of the utility of the next unit (the marginal utility) helps in understanding the diamond–water paradox, which asks why something as important to life as water could sell for such a low price (many places of business give it away) while something that most people easily live without, such as diamonds, sells for such a high price. The total utility of all the water you consume is very high; without it, you would die of dehydration. But because water is so plentiful, you are able to consume not merely the extremely valuable first gallons that keep you alive, but also the less important gallons that wash your clothes, and even relatively unimportant gallons that water your lawn. The relative abundance of water explains why it is so inexpensive, despite the fact that the first units consumed have extremely high value. Diamonds, on the other hand, are very scarce, and so people consume very few of them. Indeed, for most people the marginal utility of the first diamond they might consume is less than the utility of the other goods they would have to pass up in order to buy their first diamond, and so they don't buy any diamonds at all.

20. We have been talking up to this point about the choices of *individual* consumers. We can also ask how much of a good all the consumers together will want to purchase. This gives us the **market demand curve**. We get the quantity demanded by the market at some price by finding the quantity demanded by each individual at that price, then adding up these quantities to get the total quantity demanded at that price. Of course, not all consumers face the same price for a product. For example, the price of gasoline in Boston may be higher than the price of gasoline in Baton Rouge. This is because gasoline at these two locations is essentially two different products, selling in two different markets. They are different products because they are located in different places, and they aren't particularly close substitutes; if you lived in Boston, you wouldn't fill up your car in Baton Rouge just because gas was a few cents cheaper there.

21. Although the consumer will continue consuming until the last (least beneficial) unit has a marginal benefit that just equals the price, the previous units consumed have marginal benefits that exceed the price. The difference between total willingness to pay and the total expenditure on the good, which is the same thing as the difference between the marginal benefit and the price added up over all the units consumed, is called the **consumer surplus** that is derived from consuming that good. It is the difference between the *most* that the consumer would be willing to pay for all the units, taken one by one, and the amount that the consumer actually pays for them. We can also calculate, in principle, the consumer surplus for all the consumers in the market for that good. Consumer surplus measures (in dollars, since willingness to pay and price paid are both in dollars) the benefit to consumers of purchasing and consuming the good in question.

## ZEROING IN

1.  People often dispute the economist's assumption that people maximize utility. They simply don't believe that people go through the sort of calculations that economists use when figuring out the "utility-maximizing combination of goods and services." After all, if you have never seen the "utility-maximizing" rule or the "price equals marginal benefit" rule before now, how can you have been using it all your life? Economists don't actually claim that people make all these calculations consciously or explicitly, although people sometimes do (and maybe after taking economics, you will more often!). If you have ever said to yourself, "I was going to buy that concert ticket (or whatever), but at $30 it just wasn't worth it," you behaved like a utility-maximizing person. More generally, however, economists believe that people behave *as if* they were making the calculations explicitly, and that they make the same choices that they would have made if they followed the utility-maximizing rules. As support for the model of utility-maximizing people (and it is a *model* of human behavior, remember), economists point out that people's choices respond to changes in prices, income, and other things in much the way that the model predicts they will.

2.  The main idea in understanding consumer behavior is the idea of *constrained maximization*, or doing the best you can given the constraints you face. Consumers try to be as happy as they can be subject to the limits they face. People face many constraints in life; in studying consumer behavior, we focus on the constraints that arise because people have limited incomes and the goods that they want to buy have prices. Given the income they have and the prices they face, people choose the combination of goods that makes them as happy as possible. If the prices or their income changes, then the constraint that they face changes, and people will adjust to do the best they can under the new constraint.

3.  The notion of **marginalism**, that what matters is the *marginal* benefit (or cost, as you will see later on) of the *next* unit consumed rather than the *total* benefit of *all* the units consumed, is extremely important in economics. Thinking about the marginal unit plays an important role in knowing what's the best choice to make and in understanding how the best choice changes in response to changes in other variables. To see how marginal thinking works, first consider Edmund, who is trying to get to the top of Mount Marshall in Figure 5.1.

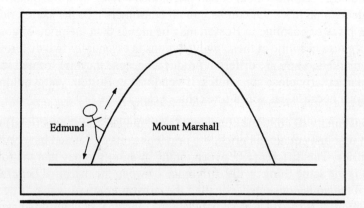

**Figure 5.1**

How will Edmund know when he has reached the top of the mountain? One way would be for him to check the altitude at each point on the mountain and then go back to the point with the highest altitude. Another way would be simply to see if a step in any direction takes him higher. If one does, then wherever he is currently standing cannot be the top of the mountain (since he can go higher by taking a step in that direction). Edmund should take a step in the direction that takes him higher and then check again to see if he can find a step in any direction that takes him higher still.

When Edmund gets to a point where a step in any direction takes him to a lower altitude, he knows that he must be at the top. In marginal terms, Edmund asks himself if the marginal change in altitude (the change in altitude from a small step in some direction) is positive. If it is, he takes a step in the indicated direction and checks again. Only when the marginal change in altitude is zero in all directions will Edmund know that he is standing on the very peak of the mountain, as in Figure 5.2.[*]

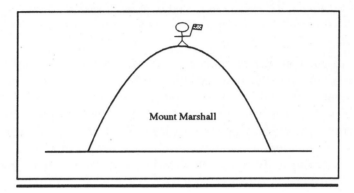

**Figure 5.2**

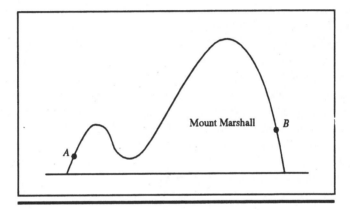

**Figure 5.3**

When a consumer chooses the combination of goods that provides the most utility, he or she could go about making the decision by considering every possible combination of goods and then choosing the one that yields the highest utility. Alternatively, the consumer could find the answer by asking whether a small change in the combination he or she is currently considering (a dollar less spent on chips, a dollar more spent on salsa) would make him or her happier. If some change raises the consumer's utility, he or she should make that change and then consider further changes. When the consumer gets to the point where the additional utility he or she gets from spending another dollar on any good is just offset by the utility he or she would give up by spending a dollar less on other goods, then the consumer knows that he or she can't do any better, and so must be doing the best he or she can. This is, of course, what the utility-maximizing rule (in its alternative form) says.

---

[*]You may have figured out that if Mount Marshall looks the way it does in Figure 5.3, Edmund's step-by-step approach won't always get him to the top. It will if he starts on the right side of the mountain, at point B, but not if he starts on the left, at point A. In cases like this, marginal analysis does not work; fortunately, most problems in economics are analogous to Figure 5.2, not Figure 5.3.

The idea of the margin is also important because it is at the margin that responses to changes take place. When your college raises its admission standards, it doesn't stop taking students; only those students at the margin (who were just barely qualified for admission previously) have their admission decision affected. When the price of something rises, people don't stop consuming altogether; they make an adjustment at the margin by buying a bit less. Similarly, when interest rates rise, people don't stop consuming today; they make a marginal adjustment by consuming a little less today and saving a little more to pay for a little more consumption in the future. The margin is where the action is; when you see the word *marginal*, you should think about change and ask yourself what variable is changing, and in response to what.

4. The concept of the marginal unit can be confusing. We say that the marginal unit is the "last" unit, and that the marginal utility of each additional unit is lower than the marginal utility of the previous one. Yet people often think that the last unit they consumed provided more, not less, satisfaction than the one before it. The problem is that they are confusing the last unit in time with the last unit in benefit. For example, suppose Amy is a college student and she likes to drink milk. Over the course of some time period (let's say the month of September), Amy has fifty cartons of milk. She has milk with many of her meals, after she plays tennis, for a midnight study break, and on other occasions. We could ask Amy to rank the fifty cartons of milk from the one she got the most satisfaction out of to the one that provided the least satisfaction (i.e., from the highest utility to the lowest). She might tell us, for instance, that the carton she had right after her tennis game on September 27, when it was 90 degrees outside, gave her the most utility, the one she had for breakfast on September 3 gave her the next most utility, and the carton she had when she was bored and looking for something to do on September 17 gave her the least utility. We would presume that Amy was willing to pay at least the price of a carton of milk on each of these occasions (i.e., her marginal benefit was greater than or equal to the price), for otherwise she wouldn't have incurred the cost. But the "last" carton in benefits (the one on September 17, for which she may have barely been willing to pay the cost of the carton) was not the last carton she consumed during the month. And had the price of milk risen enough, the carton that Amy would have chosen to do without, "because it just wasn't worth the money," would have been that least beneficial carton. That carton is the marginal unit for Amy (at least in the month of September), the one for which marginal benefit just equals price.

## ACTIVE REVIEW

## Fill-In Questions

1. The economic measurement of the amount of pleasure a person gets from the consumption of goods and services is called _____.

2. _____ is the additional utility gained from consuming one extra unit of a good or service.

3. _____ is used to indicate an addition to the thing being discussed.

4. A consumer is _____ between two combinations of goods when he gets the same amount of _____ from each.

5. The total amount that a consumer can spend on goods and services is the _____.

6. How much consumers can spend and still remain within the budget constraint depends on their _____ and the _____ of the goods they buy.

7. When you say that you are making the most out of what you've got, you are saying that you are _____ your _____, given your _____.

8.  The price of steak decreases. This leads to an increase in the quantity demanded of steak. Economists break the increase into two effects: the _____ and the _____.

9.  The _____ is the change in consumption of good because a price change has changed a consumer's _____ income.

10. _____ states that the _____ of a good should be equal to its _____.

11. If the marginal benefit of an extra pizza is $8 and the price of a pizza is $15, a utility-maximizing consumer should buy _____ pizzas.

12. When Jean-Luc states that he is willing to pay $1 for his fifth cup of Earl Gray tea, he is expressing the _____ of that cup.

13. A(n) _____ for a good can be derived from a person's willingness to pay for that good. The quantity demanded of the good is graphed on the _____ axis, and both price and _____ are graphed on the _____ axis.

14. The demand curve is downward-sloping as a result of _____.

15. To find the market _____ from the individual demand curves for a good, one should _____ all of the individual quantities demanded for that good at a given _____.

16. The difference between the price of a good and the marginal benefit of that good is called _____.

## True-False Questions

1.  T  F    When Al states that his new computer gives him 1,000 units of utility, he means that he should be able to use his computer for 1,000 useful purposes.

2.  T  F    Usually Anastasia eats 5 potato chips for a midnight snack, and that gives her 100 units of utility. However, late one night, she consumes 10 chips and gets 125 units of utility. Her marginal utility from chips is 25 units.

3.  T  F    The measurement of utility across consumers should be the same and is always given in utils.

4.  T  F    Forrest has $20 to spend on chocolate and Dr. Pepper. The cost of a pound of chocolate is $4, and Dr. Pepper costs $0.75 per can. Forrest can buy 4 pounds of chocolate and 6 cans of Dr. Pepper.

5.  T  F    An increase in a consumer's income rotates the budget line.

6.  T  F    A consumer's income does not affect his or her budget constraint.

7.  T  F    As Christa's income increases, we would expect her demand curve for tangerines (a normal good to Christa) to shift to the right.

8.  T  F    When the price of gasoline rises, Deanna takes the bus to school more often, instead of driving her car. This is an example of the substitution effect.

9.  T  F    Mitch is a utility maximizer. His total benefit from buying one CD is $20, and his total benefit from buying two CDs is $33. If CDs cost $10 each, he should buy one CD.

10. T  F    Adam Smith's diamond–water paradox helps us explain the fact that water is more useful, even though water is considerably less expensive than diamonds.

11.  T    F    A rational consumer buys more of a good if its marginal benefit is less than its price.

12.  T    F    A person's marginal benefit can be used to determine that person's individual demand curve.

13.  T    F    The market demand curve for a good is obtained by adding the heights of all the individual demand curves at each quantity.

14.  T    F    The consumer surplus for a good is the area between the supply demand curve and the price charged for that good.

15.  T    F    Consumer surplus measures what society gives up to produce a good, which is important for evaluating government policy.

## Short-Answer Questions

1.    What does it mean to get more utility from a pound of spinach than from a pound of chocolate?

2.    Explain the idea of marginal utility.

3.    Can all products eventually become bads?

4.    Explain why a consumer's budget constraint is eased when the price of something that he or she consumes falls, even though the consumer's income remains unchanged.

5.    Explain the difference between the income effect and the substitution effect of a price increase.

6.    Explain why the income effect might cause someone to buy less of a good when its price rises.

7.    Explain in words the utility-maximizing rule, *price equals marginal benefit.*

8.    Maurice would be willing to pay (at most) $5 for his first roller coaster ride of the day, $4 for his second ride, $2 for his third ride, and $0.50 for his fourth ride. If the price of a roller coaster ticket is $6, how many rides will Maurice take today? Explain your answer.

9.    Using the information given in question 8, how much consumer surplus will Maurice get from riding the roller coaster today? Explain your answer.

## WORKING IT OUT

1.    The most important things to learn in this chapter are the relationships among willingness to pay, marginal benefit, demand, and consumer surplus. Willingness to pay and marginal benefit (or marginal willingness to pay) give the value in dollars that consumers place on a good. With those valuations, they choose how much to purchase given the price they face for the good, and the difference between their total valuation and their total expenditure on the good measures in dollars the benefit they receive from their purchases. Understanding how these concepts fit together will help you to see the effects on demand of changes in other variables and to be able to evaluate the market equilibrium after all the pieces are put together (in Chapter 7).

2.    The other key concept in this chapter is the utility-maximizing rule, which is another way of thinking about the decision of how much to consume, which looks at the problem in terms of trading off one good for dollars, and which represent all other goods. If you understand the logic behind this rule, you will be able to see not only why the consumer must be maximizing utility when it holds, but what sort of combination of goods he or she should move toward in order to be better off if it doesn't hold.

# Worked Problems

1.  The following table gives Juan's utility from consumption of steak and chicken.

|  |  | | | | |
|---|---|---|---|---|---|
| | **4** | 19 | 25 | 31 | 32 |
| | **3** | 17 | 23 | 29 | 30 |
| Quantity of | **2** | 13 | 19 | 25 | 26 |
| Chicken | **1** | 8 | 14 | 17 | 18 |
| | | **1** | **2** | **3** | **4** |
| | | Quantity of Steak | | | |

a.  If Juan has $25 to spend on these two goods, and the price of steak is $5 and the price of chicken is $3 per unit, how much of each good will Juan purchase?

b.  Suppose the price of chicken falls to $2 per unit. What will happen to Juan's consumption of chicken?

**Answers**

a.  *Since Juan has only $25 to spend, he cannot afford some of these combinations. In particular, the top three combinations in the right-most column, and the top two combinations in the next column to the left all cost more than $25. Juan can afford the remaining combinations, and of these 3 steak and 3 chicken gives the highest utility (29).*

b.  *If the price of chicken falls to $2, the cost of every combination falls, and some of the combinations that Juan couldn't afford before now cost less than $25. In particular, the top combination in the next-to-last column, and the third combination down in the right-most column can now be afforded, although Juan still can't afford the top two entries in the last column. Of the affordable combinations, the combination of 3 steak and 4 chicken now gives the highest utility (31). So when the price of chicken falls from $3 to $2, Juan's demand for chicken rises from 3 units to 4 units.*

2.  The following table gives Billy's total willingness to pay for different levels of consumption of tennis balls during the summer of 1994.

| Cans of Tennis Balls | Total Willingness to Pay |
|---|---|
| 1 | $7.65 |
| 2 | $13.04 |
| 3 | $16.50 |
| 4 | $19.37 |
| 5 | $20.58 |

a.  What is the marginal benefit to Billy of the third can of tennis balls?

b.  If the price of tennis balls is $1.99 per can, how many cans will Billy wish to purchase in the summer of 1994?

c.  If the price of tennis balls is $1.99 per can, how much consumer surplus does Billy receive from the cans of tennis balls he chooses to buy?

**Answers**

a.   *Since Billy is willing to pay $16.50 for 3 cans of tennis balls, but only $13.04 for 2 cans, the third can provides him with $3.46 of marginal benefit. Marginal benefit, or marginal willingness to pay, is the increase in willingness to pay to consume an additional unit.*

b.   *To find the answer to this question, you need to know the marginal benefit of each successive can of tennis balls. The following table gives that information, which you should be able to check by subtracting successive values of willingness to pay from the table above.*

| Cans of Tennis Balls | Marginal Willingness to Pay |
|---|---|
| 1 | $7.65 |
| 2 | $5.39 |
| 3 | $3.46 |
| 4 | $2.87 |
| 5 | $1.21 |

*When the price of tennis balls is $1.99 per can, the first, second, third, and fourth cans all provide Billy a marginal benefit that exceeds their price, and so Billy will want to buy 4 cans. The fifth can provides Billy with some marginal benefit, but not enough benefit to make him willing to purchase it. The most he'd be willing to pay for the fifth can is $1.21, but it would cost him $1.99.*

c.   *We can calculate Billy's consumer surplus in two ways. The simplest way is to find the difference between the total he is willing to pay for the 4 cans of tennis balls he buys and the total amount he pays for them. From the first table, we know that the most Billy is willing to pay for 4 cans of tennis balls is $19.37. Those 4 cans cost him a total of 4 x $1.99 = $7.96, and $19.37 – $7.96 = $11.41, which is Billy's consumer surplus.*

*The other way to calculate Billy's consumer surplus is to find the difference between his marginal benefit and the price he has to pay for each can that he buys, and add them up. From the second table, we know that Billy's marginal benefit from the first can of tennis balls is $7.65, and since that can cost him $1.99, the consumer surplus he receives from that can is $7.65 – $1.99 = $5.66. We can find the consumer surplus from the second, third, and fourth cans in the same way; it is $3.40, $1.47, and $0.88, respectively (you can check this). If we add up the consumer surplus for each can that Billy buys, we find that $5.66 + $3.40 + $1.47 + $0.88 = $11.41, which is the same answer that we found before. The advantage of this second approach, even if it takes a little more time, is that it reminds you that it is the marginal consumer surplus that will determine where Billy's purchases will stop. So long as the consumer surplus of the next unit is positive (i.e., marginal benefit – price is positive, or marginal benefit is greater than the price), Billy will want to purchase that next unit.*

# PRACTICE PROBLEMS

1. The following table gives Carol's total willingness to pay for different levels of consumption of rolls of photographic film during 1995.

| Rolls of Film | Total Willingness to Pay |
|---|---|
| 1 | $6.00 |
| 2 | $10.80 |
| 3 | $14.40 |
| 4 | $16.80 |
| 5 | $18.00 |
| 6 | $18.60 |

   a. What is the marginal benefit to Carol of the fifth roll of film?

   b. If the price of a roll of film is $3.50, how many rolls of film will Carol wish to purchase in 1995?

   c. If the price of a roll of film is $3.50, how much consumer surplus does Carol receive from the rolls of film she chooses to buy?

2. Boxes of pencils cost $3 and markers cost $1.50 each. Joe, spending all of his income, buys 4 boxes of pencils and 3 markers. The last box of pencils gives him $3 of benefits, and the next marker would give him $2 of benefits. Use the utility-maximizing rule to explain whether Joe is maximizing his utility or not, and if not, explain how he might increase his utility by rearranging his consumption without spending any more money.

# CHAPTER TEST

1. The satisfaction that a person receives from the consumption of goods is called his or her

   a. budget constraint.
   b. consumer surplus.
   c. income.
   d. utility.

2. Marginal utility is *best* described as the

   a. additional satisfaction gained by consumption of the last good.
   b. per unit satisfaction of the good consumed.
   c. total satisfaction gained from the total consumption of the good.
   d. change in satisfaction from consuming one additional unit of the good.

3. When the marginal utility of a good is zero, this implies that

   a. a consumer would not spend any additional income to buy more of that good.
   b. consumption of additional units would have positive marginal utility.
   c. total utility is minimized.
   d. total utility is also zero.

4. Consumers will divide their income among all goods so that

   a. total utility is maximized.
   b. marginal utility is zero.

    c.    marginal utility is maximized.

    d.    an equal amount is spent on each good.

The following table should be used for questions 5 through 10.

| Apples | | Oranges | |
|---|---|---|---|
| Quantity | Total Utility | Quantity | Total Utility |
| 0 | 0 | 0 | 0 |
| 1 | 20 | 1 | 40 |
| 2 | 35 | 2 | 85 |
| 3 | 48 | 3 | 125 |
| 4 | 60 | 4 | 155 |
| 5 | 70 | 5 | 180 |
| 6 | 75 | 6 | 200 |
| 7 | 70 | 7 | 210 |

5.    The marginal utility of the fourth orange is

    a.    10.
    b.    12.
    c.    13.
    d.    30.

6.    If a consumer could choose any combination of apples and oranges (up to 7 of each), which combination would be preferred?

    a.    0 apples and 6 oranges
    b.    1 apple and 3 oranges
    c.    5 apples and 2 oranges
    d.    6 apples and 1 orange

7.    Johnny Appleseed has planted an apple tree in your back yard, so that apples are free to you. How many apples will you eat?

    a.    1
    b.    5
    c.    6
    d.    7

8.    The price of apples is $0.50, and the price of oranges is $1. If you have $8.50 to spend on apples and oranges, how many apples will you buy?

    a.    6
    b.    5
    c.    4
    d.    3

9.    Using the prices and budget from question 8, how many oranges will you buy?

    a.    4
    b.    5
    c.    6
    d.    7

10. Using the prices and budget from question 8, which of the following combinations of apples and oranges could the consumer *not* buy?

    a.    1 apple and 8 oranges
    b.    5 apples and 6 oranges
    c.    10 apples and 4 oranges
    d.    11 apples and 3 oranges

11. The substitution effect suggests that

    a.    as the price of a good decreases, one will buy more of that good, since in effect one has more to spend.
    b.    as the price of a good decreases, one will buy more of that good, since that good is relatively cheaper than other goods.
    c.    as the price of a good increases, one will buy less of that good, since it is more expensive.
    d.    as the price of a good increases, one will buy more of the other goods, since one has less "real" income to spend on all goods.

12. The income effect measures the change in the quantity demanded of a good resulting from the change in

    a.    the price of the good being measured.
    b.    the price of another good in a person's consumption bundle.
    c.    real income.
    d.    a consumer's tastes and preferences.

13. At a movie, you can buy a large popcorn for $1.50, a jumbo popcorn for $2.00, or a gigantic popcorn for $2.50. Your total benefit of consuming a large popcorn is $2.00, of a jumbo popcorn is $2.75, and of a gigantic popcorn is $3.00. If you are a rational consumer, you should

    a.    buy a large popcorn.
    b.    buy a jumbo popcorn.
    c.    buy a gigantic popcorn.
    d.    have bought candy instead of popcorn.

14. An individual demand curve is downward-sloping to the right because

    a.    each additional unit has a lower and lower marginal benefit.
    b.    high-priced goods mean that one has more income to spend on other low-priced goods.
    c.    the substitution effect is negated by the income effect.
    d.    the substitution effect forces one to spend more on a good as the price rises.

15. To find the market demand curve from the individual demand curves, one

    a.    adds up the marginal benefits of the individuals at each quantity.
    b.    adds up the budget constraints of the individuals.
    c.    considers only those individuals who are buying at the current price.
    d.    adds up the quantities demanded by individuals at each price.

16. The marginal benefit of a good is a measure of

    a.    the price of the good.
    b.    consumer surplus.
    c.    how much a consumer values another unit of the good.
    d.    the total utility that the consumer gets from the good.

Use the following marginal benefit schedule for questions 17 to 19.

| Quantity | Marginal Benefit |
|----------|------------------|
| 1 | $20 |
| 2 | $19 |
| 3 | $18 |
| 4 | $17 |
| 5 | $16 |
| 6 | $15 |
| 7 | $14 |
| 8 | $13 |
| 9 | $12 |
| 10 | $11 |

17.  The market price for the good is $17. A person's total consumer surplus at this price is

    a.  $0.
    b.  $6.
    c.  $17.
    d.  $64.

18.  If there are 250 people with this marginal benefit schedule in this economy and the market equilibrium price is $13, the equilibrium quantity is

    a.  2,500.
    b.  2,000.
    c.  1,000.
    d.  0.

19.  The total consumer surplus in this society at a market price of $13 is

    a.  $0.
    b.  $3,500.
    c.  $7,000.
    d.  $7,500.

20.  Consumer surplus is used by economists to

    a.  assess the benefits of government policy.
    b.  measure how much consumers gain from purchasing a product.
    c.  evaluate the performance of markets.
    d.  do all of the above.

# ANSWERS TO THE REVIEW QUESTIONS

## Fill-In Questions

1.  utility

2.  Marginal utility

3.  Marginal

4.  indifferent; utility

5.  budget constraint

6.    income; prices

7.    maximizing; utility; budget constraint

8.    income effect; substitution effect

9.    income effect; real

10.   Utility maximization; price; marginal benefit

11.   less

12.   marginal benefit

13.   individual demand curve; horizontal; marginal benefit; vertical

14.   diminishing marginal benefit

15.   demand curve; price

16.   consumer surplus

## True-False Questions

1.    **False**.    Utility is a measure of happiness or well-being.

2.    **False**.    Marginal utility is the additional utility received from consuming one more.

3.    **False**.    There is no unit of happiness that can be compared across people.

4.    **False**.    This combination violates Forrest's budget constraint.

5.    **False**.    When the income rises, the budget line shifts. Only a change in price would cause the budget line to rotate.

6.    **False.**    The budget constraint depends on both the consumers' income and the prices that they face.

7.    **True**.    Increased income shifts out her budget constraint, and she demands more of all normal goods.

8.    **True**.    The price increase leads her to switch to relatively cheaper substitutes.

9.    **False**.    His marginal benefit for the first CD ($20) exceeds its price, so he should buy it, and his marginal benefit for the second CD ($33 – $20 = $13) is greater than the price. He should buy two CDs.

10.   **True**.    The answer is that because water is less scarce, people are able to buy not only the amounts they need to survive, but also units that give much lower benefits, like water for lawns.

11.   **False**.    A rational consumer buys more of a good if the marginal benefit of the next unit exceeds its price, but if the marginal benefit of the last unit is less than its price, the consumer should consume less of that good.

12.   **True**.    Since a rational person will buy any unit that has a marginal benefit greater than the price, the person's marginal benefit curve for a good is his or her individual demand curve for that good.

13.   **False**.    The market demand curve for a good is obtained by adding the quantities from each of the individual demand curves at each given price.

14.   **False**.    Consumer surplus measures the difference between the demand curve and what they actually have to pay.

15. **False.**    Both the income effect and the substitution effect lead to more consumption in the future when the interest rate rises. You have to give up less today to get a unit of consumption in the future, so future consumption is cheaper (substitution effect); your income goes further, so you buy more of all normal goods, including future consumption (income effect).

## SHORT-ANSWER QUESTIONS

1.    Saying that you get more utility from a pound of spinach than you get from a pound of chocolate means that you would prefer a pound of spinach to a pound of chocolate. You like the former more than the latter.

2.    Marginal utility is the *additional* utility that a person gets when he or she consumes *one more* unit of a good.

3.    Yes. A bad exists when marginal utility is negative. Given that marginal utility diminishes with additional consumption, it will eventually become negative. At this point, the product has become a bad.

4.    When the price of a good that the consumer buys falls, and all else, including the consumer's income and the prices of other goods, remains the same, the consumer can now afford to buy additional goods. If the consumer was spending his or her entire income before the price fell, he or she would now be able to buy the same combination of goods and have some money left over. Thus, the budget constraint has shifted, and some combinations of goods that were not affordable before have become affordable.

5.    When the price of something you consume rises (all else equal), it has become relatively more expensive than other goods, and people will switch their consumption away from that good and toward substitutes. This is the substitution effect. In addition, the price increase means that your income won't allow you to purchase as much as you were able to at the old prices. In terms of what you can afford to buy, you are poorer (even though your income measured in dollars hasn't changed), and when people are poorer, they buy less of all normal goods (and more of all inferior goods). This is the income effect.

6.    When the price of something rises, the combinations of goods that consumers can afford are limited further. Consumers are made poorer by a price increase and will buy less of all normal goods. If the good whose price increased is a normal good, the income effect of the price increase will lead the consumer to buy less of that good. Of course, the substitution effect will lead the consumer to buy less too.

7.    The utility-maximizing rule, *price equals marginal benefit*, says that you should consume up to the point where the dollar value to you of the last (marginal) unit you consume is just equal to the price you have to pay for it. You should consume every unit for which the marginal benefit is greater than the price, since those units give you some consumer surplus. You should not consume units that have a marginal benefit that is less than their price, because although they may give you some additional benefit, the other goods you have to sacrifice in order to pay for them are worth more to you.

8.    Maurice will not ride the roller coaster because the price is always greater than the marginal benefit.

9.    Maurice gets $0 of consumer surplus.

## SOLUTIONS TO THE PRACTICE PROBLEMS

1.  a.    Marginal benefit, or marginaume an additional unit. Since Carol is willing to pay $18.00 for 5 rolls of film, but only $16.80 for 4 rolls, the fifth roll provides her with $1.20 of marginal benefit.

    b.    To find the answer to this question, you need to know the marginal benefit of each successive roll l willingness to pay, is the increase in willingness to pay to consof film. By subtracting the total utility at each level of consumption from the total utility received by consuming one less unit, we obtain the following information:

| Rolls of Film | Marginal Willingness to Pay |
|:---:|:---:|
| 1 | $6.00 |
| 2 | $4.80 |
| 3 | $3.60 |
| 4 | $2.40 |
| 5 | $1.20 |
| 6 | $0.60 |

    When the price of film is $3.50 per roll, the first, second, and third rolls all provide Carol a marginal benefit that exceeds their price, and she will want to buy those 3 rolls. The fourth roll (and the fifth and sixth) provides Carol with some marginal benefit, but not enough to make her willing to purchase it.

    c.    We can calculate Carol's consumer surplus by finding the difference between the total she is willing to pay for 3 rolls of film and the total amount she pays for them. From the first table, we know that the most Carol is willing to pay for 3 rolls of film is $14.40. Those 3 rolls cost her a total of 3 x $3.50 = $10.50, and $14.40 – $10.50 = $3.90, which is Carol's consumer surplus.

    We can also calculate Carol's consumer surplus by finding the difference between her marginal benefit and the price she has to pay for each roll that she buys, and adding them up. From the second table, we know that Carol's marginal benefit for the first roll of film is $6.00, and since that roll cost her $3.50, the consumer surplus she receives from that roll is $6.00 – $3.50 = $2.50. We can find the consumer surplus from the second and third rolls in the same way; it is $1.30 and $0.10, respectively. If we add up the consumer surplus that Carol receives from each roll that she buys, we find that $2.50 + $1.30 + $0.10 = $3.90, which is the same answer that we found before.

2.  Joe is not maximizing his utility; you can see this by using the utility-maximizing rule. While the marginal benefit of the last box of pencils he bought was just equal to its price, the marginal benefit of the next marker he would buy is greater than its price. Joe can increase his utility without spending any more money by buying one less box of pencils and buying more markers. Buying one less box of pencils loses him $3 of marginal benefits (since that's what the last box was worth to him), but saves him 3 dollars (since that's what he saves by not buying them). If he spends $1.50 of that $3 on another marker, he will get a $2 marginal benefit and still have $1.50 to spend on other things, so he will have turned that $3 into $3.50 of benefits plus money, a net gain of 50 cents.

# ANSWERS TO THE CHAPTER TEST

1. d
2. d
3. a
4. a
5. d
6. a
7. c
8. b
9. c
10. c
11. b
12. c
13. b
14. a
15. d
16. c
17. b
18. b
19. c
20. d

# APPENDIX TO CHAPTER 5

# Consumer Theory with Indifference Curves

## OVERVIEW

In Chapter 5, we used a model of utility maximization to explain consumers' buying choices and to understand how those choices respond to changes in prices and income. We used the budget constraint to describe the combinations of goods that consumers could afford, given their income and the prices of the goods, and we showed the utility-maximizing rule that must be true if consumers spend their income to make themselves as happy as possible. In this chapter, we will look at the consumer's decision more closely, using a diagram of the budget constraint and representing the consumer's tastes using something called **indifference curves**.

## REVIEW

1.  The main idea in understanding consumer behavior is the idea of *constrained maximization*, or doing the best you can under the constraints you face. There are two parts to the model of consumer choice. One part describes which combinations of goods the consumer can afford, given his income and the prices he faces. The **budget constraint** shows the limits within which the consumer can choose. The other part describes how the consumer feels about different combinations of goods. **Indifference curves** are how the consumer's tastes or preferences are represented in a diagram. We'll get to those in a little bit.

2.  In order to be able to show the consumer's decision using a diagram, we will assume that he has to choose only the amounts of two goods to consume. Call those goods $X$ and $Y$, and measure their quantities on the $X$ (horizontal) and $Y$ (vertical) axes of a diagram. We'll suppose that the consumer can purchase fractions of a unit (like a half a pound of sugar).

3.  The budget line is made up of all the combinations of $X$ and $Y$ that the consumer can just purchase with his income at the prevailing prices of $X$ and $Y$. To plot the budget line for a specific consumer, we need to know his income and the two prices. Then we can see which combinations of $X$ and $Y$ are affordable and which cost more than he has to spend. For example, suppose the consumer has $36 to spend this week on $X$ and $Y$, and the prices of $X$ and $Y$ are $2 and $3 per unit, respectively. Then one thing the consumer can afford is 18 units of $X$, because 18 units of $X$ at $2 each is just $36. Of course, if he makes this choice, he can't afford to buy any $Y$, since he has no income remaining, but the combination of 18 $X$ and 0 $Y$ is a point on the budget line. He can also afford to buy 3 units of $X$ and 10 units of $Y$, because 3 units of $X$ at $2 per unit and 10 units of $Y$ at $3 per unit also costs $36, so that's another point on the budget line. There are lots of other combinations on his budget line; for example, if he buys 6 units of $Y$, how many units of $X$ can he buy? The answer is 9 units, since 6 units of $Y$ at $3 per unit costs $18, and the remaining $18 of his income allows him to buy 9 units of $X$ at $2 per unit.

4.  If we plot all the combinations of $X$ and $Y$ that the consumer can just afford with his income, they will form a downward-sloping straight line, which is the budget line. The line slopes down because in order to purchase more $X$ (move to the right) the consumer will have to purchase less $Y$ (move down). Any combination that lies below the budget line can be afforded with income left

over, and any combination that lies above the budget line costs more than the income that the consumer has to spend.

5.  Of course, if the consumer's income rises, he will be able to afford more. The result of an increase in the consumer's income is to shift his budget line outward, parallel to the original budget line. Conversely, if the consumer's income falls, his budget line shifts inward, parallel to its original position.

6.  The slope of the budget line is given by $-(P_X/P_Y)$. To get one more unit of $X$ requires having $P_X$ dollars to spend, and if you are currently spending all your income, the only way to get that is to buy fewer units of $Y$. How many fewer units depends on the prices of $X$ and $Y$; each unit of $Y$ *not* bought frees up $P_Y$ dollars to spend on $X$. You have to forgo enough units of $Y$ at $P_Y$ each to get $P_X$ dollars, which means giving up $P_X/P_Y$ units. In the example above, where $P_X = \$2$ and $P_Y = \$3$, if you want to buy one more unit of $X$, you need \$2, which you can get by buying 2/3 of a unit less of $Y(P_X/P_Y = 2/3)$. The slope of the budget line is negative because in order to buy one *more* unit of $X$, you need to buy some amount *less* of $Y$.

7.  When the price of one good changes, holding the price of the other good constant, the budget line rotates or twists. For example, the price of $X$ rises (holding income and the price of $Y$ constant), and the budget line pivots inward around its original $Y$ intercept (the point where the budget line hits the $Y$ axis). The slope steepens because $P_X/P_Y$ rises (in order to purchase one more $X$, you need to forgo more $Y$ after the price of $X$ has risen). The reason that the $Y$ intercept doesn't change is that the amount of $Y$ that can be purchased if the consumer spends his entire income on good $Y$ and none on good $X$ (which is the combination of goods that this point represents) is unaffected by the price of $X$. Similarly, if the price of $Y$ falls (holding income and the price of $X$ constant), the budget line pivots outward around its original $X$ intercept.

8.  Now that we have seen how to show the combinations of two goods that the consumer can afford with his income, we want to see how the consumer chooses the best combination, the one that maximizes his utility. To do this, we need to know something about the consumer's preferences. Remember from Chapter 5 that economists recognize that different people have different preferences. Here, we will just assume we know what this consumer's preferences are, but the same approach will work for other preferences—we just need to know how the consumer feels about good $X$ and $Y$.

9.  We start from a pretty simple proposition—that more goods make our consumer happier. Our consumer would rather have a combination that has the same amount of $X$ and more $Y$ than a combination that has the same amount of $X$ and less $Y$, and would rather have a combination that has the same amount of $Y$ and more $X$ than a combination that has the same amount of $Y$ and less $X$. From this, we can figure out combinations that give our consumer the *same* level of utility or happiness. Start at some combination (a point on the $X$–$Y$ graph), take away some $Y$ (which makes the consumer worse off), and then make up for it by giving him more $X$ until he says he is as happy as when he started. The consumer is *indifferent* between these two combinations—they make him equally happy, and given a choice between the two, he will tell you it doesn't matter; they're equally good. If we go back to the original starting point, take away some $X$ (again making him less happy) and then make up for it by giving him more $Y$ until he says he is as happy as when he started, we can find another combination that gives him the same utility as the starting point. In fact, we can find a lot of combinations that yield the same utility as the starting point in this way. The curve that you get by connecting all these combinations is called an **indifference curve**, because the consumer is indifferent among all the combinations it represents; each makes him as happy as any other.

10.  An indifference curve is sloped downward because reduced consumption of one good must be accompanied by increased consumption of the other in order to keep the consumer at the same

level of utility. The slope of the indifference curve is called the **marginal rate of substitution**; it depends on how much utility the consumer loses when we take a little $X$ from him and how much utility he gains from each unit of $Y$ he gets in return. Recall from Chapter 5 that the extra utility that a consumer gets from one more unit of a good is the **marginal utility** of that good. Therefore, for each unit of $X$ we take away from our consumer, he loses $MU_X$ in happiness. We have to give him enough $Y$ to make up this loss in utility; since each *unit* of $Y$ gives him a gain of $MU_Y$ in utility, we need to give him enough extra $Y$ (call this amount $\Delta Y$ for "change in $Y$") so that $\Delta Y \times MU_Y$ equals the loss in utility from the units of $X$ taken away $(\Delta X \times MU_X)$. That is, between any two points on the indifference curve, $-\Delta X \times MU_X = \Delta Y \times MU_Y$ (the minus sign is because $\Delta X$ was negative—we took some $X$ away). The slope of the indifference curve, which tells us how many units of $Y$ must be given for each unit of good $X$ taken $(\Delta Y/\Delta X)$, must equal $-MU_X/MU_Y$.

11. We can interpret the marginal rate of substitution as the biggest number of units of good $Y$ our consumer is willing to trade for one more unit of good $X$. For example, if the marginal rate of substitution is 6, that means the consumer will be just willing to trade 6 units of $Y$ for 1 unit of $X$; that trade will leave him as well off as when he started. Obviously, he'd be happier if he only had to trade 5 units of $Y$ for 1 unit of $X$, but the most he'll trade is 6 units. He won't trade 6½ unit of $Y$ for an additional unit of $X$, since that would leave him worse off.

12. Notice that the indifference curves are bowed inward toward the origin. This is called "diminishing marginal rate of substitution." It occurs because people are more willing to trade things they have a lot of to get an additional unit of things they have little of. Near the $Y$ axis, where the consumer has a lot of $Y$ and not much $X$, he will be willing to give up relatively more $Y$ to get another unit of $X$, so the slope of the indifference curve (the marginal rate of substitution) is high. Near the $X$ axis, where the consumer has lots of $X$ and little $Y$, he isn't willing to trade much of his limited $Y$ to get even more of the $X$ that he has a lot of already. In fact, in order to get him to part with a little of his scarce $Y$, you have to give him a lot of $X$, so the slope of the indifference curve (the marginal rate of substitution) is low. As his consumption of $X$ has increased, his marginal rate of substitution has fallen; that's why it's called the diminishing marginal rate of substitution.

13. The indifference curve tells us all the combinations that give the same utility as the one we started with when we constructed it. What about all the other combinations? Any combination that lies above the indifference curve gives more utility than any point on the indifference curve, since it involves more of *both* goods than some points on the indifference curve, and all the points on the indifference curve give the consumer the same utility. If we pick one point above the indifference curve, we can find all the combinations that give the same utility as that combination and find another indifference curve. Similarly, any combination that lies below an indifference curve gives less utility than any point on that indifference curve, and if we start with one such point, we can find all the other combinations that give the same utility as that combination and find yet another indifference curve. So there isn't just one indifference curve; there is a whole set of them. All the combinations on an indifference curve give the consumer the same level of utility, and higher indifference curves give more utility.

14. Now we have both pieces to the puzzle: what combinations of $X$ and $Y$ our consumer can afford, and how he feels about different combinations. The question now is to find out which affordable combination of $X$ and $Y$ is the best one, the one that maximizes his utility. To do this, we put both the budget line and the set of indifference curves on the same diagram and ask which is the highest indifference curve the consumer can reach (how high his utility can get) without going outside the budget line (not spending more than he has). There will always be an indifference curve that just touches the budget line but never cuts through it, and that is the highest indifference curve the consumer can reach given his budget curve. The point at which that indifference curve and the budget line just touch, which is called the **tangency point**, represents

the combination of goods $X$ and $Y$ that is both affordable and gives the consumer the highest level of utility. If the consumer wants to maximize his utility subject to his budget constraint, this is the combination he will choose.

15. At the tangency point, the slope of the indifference curve and the slope of the budget line are equal. If they weren't, the indifference curve would cut through the budget curve, and we could find another combination that gave a slightly higher level of utility. Recall that the slope of the budget line equals $-P_X/P_Y$, and the slope of the indifference curve equals $-MU_X/MU_Y$ (the marginal rate of substitution). Therefore, at the utility-maximizing combination of $X$ and $Y$, we know that $P_X/P_Y = MU_X/MU_Y$. This is called the **utility-maximizing rule**, because it is always true at the utility-maximizing combination. If you check at some combination of $X$ and $Y$ whether $P_X/P_Y$ equals $MU_X/MU_Y$ and it doesn't, you know that combination is not the utility-maximizing combination.

16. So far, we have figured out the amounts of $X$ and $Y$ that this consumer will buy at a particular $P_X$, $P_Y$, and income. Of course, if any of those variables change, the consumer's budget curve will shift and there will be a different utility-maximizing combination. For example, this consumer's demand for good $X$ tells us how much $X$ he wants to purchase at different prices of $X$, holding other variables (such as income and the price of other goods like $Y$) constant. We can find another point on his demand curve by increasing $P_X$ and finding the amount of $X$ in the new utility-maximizing combination he chooses. Remember that when the price of $X$ increases, the budget line rotates or twists inward. This means that combinations on the old budget line can no longer be afforded, and the consumer has to pick a new utility-maximizing point. That combination is the one where a different, lower, indifference curve just touches the new budget line. The amount of $X$ in that new combination, along with the new $P_X$, gives another point on the consumer's demand curve. If the price of $X$ falls, the budget line rotates outward, and the consumer will make a new tangency point where a higher indifference curve just touches that budget line.

17. We can also use this model to see how the consumer's demand changes when his income changes. For example, if the consumer's income falls, his budget line moves inward but stays parallel to the original budget line (because the slope of the budget line depends only on the prices of $X$ and $Y$, which haven't changed). This again means that combinations on the original budget line can no longer be afforded. The consumer has to pick a new utility-maximizing combination. This means finding where an indifference curve just touches the new budget line. Generally, this will involve buying less of both goods, but if one good is an inferior good, the new combination will involve more of that good and less of the other. If the consumer's income rises, the budget line shifts outward parallel to the original budget line, and the consumer again has to find a new tangency point.

18. Recall from Chapter 5 that there are really two reasons why an increase in the price of a good leads to a decrease in the quantity demanded: the substitution effect, which shows how consumers purchase less of the good whose price has risen and more of other goods that have become relatively cheaper, and the income effect, which shows how consumers buy less of all normal goods and more of all inferior goods when the price increase lowers the purchasing power of their incomes. We can use the budget line and indifference curves to see both of these effects when the price of a good increases. To do this, we break down the move from the original tangency point before the price increase to the new tangency price after the price increase into two steps. The first step is to shift the budget line inward, parallel to the original budget line (remember, this is what happens when income falls but prices don't change), until it is just tangent to the *same* indifference curve that the new tangency point is on. This shows us a pure reduction of income that gives the consumer the same level of happiness he can achieve after the price increase; it shows us the choice that the consumer would have made if his income had been reduced (without changing prices) enough so that he could be just as happy as he is after the price change. The

difference between his original consumption of $X$ and the consumption of $X$ at this new tangency point is the income effect of the price change. The second step is to rotate the budget line around the new indifference curve until the consumer's utility-maximizing choice at the new prices is reached. This shows a pure change in prices; it keeps the consumer at the same level of happiness, so his true income isn't changing. The difference between his consumption of $X$ at the tangency point that represented only the income effect and his consumption of $X$ at the final tangency point is the substitution effect of the price change.

## ZEROING IN

1. You might think that choosing a point on your budget line and spending all your income isn't a smart choice because you'd be better off saving some for the future. But the purpose of saving is to be able to buy something in the future, which is just another good. In this model, there are only two goods. You can think of it as determining how to spend the income you have decided to spend on those goods.

2. Although we don't draw them all in, there are actually a whole set of indifference curves that entirely fill up the space in the $X$–$Y$ diagram. After all, every point in that diagram represents a combination of some amount of good $X$ and some amount of good $Y$, and if you start at *any* point, you can always find the set of other combinations that gives the consumer the same level of utility. Every point has to be on an indifference curve. That guarantees that there is some indifference curve that just touches the budget line.

3. Different people can have different indifference curves. After all, some people like pepperoni pizza and some like sausage pizza. Likewise, different people can have different budget constraints. Some are richer and others are poorer. As a result, people can make different choices. But whatever your budget constraint and whatever your preferences, this is how you would go about finding *your* utility-maximizing combination.

## ACTIVE REVIEW

## Fill-In Questions

1. The _____ line shows all the combinations of goods $X$ and $Y$ that the consumer can afford, given his _____ and the _____ of the goods he faces.

2. The _____ of the budget line is $-P_X/P_Y$. An increase in the price of one good, holding the price of the other good and income constant, causes the budget line to _____.

3. A change in the consumer's _____, holding prices constant, causes the budget line to _____ but remain _____ to the original budget line.

4. A consumer's preferences can be shown by a set of _____, which show combinations of goods that give the consumer the same _____.

5. _____ slope downward because if the consumer gives up some of one good, he must receive _____ of the other in order to achieve the same level of _____. The slope of the indifference curve is called the _____, which is given by _____.

6. In order to maximize his utility given his budget, the consumer should find the _____ indifference curve without going above the _____. This occurs at a _____ point, where an indifference curve just touches the _____.

7. The _____ rule always holds at a tangency point; at that point, _____ equals _____.

8.    Changes in _____ or _____ cause the budget line to _____, and the consumer will respond by finding a new tangency point. This lets us see how _____ responds to changes in these variables.

## True-False Questions

1.    T    F    If a consumer's income is $20 per week, the price of chips is $2 per bag, and the price of salsa is $3.50 per jar, the combination of 3 bags of chips and 4 jars of salsa lies on his budget line.

2.    T    F    A consumer can only afford combinations that lie on his budget line.

3.    T    F    If the prices of both goods go up by 50 percent, the slope of the budget line doesn't change.

4.    T    F    The price of hot dogs is $1 each, and the price of candy bars is 50 cents each. Anne's marginal utility of another hot dog is 10, and her marginal utility of another candy bar is 5. If Anne is spending all her income on these two goods, she is maximizing her utility.

5.    T    F    If we ignore the income effect, a decrease in the price of $Y$ will lead the consumer to consume more $Y$.

## Short-Answer Questions

1.    Why is the budget line a straight line?

2.    What happens to the budget line when the consumer's income increases (all else equal), and why?

3.    Why do indifference curves slope downward?

4.    Explain how you find the consumer's utility-maximizing combination of goods from his budget line and set of indifference curves.

## WORKING IT OUT

## Worked Problems

1.    Figure 5A.1 shows a consumer's budget line, some of his indifference curves, and several points representing different combinations of the goods $X$ and $Y$. What can you say about each labeled point?

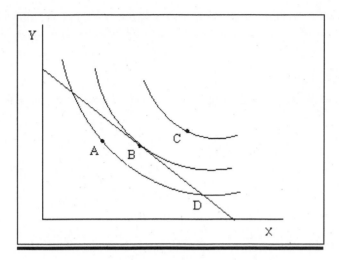

**Figure 5A.1**

**Answer**

*Point A is a combination that the consumer can afford with income left over. It cannot be the utility-maximizing combination. Point B is a tangency point. It is the where the highest indifference curve that can be reached without going above the budget line just touches the budget line. This is the utility-maximizing combination. Point C is a combination that the consumer can't afford with his income. Although it would make him happier than point B, it's too expensive. Point D is a point on the budget line, but it isn't the utility-maximizing point because the indifference curve it lies on cuts through the budget line. Moving along the budget line toward point B is still affordable and allows the consumer to reach higher indifference curves (until point B is reached).*

2.   Use a budget line and indifference curve diagram to show how the demand for $X$ changes when the price of good $X$ falls.

**Answer**

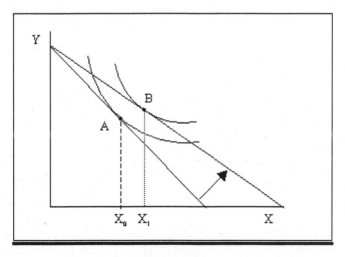

**Figure 5A.2**

*Figure 5A.2 shows what happens. The consumer's utility-maximizing combination before the price increase is at point A, where he chooses to buy $X_0$ units of $X$. The decrease in the price of $X$ causes the consumer's budget line to rotate outward around the point where it hits the Y axis. The* *consumer can now afford combinations that weren't affordable before, and he finds a new tangency point at point B. He demands a larger quantity of X, moving up to $X_1$.*

## PRACTICE PROBLEM

1.    Use a budget line and indifference curve diagram to show how the demand for Y changes when the price of good Y falls.

## ANSWERS TO THE REVIEW QUESTIONS

### Fill-In Questions

1.    budget; income; prices

2.    slope; rotate or twist

3.    income; shift; parallel

4.    indifference curves; utility

5.    Indifference curves; more; utility; marginal rate of substitution; $-MU_X/MU_Y$

6.    highest; budget line; tangency; budget line

7.    utility maximizing; $P_X/P_Y$; $MU_X/MU_Y$

8.    income; prices; shift; demand

### True-False Questions

1.    **True**.    Three bags of chips cost $6, and 4 jars of salsa cost $14, which can just be purchased with the consumer's $20 income.

2.    **False**.    A consumer can afford any combination that lies on the budget line or inside it. But points inside the budget line can't be utility maximizing, because you can always reach a higher indifference curve from those points by moving out toward the budget line and consuming more of both goods.

3.    **True**.    The slope of the budget line is given by the ratio of the prices. If both prices go up by the same proportion, their ratio doesn't change.

4.    **True**.    The utility-maximizing rule holds for Anne. The price ratio ($P_{\text{hot dogs}}/P_{\text{candy bars}} = 1/0.5 = 2$) and her marginal rate of substitution ($MU_{\text{hotdogs}}/MU_{\text{candy bars}} = 10/5 = 2$) are equal.

5.    **True**.    If we ignore the income effect, the substitution effect says that the consumer will substitute the relatively cheaper Y for the relatively more expensive X.

### Short-Answer Questions

1.    The slope of the budget line depends on the prices of the two goods. Since those prices don't change when the consumer chooses different combinations of the goods, the slope of the budget line doesn't change either. Therefore, it has to be a straight line.

2.    When the consumer's income increases, his budget line shifts out to the right, but it remains parallel to the original budget line because the slope depends only on the prices of X and Y. This happens because the increase in income makes some combinations affordable that weren't when the consumer's income was lower.

3.  Indifference curves slope downward because reduced consumption of one good must be accompanied by increased consumption of the other in order to keep the consumer at the same level of utility.

4.  In order to find the consumer's utility-maximizing combination of goods, we find the highest indifference curve that can be reached without going above the budget line. This occurs at a tangency point, where an indifference curve just touches the budget line.

## SOLUTION TO THE PRACTICE PROBLEM

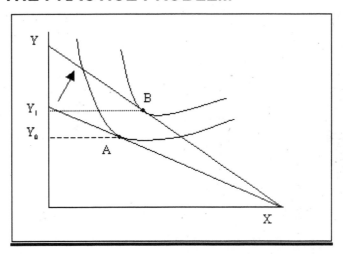

**Figure 5A.3**

1.  Figure 5A.3 shows what happens. The consumer's utility-maximizing combination before the price increase is at point $A$, where he chooses to buy $Y_0$ units of $Y$. The decrease in the price of $Y$ causes the consumer's budget line to rotate outward around the point where it hits the $X$ axis. The consumer can now afford combinations that weren't affordable before, and he finds a new tangency point at point $B$. He demands a larger quantity of $Y$, moving up to $Y_1$.

# CHAPTER 6

# The Supply Curve and the Behavior of Firms

## CHAPTER OVERVIEW

In the last chapter, we took a closer look at how consumers' decisions about how best to spend their income lead to demand curves for goods and services. In this chapter, we take a closer look at what lies behind the supply curves for those goods and services. We will turn our attention to the choices that firms make about how much to produce. We will see that firms wish to maximize their profits. In doing so they are restricted in their choices by technological limits on how much they can produce with a given amount of inputs and by the need to acquire those inputs at a price. We will see that this model of firm behavior explains the positive slope of supply curves and why the supply curve shifts when other variables change. We will also introduce some additional ideas that will play an important role when we evaluate the performance of the market system later in the text.

## CHAPTER REVIEW

1.  A **firm** is an organization that produces goods or services. Firms come in all sizes, from the small-town lawyer's practice to corporate giants like Ford Motor Company and Microsoft, some producing one good and others producing a vast array of products. For our purposes here, it is best to think of a smaller firm that produces only one good; this will keep things simple.

2.  There are several different legal arrangements under which firms can be organized. A *sole proprietorship* is a firm owned (and typically run) by a single person. The owner makes the company's decisions, earns the income that the firm makes if it has any, and is responsible for paying the firm's losses if it has any. A *partnership* is much like a sole proprietorship, except that there are two or more owners who share in the decision making, the income, and the losses. A *corporation* has stockholders who own the firm and share the income that the firm makes, and hired management that makes the decisions for the company. The majority of firms in the United States are proprietorships, but because they are typically very small, they do not account for a large percentage of the nation's economic activity. Most of the 3.5 million corporations in the United States are small as well, and most of the nation's economic activity takes place within the 14,000 largest corporations.

3.  The supply curve for a firm tells us how much the firm is willing and able to supply at different prices, much as the market supply curve that we looked at in Chapter 3 tells us how much all the firms together are willing and able to supply at different prices. If we are going to ask how much the firm will supply at different prices, then the price must be something that the firm responds to, not something that it has control over. We call a firm that takes the market price as given a **price-taker**. There are real-world instances in which this is a good description of firms; farmers, for example, can find out today's crop price on the commodity market, but they cannot change that price by their actions.

4.  A market that is made up entirely of price-taking firms is called a **competitive market**. We will see later how the choices of all the firms together in the competitive market determine the price that each firm individually takes as given.

5. Not all markets in the real world are competitive. For example, when there is only one producer of a good, that firm can alter the price by choosing a different level of output to sell. A firm that is the only seller of a product is called a *monopoly*. In that case, it doesn't make any sense to ask how much the firm will sell at different prices. The monopoly doesn't respond to the price; it determines the price. We will return to monopolies in Chapter 10.

6. Economists assume that firms make choices about how much output to produce and how to produce it with the goal of maximizing profits. **Profits** are the difference between the revenue that the firm takes in from the sale of its output and the total costs of producing that output. That is,

   Profits = Total revenue – Total costs

   When the profits that a firm earns are positive, the firm is taking in more revenue from the sale of its output than it requires to pay for the inputs used in the production of that output. When the firm is making a profit of zero, its revenues exactly cover its costs. A firm that makes a negative profit does not receive enough from the sales of its products to pay all its costs.

7. We have already discussed the concept of revenue in Chapter 4. **Total revenue** is computed by multiplying the quantity of output sold by the price at which it is sold. That is,

   Total revenue = Price × Quantity = $P \times Q$

   Since we are talking about a price-taking, competitive firm in this chapter, the only way the firm can increase its revenue is to sell more units. Revenue would also increase if the price of the good rose, but for a competitive firm, increasing the price would not be something the firm could *choose* to do.

8. Using a given amount of inputs, there is an upper limit on how much output the firm can produce. Using more inputs allows the firm to produce more output. A firm's ability to vary its inputs depends on how much time it has to make those adjustments. Changing inputs takes time, and when there isn't enough time to change all its inputs, a firm may only be able to adjust some. The time period in which some inputs are fixed is called the *short run*, and we will focus on the short run in this chapter. In Chapter 8, we will look at the *long run*, which is enough time to allow all inputs to be varied.

9. The firm's **production function** tells how much output will be produced from any given amount of inputs. We can ask how much total output will go up if another unit of one input is utilized, holding the levels of the other inputs constant. For example, we can ask how much more the firm would be able to produce if it hired one more hour of labor time. The additional output that results from this additional unit of labor is called the **marginal product of labor**.

10. Typically, each additional unit of an input increases output by less than the previous unit did. That is, the marginal product of an input gets smaller and smaller as more and more of the input is used. When labor is the input being increased, this phenomenon is known as **diminishing returns to labor**. Each successive hour of labor hired causes total output to rise, but by less than the previous hour caused output to rise. This occurs because the other inputs are being held constant, so that more and more labor is being used with a fixed amount of capital, raw materials, and so forth.

11. Production requires inputs of capital (machines, buildings, land) and labor (workers' time). These typically have to be acquired in markets; workers and owners of capital have to be paid. The more the firm produces, the more inputs it requires and the more it has to pay to acquire them. Therefore, **total costs** increase when production increases. How much total costs rise with output depends on how much more inputs are required to produce additional output.

12. All inputs must fall into one of two categories: those that vary with output in the short run, and those that are fixed in the short run. Therefore, all costs must fall into one of two categories: fixed costs and variable costs. Total cost at any level of production is the sum of the **fixed costs** (which don't change with the level of production) and the **variable costs** associated with that level of production.

13. **Marginal cost** is the change in total cost associated with a one-unit change in output. Typically, marginal cost increases as production increases; that is, the additional cost of producing another unit is higher when the level of output is greater. This is a consequence of diminishing returns to labor; if each additional unit of labor adds less to output than the previous unit of labor added, then each additional unit of output must take more labor than the previous one required, and it adds more to total cost than the previous one did.

14. We can graph the total cost of producing different levels of output. The slope of the total cost curve gives the marginal cost of each successive unit, since the slope shows how much total cost rises when output increases by one unit. Increasing marginal cost makes the total cost curve become steeper as output rises.

15. We can also graph the marginal cost at different levels of output. Increasing marginal cost means that the marginal cost curve slopes upward.

16. A price-taking firm in the competitive market has to decide how much it wants to sell at the current price. If the firm is interested in **profit maximization**, as we have assumed, then it should produce and sell any unit of output that adds to its profits (or reduces its losses), but not any unit that reduces its profits (or increases its losses). A unit of output adds to the firm's profits (or reduces its losses) if selling it adds more to revenue than the additional costs that are incurred in producing it. Conversely, a unit reduces the firm's profits if selling it adds less to revenue than the additional costs of its production. The additional revenue that comes from selling one more unit is called the **marginal revenue**. For a price-taking firm, the additional revenue that is received when the firm sells one more unit is simply the price at which the firm can sell. The additional costs incurred when another unit is produced are the marginal cost. Therefore, if we plot the marginal cost of different amounts of output and choose a price for the firm to respond to, the profit-maximizing firm will produce each unit that has a marginal cost less than the price and will stop when the marginal cost of the next unit would be above the price.

This is shown in Figure 6.1; the marginal cost of each of the first two units is below the price of $5, so producing and selling them adds to profit. The third and subsequent units have marginal costs that exceed the $5 price; producing and selling the third unit would not add to profits, and so the firm chooses to sell 2 units at the price of $5.

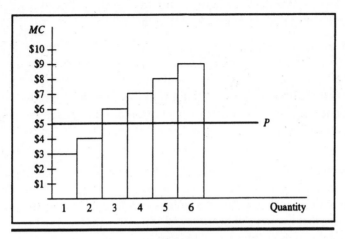

**Figure 6.1**

If the price rises, then some additional units that had a marginal cost above the old price will now have a marginal cost below the new price, and the firm will be able to earn some additional profit by producing them. The firm will now produce up to the unit of output whose marginal cost exceeds the new price. This is shown in Figure 6.2. When the price rises from $P_{old}$ of $5 to $P_{new}$ of $7.50, the third and fourth units, which have marginal costs greater than $5 but less than $7.50, now add something to profit when they are produced and sold. The fifth and sixth units have marginal costs that still exceed the price and would reduce profits if sold. In response to the increase in price, the firm will now choose to expand its sales from 2 units to 4 units.

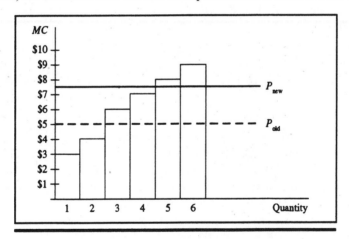

**Figure 6.2**

We can find out how much the firm will want to sell at other prices in the same way. Doing this for many prices traces out the firm's supply curve, which tells how much the firm will want to sell at each different price.

17. If the price-taking firm maximizes its profits by producing up to the point where the marginal cost of the next unit is just greater than the price, and if production can be increased in relatively small steps, then the firm will produce up to the point where the **price equals the marginal cost** of the last unit produced. The supply curve will be a smooth curve of many small steps. The rule that the price-taking firm uses is to choose a quantity to produce so that price equals marginal cost. Actually, the basic logic, which is to produce any unit that adds more to revenue than it adds to cost, holds for other firms besides the price-taking firms in competitive markets that we are considering here, and so the rule can be stated more generally as, choose a quantity to produce so

that marginal revenue equals marginal cost. In the case of the price-taking firm in a competitive market, however, the marginal revenue is equal to the price.

18. The quantity that maximizes profit for a price-taking firm can also be found by looking either at a table of total revenue and total costs at different levels of output or at a graph of the same information. If we list the total revenue from selling different levels of output (which will depend on the price at which the good sells) and the total costs of producing those levels of output, we can take the difference to get profit and find the level of output that yields the highest profit. Changing the price at which the good sells will change the numbers in the revenue column, and therefore also change the profit column, so that a different level of output will provide the highest profit.

19. We can also graph total costs and total revenue at different levels of output. For a price-taking firm, the total revenue curve will be an upward-sloping straight line whose slope is the price of the product, since selling one more unit always increases total revenue by the price of the product. We can find the quantity that maximizes profits by finding the quantity that yields the largest vertical gap between the total revenue and total costs lines, since that gap is total revenues minus total costs or profits. Changing the price at which the good sells changes the slope of the total revenue curve, so that a different level of output will provide the highest profit.

20. The **market supply curve** gives the quantity that all the firms together want to sell at different prices. It is obtained by adding up the individual supply curves; that is, at each price, we add up the quantities that each firm is willing to supply at that price.

21. Since the slope and position of the individual firms' supply curves depend on their marginal cost curves, anything that affects the firms' marginal costs will shift the firms' supply curves. Furthermore, since the market supply curve is the sum of the firms' supply curves, those same things will shift the market supply curve as well. For example, a change in technology that saves variable inputs and lowers marginal cost will shift the firms' marginal cost curves down and will lead to more output being supplied at any price. Therefore, this change in technology will cause the market supply curve to shift to the right. Similarly, an increase in the price of labor (a variable input) will raise the marginal cost curves of the firms. Firms will find fewer units profitable to sell at each price, and both the firms' supply curves and the market supply curve will shift to the left.

22. **Producer surplus** is the difference between the price at which each unit sells and its marginal cost, added up over all the units that the firm sells. Graphically, producer surplus is the area under the price line and above the marginal cost curve from the vertical axis out to the quantity that the firm sells. Producer surplus is a measure of how much the firm gains from selling at the given price, because the total amount by which the revenue the firm receives for selling each unit exceeds the additional cost of producing that unit. Producer surplus is not the same thing as profit, however, because the sum of the marginal costs of all the units produced is not equal to total costs. Total costs are the sum of the marginal costs plus the fixed costs. Therefore, profit is producer surplus minus fixed costs, and producer surplus is profit plus fixed costs.

# ZEROING IN

1. This chapter focuses on the supply decisions of *price-taking firms* in *competitive markets*. There are other factors that enter into supply in the long run but not in the short run. We will take up those factors in Chapter 8. Not all firms are price-taking firms; many can raise their prices within limits without losing all their customers. We will return to those firms later, in Chapters 10 and 11. Furthermore, not all price-taking firms are in competitive markets. A competitive market is one that consists *entirely* of price-taking firms, and there are markets in which there are one or more large firms that can raise their prices without losing all their customers and other firms that are smaller and have to take the large firms' price as given.

Why do we spend so much time on competitive markets? When we evaluate the performance of competitive markets in Chapters 8 and 9, we will see that they do a particularly good job of allocating resources to firms and goods to people. We can use competitive markets as a benchmark against which to evaluate the performance of other sorts of markets. To do that, we need a good understanding of how a competitive market works. Also, many of the cost concepts that we address here are important when we analyze firms that don't take prices as given.

2.    While it is often difficult to ignore sunk costs, they really should not play a role in your decision making. A sunk cost is money that has been spent and can't be recovered. Nothing you do can change that fact, so you should ignore sunk costs. Consider the following example.

You have planned a trip to Savannah and paid $100 in a nonrefundable advance for your hotel room for the week. You have also paid $250 for your airplane ticket, but this is refundable if you choose not to use it. Assume that you see the weather forecast and it will be raining all weekend in Savannah. Should you go to Savannah?

It depends on the value to you of going to Savannah. Even with the rain, if it is worth more than $250, then you should go. What about the $100? Should the value of going to Savannah be more than $350? The $100 nonrefundable advance is a sunk cost. You can't get it back. What matters is the additional cost, not the total cost. It is the $250 that matters.

3.    The price equals marginal cost rule for finding the profit-maximizing quantity to produce is just like the price equals marginal benefit rule for finding the utility-maximizing amount to consume that we looked at in Chapter 5. The logic is the same; if price is greater than marginal cost, then producing and selling the next unit brings in enough additional revenue (the price) to cover the added costs (marginal cost) and have something left over that can be added to profits. On the other hand, if price is less than marginal cost, then producing and selling the last unit didn't bring in enough additional revenue to cover the additional costs of producing it, and the difference had to be taken from profits. Cutting back production by one unit means that those funds can remain as part of profits, so that profits are higher.

## ACTIVE REVIEW

### Fill-In Questions

1.    There are several different types of firms, including _____, _____, and _____.

2.    When analyzing the decisions of firms, economists generally assume that the firm's goal is to maximize _____.

3.    When there are many small firms in a market, no single firm can successfully charge a price much above what others are charging. Economists refer to each firm in this situation as _____.

4.    A market that consists entirely of _____ firms is called a(n) _____ market.

5.    Total profit is the difference between a firm's _____ and its _____.

6.    Capital and labor are considered to be _____. As you increase either or both of these inputs, the total _____ of the firm increases.

7.    The additional output created by adding one more worker to the production of a good is called the _____ of labor.

8. When diminishing returns to labor occur, successive increments of labor lead to _____ increments of _____.

9. All costs can be broken into two categories. _____ are the costs of _____ inputs, such as the amount of labor that goes into producing a good or the amount of raw materials needed to produce the good. On the other hand, _____ are the costs of the inputs that have to be paid regardless of the level of output, such as rent on land and buildings and the pay of the manager of a plant.

10. Marginal cost is the change in total costs due to the production of _____ unit of output.

11. The additional revenue from selling one more unit of a good is called _____.

12. To maximize its profits, a competitive firm should produce the quantity for which _____ equals _____.

13. An upward-sloping _____ implies a(n) _____ supply curve.

14. The market supply curve is the sum of the _____ supply curves.

15. _____ is the difference between the _____ of a good and the _____ of producing the good.

## True-False Questions

1. T F Things that affect the shape of the supply curve for a good include technology, weather, and the price of the good.

2. T F One of the principal assumptions in economic analysis is that firms try to sell as much as possible.

3. T F Markets in which no single firm is big enough to affect the price of the product are considered to be competitive markets.

4. T F Firms in a competitive market do not determine prices when they maximize profits.

5. T F Alice's Flower Shop shows total revenue of $50,000 for the month of May, while the total costs in May were $40,000. In the month of May, Alice made a positive profit.

6. T F In the long run, all inputs can be varied.

7. T F One worker is able to produce 4 widgets, 2 workers can produce 9 widgets, and 3 workers can produce 13 widgets. Diminishing returns to labor begin when the firm hires the third worker.

8. T F The idea of diminishing returns to labor implies that the marginal cost of producing more and more output is increasing.

9. T F The marginal cost curve for a firm provides all the information needed to find that firm's supply curve.

10. T F The price of a good is $100, and the marginal cost of the good is $90. A competitive firm should produce that unit.

11. T F A more general rule about production decisions is that a firm wishes to equate marginal revenue and marginal costs.

12. T F Another way to find the profit-maximizing output is to take a profit table and find the quantity of output that is associated with the highest level of profit.

13.   T   F      A reduction in the price of a variable input will shift an individual firm's supply curve to the right, but will not affect the market supply curve.

14.   T   F      The price of a good is $10. The marginal cost for the first unit is $1, and the marginal cost for the second unit is $4. The producer surplus for the first two units is $15.

15.   T   F      If one knows the producer surplus and the profits for a firm, one can find the fixed costs for that firm.

## Short-Answer Questions

1.      Why are some inputs fixed in the short run?

2.      In what sense are firms in competitive markets price-takers?

3.      What is the production function?

4.      What is meant by diminishing returns to a variable input?

5.      What is marginal cost?

6.      Why does diminishing returns to a variable input imply increasing marginal cost?

7.      Explain why a profit-maximizing competitive firm would produce up to the point where price equals marginal cost.

8.      Explain why marginal revenue is equal to price for a price-taking firm.

9.      What is producer surplus, and how is it related to a firm's profits?

## WORKING IT OUT

1.      It is important to understand the relationship between total costs, fixed costs, variable costs, and marginal cost. First, remember that at any level of output, all the inputs are either fixed or variable in the short run. That is, either they can be adjusted or they can't. Therefore, all the costs can be separated into the two categories of fixed costs and variable costs, and

Total costs = Fixed costs + Variable costs

Second, recall that marginal cost means the *additional* cost of producing one *more* unit, so that it involves *differences* in total costs. Since fixed costs don't increase when the firm increases output (they are fixed, remember), the amount by which variable costs rise when output rises must also be the amount by which total costs rise when output rises.

2.      It is also important to be able to apply the price = marginal cost rule to figure out the profit-maximizing output level for the firm, and to be able to calculate producer surplus once you know how much the firm will produce at the given price. Just remember the logic of the rule: Produce every unit that has a marginal cost less than the price. When the marginal cost of the next unit exceeds the price, producing that next unit is not profitable, because it adds more to costs than it adds to revenue. Once you know how many units the firm will produce, producer surplus can be calculated by subtracting the marginal cost for each unit produced from its price.

## Worked Problems

1.      The following table contains some incomplete total costs, fixed costs, variable costs, and marginal cost information for a firm. Fill in the missing values (a through e) and explain how you arrived at your answers.

| Output | Total Costs | Fixed Costs | Variable Costs | Marginal Costs |
|---|---|---|---|---|
| 1 | 20 | a | 5 | 2 |
| 2 | 23 | a | 8 | C |
| 3 | B | a | 12 | 4 |
| 4 | 34 | a | 19 | 7 |
| 5 | 43 | a | d | E |

**Answers**

a. *The fixed costs at every level of output are 15 (since fixed costs don't change with output). This can be found by subtracting variable costs from total costs at 1, 2, or 4 units of output.*

b. *Total costs for 3 units are 27. There are two ways to find this: by adding the fixed costs of 15 from the previous answer to the variable costs of 12, or by adding the marginal cost of the third unit, which is 4, to the total costs of the second unit, which are 23.*

c. *The marginal cost of the second unit is 3. This can be found by subtracting the total costs of 1 unit from the total costs of 2 units, or by subtracting the variable costs of 1 unit from the variable costs of 2 units.*

d. *The variable costs of the fifth unit are 28. This can be found by subtracting fixed costs, which are 15, from part a, from total costs, which are 43.*

e. *The marginal cost of the fifth unit is 9. This can be found by subtracting the total costs of 4 units from the total costs of 5 units, or by subtracting the variable costs of 4 units from the variable costs of 5 units, which you found in part d.*

2. The following table gives the short-run marginal cost of producing different levels of insulated coffee mugs.

| Output | Marginal Cost |
|---|---|
| 1 | $2.75 |
| 2 | $3.00 |
| 3 | $3.50 |
| 4 | $4.50 |
| 5 | $5.75 |
| 6 | $7.25 |
| 7 | $9.25 |

a. If Mugs ' R Us is a price-taking firm with the above marginal costs and the price of insulated coffee mugs is $4.00, what is the profit-maximizing level of output for the company, and what producer surplus will it earn?

b. If the price rises to $7.50, what is the profit-maximizing level of output, and what is the producer surplus?

c. Suppose the price remains at $4.00 per mug, but an increase in the price of plastic used to make the mugs adds $1.00 to marginal cost at every level of output. What effect does this have on the profit-maximizing level of production and on producer surplus?

**Answers**

a. *If the price of mugs is $4.00, then Mugs 'R Us should sell 3 mugs. The first mug costs $2.75 to produce, but can be sold for $4.00, adding $1.25 to producer surplus. The second mug* costs an additional $3.00 to produce, and selling it for $4.00 adds another $1.00 to producer surplus. The third mug costs $3.50 to produce and adds $0.50 when sold at $4.00. The fourth mug, however, would cost an additional $4.50 to produce, and the $4.00 that would be added to revenue by its sale wouldn't cover those costs. Hence 3 units is the profit-maximizing output, and the total producer surplus from producing and selling those 3 units is $1.25 + $1.00 + $0.50 = $2.75.

b.    If the price rises to $7.50, the fourth, fifth, and sixth mugs are now profitable to produce. Each adds less to total cost than the additional revenue that is obtained from its sale. The seventh mug, however, has a marginal cost that exceeds the $7.50 price, so 6 units is the profit-maximizing output level. Producer surplus can be calculated by subtracting marginal cost from price for the 6 units that are produced and adding up the results. The following table shows the calculation.

| Output | Marginal Cost | Price | Producer Surplus |
|---|---|---|---|
| 1 | $2.75 | $7.50 | $4.75 |
| 2 | $3.00 | $7.50 | $4.50 |
| 3 | $3.50 | $7.50 | $4.00 |
| 4 | $4.50 | $7.50 | $3.00 |
| 5 | $5.75 | $7.50 | $1.75 |
| 6 | $7.25 | $7.50 | $0.25 |
| | | | Total Producer Surplus $18.25 |

c.    If the price remains at $4.00 but the marginal cost at each level of output increases by $1.00, then the company will want to produce either 1 or 2 mugs. The first mug has a marginal cost of $3.75 after the cost increase, and if it is sold for $4.00, the firm receives a producer surplus of $0.25 from its sale. The second mug now costs $4.00 after the cost increase, so that selling it for $4.00 adds just enough to revenue to cover the additional cost of producing it. The firm earns no additional producer surplus from the second mug, but it doesn't lose any either, so the firm should be indifferent about producing or not producing the second mug. The third mug, which cost $3.50 before the cost increase and was profitable at a $4.00 price, now costs $4.50 and is no longer profitable. Total producer surplus is $0.25 from the sale of the first mug (plus $0 from the sale of the second if the firm chooses to sell it, and so $0.25 in either case).

## PRACTICE PROBLEMS

1.    The following table contains some incomplete total costs, fixed costs, variable costs, and marginal cost information for a firm. Fill in the missing values (a through e) and explain how you arrived at your answers.

| Output | Total Costs | Fixed Costs | Variable Costs | Marginal Costs |
|---|---|---|---|---|
| 0 | 12 | b | 0 | — |
| 1 | e | b | 5 | 5 |
| 2 | 20 | b | 8 | 3 |
| 3 | 26 | b | 14 | A |
| 4 | d | b | c | 9 |
| 5 | 46 | b | 34 | 11 |

2.    Suppose a price-taking firm has the following total costs.

| Output | Total Costs | Marginal Costs |
|---|---|---|
| 0 | 4 | — |
| 1 | 14 | |
| 2 | 21 | |
| 3 | 29 | |
| 4 | 38 | |
| 5 | 48 | |
| 6 | 60 | |
| 7 | 85 | |
| 8 | 104 | |

a.    Calculate the marginal cost at each level of output.

b.    If the price is $11 per unit, what is the profit-maximizing quantity, and how much are producer surplus and profits at that output?

c.    If a new production technique lowers marginal cost by $6 at each level of output, what is the new profit-maximizing quantity, and how much are producer surplus and profits, assuming that the price remains at $11 per unit?

# CHAPTER TEST

Use the following incomplete chart to answer questions 1 through 5.

| Q | P | Fixed Cost | Variable Cost | Total Cost |
|---|---|---|---|---|
| 0 | 100 | ??? | ??? | 50 |
| 1 | 100 | ??? | 70 | ??? |
| 2 | 100 | ??? | ??? | 200 |
| 3 | 100 | ??? | 250 | ??? |
| 4 | 100 | ??? | 400 | ??? |

1.    The total fixed cost in this example is

a.    0.
b.    50.
c.    100.
d.    300.

2.    The total costs of producing no output are

a.    50.
b.    100.
c.    400.
d.    incalculable from the information given in this question.

3.    The total variable costs of producing 2 units are

a.    150.
b.    190.

c.   240.
d.   300.

4.   The total revenue from producing 4 units of the good is

a.   3.
b.   100.
c.   300.
d.   400.

5.   The profits from producing 3 units of the good are

a.   -50.
b.   100.
c.   50.
d.   100.

6.   In a competitive market, firms are price-takers because

a.   they can set whatever price they choose.
b.   prices are set by the government.
c.   any firm that charges more than the market price will lose its customers.
d.   prices are set by the biggest firm in the market.

7.   The relationship between levels of inputs and the level of output those inputs achieve is called

a.   the marginal product.
b.   the production function.
c.   the production possibility curve.
d.   external economies of scale.

8.   Diminishing returns to labor imply that

a.   the marginal cost curve for a firm is downward-sloping.
b.   the output of a firm will eventually decrease.
c.   producing more of a product means having to produce less of another good.
d.   each additional unit of variable inputs increases the amount of output by a lesser amount than the previous units of inputs increased output.

Use the following table for questions 9 through 12.

| Input of Labor | Output of Baskets |
|---|---|
| 1 | 10 |
| 2 | 25 |
| 3 | 41 |
| 4 | 52 |
| 5 | 62 |
| 6 | 70 |
| 7 | 75 |
| 8 | 75 |

9.   Diminishing returns to labor occur at the _____ unit of input.

a.   second
b.   third

   c.   fourth
   d.   fifth

10.  The marginal product of labor for the sixth unit of labor is

   a.   0.
   b.   5.
   c.   8.
   d.   10.

11.  The marginal product of labor for the eighth unit of labor is

   a.   0.
   b.   10.
   c.   11.
   d.   16.

12.  Increasing returns to labor occur for the following units of inputs:

   a.   none.
   b.   1.
   c.   1 and 2.
   d.   1, 2, and 3.

13.  The supply curve is upward-sloping due to all of the following *except*

   a.   marginal cost is increasing as output increases.
   b.   the shape of the production function.
   c.   diminishing returns to labor.
   d.   the production possibilities curve.

14.  The assumption that business firms seek to maximize profits implies that

   a.   they will be concerned with profits only if the industry structure is competitive.
   b.   they wish to achieve positive profits, but after achieving that goal, they concentrate on other, noneconomic goals.
   c.   they seek the greatest difference between total revenue and total costs.
   d.   they never lose money.

15.  When a firm is maximizing profits,

   a.   it will never produce an economic loss.
   b.   average costs will be at a minimum.
   c.   marginal revenue equals marginal cost.
   d.   marginal revenue equals zero.

16.  If the price of a good is less than the marginal cost of producing it at the current level of output, the profit-maximizing firm should

   a.   expand output.
   b.   lower the price.
   c.   shut down operations.
   d.   decrease output.

17.  The market supply curve is

   a.   found by comparing the marginal costs of different firms at the same level of output.
   b.   found by adding the individual firms' supply curves at each price.
   c.   the highest individual supply curve.

    d.    unrelated to the profit-maximizing decisions of the firms.

18.   Producer surplus is

    a.    the difference between the price and the costs of producing the last unit of the good.

    b.    the summation of the difference between the price of the output and the marginal cost of producing each unit of the good.

    c.    what producers wish to maximize, so that they can maximize profits.

    d.    the amount that producers have left over after producing the good.

# ANSWERS TO THE REVIEW QUESTIONS

## Fill-In Questions

1.   proprietorships; partnerships; corporations

2.   profits

3.   price-taker

4.   price-taking; competitive

5.   total revenue; total costs

6.   inputs (or factors of production); output

7.   marginal product

8.   smaller; output

9.   Variable costs; fixed costs

10.  an additional

11.  marginal revenue

12.  price; marginal cost

13.  marginal cost curve; upward-sloping

14.  individual firms'

15.  Producers surplus; price; marginal cost

## True-False Questions

1.   **False**.    The price of a good does not affect the shape of the supply curve.

2.   **False**.    Economists assume that firms try to maximize their profits.

3.   **True**.    Competitive markets are markets in which there are large numbers of firms, each so small compared to the market that its output has no perceptible effect on the total and therefore no perceptible effect on the price.

4.   **True**.    Firms in a competitive market are price-takers. They can only determine the quantity that maximizes profits for a given market price.

5.   **True**.    Profits equal revenue minus total costs.

6.   **True**.    In the long run, there is enough time to vary all inputs. There are no fixed inputs in the long run.

7. **True.**  The marginal product of labor is 4 for the first worker, increases to 5 for the second worker, but then decreases to 4 for the third worker.

8. **True.**  If each successive worker adds less to output than the previous worker added, then each successive unit of output requires more additional labor than the previous unit required.

9. **True.**  The marginal cost curve tells us everything we need to know in order to find out how much the firm will produce at different prices.

10. **True.**  Price exceeds marginal cost, so the additional revenue from selling the unit will cover the additional cost, with $10 to be added to profit.

11. **True.**  The firm should produce up to the point where marginal revenue equals marginal cost. For a competitive firm, marginal revenue equals price, so a competitive firm should produce up to the point where price equals marginal cost.

12. **True.**  Choose the level of output where the difference between total revenue and total cost is the greatest.

13. **False.**  Since the market supply curve is the sum of the individual firms' supply curves, anything that shifts the firms' supply curves shifts the market supply curve, too.

14. **True.**  The difference between price and marginal cost is $9 for the first unit and $6 for the second, giving a total producer surplus of $15.

15. **True.**  From the producer surplus and the profits, you can calculate the fixed costs of the firm (since producer surplus equals profits plus fixed costs).

## Short-Answer Questions

1. It takes time to vary some inputs; for example, it could take a year or more to build a new factory. A firm that was deciding how much to produce in the next few months in that case might be able to hire more workers or buy more raw materials, but would have to work with whatever factory it currently has.

2. A firm in a competitive market (one that includes many other small producers of the same product) can set whatever price it wants, but if it sets a price above what the other firms are charging, it will sell nothing. Thus, firms are competing to see if they can sell at the market price. They are not trying to beat the others like in a sports competition.

3. The production function is a curve that shows the amount of output that can be produced from any combination of inputs using the technology available to the firm.

4. Diminishing returns to a variable input refers to the fact that as more units of the variable input are employed along with a given amount of a fixed input, output increases by less and less with each successive unit of variable input used.

5. Marginal cost is the amount by which total costs change when output is changed by one unit.

6. If each additional unit of a variable input that is employed along with a given amount of fixed input adds less to total production than the previous unit of variable input added (diminishing returns to a variable input), then producing each additional unit of output with the given amount of the fixed input requires a larger addition of the variable input. Therefore, the amount by which total costs increase when output is increased unit by unit must be rising (that is, increasing marginal cost).

7. If price is greater than marginal cost, then selling the next unit increases revenue by enough to cover the added costs (marginal cost) of producing it and to have something left over that can be

added to profits. On the other hand, if price is less than marginal cost, then selling the last unit didn't bring in enough additional revenue to cover the additional costs of producing that unit, and the difference had to be taken from profits. In this case, cutting back production by one unit means that those funds can remain as part of profits, so profits are higher. If profits can be increased by increasing production whenever price is greater than marginal cost and by reducing production whenever price is less than marginal cost, then profits will be maximized when price equals marginal cost.

8. For a price-taking firm, the price that the firm receives when it sells another unit is unrelated to the number of units it sells. If it sells one more unit, its revenue increases by the price at which it sells that unit. If it sells 10 more units, its revenue increases by 10 times that same price. The change in total revenues due to the sale of one more unit (marginal revenue) is always the price, no matter how many units the price-taking firm chooses to sell.

9. Producer surplus is the amount by which price exceeds marginal cost for each unit that the firm produces, added up over all the units the firm chooses to produce. It is a measure of how well the firm does from its sales, but it is not quite the same thing as profits. Adding up the marginal costs of all the units produced gives the variable costs of that level of output, but it does not give the total costs because fixed costs are not included. Therefore, producer surplus, which is revenue minus variable costs, is not profits, which would be revenue minus total costs. Instead, producer surplus minus fixed costs equals profits, or put differently, producer surplus equals profits plus fixed costs.

# SOLUTIONS TO THE PRACTICE PROBLEMS

1.

    a. The marginal cost of the third unit is $6, which can be found by subtracting the total costs of 2 units ($20) from the total costs of 3 units ($26), or by subtracting the variable costs of producing 2 units ($8) from the variable costs of producing 3 units ($14).

    b. The fixed costs are $12 at every level of output. This can be found by looking at the total costs of 0 units, or by subtracting variable costs from total costs at 2, 3, or 5 units.

    c. The variable costs of producing 4 units are $23, which is found by adding the marginal cost of the fourth unit ($9) to the variable costs of producing 3 units ($14). Remember that the increase in cost from producing one more unit (marginal cost) is entirely an increase in the variable costs, because fixed costs don't change when you change the output level.

    d. The total costs of producing 4 units are $35. This can be found by adding the marginal cost of the fourth unit ($9) to the total costs of producing 3 units ($26), or by adding the variable costs of producing 4 units ($23 from part c) to the fixed costs ($12 from part b), or even by subtracting the marginal cost of the fifth unit ($11) from the total costs of producing 5 units ($46).

    e. The total costs of producing 1 unit are $17, which can be found by adding the marginal cost of the first unit ($5) to the total costs of producing 0 units ($12), or by adding the variable costs of the first unit ($5) to the fixed costs of the first unit ($12), or by subtracting the marginal cost of the second unit ($3) from the total costs of producing 2 units ($20).

2.  a.  Looking at the increase in total costs at each successive level of output gives the following marginal costs:

| Output | Total Costs | Marginal Cost |
|---|---|---|
| 0 | 4 | — |
| 1 | 14 | 10 |
| 2 | 21 | 7 |
| 3 | 29 | 8 |
| 4 | 38 | 9 |
| 5 | 48 | 10 |
| 6 | 60 | 12 |
| 7 | 75 | 15 |
| 8 | 94 | 19 |

b.  If the price is $11 per unit, this firm will maximize its profits by selling 5 units. Producing each of the first 5 units adds less to cost than its sale adds to revenue (marginal cost is less than the price), so these units add to profit. The sixth unit has a marginal cost that exceeds the price at which it can be sold, and so would reduce profit. Producer surplus, which is the difference between price and marginal cost added up over all the units produced, is $1 + $4 + $3 + $2 + $1 = $11. Since total costs are $4 even when no output is produced, we know that fixed costs equal $4, and since profits equal producer surplus minus fixed costs, profits = $7. We can also calculate profits by subtracting the total costs of producing 5 units ($48) from the total revenue received from selling 5 units at $11 each ($55), which also gives profits of $7.

c.  If the new production technique lowers marginal cost by $6, then the new marginal costs are as given below, and adding the marginal cost to the previous unit's total costs gives new total costs as well.

| Output | Total Costs | Marginal Cost |
|---|---|---|
| 0 | 4 | — |
| 1 | 8 | 4 |
| 2 | 9 | 1 |
| 3 | 11 | 2 |
| 4 | 14 | 3 |
| 5 | 18 | 4 |
| 6 | 24 | 6 |
| 7 | 33 | 9 |
| 8 | 46 | 13 |

If the price remains at $11, the firm will maximize its profits by selling 7 units. The first 7 units all have marginal costs below the price, but the eighth unit has a marginal cost that exceeds the price. Producer surplus is $7 + $10 + $9 + $8 + $7 + $5 + $2 = $48. Profits equal $44, which can be calculated either by subtracting fixed costs ($4) from producer surplus ($48) or by subtracting total costs at 7 units ($33) from the revenue received from the sale of 7 units at $11 each ($77).

## ANSWERS TO THE CHAPTER TEST

1. b
2. a
3. a
4. d
5. b
6. c
7. b
8. d
9. c
10. c
11. a
12. d
13. d
14. c
15. c
16. d
17. b
18. b

# CHAPTER 7

# The Interaction of People in Markets

## CHAPTER OVERVIEW

One of the most significant contributions of Adam Smith, author of the *Wealth of Nations*, was that as people pursue their own interests in a market, they are guided by an **invisible hand** to produce and consume a quantity that is efficient. The fundamental market model of supply and demand was introduced in Chapter 3. We learned that a market is an arrangement by which people, as consumers or producers, exchange goods and services. In Chapters 5 and 6, we explored the microeconomic foundations of consumer and firm behavior through the concepts of utility and profit maximization. In Chapter 7, we turn to the competitive equilibrium model of supply and demand, armed with a better understanding of the motives and goals of consumers and firms, in order to enhance our understanding of economic efficiency.

A tremendous amount of information is required to coordinate and motivate the production and consumption decisions that occur in a market economy. Prices provide this information in the competitive equilibrium model. A market price adjusts until it equals the equilibrium price, the price at which the quantity demanded equals the quantity supplied. While the competitive equilibrium model is theoretical in nature, results from experimental markets, like a double-auction experiment, support its general conclusions.

An outcome of the competitive equilibrium model is that the market is efficient; it creates Pareto efficiency. In such a state, the marginal benefit equals the marginal cost of the last item produced, the marginal cost of the good is the same for every producer, and the marginal benefit of consuming the good is equal for all consumers. This outcome is assured because each producer and consumer faces the same market price in a competitive market; each is a price-taker. An alternative way to describe an efficient outcome is that the sum of consumer and producer surplus is maximized. From this view, economists measure inefficiency by the consumer and producer surplus lost as a result of some action. This is called the deadweight loss.

## CHAPTER REVIEW

1.  Markets process information and coordinate and motivate economic activity. The **competitive equilibrium model** begins with the common model of supply and demand, and then explicitly incorporates utility-maximizing consumers and profit-maximizing producers. A key feature of the competitive equilibrium model is that a price that equates quantity demanded and quantity supplied—the *equilibrium price*—emerges from the free interaction of buyers and sellers (Adam Smith called this the **invisible hand**). The presence of a surplus or a shortage causes the market price to adjust toward equilibrium.

2.  Economists have begun to construct experimental markets in order to test the predictions of the theoretical competitive equilibrium model. In a **double-auction market**, both buyers and sellers call out prices; buyers call out **bids** and sellers call out **asks**. Consumers are motivated by the desire to maximize the difference between the marginal benefits associated with an item and the price paid for it. Producers are motivated by the desire to maximize the difference between the price at which they sell an item and the marginal cost of producing it. The results of such

experiments show that individuals motivated by self-interest interact (compete) so as to create an equilibrium price, even though no one individual is in charge of the market process (sets a price).

3. Ticket scalping generally arises when a market allocation system is not allowed to work. Scalping helps to create a **Pareto efficient outcome**.

4. The competitive equilibrium model shows that the market works well (the outcome is efficient). In an efficient outcome it is not possible to make someone better off without hurting someone else; this is called **Pareto efficiency**. In general, three conditions are required for Pareto efficiency. First, the marginal benefit ($MB$) must equal the marginal cost ($MC$) of the last item produced. Second, the marginal cost of a good should be equal for every producer. Third, the marginal benefit of consuming the same good should be equal for all consumers. The conclusion that a competitive market produces an efficient outcome is called the **first theorem of welfare economics**.

5. The model of consumer behavior showed that consumers maximize utility by purchasing goods until $MB = P$. The model of firm behavior showed that competitive firms maximize profits by expanding production until $MC = P$. *All participants in a competitive market face the same price.* Therefore, the marginal benefits of all consumers of a product are equal, the marginal costs of the producers of the product are equal, and marginal benefits equal marginal costs; competitive markets are efficient.

6. Reducing **income inequality** is also a desirable goal of an economic system. Efficiency and income equality are not the same thing. Greater income equality may be promoted through a system of taxes and transfer payments.

7. The sum of consumer and producer surplus is a measure of economic well-being. (Recall that consumer surplus is the area below the demand curve and above the price line, and producer surplus is the area above the supply curve and below the price line.) Efficient competitive markets maximize this total. Deviations from this are called **deadweight losses**, and represent a measure of the waste from inefficient production. A tax on a commodity (an **ad valorem tax** or a **specific tax**) causes a competitive market to diverge from the efficient level of production resulting in a deadweight loss. This outcome is independent of who pays the tax (buyers or sellers). Even though taxes raise revenue that may be used for public infrastructure projects, they still cause a loss in consumer and producer surplus that is greater than the value of the taxes collected.

8. The market also appears to be *informationally efficient*. This is to say, one person or agency (the government) could not possibly know all the information that is processed in the market interaction. However, there are instances where great precision in coordination may be required. Here, the informational advantage of the market and the price system is not very great. In these cases, other organizations arise that address the issues of coordination and motivation.

## ZEROING IN

1.

    a. In the competitive equilibrium model, prices adjust to equilibrium, *ceteris paribus*. This occurs automatically. No one individual is in charge of the adjustment process. Consider the information that is transmitted when there is a shortage in a market like that shown in Figure 7.1.

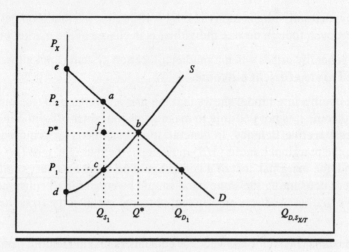

**Figure 7.1**

b.   Equilibrium is shown by $P^*$ and $Q^*$. Suppose, however, that the *current* market price is $P_1$. At this price, the quantity demanded ($Q_{D1}$) is greater than the quantity supplied ($Q_{S1}$). Firms can sell all they want and profits are being maximized; firms are in equilibrium. This is true because the quantity $Q_{S1}$ is determined by the point where $P_1$ crosses the supply curve. Because $P_1 = MC$, firms are supplying the quantity they want to at the current price.

c.   Now consider consumers. At $P_1$ they would maximize utility by purchasing the quantity $Q_{D1}$. This is determined from their demand curve. However, they cannot do this because firms are offering only $Q_{S1}$. Viewed another way, $Q_{S1}$ would be an equilibrium quantity for consumers if the market price were $P_2$. At the quantity $Q_{S1}$, $P_2 = MB$, consumers would be maximizing utility at $P_2$. Given this information, the marginal benefit to consumers of $Q_{S1}$ is greater than $P_1$. Consumers would like to buy more; this is the nature of a shortage.

d.   How do buyers communicate their disequilibrium to firms? They do it by disturbing the firms' equilibrium by offering to pay a higher price; they bid the price up above $P_1$. When they do so, price rises above marginal cost, and the quantity supplied will increase beyond $Q_{S1}$.

e.   A similar story could be told for a beginning surplus. In this case, firms would communicate their disequilibrium to consumers by lowering price. In either case, price is the common denominator. It is, through the market, a mechanism of communication.

2.   Competitive markets create efficient outcomes. Why? First, consider the three conditions of Pareto efficiency: The marginal cost for producers of the same item must be equal, the marginal benefit for consumers of the same item must be equal, and the marginal cost must equal the marginal benefit.

Marginal costs are equated because each firm, independent of the others in the market, attempts to maximize profits. Each firm tries to find the level of production at which the market price equals the marginal cost. *In a competitive market, all firms face the same price.* Thus, by being profit maximizers facing a common price, firms end up equating their marginal costs without communicating with one another.

Consumers act in a similar way. Each consumer independently tries to maximize utility; he or she seeks a level of purchases at which the market price equals the marginal benefit of the last unit purchased. *Again, in a competitive market, all consumers face the same price.* So, as each consumer maximizes utility given a common price, all consumers end up equating marginal benefits.

Finally, because all market participants, buyers and sellers, face a common price and because all of them are trying to maximize profits or utility, buyers and sellers end up equating marginal cost with marginal benefit.

Why do competitive markets create efficient outcomes? It is because of the common motivation (maximizing something) and because of the common price in a competitive market. Again, price is information that serves as a common denominator for all those choosing to participate in a market.

3. Deadweight loss is an important tool of economists. More time will be spent in its calculation in "Working It Out." For now, consider Figure 7.1 again.

Suppose $D$ and $S$ depict the self-interest of buyers and sellers, and that the government limits the production of the product to $Q_{S1}$. If the market were free of the limit, equilibrium would be achieved at $P^*$ and $Q^*$. Here, consumer surplus is equal to the area $eP^*b$, and producer surplus is equal to $dP^*b$. As described in point 2, this is efficient because $MB = P^* = MC$. The limit, however, takes away the incentive for firms to offer $Q^*$ to the market. Firms now offer $Q_{S1}$. Thus, firms lose $fbc$ in producer surplus. In addition, this action on the part of the sellers forces consumers to purchase less. Consumers can purchase only what firms offer. The production limit reduces consumer surplus by the area $fba$. The total deadweight loss is shown by $acb$, the sum of the two areas lost. Consumers and producers can no longer communicate through price, and they are forced to do things that they would not have chosen to do. This is the perversion beneath the graphical depiction of deadweight loss and the nature of economic inefficiency.

## ACTIVE REVIEW

## Fill-In Questions

1. With the explicit addition of the behavior of consumers and firms, the simple model of supply and demand becomes the _____.

2. An individual _____ depends on the _____ a consumer gets from consuming a good.

3. Marginal cost is used to create the_____ of a firm.

4. As people interact in a market, price moves toward the _____.

5. Adam Smith argued that by individual consumers and firms pursuing their own self-interest, they were guided by a(n) _____ to consume and produce an efficient quantity.

6. A market in which both buyers and sellers call out prices is called a(n) _____.

7. In a double-auction market, buyers call out _____, and sellers call out _____.

8. A double-auction market is a simple form of a(n) _____ market.

9. A situation of _____ exists when market participants know only their own preferences or costs.

10. Double-auction markets tend to find prices through a process described as _____.

11. In an efficient outcome, the _____ equals the _____ of the last unit, the _____ is equal for every producer, and the _____ is equal for every consumer.

12. The three conditions of an efficient outcome are satisfied in a competitive market because consumers and firms face the same _____.

13. The area below a demand curve and above the market price line is called _____.

14. The area above a supply curve and below the market price line is called _____.

15. The _____ is used to measure the waste from inefficient production.

16. In a competitive market, _____ and _____ are maximized.

17. A major disadvantage of central planning is that it is _____.

## True-False Questions

1. T F The competitive equilibrium model does not explicitly account for the utility-maximizing behavior of consumers and the profit-maximizing behavior of sellers.

2. T F The competitive equilibrium model does not explain the determination of an equilibrium price.

3. T F Experimental markets, like a double-auction market, are used to test the predictions of the competitive equilibrium model.

4. T F Competition plays no role in the determination of an equilibrium price during a market experiment.

5. T F A characteristic of an efficient outcome is that the marginal cost of producing a good is minimized by all producers.

6. T F A characteristic of an efficient market outcome is that the marginal benefit of consuming each good is the same for all consumers.

7. T F The three conditions for an efficient outcome hold in a competitive market because each consumer and each producer consumes or produces the same quantity.

8. T F Competitive markets are efficient.

9. T F Economic efficiency has nothing really to do with income equality.

10. T F A deadweight loss is associated with an efficient competitive market.

11. T F The loss to society from producing more or less than the efficient amount is called a deadweight loss.

12. T F A deadweight loss can be associated with taxation.

13. T F Ticket scalping is always efficient.

14. T F Market-based activity is always informationally efficient.

## Short-Answer Questions

1. What distinguishes the competitive equilibrium model from the simpler model of supply and demand?

2. What do shortages and surpluses do?

3. What is the purpose of a market experiment?

4. What is a double-auction market?

5. Why are buyers motivated to pay the lowest price?

6. What are the three conditions for efficient economic outcomes, and what is common among each of them?

7. Briefly, what is the meaning of Pareto efficiency?

8. Graphically, what is consumer and producer surplus?

9. What is a deadweight loss?

10. Why does a tax create a deadweight loss?

11. What is ticket scalping?

12. When might a market and the price system fail to offer an informational advantage over an alternative form of organization?

## WORKING IT OUT

Deadweight loss is a very important economic tool. It is one way in which economists measure economic inefficiency. A little high school geometry within the context of consumer and producer surplus may aid us in its calculation and help convey its meaning.

Figure 7.2 shows the standard diagram of a competitive market. The efficient competitive equilibrium is shown by $P^*$ and $Q^*$. For simplicity, the supply and demand curves have been extended to touch the vertical axis. Also, let us assume that infinitesimally small units can be purchased; this lets us use geometry.

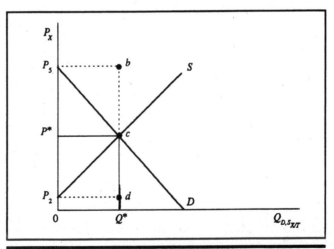

**Figure 7.2**

It was argued in the text that the sum of consumer and producer surplus is maximized at equilibrium. How do you measure this? Let us develop a general way to measure the two surpluses. First, let us measure consumer surplus. Remember that it is the area below the demand curve and above the market price line. In Figure 7.2, this is shown by $P_5P^*c$. What is the value of this area? If we look at the box formed by the dashed lines in the figure, we can easily see that consumer surplus is one-half (0.5) of the total area of the box. From basic geometry, you will remember that the area of a box is found by multiplying the *height* times the *base*. Here, the height is the distance $P_5P^*$, or the value $P_5 - P^*$. The base is $P^*c$, or the value of $Q^*$. Thus, consumer surplus equals $0.5[(P_5 - P^*) \times Q^*]$. A similar approach can be used to determine producer surplus. Its value equals $0.5[(P^* - P_2) \times Q^*]$. The sum of these two values is greatest when the market is efficient.

Now, let us levy a tax, calculate the deadweight loss, and determine the revenue collected by the government.

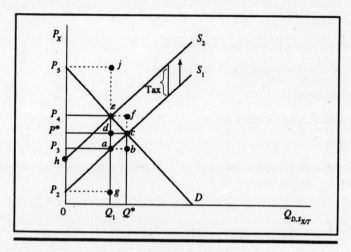

**Figure 7.3**

Consider Figure 7.3. The original supply and demand curves are given by $S_1$ and $D$, respectively. The initial efficient equilibrium is $P^*$ and $Q^*$. As in Figure 7.2, consumer surplus is shown by the area $P_5P^*c$, and producer surplus is shown by the area $P^*P_2c$.

Assume that a per-unit tax is levied on sellers. This shifts the supply curve up by the amount of the tax, as shown by the movement of the supply curve from $S_1$ to $S_2$; the tax determines the vertical distance between the two supply curves. The amount of the tax is $P_4 - P_3$ (which equals the distance $ea$ and the distance $hP_2$). As shown, the tax reduces the equilibrium quantity to $Q_1$ and raises the price consumers pay to $P_4$.

Consumer surplus is now the area $P_5P_4e$. Using the box $P_5P_4ej$, the value of the consumer surplus equals $0.5[(P_5 - P_4) \times Q_1]$; consumer surplus has been reduced by the area $P^*P_4ec$.

Firms collect $P_4$ from buyers for every unit they sell. But remember that they must pay $ea$ to the government. This means that they get to keep only $P_3$. After the tax, producer surplus is shown by the area $P_2P_3a$. The value of this (again, visualize the box $P_2P_3ag$) is equal to $0.5[(P_3 - P_2) \times Q_1]$. The tax has reduced producer surplus by the area $P_3P^*ca$.

The revenue collected by the government is the per-unit tax multiplied by the number of units traded on the market. This is shown by the area $P_3P_4ea$ and is calculated by $(P_4 - P_3) \times Q_1$.

The deadweight loss is the area remaining after we account for the *new* producer and consumer surplus and the tax revenues. This remainder is shown by the triangle *eac*. What is its value? Again, it helps to visualize some boxes and use a little geometry. Segment *cd* divides the deadweight loss into two parts. The area *edc* is the part of the deadweight loss lost by consumers, and the area *adc* is the part lost by producers. The boxes *defc* and *adcb* remind us of the geometry we have been using. So the deadweight loss is equal to the sum of $0.5[(P_4 - P^*) \times (Q^* - Q_1)]$ and $0.5[(P^* - P_3) \times (Q^* - Q_1)]$.

## Worked Problems

1.  Assume that Figure 7.4 depicts a competitive market for some product. The original market demand and supply curves are shown by $S_1$ and $D_1$.

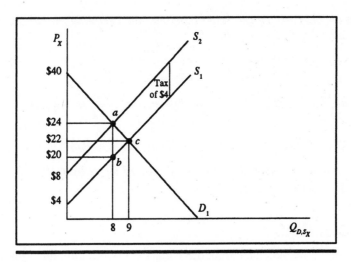

**Figure 7.4**

a. What are the efficient market equilibrium price and quantity?

b. What is the value of the consumer surplus?

c. What is the value of the producer surplus?

d. What is the sum of consumer and producer surplus for this product?

**Answers**

a. *This is determined by the intersection of the original demand and supply curves. The equilibrium price is $22, and the equilibrium quantity is 9 units.*

b. *This is the area below the demand curve and above $22.*

   *Consumer surplus = 0.5[($40 – $22) × 9] = $81.*

c. *Producer surplus = 0.5[($22 – $4) × 9] = $81.*

d. *$81 + $81 = $162.*

2. Assume that the local government levies a tax of $4 per unit that is paid by sellers.

   a. How does the tax affect Figure 7.4?

   b. What are the new equilibrium price and quantity?

   c. What price do sellers collect from buyers, and what do they keep to cover their costs and profit?

   d. What is the new consumer surplus?

   e. What is the new producer surplus?

   f. What revenue does the government collect?

   g. What is the deadweight loss?

**Answers**

a. *The tax shifts the supply curve to $S_2$. The vertical distance between the two supply curves is $4. This can be seen where they intersect the vertical axis. Also, $S_2$ and $S_1$ are parallel.*

b. *The equilibrium quantity is now 8 units. The equilibrium price increases to $24. It did not rise by the full amount of the tax ($4) because the demand curve is not vertical.*

c.   *Consumers pay $24 per unit to sellers. Sellers must send $4 per unit to the government. Thus, they keep $20 per unit.*

d.   *This is the area below the demand curve and above $24.*
     *Consumer surplus = 0.5[($40 − $24) × 8] = $64.*

e.   *This is the area above the original supply curve (S₁) and below $20.*
     *Producer surplus = 0.5[($20 − $4) × 8] = $64.*

f.   *After the $4 per unit tax, 8 units are sold. Thus, the government collects $32 in revenue.*

g.   *This is seen by the area acb. The loss is calculated as follows:*
     *0.5[($24 − 22) × 1] + 0.5[($22 − $20) × 1] = $2.*

## PRACTICE PROBLEMS

1.   Assume that Figure 7.5 depicts the competitive market in your college town for pairs of running shoes per week. *D* and *S* are the initial demand and supply curves.

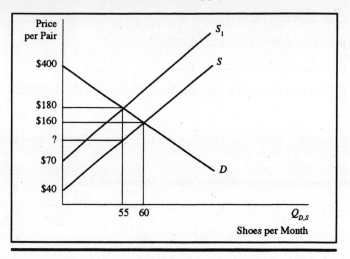

**Figure 7.5**

a.   What are the efficient market equilibrium price and quantity?

b.   What is consumer surplus?

c.   What is producer surplus?

d.   What is the sum of producer and consumer surplus?

2.   Assume that your local government plans a tax of $30 per pair of running shoes sold. The proceeds of the tax will be used to improve a local park.

a.   How does this affect Figure 7.5?

b.   What are the new equilibrium price and quantity?

c.   What price do sellers get to keep to pay costs?

d.   What is the new consumer surplus?

e.   What is the new producer surplus?

f.   What are the revenues collected by the government over an average month?

g.   Does the tax create a deadweight loss? If yes, what is its value? How much of it do consumers pay?

# CHAPTER TEST

1.   Prices

   a.   provide information to buyers and sellers.
   b.   coordinate changes in consumption and changes in production.
   c.   motivate changes in production.
   d.   do all of the above.

2.   The _____ incorporates utility-maximizing consumers and profit-maximizing firms in competitive markets.

   a.   model of consumer behavior
   b.   model of firm behavior
   c.   first theorem of welfare economics
   d.   competitive equilibrium model

3.   A surplus or a shortage causes price to adjust to the

   a.   equilibrium price.
   b.   true price.
   c.   fair price.
   d.   only price.

4.   In a double-auction market, the offer of a buyer is called a(n) _____ and the offer of a seller is called a(n) _____.

   a.   ask, bid
   b.   put, call
   c.   bid, ask
   d.   outcry, call

5.   In a double-auction market, each seller tries to maximize the difference between

   a.   the ask and the bid.
   b.   the price of the item sold and the marginal cost of the item.
   c.   the price of the item purchased and the marginal benefit of the item.
   d.   marginal utility and marginal cost.

6.   In a double-auction market, each buyer tries to maximize the difference between

   a.   the ask and the bid.
   b.   the price of the item sold and the marginal cost of the item.
   c.   the price of the item purchased and the marginal benefit of the item.
   d.   marginal utility and marginal cost.

7.   Ticket scalping will not arise

   a.   when market allocations occur.
   b.   when the marginal benefit of an item is different between two people.
   c.   when the marginal benefit of an item is zero people with low incomes.
   d.   when buyers can exploit sellers.

8. An economic outcome is not Pareto efficient if

    a. someone could be made better off only if someone else was hurt.
    b. someone could be made better off without others being hurt.
    c. everyone has the same total utility.
    d. there is perfect income equality.

9. An efficient economic outcome requires that

    a. the marginal benefit be greater than the marginal cost of the last item produced.
    b. the marginal benefit equal the marginal cost of the last item produced.
    c. the marginal benefit be less than the marginal cost of the last item produced.
    d. total utility equal profit.

10. If the marginal cost of a good is not equal for every producer, then

    a. the market must be in equilibrium.
    b. the marginal benefit must equal the market price.
    c. production could be increased without cost.
    d. production could be increased only with extra cost.

11. The proof that competitive markets are efficient is referred to as

    a. the model of consumer behavior.
    b. the third law of thermodynamics.
    c. the model of firm behavior.
    d. the first theorem of welfare economics.

12. The common element in the three criteria for an efficient outcome is that

    a. all market participants face the same market price.
    b. sellers are not price-takers.
    c. buyers dominate the market process.
    d. market participants face different prices.

13. Graphically, consumer surplus is the area

    a. below the demand curve and above the market price line.
    b. below the demand curve and above the horizontal axis.
    c. above the supply curve and below the market price line.
    d. above the supply curve and below the demand curve.

14. Graphically, producer surplus is the area

    a. below the demand curve and above the market price line.
    b. below the demand curve and above the horizontal axis.
    c. above the supply curve and below the market price line.
    d. above the supply curve and below the demand curve.

15. A feature of an efficient competitive market is that

    a. the sum of consumer and producer surplus is minimized.
    b. the sum of consumer and producer surplus is maximized.
    c. consumer surplus becomes the entire area below the demand curve.
    d. consumer surplus equals producer surplus.

16. The demand curve represents _____, and the supply curve represents _____.

    a. marginal costs, marginal benefits
    b. marginal benefits, total costs

    c.    total utility, marginal costs
    d.    marginal benefits, marginal costs

17.  A deadweight loss results from

    a.    deviating from the competitive equilibrium.
    b.    being in competitive equilibrium for too long.
    c.    Pareto efficiency.
    d.    a double-auction market.

18.  A tax creates a deadweight loss because it

    a.    forces an efficient outcome rather than allowing one to occur voluntarily.
    b.    increases producer surplus at the expense of consumer surplus.
    c.    causes the market to deviate from equilibrium.
    d.    increases consumer surplus at the expense of producer surplus.

19.  Markets are

    a.    always informationally more efficient than anything else.
    b.    informationally efficient, except possibly in cases where great precision in coordination is required.
    c.    never informationally efficient.
    d.    informationally efficient if taxes are imposed on sellers.

20.  The sum of consumer surplus plus producer surplus equals

    a.    marginal benefit plus marginal cost of all items.
    b.    marginal benefit divided by marginal cost of all items.
    c.    marginal benefit minus marginal cost of all items.
    d.    zero.

# ANSWERS TO THE REVIEW QUESTIONS

## Fill-In Questions

1.  competitive equilibrium model
2.  demand curve; marginal benefit
3.  supply curve
4.  equilibrium price
5.  invisible hand
6.  double-auction market
7.  bids; asks
8.  experimental
9.  imperfect information
10.  price discovery
11.  marginal benefit; marginal cost; marginal cost; marginal benefit
12.  market price
13.  consumer surplus

14.  producer surplus

15.  deadweight loss

16.  consumer surplus; producer surplus

17.  informationally inefficient

## True-False Questions

1.  **False**.    The explicit inclusion of utility-maximizing consumers and profit-maximizing firms is what distinguishes the competitive equilibrium model from the simple supply and demand model developed in Chapter 3.

2.  **False**.    The competitive equilibrium model describes the process by which an equilibrium price is established. The market price will rise in response to a market shortage and fall in response to a market surplus. The equilibrium price will equate the quantity demanded and the quantity supplied.

3.  **True**.    In a double-auction market experiment, individuals play the roles of buyers and sellers. Buyers call out bids, and sellers call out asks. In determining the quantity bought and sold, buyers consider the difference between the marginal benefit and the amount paid for a product, whereas sellers consider the difference between the marginal cost and the price at which a product is sold. The result of this "open outcry" market experiment is a convergence to an equilibrium price.

4.  **False**.    A single seller or buyer finds it impossible to influence the outcome of the experiment when others are free to holler out their own bids or asks. The freedom of others to do this is the essence of competition.

5.  **False**.    This characteristic is that the marginal cost is the same, not minimized, across all producers. This is not necessarily the lowest possible marginal cost.

6.  **True**.    If this were not true, a redistribution of goods would produce a gain for some people with no loss to anyone else.

7.  **False**.    The three conditions hold because all participants (buyers and sellers) in a competitive market face the same price.

8.  **True**.    This is the conclusion of the first theorem of welfare economics. The competitive market is said to be Pareto efficient.

9.  **True**.    Reducing income inequality is a desirable goal in an economic system, but is not necessarily related to economic efficiency. As a result, government income transfer programs often have the reduction of income inequality as their goal.

10. **False**.    A feature of competitive markets is that the sum of consumer and producer surplus is maximized. Thus, a deadweight loss would not exist.

11. **True**.    Any amount produced that differs from that produced by an efficient competitive market reduces consumer and producer surplus. The result is a deadweight loss.

12. **True**.    Taxation prevents a competitive market from producing an efficient quantity. As a result, taxation reduces producer and consumer surplus.

13. **True**.    Ticket scalping often arises when a market allocation scheme is not allowed to work. Scalping can create a Pareto efficient outcome.

14. **False.**    There are occasions when great precision in coordination is required (like a marching band). In these cases, the informational advantage of the price system and the market may not be large.

## Short-Answer Questions

1.    The competitive equilibrium model explicitly accounts for utility-maximizing consumers and profit-maximizing firms. A richness is added to market analysis when these foundations of demand and supply are included.

2.    Shortages and surpluses cause price to move toward equilibrium. In a shortage, the quantity demanded exceeds the quantity supplied at the current market price; the price is below equilibrium. As a result, price rises. A surplus is associated with a price above equilibrium. Here, quantity supplied exceeds quantity demanded, and price falls.

3.    Market experiments offer an opportunity to observe the process described in the competitive equilibrium model. They are an economist's version of a laboratory experiment.

4.    A double-auction market is one where *both* buyers and sellers call out prices. The buyers call out bids, and the sellers call out asks. Double-auction markets are also called "open outcry" markets.

5.    A buyer's gain on each item purchased is the difference between the marginal benefit received from that item and the price paid for it. By trying to pay the lowest price, the buyer maximizes net gain.

6.    First, the marginal benefit must equal the marginal cost of the last unit produced. Second, the marginal cost of a good should be equal for every producer. Third, the marginal benefit of consuming a good should be equal for all consumers. These are the foundations of the first theorem of welfare economics. The equality between outcomes is ensured because all producers and all consumers face the same market price.

7.    This is a way to define an efficient outcome. It states that an efficient outcome is one for which it is impossible to make someone better off without hurting someone else.

8.    Consumer surplus is the area below the demand curve and above the market price line. Producer surplus is the area above the supply curve and below the market price line.

9.    A deadweight loss is a measure of the waste from inefficient production. It is the sum of the consumer and producer surplus lost as a result of not producing the efficient equilibrium quantity.

10.    A tax causes the market to move away from the economically efficient quantity. Therefore, the sum of producer and consumer surplus is not maximized.

11.    Ticket scalping is selling a ticket to an event at a higher price than the face value of the ticket.

12.    This may occur in areas where great precision is required. A good example is in the direction of a marching band.

## SOLUTIONS TO THE PRACTICE PROBLEMS

1.    a.    $160 per pair and 60 pairs

b.    $7,200

c.    $3,600

d.    $10,800

2.  a.   The supply curve shifts up by the amount of the tax. The vertical distance between $S_1$ and $S$ is $30.

    b.   $180 per pair and 55 pairs

    c.   $150 per pair

    d.   $6,050

    e.   $3,025

    f.   $1,650

    g.   The tax does create a deadweight loss. The value of the loss is $75. Consumers lose $50, and producers lose $25.

# ANSWERS TO THE CHAPTER TEST

1.  d
2.  d
3.  a
4.  c
5.  b
6.  c
7.  a
8.  b
9.  b
10. c
11. d
12. a
13. a
14. c
15. b
16. d
17. a
18. c
19. b
20. c

# PART 2

# Sample Test: (Chapters 5–7) Principles of Microeconomics

## SAMPLE TEST QUESTIONS

1. As more of a good is consumed by an individual,

   a. total utility increases.
   b. marginal utility increases.
   c. total utility stays constant.
   d. price increases.
   e. price falls.

2. Suppose a consumer is spending all of his income. The marginal utility of bread is 20, the price of bread is $0.10, the marginal utility of honey is 30, and the price of honey is $0.20. The consumer

   a. is maximizing utility.
   b. should consume more honey and less bread to maximize utility.
   c. should consume less honey and more bread to maximize utility.
   d. should consume more honey and more bread to maximize utility.
   e. should consume less honey and less bread to maximize utility.

3. Consumer surplus is

   a. equivalent to value in use.
   b. equivalent to value in exchange.
   c. total expenditure divided by the price per unit.
   d. the difference between what consumers would be willing to pay and what they have to pay.
   e. the difference between total expenditure and what consumers have to pay per unit.

4. A market demand curve

   a. is derived by the process of vertical summation.
   b. graphically illustrates increasing marginal utility.
   c. is derived from the law of diminishing returns.
   d. is based on consumer utility maximization.
   e. can be derived only if market price actually falls.

5. A firm that considers price a given and chooses quantity of output accordingly is called a

   a. market-taker.
   b. monopoly.
   c. quantity-setter.
   d. profit-maximizer.
   e. price-taker.

6. Marginal cost

   a. represents the increase in benefit from one more unit of a good.

b.   represents the increase in cost when an additional unit is produced.
c.   is likely to diminish as more and more of a good is produced.
d.   All of the above statements are true.
e.   Only (a) and (b) are true.

7.   The key condition for profit maximization for a firm in a competitive market is to

a.   choose a quantity to produce so that price equals marginal cost.
b.   choose a quantity to produce so that the price is greater than marginal cost.
c.   choose a quantity to produce so that the price is less than marginal cost.
d.   choose a quantity to produce so that marginal revenue is greater than marginal cost.

8.   Profit-maximizing firms respond to higher prices by

a.   increasing the quantity they are willing to produce.
b.   decreasing the quantity they are willing to produce.
c.   producing the same quantity.
d.   discounting the goods they produce.

9.   Since marginal product decreases as input is increased,

a.   it takes increasing amounts of input to produce one more unit of output.
b.   it takes decreasing amounts of input to produce one more unit of output.
c.   nothing is implied about how much input is required to produce one more unit of output.
d.   the amount of input it takes to produce one more unit of output does not change.

10.   Double-auction market experiments indicate that

a.   the competitive equilibrium model is not a good predictor of real-world phenomena.
b.   only centrally directed economies can result in anything resembling equilibrium.
c.   markets like the New York Stock Exchange frequently result in equilibrium, but others do not.
d.   economic supply and demand theory does a remarkably good job of predicting real-world phenomena.
e.   auction markets are nearly impossible to manage.

11.   When marginal product increases,

a.   total product falls.
b.   marginal costs fall.
c.   total costs fall.
d.   too much capital is used.

12.   The area below the price line and above the supply curve is called

a.   the deadweight loss.
b.   consumer surplus.
c.   producer surplus.
d.   profit.

13.   The area above the price line and below the demand curve is called

a.   the deadweight loss.
b.   consumer surplus.
c.   producer surplus.
d.   total utility.

14. When a market is competitive,

    a.    the deadweight loss is minimized.
    b.    the deadweight loss is equal to profit.
    c.    the deadweight loss is maximized.
    d.    the deadweight loss is equal to the inverse of the elasticity of demand.

15. If the deadweight loss is positive,

    a.    the market is efficient.
    b.    the market is competitive.
    c.    the market is not efficient.
    d.    consumer surplus is smaller than producer surplus.

# ANSWERS TO THE SAMPLE TEST

1.  a
2.  c
3.  d
4.  d
5.  e
6.  b
7.  a
8.  a
9.  a
10. d
11. b
12. c
13. b
14. a
15. c

# PART 3

# The Economics of the Firm

Markets are arrangements by which people meet for the purpose of exchanging goods and services. Prices, the result of this interaction, represent information about relative scarcity, and are central to the incentives that exist in our economy. Part 3 begins with the development of a formal model of producers by examining the costs of production. Next, this presentation is extended to the behavior of product markets, markets where goods and services are exchanged. This examination includes theoretical foundations and real-world performance. The markets that are examined include the extremes of perfect competition and monopoly, as well as the widely observed forms of monopolistic competition and oligopoly. All markets, and the prices created in them, allocate limited resources among competing uses. The ability to do this efficiently is affected by the features that characterize each type of market. In virtually all instances, a reduction in market power and an increase in competition help the market economy maximize social welfare and improve economic efficiency.

# CHAPTER 8

# Costs and the Changes at Firms over Time

## CHAPTER OVERVIEW

All forms of businesses, from proprietorships and partnerships to domestic and multinational corporations, face decisions concerning start-up, expansion, and shutdown. These choices are one dimension of the change that occurs in a market economy. A crucial component of these decisions is the nature and behavior of the costs of production. This chapter examines the relationship between costs and production over the short run and the long run. Also, standard graphs are developed that permit the determination of profit, loss, breakeven, and shutdown.

First, the various short-run costs of production are defined and graphed. Interrelationships within these costs are described from two perspectives: a total view and a per-unit view. The costs discussed include total costs, variable costs, fixed costs, average total cost, average variable cost, and average fixed cost. Marginal cost is of particular importance for several reasons. It is a component of profit maximization decisions, and its location and shape determine the location and shape of virtually all the other cost functions. Also, marginal cost can be traced back to the production function, the marginal product of labor, and diminishing returns. Next, graphical representations of the costs of production (cost curves) and market-determined revenues are used to identify profit, loss, and the breakeven and shutdown points. Here the per-unit perspective is particularly useful. At this point, the relationship between a firm's supply curve and its marginal cost curve is developed. The examination of costs is carried into the long run through the construction of the long-run average total cost curve from short-run average total cost curves. Economies of scale are introduced at this point. Mergers and economies of scope are discussed. Of particular importance in such situations is the issue of the internal coordination of business activities.

## CHAPTER REVIEW

1.

    a.    Many of the definitions of the costs of production were originally discussed in Chapter 6. Recall that total costs (*TC*) are the sum of variable costs (*VC*) and fixed costs (*FC*). Figure 8.2 in the text is a graphical representation of these costs.

    b.    It is natural to present the economist's view of time in a discussion of costs. Over the **short run**, only the inputs that generate variable costs can be changed. The inputs that generate fixed costs cannot be altered. **Sunk costs** are costs that are committed and that cannot be recovered in the short run. However, over the **long run**, both fixed and variable costs can be changed.

    c.    In addition to *TC*, *FC*, and *VC*, other costs of interest are **average total cost (*ATC*)** and **average variable cost (*AVC*)**, both of which first decrease and then increase as production increases, and **average fixed cost (*AFC*)**, which declines with increases in production. *Marginal cost* (*MC*) is the change in *TC* divided by the change in the quantity produced.

2.    It is important to see the linkage between production and costs. For example, if a company wishes to expand production in the short run, it needs to add variable inputs. As a result, variable costs

will rise. Also, this is seen in the connection between marginal cost and the decreasing marginal product of labor, or diminishing returns to labor. Recall from Chapter 6 that as labor is added to a fixed amount of capital, the marginal product of labor rises at first and then falls. Alternatively, if the marginal product of labor is rising, it takes fewer and fewer workers to expand production by a certain amount (such as one unit). When the marginal product of labor falls, it takes increasing amounts of labor to produce the same increase in output. From this perspective, as the marginal product of labor rises, the marginal cost of production falls. The link between diminishing returns to labor and the costs of production is marginal cost. It is also important not to confuse average product of labor with marginal product of labor. The **average product of labor** is the quantity produced, or *total product*, divided by the amount of labor input. The marginal product of labor is the *change* in quantity produced from a *change* in labor input.

3.  Figures 8.4 and 8.5 in the text are very important. Both figures show per-unit costs. When placed on the same graph, the generic curves for *ATC*, *AVC*, and *MC* must be drawn in a particular way. The *MC* curve cuts through the *ATC* and *AVC* curves from below and crosses each at its lowest point. This is due to the mathematical relationship between marginals and averages.

4.  Figures 8.6 to 8.10 in the text use the *ATC, AVC,* and *MC* curves to show profit, loss, breakeven, and shutdown for a competitive business. In each diagram, the profit-maximizing level of production is the quantity at which the price line crosses the marginal cost curve. Once this quantity has been located, profit, loss, and breakeven can be determined by comparing price ($P$) with *ATC*. If $P > ATC$, an economic profit is earned. If $P = ATC$, the business is at the **breakeven point**. Even though profits are zero at this point, the owner still earns a normal return. A loss occurs when $P < ATC$, and the owner must determine whether the firm should shut down. The general rule is that an operating loss should never exceed fixed costs. This is true if $P > AVC$. Once $P = AVC$, the firm has reached the **shutdown point**. If the price falls below *AVC*, the firm should cease operations and pay only fixed costs during the short run. In the short run, fixed costs are sunk costs.

5.  The supply curve of a single firm tells us the quantity of a good that the firm will produce at various prices. By using the shutdown point, you can see that the firm will produce nothing until price is greater than the minimum value of average variable cost. Once this point is reached, the firm's level of production is found by equating price with marginal cost. Thus, the firm's supply curve is the same as the portion of the firm's marginal cost curve that rises above the shutdown point (the minimum of *AVC*).

6.

a.  Capital (the generic term for fixed inputs) can vary in the long run. As the amount of capital changes, the productivity of labor (the generic term for variable inputs) changes. Initially, as capital increases, labor productivity increases. This results in an increase in fixed costs but a decrease in variable costs at all levels of production.

b.  Graphically, a change in capital causes the short-run average total cost curve to shift positions. This is shown in Figures 8.11 to 8.13 in the text. As capital continues to increase, the short-run *ATC* curve continues to shift. The **long-run average total cost curve** traces out the points on the lowest short-run average total cost curves.

c.  The slope of the long-run average total cost curve reflects the nature of the returns to scale a firm experiences as it expands capital. More formally, **economies of scale**, or *increasing returns to scale*, are shown by a declining long-run *ATC*, and **diseconomies of scale**, or *decreasing returns to scale*, are shown by an increasing long-run *ATC*. The long-run *ATC* is horizontal under **constant returns to scale**. Most firms initially experience falling long-run average total costs with expansion and then enter a range of constant long-run average total costs. The point of transition is referred to as the **minimum efficient scale**. Eventually, increasing long-run average costs are experienced.

7. Firms can expand by adding capital over the long run through a merger. Combining different types of firms to lower costs or to promote the creation of a new product is called **economies of scope**.

## ZEROING IN

1.

   a. A theme throughout the text is the use and usefulness of marginal analysis—making decisions sequentially by comparing marginal revenue to marginal costs. As noted, marginal cost is one of the components of this methodology. It is defined as the change in total cost divided by the change in production. From this definition, it is apparent that marginal cost is the *additional* cost resulting from the production of the *next* unit.

   b. Graphically, marginal cost is shown falling at first, reaching a minimum, and then rising steeply. This short-run shape can be traced back to the production function and the marginal product of labor.

   c. The marginal product of labor is defined as the change in total product divided by the change in labor. Accordingly, the marginal product of labor is the *additional* output resulting from hiring the *next* worker. The inverse of this is the change in labor divided by the change in total product, or the *additional* labor needed to produce the *next* unit of output. If this is multiplied by the market wage of each worker, the result is marginal cost. As marginal product *rises*, its inverse *falls*; it takes fewer and fewer workers to produce another unit of output. As a result, marginal cost *falls*. When diminishing returns set in and marginal product *falls*, it takes increasing amounts of labor to produce another unit of output, and marginal cost *rises*. In the end, the behavior of costs and the behavior of production are two sides of the same coin.

2. Graphs of per-unit costs include *ATC, AVC,* and *MC.* Because of the mathematical interrelationship between them, these per-unit cost curves must be drawn in a special way. By this stage in the term, you have had a few tests or quizzes and can probably compute an average score. How do you make this average rise? You need to score higher on the *next* test than your average on the previous tests. *Next* is another word for *marginal.* Now, look at Figure 8.5 in the text closely, particularly where *MC* crosses *AVC* and *ATC.* To the left of these points, both *AVC* and *ATC* are falling and *MC* is below them—when the *next* product costs less than the average, the average must fall. To the right of these points, *MC* exceeds (is above) the averages, and, as a result, the averages rise. Thus, the special construction of the per-unit graph is due to the fundamental mathematical relationship between marginals and averages.

3. It is important to distinguish between *profit maximization* and *making a profit.* The former is a rule or a process, and the latter is a result or an outcome. This distinction makes Figures 8.6 to 8.10 in the text easier to understand. Profit maximization is the application of *marginal analysis* to a firm's selection of a quantity to produce. The revenue from each additional unit (marginal revenue) is compared with the cost of producing the same unit (marginal cost). A firm selling in a competitive market will maximize profit at the quantity where $P = MC$. Of all the possible levels of output from which a firm could choose, this rule takes the firm to the best one. Once this quantity has been determined, profits and losses are determined by comparing $P$ and $ATC$. This amounts to comparing total revenue with total cost. Thus, the process (profit maximization) uses marginals, whereas the result (making a profit) uses totals.

## ACTIVE REVIEW

### Fill-In Questions

1. _____ are the sum of fixed costs and _____.

2. The _____ is the period of time during which the inputs that generate fixed costs cannot be altered._____ inputs are variable over the long run.

3. In the_____ , only those inputs that generate variable costs can be changed.

4. Frequently, economists refer to fixed factors of production as _____ and to variable factors of production as _____.

5. _____ is defined as the change in _____ divided by the change in _____.

6. _____, _____, and _____ can each be divided by the quantity produced to give the _____, _____, and _____.

7. The general shape of the _____ curve is that it rises and then _____.

8. The _____ shows the change in output when inputs change.

9. _____ is the change in production obtained by adding labor. When it decreases, _____ are said to occur.

10. When marginal product_____ , marginal cost rises.

11. When marginal cost is below average total cost, average total cost must _____ when production increases.

12. The marginal cost curve cuts through the *ATC* and *AVC* curves at the _____ of these curves.

13. A competitive firm maximizes profits by finding the level of _____ at which _____ equals _____.

14. Profits and losses can be determined by comparing _____ and _____ or _____ and _____ at profit-maximizing output.

15. When $P = ATC$, _____ are zero, but when $P > ATC$, they are positive.

16. Shutdown should occur when _____ is less than _____ or when _____ exceed _____.

17. The firm's supply curve is the same as that portion of _____ that rises above the minimum of _____.

18. If price is below the minimum value of _____, the quantity supplied by a firm will be _____.

19. The _____ traces out the points on the lowest _____.

20. Over the long run, _____ can change.

21. When all inputs change, the _____ of the firm changes.

22. _____ occur when the long-run average total cost curve falls.

23. _____ are costs that you have committed that cannot be recovered in the short run.

## True-False Questions

1.  T  F    All inputs to a production process are variable in the long run.
2.  T  F    Marginal cost is the change in total costs divided by the change in output.
3.  T  F    ATC = AVC + AFC = (TVC/Q) + (FC/Q)
4.  T  F    The costs of production are related to the production function.
5.  T  F    Marginal cost of output and the marginal product of labor are related.
6.  T  F    Average variable cost cuts marginal cost at the low point of marginal cost.
7.  T  F    When total revenue equals total costs, the firm earns no economic profit.
8.  T  F    If a firm is losing money but the loss is less than total fixed costs, the firm should continue production and not shut down.
9.  T  F    If price falls below *ATC*, the quantity supplied by a firm will be zero.
10. T  F    The supply curve of a firm is the same as the rising portion of its *AVC* curve.
11. T  F    As capital changes, the short-run average total cost curve will shift.
12. T  F    The long-run average total cost curve is traced out by finding the midpoints of the upward-sloping portion of short-run average total cost curves.
13. T  F    A horizontal long-run average total cost curve is indicative of increasing returns to scale.
14. T  F    For most firms, the long-run average total cost curve eventually starts to turn upward.
15. T  F    Economies of scale and economies of scope are synonymous.
16. T  F    Sunk costs can be recovered in the short run.

## Short-Answer Questions

1.  Differentiate between the short run and the long run.
2.  How is marginal cost derived from the production function? (Assume the short run.)
3.  What is the mathematical relationship between averages and marginals?
4.  How are the average and marginal cost curves related?
5.  How do you calculate profit or loss by using the generic short-run cost curve diagram?
6.  How are a firm's supply curve and its marginal cost curve related?
7.  Short-run average cost curves shift over the long run. Why?
8.  What is the relationship between the shape of the long-run average total cost curve and economies of scale?
9.  What are sunk costs?

## WORKING IT OUT

1.  Two views of the costs of production are introduced in Chapter 8. There is the total view (*TC*, *VC*, and *FC*), and there is the per-unit view (*AFC*, *AVC*, *ATC*, and *MC*). It is important to see that they are all linked together; knowing one of them allows you to determine the rest. For example, suppose you know only a firm's short-run total costs (*TC*) of producing a continuous number of units beginning with zero. The first thing you should notice is that the total cost of producing no units is not zero. While no *variable* inputs are used at this level of production, *fixed* inputs are still employed. This is the nature of the short run. Thus, the total cost of producing nothing equals a firm's total fixed cost (*FC*). This cost is a sunk cost and cannot be recovered and is the same regardless of the amount produced. Subtracting this from total cost gives total variable cost (*VC*). The next point in the linkage is marginal cost (*MC*). This begins the connection to the per-unit view. Recall that *marginal* is synonymous with *change*. The costs that change with changes in production are *TC* and *VC*. Marginal cost is calculated by subtracting consecutive values for either *TC* or *VC*. The remaining per-unit costs are computed by dividing *TC*, *VC*, and *FC* by the associated level of production.

2.  Another important linkage presented in the chapter is the one between marginal cost and the marginal product of labor. This is the connection between the production function and the costs of production. Suppose you want to know the cost of producing one more unit of output—the marginal cost. You need to know two things. The first is the number of additional variable inputs that need to be hired to produce the additional unit. This is given by the marginal product of labor. The second thing you need to know is the market price of each variable input. This is given by the market wage. So, when marginal product *diminishes*, it takes *increasing* amounts of the variable input to produce another unit. Given the market wage, marginal cost *rises*.

3.  In the long run, a firm is able to add capital to the production process. This raises fixed costs, *and* it raises the productivity of variable inputs; marginal product shifts to the right. The shift in marginal product causes a shift in marginal cost. Following the connections described in the first point of "Working It Out," a shift in *MC* causes shifts in all the other cost curves, both total and per-unit measures.

## Worked Problems

Assume that every day you walk past a business named Teak-Your-CPU. You hear saws, drills, and rock-and-roll, and you are curious about the name. One day, after hearing a lecture on the costs of production, you build up courage and walk in to look around. You meet the owner, and she tells you that the business produces handmade, custom teak computer desks. She then gives you a tour. You see wood being cut, sanded, stained, and assembled by skilled workers. Raw materials, capital, and labor come together, and a teak desk is created.

Did your professor talk about the things you see on the tour? Essentially, you are seeing how Teak-Your-CPU uses inputs to assemble output (desks); you are observing the *production function*. You also see that some of the inputs would take time to change. The factory is only so big; the saws and drills are heavy, look expensive, and are bolted to the floor. These are *fixed inputs* (*capital*). There are also some inputs that can change quickly. Because your host is considered to be a good employer, she can hire new workers pretty quickly. Also, new supplies of teak can be found and delivered with little delay. These are *variable inputs* (*labor*). At the end of your tour, you ask your host, "Do you have all those confusing costs we talk about in class?"

Your host does not understand your question, but she says that the following data are recent cost figures calculated by her sister, who happens to be the firm's accountant.

| Desks per Day | Total Costs |
|---|---|
| 0 | $1,000 |
| 1 | $1,500 |
| 2 | $1,750 |
| 3 | $1,850 |
| 4 | $2,000 |
| 5 | $2,200 |
| 6 | $2,500 |
| 7 | $2,900 |
| 8 | $3,500 |
| 9 | $4,200 |
| 10 | $5,000 |

1.

     a.    Calculate short-run *VC, FC,* and *MC* for Teak-Your-CPU.

     b.    Calculate *ATC, AVC,* and *AFC.*

**Answers**

     a.    *You have been given levels of output and the total cost associated with each level. Remember that TC = VC + FC. Also, recall that FC is constant in the short run and exists at every level of output. So, when no desks are produced, the owner still must pay $1,000 in fixed costs. MC is the change in TC or VC when another desk is produced. Thus, the following can be calculated from the above table.*

| Desks | TC | FC | VC | MC |
|---|---|---|---|---|
| 0 | $1,000 | $1,000 | 0 | |
| 1 | $1,500 | $1,000 | $500 | $500 |
| 2 | $1,750 | $1,000 | $750 | $250 |
| 3 | $1,850 | $1,000 | $850 | $100 |
| 4 | $2,000 | $1,000 | $1,000 | $150 |
| 5 | $2,200 | $1,000 | $1,200 | $200 |
| 6 | $2,500 | $1,000 | $1,500 | $300 |
| 7 | $2,900 | $1,000 | $1,900 | $400 |
| 8 | $3,500 | $1,000 | $2,500 | $600 |
| 9 | $4,200 | $1,000 | $3,200 | $700 |
| 10 | $5,000 | $1,000 | $4,000 | $800 |

b.    *Divide each of the above columns by the associated quantity of desks.*

| Desks | AFC | AVC | ATC |
|---|---|---|---|
| 1 | $1,000 | $500 | $1,500 |
| 2 | $500 | $375 | $875 |
| 3 | $333.33 | $283.33 | $616.66 |
| 4 | $250 | $250 | $500 |
| 5 | $200 | $240 | $440 |
| 6 | $166.66 | $250 | $416.66 |
| 7 | $142.86 | $271.43 | $414.29 |
| 8 | $125 | $312.50 | $437.50 |
| 9 | $111.11 | $355.55 | $466.66 |
| 10 | $100 | $400 | $500 |

2.

a.    The owner tells you that the initial price was $400 per desk. Was Teak-Your-CPU profitable?

b.    Should Teak-Your-CPU have shut down?

c.    After a year or so, word of the beauty and unique character of the desks spread, and the company experienced an increase in demand. As a result, it can now charge $600 per desk. How many desks should Teak-Your-CPU produce to maximize profits, and is the company making a profit?

## Answers

a.    *First, you need to determine how many desks maximize profit. This is the number at which MC is $400, or 7 desks per day. At this level, total revenue was $2,800 (7 × $400), and total costs were $2,900. Teak-Your-CPU was losing money.*

b.    *The rule concerning shutdown is to compare P and AVC at the profit-maximizing quantity. If P > AVC, the loss from producing is less than the fixed costs that would need to be paid if the company shut down. At 7 desks, AVC is $271.43. Thus, Teak-Your-CPU was smart to continue operations.*

c.    *At $600 per desk, profits are maximized at 8 desks per day. At this quantity, price and marginal cost are equal. Total revenue is $4,800 (8 × $600), and total costs are $3,500. Profits are $1,300 ($4,800 − $3,500).*

## PRACTICE PROBLEMS

1.    Assume that some time passes before you return to Teak-Your-CPU. The owner tells you that two things have happened since your first visit. First, certain saws and drill presses have been coordinated through the use of a new computer. This has resulted in a doubling of the marginal product of the workers, but it has also raised fixed costs by $500. Second, new competitors have opened up, and the market price has fallen to $300 per desk.

a.    Calculate TC, VC, FC, MC, ATC, AVC, and AFC.

b.    What quantity maximizes profits?

c.    Is Teak-Your-CPU profitable?

    d.    Does your answer to part (c) prompt another question?

2.

    a.    Describe how these cost curves differ from those in Worked Problem 1.

    b.    Would Teak-Your-CPU be better off if it expanded output beyond profit maximization?

    c.    Where does *MC* cut through *AVC* and *ATC*?

# CHAPTER TEST

1.    Total costs equal

    a.    variable costs minus fixed costs.
    b.    average variable cost plus marginal cost.
    c.    variable costs divided by output.
    d.    variable costs plus fixed costs.

2.    The time period over which only some inputs are variable is the

    a.    long run.
    b.    short run.
    c.    market period.
    d.    adjustment period.

3.    Total costs divided by the quantity produced is

    a.    marginal cost.
    b.    average total cost.
    c.    marginal product.
    d.    marginal fixed cost.

4.    If $MC < AVC$, then

    a.    *AVC* will fall with increased production.
    b.    *MC* is at its lowest point.
    c.    *AVC* is minimized.
    d.    *AVC* will rise with increased production.

5.    If the marginal product of labor is falling,

    a.    marginal cost is rising.
    b.    average total cost is rising.
    c.    marginal cost is falling.
    d.    total fixed cost is falling.

6.    Graphically, the *MC* curve cuts through the *ATC* curve at

    a.    the lowest point on the *MC* curve.
    b.    the highest point on the *MC* curve.
    c.    the lowest point on the *ATC* curve.
    d.    the middle of the upward-sloping portion of the total cost curve.

7.    As production increases, the gap between *ATC* and *AVC*

    a.    increases.
    b.    diminishes.
    c.    remains constant.

    d.    is proportional to *MC*.

8.    A competitive firm maximizes profits by finding the level of production at which

    a.    $P = MC$.
    b.    $P = ATC$.
    c.    $ATC = MC$.
    d.    $P < MC$.

9.    If, at the profit-maximizing quantity, profits are zero,

    a.    $P < ATC$.
    b.    $P = ATC$.
    c.    $P > ATC$.
    d.    $P = MC$.

10.    If, at the profit-maximizing quantity, losses are earned, the firm should shut down if

    a.    $P < ATC$.
    b.    $P < AVC$.
    c.    $P < MC$.
    d.    $MC < AVC$.

11.    In the short run, a firm should shut down when

    a.    production losses are less than fixed costs.
    b.    only normal profits are earned.
    c.    production losses exceed fixed costs.
    d.    fixed costs are zero.

12.    The supply curve of a firm is the same as the part of

    a.    *MC* that rises above *AVC*.
    b.    *MC* that rises above *ATC*.
    c.    *AVC* that is rising.
    d.    *ATC* that is rising.

13.    The part of *MC* that rises above the minimum value of *AVC* is the same thing as a firm's

    a.    demand curve.
    b.    supply curve.
    c.    long-run average cost curve.
    d.    total revenue.

14.    If a firm experiences increasing returns to scale, then the

    a.    long-run average total cost curve is equal to the economies of scope.
    b.    long-run average total cost curve is positively sloped.
    c.    long-run average total cost curve is horizontal.
    d.    long-run average total cost curve is negatively sloped.

15.    The long-run average total cost curve

    a.    traces out the points on the lowest short-run average total cost curve for each level of production.
    b.    is inversely related to the depth of the short-run marginal cost curve.
    c.    traces out the midpoints on an average of several short-run average total cost curves.
    d.    is downward-sloping under decreasing returns to scale.

16. If owners direct a division to produce a certain quantity, then

    a.    a price-directed approach to management is being used.
    b.    a quantity-directed approach to management is being used.
    c.    a service management approach is being used.
    d.    a transfer price must be specified before production can begin.

17. When *ATC* declines as a result of a merger of two firms, the new firm experiences

    a.    economies of scale.
    b.    diminishing returns to labor.
    c.    mystic revelations.
    d.    economies of scope.

18. Costs that are committed in the short run which cannot be recovered are

    a.    variable costs.
    b.    total costs.
    c.    sunk costs.
    d.    average variable costs.

# ANSWERS TO THE REVIEW QUESTIONS

## Fill-In Questions

1.    Total costs (*TC*); variable costs (*VC*)

2.    short run; all

3.    short run

4.    capital; labor

5.    Marginal cost (*MC*); total costs; quantity

6.    Total costs; variable costs; fixed costs; average total cost (*ATC*); average variable cost (*AVC*); average fixed cost (*AFC*)

7.    marginal cost; rises

8.    production function

9.    The marginal product of labor; diminishing returns to labor

10.   falls

11.   fall

12.   low points

13.   output; price; marginal cost

14.   price; average total cost; total revenue; total cost

15.   economic profits

16.   price; average variable cost; losses; fixed costs

17.   *MC; AVC*

18.   *AVC;* zero

19.   long-run average total cost curve; short-run average total cost curves

20. capital

21. scale

22. Increasing returns to scale

23. Sunk costs

## True-False Questions

1.  **True.**    This is a characteristic of the long run. In the short run, the inputs that generate fixed costs cannot be altered.

2.  **True.**    The words marginal, change, and additional are synonymous in economics.

3.  **True.**    The sum in the far right brackets uses totals and quantities to create the averages that are shown in the middle of the equalities.

4.  **True.**    The production function provides information on the ways in which inputs should be combined to produce output. Thus, it provides information on the costs associated with producing a given level of output once input prices are known.

5.  **True.**    The marginal product of labor describes the change in output when labor is added to production. Marginal cost describes the change in total costs when output is changed. For example, when the marginal product of labor rises, the marginal cost of production falls.

6.  **False.**    Because of the relationship between averages and marginals, the marginal cost curve cuts the average variable cost curve from below at the lowest average variable cost.

7.  **True.**    It is important to remember that economists include the opportunity cost of the owner in the costs of production. This is called normal profit. At economic breakeven, the owner is covering all costs, including her opportunity cost.

8.  **True.**    If P < ATC but P > AVC, it is better to continue production. If the business shut down, it would pay out more in fixed costs than it would lose if it continued production.

9.  **False.**    If P < ATC, a firm is experiencing a loss but it might not need to shut down. This decision depends on whether or not the loss from operating is greater than its fixed costs. The firm will be better off if it shuts down and supplies nothing if the loss is greater than its fixed costs. Otherwise, the firm should continue producing goods.

10. **False.**    The supply curve of a firm is the same as the portion of MC that rises above the minimum of AVC.

11. **True.**    The short-run average total cost curve is built on the assumption that capital is fixed. Thus, when capital changes, the short-run average total cost curve will shift.

12. **False.**    The long-run average total cost curve traces out the points on the lowest short-run average total cost curves.

13. **False.**    The zero slope indicates constant returns to scale.

14. **True.**    Eventually, diseconomies of scale set in, especially at high levels of production.

15. **False.**    Economies of scope occur when average total costs decline as a result of a merger of two firms that are not producing the same product. Economies of scale are related to the change in production that results when all inputs are increased.

16. **False.**    Sunk costs have been committed and, as such, cannot be recovered. Fixed costs are sunk costs in the short run.

Chapter 8: Costs and the Changes at Firms over Time

# Short-Answer Questions

1.  The short run is the period of time during which it is not possible to change the things that generate fixed costs. The long run is the period of time during which all inputs can be changed.

2.  Marginal cost is defined as the change in total costs (and the change in variable costs) when output changes. It is related to the marginal product of labor, which is defined as the change in output when labor input (the variable input) changes. This identifies the number of workers needed to increase output by one unit. Knowing this number and the market wage, it is possible to calculate marginal cost.

3.  An average is a total divided by the number of observations or units. A marginal is a change in a total when observations or units change. For example, your test average is the total number of points scored on all tests divided by the number of tests. Your *next* test is the marginal test. If your marginal test score exceeds your average score on past tests, then your average score must rise.

4.  The marginal cost curve cuts the average total cost and average variable cost curves from below and passes through their lowest points. This is true because of the mathematical relationship between marginal cost and average costs.

5.  First, determine the profit-maximizing level of production ($Q^*$). Then, for this quantity, determine $ATC$. Total costs equal $ATC \times Q^*$. Total revenue P is multiplied by $Q^*$. Note that $Q^*$ is used in both calculations. Thus, you may simply compare $P$ and $ATC$ in the per-unit diagram to determine whether total revenue exceeds (profit), equals (breakeven), or is less than (loss) total costs.

6.  The supply curve of a firm shows the relationship between the quantity the firm will offer to the market and various prices. A firm determines the quantity it will offer to the market by equating a given price to its marginal cost. This is always true unless price falls below the minimum value of $AVC$, the point of shutdown. Thus, the supply curve of a firm is the same as the portion of $MC$ that rises above $AVC$.

7.  Short-run average cost curves are constructed assuming that capital is fixed. Capital is no longer fixed over the long run. Accordingly, the assumption no longer holds, and the $ATC$ and $AVC$ curves will start to move or shift.

8.  The long-run $ATC$ curve describes what happens to a firm's $ATC$ when its scale increases. A horizontal long-run $ATC$ curve reflects constant returns to scale. A downward-sloping long-run $ATC$ curve is indicative of increasing returns to scale, and an upward-sloping long-run $ATC$ curve indicates decreasing returns to scale.

9.  Sunk costs are costs that cannot be recovered. They have been committed and, as such, are sunk.

Copyright © Houghton Mifflin Company. All rights reserved.

## SOLUTIONS TO THE PRACTICE PROBLEMS

1.    a.    There are two factors to take into account in answering the question. The first is the doubling of marginal product. Recall that when marginal product rises, marginal cost falls. Thus, a doubling of marginal product will cut marginal cost by half. (Remember that $MC$ is the additional cost of producing the *next* unit, not the cost of producing a total number of units.)

| Desks | MC |
|:-----:|:-----:|
| 1 | $250 |
| 2 | $125 |
| 3 | $50 |
| 4 | $75 |
| 5 | $100 |
| 6 | $150 |
| 7 | $200 |
| 8 | $300 |
| 9 | $350 |
| 10 | $400 |

The second factor is the increase of $500 in $FC$ at each level of output.

| Desks | FC |
|:-----:|:-----:|
| 0 | $1,500 |
| 1 | $1,500 |
| 2 | $1,500 |
| 3 | $1,500 |
| 4 | $1,500 |
| 5 | $1,500 |
| 6 | $1,500 |
| 7 | $1,500 |
| 8 | $1,500 |
| 9 | $1,500 |
| 10 | $1,500 |

Remember that $TC = VC + FC$. So, if you add the $MC$ of the first desk to the $FC$ for 0 desks, you will have $TC$ for the first desk. $MC$ for the first desk is also $VC$ for the first desk. In fact, addition of $MC$ to a previous $VC$ gives the new $VC$.

| Desks | FC | MC | VC | TC |
|---|---|---|---|---|
| 0 | $1,500 | | | |
| 1 | $1,500 | $250 | $250 | $1,750 |
| 2 | $1,500 | $125 | $375 | $1,875 |
| 3 | $1,500 | $50 | $425 | $1,925 |
| 4 | $1,500 | $75 | $500 | $2,000 |
| 5 | $1,500 | $100 | $600 | $2,100 |
| 6 | $1,500 | $150 | $750 | $2,250 |
| 7 | $1,500 | $200 | $950 | $2,450 |
| 8 | $1,500 | $300 | $1,250 | $2,750 |
| 9 | $1,500 | $350 | $1,600 | $3,100 |
| 10 | $1,500 | $400 | $2,000 | $3,500 |

Note that VC is also half of the old VC. Now, divide each column by the number of desks.

| Desks | AFC | AVC | ATC |
|---|---|---|---|
| 1 | $1,500 | $250 | $1,750 |
| 2 | $750 | $187.50 | $937.50 |
| 3 | $500 | $141.66 | $641.66 |
| 4 | $375 | $125 | $500 |
| 5 | $300 | $120 | $420 |
| 6 | $250 | $125 | $375 |
| 7 | $214.28 | $135.71 | $349.99 |
| 8 | $187.50 | $156.25 | $343.75 |
| 9 | $166.66 | $177.77 | $344.33 |
| 10 | $150 | $200 | $350 |

b.  At a price of $300 per desk, the firm will maximize profits at 8 desks per day. Price equals marginal cost at this quantity.

c.  For 8 desks, the total revenue is $2,400 (8 x $300), and total costs are $2,750. Teak-Your-CPU is losing money again. The loss is $350.

d.  Given the loss, the next question is whether the company should shut down. The price exceeds the AVC of $156.25. Also, FC are $1,500 at this level of output, which is less than the loss of $350. Therefore, Teak-Your-CPU should not shut down.

2.  a.  First, consider the total view. The second FC curve is clearly above the first. Also, the second VC curve is below the first. The second TC curve crosses the first at 4 desks. After this point, the second TC curve falls below the first. From a per-unit view, the second AFC curve is above the first at all levels of output, and the second AVC curve is below the first. Graphically, the per-unit cost curves have shifted down and to the right. This confirms the discussion in the text.

b.  The total revenue for 9 desks is $2,700, and the total costs are $3,100. The loss is $400. No, the company would not be better off beyond 8 units.

c.  Recall that average costs fall if marginal cost is lower than the average and rise when marginal cost is higher than the average. AVC rises after 5 desks. Thus, MC must cut through AVC at about this quantity. ATC rises after 8 desks. This suggests that MC cuts through ATC at about this quantity.

## ANSWERS TO THE CHAPTER TEST

1.  d
2.  b
3.  b
4.  a
5.  a
6.  c
7.  b
8.  a
9.  b
10.  b
11.  c
12.  a
13.  b
14.  d
15.  a
16.  b
17.  d
18.  c

# APPENDIX TO CHAPTER 8

# Producer Theory with Isoquants

## OVERVIEW

This appendix presents a formal graphical treatment (using isoquants and isocost lines) of cost minimization.

## REVIEW

1.   A long-run decision concerns the determination of the combination of labor *and* capital that minimizes total costs. In the long run all inputs are variable. The theoretical foundations of an answer may be found by using isoquants and an isocost line.

     a.   An **isoquant** is a graphical representation of the production function. It shows all the possible combinations of labor and capital that result in the same quantity of production. There is a unique isoquant for each level of production. Its slope is called the **rate of technical substitution**. An **isocost** line shows the combinations of labor and capital that have the same total costs. The slope of the isocost line depends on the ratio of the price of labor to the price of capital.

     b.   The combination of labor and capital that minimizes total costs for a specific level of production is found where an isocost line is tangent to the specific isoquant. A different combination would be associated with higher total costs or lower levels of production. A change in the price of labor or capital alters the slope of the isocost line and therefore alters the point of tangency. In general, firms will substitute away from those inputs that have become relatively more expensive.

## ACTIVE REVIEW

### Fill-In Questions

1.   A(n) _____ shows all possible combinations of labor and capital that produce a certain level of production.

2.   Different combinations of labor and capital that have the same total costs can be shown by a(n) _____.

### True-False Questions

1.   T   F   Isoquant lines show combinations of labor and capital that will produce the same quantity of output.

2.   T   F   In the long run, costs are minimized by finding the combination of labor and capital for which the rate of technical substitution equals the ratio of the price of labor to the price of capital.

3.   T   F      An important finding in this advanced topic is that firms reduce the use of an input as the price of that input rises.

## Short-Answer Questions

1.   How is the least-cost combination of labor and capital determined? You may assume that the quantity has already been determined.

2.   What is the slope of an isocost line?

## CHAPTER TEST

1.   Combinations of labor and capital that produce the same level of output can be depicted by a(n)

   a.   isocost line.
   b.   indifference curve.
   c.   isoquant.
   d.   point of tangency between a production function and a utility function.

2.   Combinations of labor and capital that have the same total cost can be depicted by a(n)

   a.   isocost line.
   b.   indifference curve.
   c.   isoquant.
   d.   point of tangency between a production function and a utility function.

3.   Costs are minimized for a given quantity when, at a point,

   a.   the isoquant for that quantity and an isocost line are tangent.
   b.   the slope of the isoquant for that quantity equals the slope of an isocost line.
   c.   the rate of technical substitution equals the input price ratio.
   d.   all of the above are true.

## ANSWERS TO THE REVIEW QUESTIONS

### Fill-In Questions

1.   isoquant

2.   isocost line

### True-False Questions

1.   **True**.      This is a definition of an isoquant.

2.   **True**.      This is a description of a point of tangency between an isoquant and an isocost line.

3.   **True**.      This is the result of profit-maximizing behavior over the long run, when all inputs can be substituted for each other.

### Short-Answer Questions

1.   An isoquant shows all the combinations of labor and capital that can produce a given quantity of output. The rate of technical substitution is the slope of an isoquant. It tells the rate at which labor and capital may be substituted for each other while holding production constant. This can be

determined by locating the point at which the lowest isocost line is tangent to the desired isoquant. At this point, the rate of technical substitution is equal to the input price ratio.

2.    An isocost line represents all the combinations of labor and capital that have the same total cost. The slope of an isocost line is –1 times the ratio of the price of labor to the price of capital.

## ANSWERS TO THE CHAPTER TEST

1.    c

2.    a

3.    d

# CHAPTER 9

# The Rise and Fall of Industries

## CHAPTER OVERVIEW

The competitive market adjustment process has been referred to as creative destruction. Some industries expand, whereas others decline and possibly disappear. This chapter uses the tools of economic analysis developed in previous chapters to examine the rise and fall of industries.

In general, the rise and fall of industries is examined as movements between long-run competitive equilibriums. This approach uses two familiar diagrams: a supply and demand diagram and the per-unit view of a single competitive firm. Change is introduced into this system through changes in the determinants of market demand and/or market supply. These changes introduce either economic profits or losses into the model, creating incentives for firms to either enter or exit the market. The adjustment process is modified if there are external economies or diseconomies of scale.

Two important characteristics of final long-run equilibrium are that average total costs are minimized and that resources have been guided to their most efficient use.

## CHAPTER REVIEW

1. The competitive model of Chapter 8 is expanded to include the free entry and exit of firms in an industry; they enter when economic profits are positive and exit when economic profits are negative. This extension is called the **long-run competitive equilibrium model**. This model is made up of two graphs, as shown in Figure 9.1.

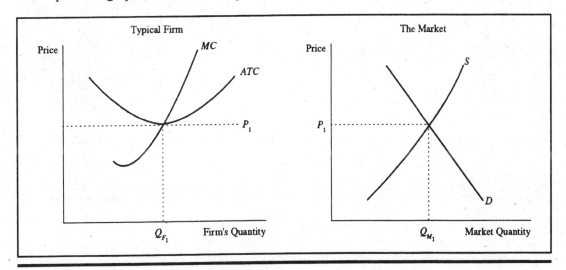

**Figure 9.1**

The graph on the right is the familiar diagram of supply and demand. The market demand curve is downward sloping, and the market supply curve is upward sloping. Market equilibrium is shown at price $P_1$ and quantity $Q_{M1}$. The other graph is the per-unit view of a single firm as presented in

Chapter 8. The firm takes price as given (seen in the horizontal price line at $P_1$). This is how an individual firm in a competitive market perceives market demand. Given this market price, the firm maximizes profits by producing the quantity $Q_{F1}$. Because $P = ATC$ at this quantity, the firm earns only normal profits.

2.  The new feature of this model is the **free entry and exit** of firms. Entry shifts the market supply curve to the right, whereas exit shifts it to the left. A firm's decision to enter a new market, or to exit a market it is currently in, is based on economic profits, which are different from the accountant's definition of profits. **Accounting profits** are defined as total revenue minus total costs, where total costs do *not* include the opportunity cost of the owner's time or the owner's funds. When computing **economic profits**, however, implicit opportunity costs are included in total costs, and so economic profits are lower than accounting profits. The term **normal profits** refers to the amount of accounting profits that exist when economic profits are equal to zero. Thus, economic profits represent earnings in excess of normal profits; the owner is making a profit above her opportunity cost. The existence of economic profits encourages new firms to enter the market. If economic profit is negative, a normal profit is not being earned; the owner is not covering opportunity cost. In this case, the firm would exit the market.

3.

   a.  A way to show the long-run adjustment of an industry is to shift the demand curve to the right. Figure 9.2 duplicates Figure 9.1 and shows a shift to the right in the market demand curve, to $D_1$. Given the market supply curve $S$, the market price rises to $P_2$. In the per-unit view of a typical firm, the price increase creates an incentive for the firm to increase production to $Q_{F2}$. At this profit-maximizing quantity, price ($P_2$) exceeds the average total cost ($ATC_2 = a$). Thus, the firm earns economic profits, shown by the area $abcd$.

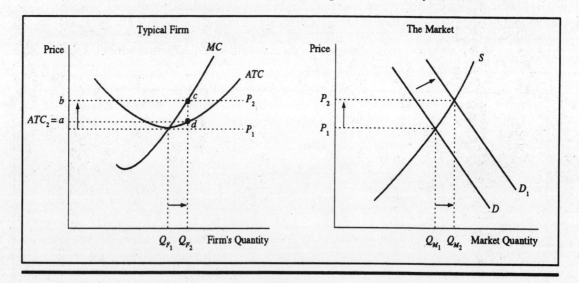

**Figure 9.2**

   b.  Economic profits create an incentive for firms outside the market to enter it. This is seen as a shift to the right in the market supply curve (Figure 9.3). As a result, price falls. Entry continues until economic profits are zero, so that all incentive to enter is removed. Assuming that $ATC$ and $MC$ do not shift, economic profits are eliminated when price returns to $P_1$. Suppose the market supply curve moves from $S$ to $S_1$ and price returns to $P_1$. Each firm returns to $Q_{F1}$, but the market quantity grows to $Q_{MB}$; there are more firms in the market. This is the new **long-run equilibrium**. It is not necessary that all firms be the same size. It is reasonable to expect firms to expand, especially ones that were already in the market. New products and changes in cost also affect the market in ways that create a long-run adjustment.

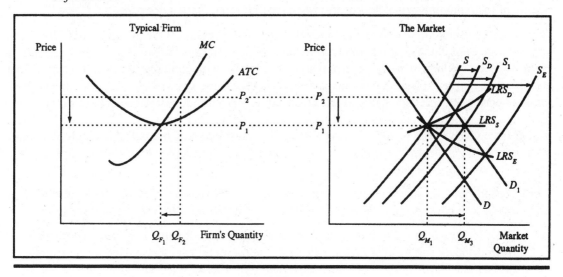

**Figure 9.3**

4.  An important feature of the adjustment process is that *ATC* is minimized in long-run equilibrium; the horizontal demand curve facing each firm is tangent to the lowest point of the firm's *ATC* curve. Goods are being produced at the lowest cost, and consumers are paying the lowest price. Also, with free entry and exit, capital is directed toward its most efficient use.

5.  The long-run adjustment process is altered if **external diseconomies of scale** or **external economies of scale** are present. External diseconomies of scale occur when expansion of an industry causes input prices to rise. This prevents the market supply curve in Figure 9.3 from shifting to $S_1$. It may only shift to $S_D$, so that the **long-run industry supply curve** will be upward sloping ($LRS_D$). In the case of external economies of scale, expansion of an industry results in the market supply curve shifting beyond $S_1$ to $S_E$ and the long-run supply curve will be downward sloping, shown by $LRS_E$. This form of industry expansion may also result in further specialization, which could lead to even lower costs of production. $LRS_S$ is the standard long-run supply curve when neither economies of scale nor diseconomies of scale are present.

# ZEROING IN

1.  The main topic of this chapter is the expansion and contraction of industries. As industries change, limited resources move among alternative uses. It is important to see the central role played by economic profits in this adjustment process. First, what do business owners or entrepreneurs do? In general, they pursue their own interests by seeking out profit opportunities. In doing this, they give other resources (like land, labor, and capital) place and purpose, and they assume risk. How do business owners and entrepreneurs know where to go, or when to change what they are doing? For that matter, how does any worker or resource owner know where to go, or when to change what he or she is currently doing? All look for the use that pays them the most. This is where economic profits come into play. Recall that a firm's total cost includes all implicit and explicit opportunity costs, including that of the owner, the normal profit. Economic profits represent profit earned above normal profit. If firms in an industry earn economic profits, others outside the industry will, in some way, see this as they seek the uses for their resources that pay the most. Alternatively, if the original enterprises in an industry earn economic profits because they hit on a unique idea or an unfilled need, others will be attracted to their success. Because owners and

entrepreneurs give land, labor, and capital place and purpose, their movement toward areas of economic profits creates the movement of resources. Thus, the freedom to earn economic profits is one of the main things that reallocates resources in a free market economy.

2. The long-run competitive equilibrium model employs two graphs. One is the familiar diagram of a competitive market made up of supply and demand. The other is the per-unit view of an individual firm. Why do we look at only *one* firm when a competitive market consists of *many* firms? In a competitive market, it is assumed that each firm has the same knowledge as all the other firms; there is perfect knowledge. With perfect knowledge, every producer will select the same technique of production in the search for maximum profits. In a sense, all producers will look the same; once you've seen one, you've seen them all. Thus, by using the per-unit graph of a *single* firm to see how *that* firm responds to market changes, we are seeing what *all* firms are doing under the same circumstances.

3. Over the long run, the market supply curve moves for three reasons. It will be helpful if we relate these reasons to concepts developed in past chapters, particularly Chapters 6 and 8.

   a. First, let's recall a definition of the market supply curve. It is the horizontal summation of the individual supply curves of the firms in the market. From this, it is pretty easy to see why the market supply curve shifts with entry and exit. The sum increases with entry because there are more firms, and it decreases with exit because there are fewer firms.

   b. The other two reasons involve external economies and external diseconomies of scale. To see these, remember that the supply curve of an individual firm is that portion of the marginal cost curve that rises above the average variable cost curve. Therefore, things that affect marginal cost affect *individual* supply curves and, through the summation process, affect the *market* supply curve.

   What are some things that cause shifts in the marginal cost of an individual firm? First, if the marginal product of labor shifts, marginal cost shifts. External economies of scale raise productivity. Thus, marginal product rises and marginal cost decreases, or shifts to the right. This produces a shift to the right in a firm's supply curve and, eventually, a shift to the right in the market supply curve. Another factor that affects the marginal cost curve is a change in the price of variable inputs. Here is where external diseconomies of scale may be seen. External diseconomies of scale raise input prices. This causes marginal cost to rise, or to shift left. This creates a shift to the left in a firm's supply curve and, eventually, a shift to the left in the market supply curve. In summary, the movements of the market supply curve described in the long-run equilibrium model have roots in the theories of costs and production.

## ACTIVE REVIEW

### Fill-In Questions

1. A(n) _____ is a group of firms producing a similar product.

2. Firms in an industry produce _____ and/or _____.

3. The _____ assumes that firms can enter and leave an industry over the long run.

4. The competitive *market demand* curve is _____, whereas a *single firm* in the market sees its demand curve as _____.

5. _____ into or _____ from an industry causes the market supply curve to shift.

6. _____ are calculated by including _____ and _____ opportunity costs in total costs.

7. Entry occurs when _____ are positive, and exit occurs when they are _____.

8. If $P = ATC$, _____ are zero and there will be neither _____ nor _____.

9. The _____ is the horizontal summation of individual supply curves. Thus, it moves with either _____ or _____ of firms.

10. _____ and _____ can cause changes in the long-run competitive model.

11. In long-run competitive equilibrium, _____ equals _____ and also equals _____.

12. In a competitive market, over the long run, _____ is minimized.

13. An upward-sloping long-run supply curve indicates the presence of _____, whereas a downward-sloping long-run supply curve suggests the presence of _____.

14. A standard practice is to assume that the long-run supply curve is _____.

## True-False Questions

1. T F The short-run competitive model takes into account the entry of firms into an industry and their exit from it.

2. T F A single firm in a competitive market perceives demand as downward sloping.

3. T F Entry causes a decrease in market supply.

4. T F Economic profits are not an implicit opportunity cost included in total costs.

5. T F Entry occurs in response to positive economic profits.

6. T F Exit causes a decrease in market demand.

7. T F When a market expands, only the number of firms increases.

8. T F New products and changes in costs can stimulate entry into a market.

9. *T F* $AVC$ is minimized in long-run equilibrium in a competitive market.

10. T F The long-run industry supply curve is downward sloping when external diseconomies of scale are present.

11. T F The long-run industry supply curve is downward sloping when external economies of scale are present.

## Short-Answer Questions

1. Describe the generic graphs used in the long-run equilibrium model.

2. What does entry do to the competitive market diagram?

3. What role do economic profits and losses play in the long-run competitive equilibrium model?

4. When does long-run equilibrium exist?

5.    Can the introduction of a new product cause entry?

6.    Why is *ATC* minimized in long-run equilibrium in a competitive market?

7.    Do external diseconomies of scale affect the long-run supply curve?

# WORKING IT OUT

The long-run competitive equilibrium model consists of two familiar diagrams. One is the model of a competitive market, with a downward-sloping demand curve and an upward-sloping supply curve. The other is the per-unit representation of a competitive firm. This consists of a market price (marginal revenue), marginal cost curve, average total cost curve, and (if necessary) average variable cost curve. These models are interrelated in that each provides information to the other. Let us use Zinfandel grapes as an example. Initially, both diagrams are assumed to be in equilibrium. In the market, this occurs when a price equates the quantity demanded and the quantity supplied. Equilibrium for the firm is described as a profit-maximizing level of production (where price equals marginal cost) with zero economic profit (average total cost equals price). When something in one (or both) of the diagrams changes, equilibrium is disturbed. Suppose the equilibrium-disturbing influence is an increase in the demand for Zinfandel grapes. This causes the market price to rise. This feeds over to the per-unit diagram; each firm expands production, and economic profits are earned. These profits feed over to the market diagram; new firms are attracted into the market, and the market supply curve shifts to the right. The price falls, and economic profits are reduced to zero. Long-run equilibrium is restored, and entry stops. Thus, these diagrams are an interrelated system depicting the movement between two equilibriums.

# Worked Problem

1.    Assume that Zinfandel grapes are bought and sold on a competitive market. Further assume that the market is in equilibrium and that the economic profits of existing vineyards are zero.

a.    Draw the initial long-run equilibrium.

b.    Discuss the short-run effects of a root disease that wipes out one-third of the growers. Assume that demand remains constant.

c.    What are the long-run effects on the market and firms, assuming no external economies or diseconomies of scale?

d.    How would your answer to part (c) change if sprays needed to fight the disease became more expensive?

**Answers**

a.    *Figure 9.4 depicts the market for Zinfandel grapes and the situation facing a representative grower. $S_1$ and $D_1$ are the initial market supply and demand curves, with equilibrium price $P_1$ and quantity $Q_{M1}$. The representative grower takes $P_1$ as given (shown by the horizontal line) and maximizes profits by producing $Q_{F1}$. Only normal profits are earned at this quantity because $P_1 = ATC$.*

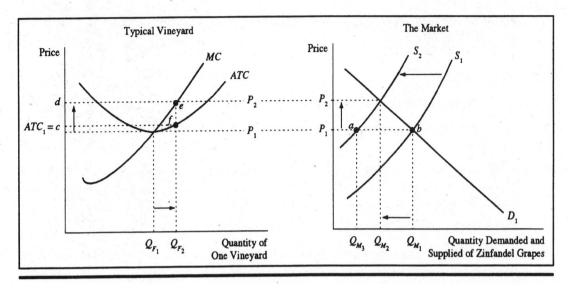

**Figure 9.4**

b.   *The root disease removes some of the vineyards from the market. This is first shown by a decrease in market supply. Assuming that demand is constant, the decrease in supply creates a shortage of grapes on the market equal to ab. Vineyards unaffected by the disease provide $Q_{M3}$ to the market, but buyers still demand the quantity $Q_{MI}$. Thus, the market price rises to $P_2$. The higher price feeds over to the remaining growers. At $P_2$ profits are maximized at $Q_{F2}$. At this quantity, price exceeds average total cost and economic profits are earned (as shown by the area cdef).*

c.   *The short-run economic profits attract other vineyards to Zinfandel grapes and encourage existing growers to expand production. This can be seen in Figure 9.5. This shifts the supply curve back to $S_1$, and the market price returns to $P_1$. At this price, economic profits return to zero.*

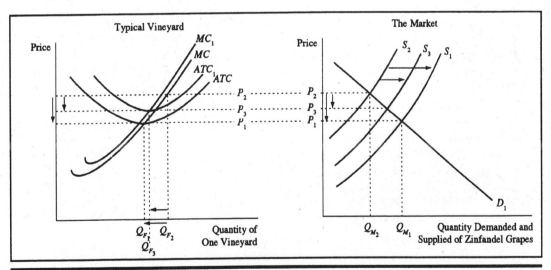

**Figure 9.5**

d.   *This suggests the existence of external diseconomies of scale. The increase in spraying costs would raise MC and ATC to $MC_1$ and $ATC_1$. The increase in marginal cost limits the* *movement of the market supply curve to $S_3$. Thus, $S_1$ is not attained. Entry stops at a higher price ($P_3$ instead of $P_1$).*

# PRACTICE PROBLEM

1.  Let's start with the information in the Worked Problem.

    a.  Draw and explain the initial equilibrium again and show the short-run effects of the root disease.

    b.  The root disease causes the price of Z infandel grapes to rise. Grape buyers see this and realize that other grapes are now relatively less expensive. What might happen over the short run to the market for red grapes, a well-known substitute for Z infandel grapes?

    c.  Describe the long-run effects in the red grape market.

    d.  Assume that red grape growers experience external economies of scale as the market expands. How does this alter your answer to part (c)?

    e.  What possible effects could the external economies of scale have on the Z infandel grape market?

# CHAPTER TEST

1.  Fred Smith founded

    a.  Federal Express.
    b.  UPS.
    c.  Disneyland.
    d.  Houghton Mifflin Company.

2.  A group of firms producing a similar product is a(n)

    a.  industry.
    b.  manufacturing sector.
    c.  entire market.
    d.  sign of collusion.

3.  In a competitive market,

    a.  a single firm perceives its demand curve as the market demand curve.
    b.  a single firm perceives market demand as a horizontal line, even though the actual market demand curve is downward sloping.
    c.  a single firm perceives market demand to be perfectly inelastic.
    d.  a single firm perceives market demand to be unit elastic.

4.  In long-run competitive equilibrium,

    a.  individual firms can earn economic profits.
    b.  individual firms earn normal profits and the entire market is in equilibrium.
    c.  individual firms earn normal profits and the entire market maintains excess demand.
    d.  individual firms earn economic profits and the entire market is in equilibrium.

5.  Normal profits

    a.  are equal to zero in long-run equilibrium.
    b.  are an explicit opportunity cost to the business.
    c.  are an implicit opportunity cost to the business.

    d.    must be greater than zero to encourage entry.

6.    The actual market demand curve is

    a.    horizontal at the market price.
    b.    always vertical in the long run.
    c.    downward sloping.
    d.    upward sloping.

7.    Exit

    a.    causes a decrease in supply.
    b.    causes a decrease in demand.
    c.    causes an increase in demand.
    d.    causes an increase in supply.

8.    *Ceteris paribus*, an increase in demand results in

    a.    an increase in price.
    b.    an increase in supply.
    c.    a decrease in the quantity demanded.
    d.    a decrease in supply.

9.    If economic profits are zero,

    a.    firms exit the market.
    b.    firms enter the market.
    c.    normal profits are zero.
    d.    then $P > ATC$ and $P = MC$.

10.    _____ provide the incentive for firms to enter a market.

    a.    Positive normal profits
    b.    Zero economic profits
    c.    Positive economic profits
    d.    Zero normal profits

11.    If economic profits are greater than zero,

    a.    firms exit the market.
    b.    firms enter the market.
    c.    firms remain in the market as long as normal profits are positive.
    d.    then normal profits must be zero.

12.    Economic profits

    a.    can result only from an increase in demand.
    b.    can result if $ATC$ falls below the original market price.
    c.    are an implicit opportunity cost to the owner.
    d.    result if $P = ATC$.

13.    In a competitive market,

    a.    $MC$ is minimized over the long run.
    b.    $AVC$ is equal to the market price over the long run.
    c.    entry will never stop.
    d.    $ATC$ is minimized over the long run.

14. In a competitive market, over the long run, *ATC* is minimized because

    a. individual firms perceive the market demand curve to be perfectly inelastic.
    b. individual firms perceive the market demand curve to be unit elastic.
    c. individual firms perceive the market demand curve to be vertical.
    d. individual firms perceive the market demand curve to be horizontal.

15. With external economies of scale present,

    a. the long-run industry supply curve will be downward sloping.
    b. the long-run industry supply curve will be horizontal.
    c. the long-run industry supply curve will be upward sloping.
    d. the long-run industry supply curve will be a hyperbola.

16. With external diseconomies of scale present,

    a. the long-run industry supply curve will be downward sloping.
    b. the long-run industry supply curve will be horizontal.
    c. the long-run industry supply curve will be upward sloping.
    d. the long-run industry supply curve will be a hyperbola.

# ANSWERS TO THE REVIEW QUESTIONS

## Fill-In Questions

1. industry
2. goods; services
3. long-run competitive equilibrium model
4. downward sloping; horizontal or perfectly elastic
5. Entry; exit
6. Economic profits; implicit; explicit
7. economic profits; negative
8. economic profits; entry; exit
9. market supply curve; entry; exit
10. New products; changes in costs
11. price; marginal cost; average total cost
12. average total cost
13. external diseconomies of scale; external economies of scale
14. horizontal

## True-False Questions

1. **True**.    This is only true in the long run.
2. **False**.    A single firm in a competitive market perceives demand to be perfectly elastic, or horizontal at the market price. This is based on the notion that a single firm in a competitive market takes price as given.

3.    **False.**    The market supply curve is the horizontal summation of the individual firms' supply curves. Entry increases the number of firms, thereby increasing the sum.

4.    **True.**    Economic profits are earnings in excess of total costs. Normal profit is an implicit opportunity cost that is included in total costs.

5.    **True.**    Firms not in a market are attracted to that market by the economic profits of those in it.

6.    **False.**    Exit causes a decrease in market supply.

7.    **False.**    It is true that the entry of new firms causes the total number of firms to increase. However, existing firms may expand by investing in new capital. Thus, existing firms can get larger.

8.    **True.**    Both of these factors can create economic profits. This would stimulate entry.

9.    **False.**    Entry stops when economic profits are zero. This occurs when P = ATC. Because competitive firms face a horizontal price line, the only possible point of tangency would be at the lowest point on ATC. So, ATC is minimized and not AVC.

10.    **False.**    The long-run industry supply curve is upward-sloping when external diseconomies of scale exist.

11.    **True.**    External economies of scale shift the market supply curve to the right. This complements the effects of entry. The net result is a downward-sloping long-run industry supply curve.

## SHORT-ANSWER QUESTIONS

1.    Two basic graphs are used simultaneously. First, there is the supply and demand diagram representing a generic market. The market demand curve is downward sloping, and the market supply curve is upward sloping. This graph is used to determine market price. The second generic diagram is the per-unit view of a representative competitive firm. The market price is depicted by a horizontal line, and *ATC* and *MC* are represented as described in Chapter 8. Initial equilibrium is found where $P = MC = ATC$.

2.    The market supply curve is the horizontal summation of the supply curves of the individual firms in the market. When new firms enter, the sum increases, and the market supply curve shifts to the right. Holding demand constant, an increase in supply will result in a decrease in the market price.

3.    Economic profits and losses create the incentive for entry into or exit from a market. In the case of profits, owners of existing firms are earning above-normal returns. This attracts others into the market. Losses represent failure to earn normal profits, and exit results.

4.    Long-run equilibrium exists when there is no incentive for either entry or exit. Existing firms earn only normal profits, and economic profits are zero. This occurs when $P = ATC$.

5.    Yes. A firm producing a new product, especially one that is well received, probably earns economic profits. These profits attract others into the market.

6.    Economic profits are zero in long-run equilibrium. Firms in a competitive market perceive demand to be perfectly elastic (horizontal) at the market price. Graphically, the lowest point on *ATC*, its minimum, is the only point where it will be tangent to the horizontal price line, and so $P = ATC$.

7.    Yes. As a market expands, costs may rise for some reason external to the firm. This serves to slow or limit the shift of the market supply curve that results from entry. In the new equilibrium, the market price is higher than the beginning equilibrium price; the long-run supply curve is upward sloping. External economies of scale result in a downward-sloping long-run supply curve.

## SOLUTION TO THE PRACTICE PROBLEM

1.  a.   Figure 9.6 shows the market for Zinfandel grapes and a per-unit view of a representative vineyard. Initial equilibrium price and quantity in the market are given by $P_1$ and $Q_{M1}$. These values are determined by the intersection of the initial market demand $(D_1)$ and market supply $(S_1)$ curves. For a representative vineyard, at the beginning price $P_1$, the grower is maximizing profits $(P_1 = MC)$ by producing the quantity $Q_{F1}$ and making zero economic profits $(P_1 = ATC)$. The root disease causes the market supply curve to shift to the left to $S_2$. As a result, the market price rises to $P_2$. At this price, the representative vineyard expands production to $Q_{F2}$ and earns economic profits, shown by the area *abcd*.

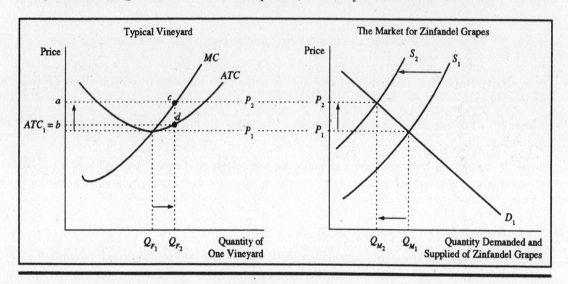

**Figure 9.6**

   b.   Because Zinfandel grapes are now relatively more expensive, the market demand curve for red grapes will shift to the right. This is shown in Figure 9.7. Initial equilibrium is shown at $P_3$ and $Q_{M3}$. The representative red grape vineyard is maximizing profits at $Q_{F3}$ and is earning only normal profits. With the root disease driving Zinfandel prices up, the demand for red grapes increases because red grapes are now relatively less expensive. This is shown by an increase in demand to $D_4$. As a result, the market price for red grapes rises to $P_4$ and market output expands to $Q_{M4}$. The representative red grape grower expands production and earns economic profits, shown by *efgh*.

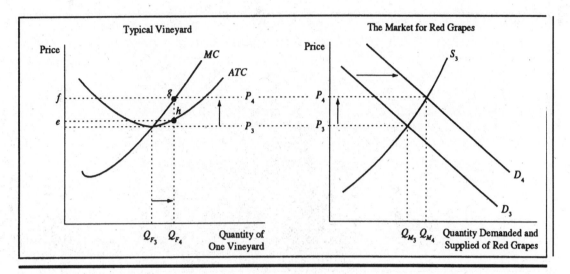

Figure 9.7

c.  New growers will be attracted to the red grape market by the economic profits. This shifts the market supply curve to the right, driving prices down. This will continue until economic profits are zero. Assuming that no external economies or diseconomies of scale exist, entry stops when price returns to $P_3$, or the supply curve shifts to $S_4$ (Figure 9.8). At this price, the representative grower reduces output back to $Q_{F3}$, and normal profits return. However, more red grapes are traded on the market ($Q_{M5}$) because there are more red grape growers.

d.  External economies of scale would cause the $MC$ and $ATC$ curves to shift to the right, as shown by $MC_1$ and $ATC_1$ in Figure 9.8. This $Q_{Fi}$ affects the market by shifting the supply curve out past $S_4$ to $S_5$. Thus, the market price falls below $P_3$ over the long run, and more red grapes are produced ($Q_{M6}$).

e.  Many effects are possible, but two relate to the events described in the exercise. The first is that the price of red grapes continues to fall as a result of the external economies of scale. In this case, the external economies contribute to making Zinfandel grapes relatively even more expensive as seen by the buyer. This may cause the demand for Zinfandel grapes to fall farther, so that the market continues to decline. A second possible effect is that the external economies experienced in the red grape market are transferable to the Zinfandel vineyards. In this case, the $MC$ and $ATC$ curves of Zinfandel growers would shift to the right. Economic profits would be earned again, which, over the long run, would encourage entry. The Zinfandel market would expand. Which of these two effects is likely? It is not possible to tell without more information. Can Zinfandel growers adopt the new methods quickly, or is their production function too specific? Also, what is the cross-price elasticity of demand between red grapes and Zinfandel grapes for buyers?

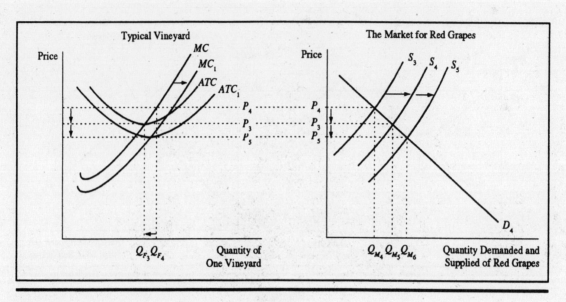

Figure 9.8

# ANSWERS TO THE CHAPTER TEST

1.  a
2.  a
3.  b
4.  a
5.  c
6.  c
7.  a
8.  a
9.  a
10. c
11. b
12. b
13. d
14. d
15. a
16. c

# CHAPTER 10

# Monopoly

## CHAPTER OVERVIEW

In this chapter, we turn to an evaluation of markets that are dominated by a single firm, or what economists call monopolies. To compare monopolies to competitive markets in terms of price, quantity, and efficiency, we need to understand how the monopoly decides how much to sell and at what price. In this discussion, we use much of the same logic that we used in Chapter 6 to understand the decisions of competitive firms. Monopolies, like competitive firms, are assumed to maximize profits, and they face costs just like other firms. The main difference, we will see, is that the monopoly has a certain amount of control over the price at which it will sell its product. As a result, a monopoly will sell a lower quantity at a higher price than would prevail if the same market were competitive, and as a result, markets that are monopolized do not yield an efficient outcome.

## CHAPTER REVIEW

1.  Economists classify industries into four different types, based on the number of firms that produce and sell the product, the ease of entry into and exit from the industry, and the degree of *product differentiation*, which refers to how similar or different are the products that the firms sell. We have already considered one type of market, the competitive industry, in which there are many firms selling the same product and free entry and exit of firms.

2.  A **monopoly** occurs when there is only one firm in an industry selling a product for which there are no close substitutes, and other firms are not free to enter the industry. Whatever prevents other firms from entering the industry is called a **barrier to entry**.

3.  To the economist, the difference between a monopoly and a competitive firm is not in the firm's goals. Both are assumed to maximize profit. Instead, the difference lies in how the firm can achieve that goal. The competitive firm is a price-taker; it can choose how much to sell at the market price, but its output is so small compared to the total in the market that its decision concerning how much to sell has no perceptible effect on the price. The monopoly, on the other hand, has **market power**; it can set the market price without reducing its sales to zero. Or, put somewhat differently, the monopoly can choose the price at which it wishes to sell, and is therefore a **price-maker**. The monopoly takes into account the effect of its sales on the price it receives for its output, something the competitive firm doesn't need to do because there is no such effect for a competitive firm.

4.  The monopoly can control the amount it sells or the price at which it sells its output, but not both independently. If the monopoly chooses to set the price, consumers' demand will determine how much gets purchased, and if the monopoly chooses a quantity to supply, consumers' demand will determine what price it can charge in order to sell that quantity. But, unlike the competitive firm, the monopoly can raise the price of its product without losing all of its customers because there are no other sellers for customers to switch to and no close substitutes for the product. Similarly, unlike the competitive firm, whose sales are only a tiny fraction of the total market supply, the monopoly's decision to restrict the quantity it offers for sale by a considerable amount has a

considerable effect on the total quantity available to consumers because its output is all the output available.

5.  One way to see that the monopoly can choose price or quantity, but not both independently, is to look at the demand curves for their output that the competitive firm and the monopoly see. The demand curve for its output that the competitive firm sees is horizontal (perfectly elastic) at the market price. Customers are willing to buy any amount the competitive firm wishes to sell at that price, but if it tries to sell at even a slightly higher price, it loses all its customers to other firms in the market. The monopoly, on the other hand, faces a demand curve for its output that is the same as the downward-sloping market demand curve for the product, because it is the only supplier in the market. If the monopoly chooses higher prices, then consumers won't want to buy as much, but because there are no other suppliers and limited substitutes for the product, quantity demanded will not drop to zero.

6.  As we saw in Chapter 6, each additional unit the competitive firm sells is sold for the same price, so that revenue increases by the price when one more unit is sold. In other words, for the competitive firm, the marginal revenue equals the price. But for the monopoly, which faces a downward-sloping demand curve, things are different. In order to sell another unit, the monopoly has to charge a lower price. Thus, selling another unit has two effects on the monopoly's revenues. First, revenue is increased by the sale of the additional unit at the slightly lower price. Second, revenue is decreased because in order to sell the additional unit, the monopoly has to charge a lower price for all its output, not just the last unit. As a result of these two effects, we know that marginal revenue for a monopoly must be less than the price at which it is selling its output. That is, if the monopoly is currently selling output for $P$ per unit, then if it lowers the price enough to sell one more unit, its total revenue will increase by less than $P$. In fact, if the second effect is large enough, total revenue can actually *fall* when the monopoly sells one more unit, although, as we will see shortly, no profit-maximizing monopoly will choose to produce an output so large that marginal revenue is negative.

7.  Since price declines as the monopoly's output rises, and since marginal revenue for a monopoly is lower than price, marginal revenue must also decline as output increases.

8.  The effect that selling one more unit has on total revenue depends on how much the price has to be reduced in order to sell that unit. In Chapter 4, we measured the effect of a change in price on the quantity demanded using the price elasticity of demand, and in fact, there is a relationship between the marginal revenue for a monopoly and the elasticity of demand that it faces for its output. Marginal revenue is negative when the demand for the product is inelastic, or in other words has a price elasticity less than 1. A monopolist will never produce a quantity in the inelastic portion of its demand curve; since increasing output lowers revenue in that portion, *reducing* output increases revenue and lowers cost, and therefore clearly makes profit go up.

9.  Another way to see that marginal revenue is less than the price at every quantity (except the first unit of output) is to recognize that the price the firm charges is also the firm's **average revenue**. This is easy to see; since total revenue is price times quantity, average revenue, which is total revenue divided by quantity, equals price. Recall that any time an average is falling as additional units are added, the marginal contribution of those additional units must be less than the average. So if average revenue, which is price, is falling (downward-sloping demand), then marginal revenue must be below average revenue.

10. We can now put together the revenue that the monopoly receives from its sales with the costs that the monopoly incurs to produce its output. Monopolies have to acquire inputs in order to produce their products just as competitive firms do, and so we can use the same cost measurements (average cost, marginal cost) that we discussed in Chapters 6 and 8 to describe the monopoly's

costs. Like that for a competitive firm, the monopoly's total cost curve is rising as output rises, and marginal cost also increases as output increases.

11. To find the monopoly's profit-maximizing level of output, we can look at a table of total revenue and total costs for different levels of output and find the one that gives the largest difference between revenue and cost. We can also do this graphically by plotting total revenue and total costs at different levels of output and looking for the output that gives the greatest vertical distance between the two curves.

12. We can also apply the logic that we developed in Chapter 6 to find the profit-maximizing output level for a monopoly. Remember, in order to maximize profit, a firm should sell any unit that adds more to revenue than it adds to cost. We stated that rule as *produce that quantity for which marginal revenue equals marginal cost*, and we said that in the case of the price-taking firm, marginal revenue is equal to price. This logic and rule still hold for a monopoly; the only difference is that the monopoly is not a price-taking firm and so marginal revenue for the monopoly is below price. But the monopoly can still find its profit-maximizing output level by *producing up to the level of output where marginal cost equals marginal revenue (MR = MC)*.

13. We can combine the demand and marginal revenue curves facing a monopoly with the cost curves facing the monopoly in the same way that we combined the demand curve and cost curves facing a competitive firm in Chapter 8. Figure 10.1 shows this information on one diagram.

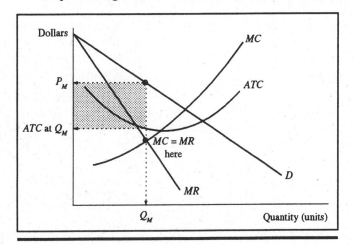

**Figure 10.1**

14. From Figure 10.1, we can find the monopoly's profit-maximizing output. First, find the point where the marginal revenue curve and the marginal cost curve cross. Draw a vertical line down from this point to the horizontal axis. The quantity at which this line hits the axis ($Q_M$) is the quantity for which marginal cost equals marginal revenue, so it is the profit-maximizing quantity.

15. To find the price at which the monopoly sells, extend the vertical line above the monopoly quantity up to the demand curve, and then go horizontally to the left to the vertical axis. Since the demand curve tells us how much will be demanded at each price, this price ($P_M$) is the price that the monopoly must charge if it wants to sell the profit-maximizing quantity.

16. To measure the profits that the monopoly makes by selling the monopoly quantity at the monopoly price, we need to find the monopoly's total revenue and total costs. Total revenue is simply price times quantity, so it appears on the diagram as the area of the rectangle with a height equal to the monopoly price and a base equal to the monopoly quantity. Total costs can be calculated by multiplying average total costs (that is, total costs divided by output) by the number of units produced. Total costs are thus equal to the area of a rectangle with a base equal to the

monopoly quantity and a height equal to the average total cost associated with producing that quantity (labeled "$ATC$ at $Q_M$" in Figure 10.1). The difference between these rectangles in the diagram is the shaded rectangle with a base equal to the monopoly quantity and a height equal to monopoly price minus average total cost at the monopoly quantity. The area of this rectangle measures the monopoly's profits. It is the amount by which each unit sells above average cost times the number of units sold.

17.   If there are barriers to the entry of new firms, the monopoly can earn these profits year after year. Remember that total costs (and therefore average total cost) already include the opportunity cost of capital, so these profits are economic profits; that is, they are above and beyond the ordinary return that investors can get by investing their capital in the next best alternative. If costs other than the costs of production, such as research and development costs or license fees that have to be paid to the government, are not included in total costs, they have to be subtracted from the profits computed in Figure 10.1 to get true profits.

18.   When the monopoly finds the quantity at which marginal revenue equals marginal cost, it may find that the price needed to sell that quantity is below average cost. This happens if the average cost curve is above the demand curve at that quantity. In that case, total revenue at the profit-maximizing quantity is below total costs, and the firm makes a negative profit. In that case, the firm will shut down in the short run, if the monopoly price is less than the average variable cost, and will exit the market if negative profits are expected to persist.

19.   In Chapter 7, we saw that competitive markets were efficient and maximized the sum of producer and consumer surplus. How does a market supplied by a monopoly compare with a competitive market in terms of equilibrium price, quantity, and consumer and producer surplus? We can evaluate the monopoly outcome by looking at Figure 10.2, which shows the monopoly's demand, marginal revenue, and marginal cost curves (we leave out the average total cost curve to avoid cluttering up the diagram too much). The monopoly quantity and price are found in the usual way: Find the point at which marginal revenue and marginal cost cross; then go down to the quantity axis and up to the demand curve and over to the price axis.

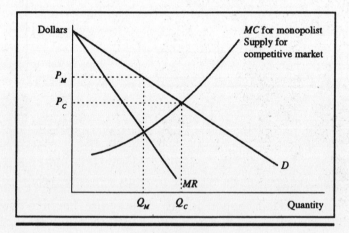

**Figure 10.2**

20.   Now suppose the monopoly were broken up into many small, price-taking firms. This would mean creating many new firms, each with its own marginal cost curve. These marginal cost curves would have to add up to the former monopoly's marginal cost curve, since that was what was broken up in the first place, and we know from Chapter 6 that the sum of the competitive firms' marginal cost curves is the market supply curve. So the monopolist's marginal cost curve in Figure 10.2 is also the competitive market's supply curve. We can find the equilibrium price ($P_C$) and quantity ($Q_C$) in the competitive industry in the usual way, by finding the intersection of the

supply and demand curves. Compare the monopoly price ($P_M$) and quantity ($Q_M$) with the competitive equilibrium price and quantity. The monopoly sells less output and charges a higher price than the competitive industry would.

21.  In Chapter 7, we saw that a competitive market maximized the sum of producer and consumer surplus, which was a measure of the benefits to producers and consumers from the good. The competitive market produces every unit that provides a marginal benefit to consumers that is greater than the marginal cost of producing that unit. We have just seen that the monopoly doesn't produce as much as the competitive market does, so there must be some units that the monopoly chooses not to produce that would add to consumer plus producer surplus if they were produced. This reduction in consumer plus producer surplus is called the *deadweight loss due to monopoly*. We can see how much it is, in dollar terms, by looking at Figure 10.3.

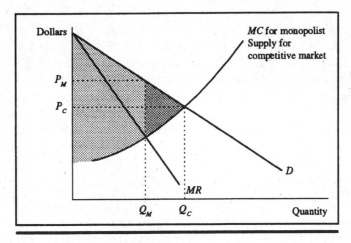

**Figure 10.3**

Recall that the sum of consumer and producer surplus is the area under the demand curve and above the marginal cost curve from the vertical axis out to the quantity that is sold. In a competitive market, the quantity sold is $Q_C$, and the sum of producer and consumer surplus is all of the shaded area, both lightly shaded and darkly shaded. A monopoly will sell only $Q_M$ units, and the sum of consumer and producer surplus is only the lightly shaded area. The darkly shaded area is the amount of producer and consumer surplus that is lost as a result of the monopoly, or the deadweight loss.

22.  Another thing that can be seen in Figure 10.3 is how the monopoly results in some consumer surplus being converted into producer surplus. The consumer surplus part of the total of producer and consumer surplus is the area under the demand curve and above the price that consumers are paying ($P_C$ in the case of competition, $P_M$ in the case of monopoly). Some part of the surplus that would be received by consumers if the market were competitive is lost in the deadweight loss, but another part is transferred to the monopoly. This is measured by the area of the rectangle between $P_M$ and $P_C$ vertically and out to $Q_M$ horizontally. This isn't a loss to society, since the monopolist is a member of society too, but it is a change in the distribution of income.

23.  Remember that it makes sense to compare monopoly provision of a good with competitive provision of that good only if competition really is a viable alternative. For example, in the case of natural monopolies, where costs would be much higher if the firms were small, it wouldn't be desirable to break up the monopoly.

24.  Another way to think about the harm done by a monopoly is to think about the fact that in the monopoly equilibrium, price is greater than marginal cost. Recall from Chapter 5 that consumers buy up to the point where the marginal benefit of another unit equals the price they have to pay for

it; this is true whether the market is competitive or a monopoly. In a competitive market, price also equals marginal cost, so consumers buy up to the point where the additional benefit they get from the last unit they consume just equals the cost of producing it. In a monopoly, however, price is above marginal cost, so when consumers purchase up to the point where the marginal benefit equals the price, the marginal benefit is above the marginal cost. As a result, the next unit would bring more additional benefit to the person who would consume it than it would cost society to produce it, which is inefficient.

25. Economists often measure the difference between price and marginal cost by looking at the **price-cost margin**. This is given by

$$\frac{\text{Price - Marginal Cost}}{\text{Price}}$$

The difference between price and marginal cost is divided by price because a $1 difference is a lot on a $5 paperback book, but virtually nothing on a $10,000 car. If the price-cost margin is 0.25, that means that 25 percent of the price is a markup over marginal cost. For a competitive firm, price equals marginal cost and the price-cost margin is zero. The size of the price-cost margin depends on the elasticity of demand that the firm faces, because that determines how much the price has to be lowered to sell another unit and therefore by how much marginal revenue falls below the price. In fact, there is an inverse relationship between the price-cost margin and the price elasticity of demand facing the firm:

$$\text{Price elasticity of demand} = \frac{1}{\text{Price cost margin}}$$

A perfectly competitive firm faces a perfectly elastic demand curve (infinitely large elasticity) and therefore has a price-cost margin of zero. A monopoly facing a demand curve with an elasticity of 3 would have a price-cost margin of 0.33, meaning that 33 percent of the price was markup over marginal cost.

26. There are several reasons why monopolies might exist. A key issue is the extent of *economies of scale*. As we saw in Chapter 8, when there are economies of scale, there is a minimum size that firms have to attain if they are to have average costs as low as possible; that size is called the *minimum efficient scale*. If the minimum efficient scale is so large that one firm of that size can serve the entire market, there will probably be a monopoly in the market. Any smaller firm would not be able to survive alongside the larger firm. A **natural monopoly** occurs when average total cost is declining at every level of demand and the minimum efficient scale is larger than the size of the market.

27. Markets may be monopolized by firms that have patents or copyrights. A patent is a legally recognized monopoly in the production of a good or the use of a technology that is granted to the inventor by the government for a limited length of time (17 years) in order to encourage innovation. A patent prohibits others from selling that good or using that process without permission from (and often payment to) the holder of the patent. A copyright is a legally recognized monopoly for the author on the use of books, pictures, computer programs, movies, songs, and so on that is also granted by the government. It makes it illegal to reproduce and sell those writings without permission from the copyright holder. Copyrights and patents do not guarantee a profitable monopoly; there may be similar but different products that satisfy the same needs or other ways to accomplish the same task.

28. The government can also create a monopoly by giving one firm a license to produce some good or service and excluding other firms from producing that good or service. Again, there is no

guarantee that a monopoly created by a license will be profitable, as there may be substitutes available to consumers.

29.   Firms may also attempt to create their own monopolies by merging into a single firm or by driving their rivals out of business and then erecting barriers to entry to prevent other firms from entering the market. However, simply observing that there is only a single firm providing a good or service does not mean that the firm is a monopolist secure behind a barrier to entry. In fact, if entry is very easy, the mere threat of entry by other firms may be sufficient to induce the sole producer of a product to produce the competitive quantity and sell it at the competitive price. If the firm were to raise its price above cost, new entrants would jump into the market to steal the firm's customers and drive the price back down to the competitive level. When entry into a market is very easy, economists refer to it as a **contestable market**, and they are less concerned about the power of a single seller to raise price.

30.   So far, we have been talking about a monopoly that can only charge a single price for all the units of output that it sells. In that case, when the monopoly lowers the price a little to increase sales by another unit, it has to lower the price on all the units sold, not merely on the last one. But some monopolies are able to charge different prices for the same item. This is called **price discrimination**. Price discrimination can take several forms: selling the same product at different prices in different locations (so long as the difference in price doesn't reflect different shipping costs), charging different prices to customers who buy different amounts, or charging different prices to different types of buyers.

31.   If a monopoly can distinguish between consumers with more elastic demand and those with less elastic demand, and if it can keep those customers separate, it will be profitable to charge them different prices. Consumers with relatively inelastic demands won't reduce their consumption as much in the face of a price increase, and they can be charged a higher price. But if customers with relatively elastic demand are charged that higher price, it will lead more of them to stop consuming. Hence, it is more profitable to charge them a somewhat lower price. In order to price-discriminate successfully according to customers' demand elasticities, the monopoly must be able to distinguish those customers with relatively inelastic demand from those with relatively elastic demand and then prevent the latter from buying output and reselling it to the former.

32.   Another way for monopolies to price-discriminate is to charge different prices depending on how much is purchased. The monopoly can do this by offering customers the first units they buy, for which their marginal benefit is higher, at a high price, and the remaining units, which have a lower marginal benefit, at a lower price. To do this successfully again requires that consumers not be able to easily resell the item; otherwise, consumers would get together and have one of the group do all the purchasing to take advantage of the lower price. Price discrimination of this sort can lead to additional sales being made; after selling the monopoly quantity at the monopoly price, the monopoly can sell some additional units at a lower price without lowering the price on the first units sold. In this case, the total output sold moves closer to the competitive quantity, so deadweight loss is reduced, but more of the consumer surplus is transferred to the monopoly's profits. Price discrimination isn't *always* bad from an efficiency standpoint (at least, compared to a monopoly that can't price-discriminate).

33.   Any firm that faces a downward-sloping demand curve, not just a monopoly that has the entire market to itself, can benefit from price discrimination if the conditions are right (i.e., it can prevent reselling, etc.). Thus, we often see price discrimination in markets that have several rival firms.

# ZEROING IN

1.  First, recognize that most markets in our economy fall somewhere between the extremes of perfect competition and true monopoly. We will discuss some of the issues that arise when products are differentiated or when there are several producers but not enough to ensure competitive behavior in the next chapter. Nevertheless, the ideas you will learn from understanding how a monopoly determines its profit-maximizing price and quantity, and how that choice falls short of the efficient result that a competitive market could achieve, will help you to understand the outcomes in other market structures and other sorts of deviations from the efficient outcome.

2.  Remember that the difference between a firm with market power and a competitive firm is that the former faces a downward-sloping demand curve, whereas the latter faces a flat (perfectly elastic) demand curve. Both the monopoly and the competitive firm have production costs, and the same cost concepts (fixed costs, variable costs, average costs, marginal cost, and so on) apply to both types of firms. Both are assumed to be equally profit oriented. Economists don't assume that monopolies are greedier than competitive firms; each is trying to make as much profit as possible. Monopolies, however, are in a better position to make a profit because their consumers have few substitutes to switch to when the price is increased. The customers of a competitive firm have lots of alternatives (the other competitive firms producing the same product) if their supplier tries to raise price.

3.  The key to understanding the relationship between the downward-sloping demand curve facing the monopoly and the marginal revenue curve that lies below it is to recognize that we are thinking about a monopoly that cannot price-discriminate. When the monopoly lowers the price a little to sell a little more, it has to lower the price on *every* unit that it sells. You should think of the calculation "What would happen to my revenue if I lowered the price enough to sell one more unit than I am currently selling?" as going on in the monopolist's head *before* anything is sold. People sometimes get confused because they think that the monopoly has *already* sold the first $X$ units (and has the revenue received from their sale safely tucked away) before it lowers the price a little to sell the $X + 1$st unit, but that would be price discrimination—selling the same thing to different customers at different prices.

4.  Remember that the logic behind finding the monopoly's profit-maximizing level of output and price is exactly the same as that which lies behind the competitive firm's profit-maximizing output decision. If marginal revenue is greater than marginal cost, then producing and selling the next unit will bring in enough additional revenue to cover the added costs and have something left over that can be added to profits. On the other hand, if marginal revenue is less than marginal cost, then producing and selling the last unit didn't bring in enough additional revenue to cover the additional costs of producing it, and the difference had to be taken from profits. Cutting back production by one unit means that those funds can remain as part of profits, so profits will be higher. Following this logic always leads marginal revenue toward marginal cost.

5.  People often wonder where the deadweight loss due to monopoly "goes." The loss can be measured in dollars (as the area of the deadweight loss triangle in Figure 10.3, for instance), but it doesn't go anywhere or to anyone. It is a lost opportunity to provide output that has benefits to people that outweigh the cost of producing the goods. Efficiency requires taking advantage of any chance to make someone in society better off by an amount that exceeds the cost of doing so. By failing to provide units of output whose benefits outweigh their costs, the monopoly misses such a chance, and the result is an inefficient outcome.

6.  At the monopoly's profit-maximizing equilibrium, the next unit is worth more to some consumer than it would cost to produce it, although it is worth somewhat less than the monopoly price (which is why that consumer doesn't buy the next unit at the monopoly price). Why doesn't the

monopoly strike a deal with that consumer and sell him or her the next unit at some price above marginal cost but below the most that the consumer would be willing to pay? The answer is that if the monopoly cannot price-discriminate, it would have to lower the price to every buyer in order to make that additional sale, and the lost revenue from that price reduction would outweigh what it could gain by selling another unit. That is why marginal revenue is less than price (and at the monopoly's equilibrium is equal to marginal cost). But if the monopoly *can* price-discriminate, it can strike the deal just described, which would make both the monopoly and the consumer better off and not make anyone else worse off. That is why price discrimination *can* lead to a more efficient level of output.

## ACTIVE REVIEW

## Fill-In Questions

1.  A _____ is a market which consists of only one firm that is protected by a(n) _____.

2.  Monopolies are called _____, since they can decide what price to charge for their good.

3.  _____ is a firm's ability to _____ without losing all its customers.

4.  Marginal revenue is the _____generated from selling _____ .

5.  In a competitive industry, each firm's marginal revenue equals _____. For a monopoly, marginal revenue is _____ than the _____, and the marginal revenue curve lies _____ the demand curve.

6.  One way to determine the profit-maximizing output is by comparing total _____ and total _____. Another way is by equating _____ revenue and _____ cost.

7.  To maximize _____, a monopoly should produce up to the level of output where the _____ from the last unit sold just _____ the _____ of producing the last unit of the good.

8.  The monopolist's profit-maximizing price is *not* where _____ and _____ intersect; instead, it is found by finding the price on the _____ above the monopolist's profit-maximizing output.

9.  When we compare a competitive industry to a monopoly, we find that the price is _____ in a monopoly and that quantity produced is _____.

10. The decrease in _____ and _____ surplus that results from a monopoly's producing less output than a competitive market would produce is called the _____ loss due to monopoly.

11. Another way to see the inefficiency created by a monopoly is to see that the marginal _____ of the last unit of the good to the consumer is greater than the _____ of producing that unit.

12. The difference between the _____ of a good and its _____ (as a fraction of the price) is called the _____ margin. For a competitive industry, this is _____.

13. A _____ is an industry in which economies of scale persist at every level of demand. In this case, the _____ is as large as the market, and there will probably be _____ in the market.

14. Cable television companies and the U.S. Postal Service are monopolies as the result of the government's granting an exclusive _____ to particular companies.

15. _____ occurs when a firm charges different customers different prices for the same good.

16. Price discrimination can help a monopoly increase its _____ if the monopoly can capitalize on the fact that different groups of customers have different _____ of demand.

## True-False Questions

1.  T  F  A firm will have market power when there are good substitutes for the good being produced and entry into the industry is relatively easy.

2.  T  F  A monopoly can charge any price that it wishes without regard to the market or the demand for the good.

3.  T  F  Competitive firms can't raise their price above the competitive level without losing all their customers to other sellers, but a monopolist doesn't face this constraint.

4.  T  F  When a monopoly raises its price, the quantity demanded of the good will decrease to zero.

5.  T  F  Marginal revenue increases as more is produced, since the firm is selling more of the good.

6.  T  F  A monopolist's price lies below the demand curve.

7.  T  F  A monopoly maximizes profits when its price equals its marginal cost.

8.  T  F  If the marginal revenue for a good is less than the marginal cost of the good, the firm will produce at least one more unit of the good.

9.  T  F  A monopoly will never have negative profits.

10. T  F  The loss created by a monopoly is measured by the reduction in consumer and producer surplus.

11. T  F  The price-cost margin for a monopoly can be determined through the use of the price elasticity of demand.

12. T  F  The XYZ Corporation is a pioneer in the field of virtual reality. One way in which it could gain a monopoly position in the industry would be by patenting its innovations in this field.

13. T  F  Examples of price discrimination are early bird specials at restaurants, student discounts for movies, and AAA discounts on hotel rooms.

14. T  F  The practice of price discrimination can be effective if the monopoly is unable to prevent consumers from reselling the good or cannot distinguish between groups of consumers.

## Short-Answer Questions

1.  Explain what is meant by market power.

2.  Why are barriers to entry essential for a monopoly to persist?

3.  Explain why marginal revenue is less than price for a monopoly.

4.  Explain how a profit-maximizing monopolist would decide what amount of product to sell.

5.  Do all monopolies make economic profits? Why or why not?

6.  When economists say that a monopoly is harmful to society because it is inefficient, what do they mean? Explain the inefficiency of a monopoly, using the ideas of marginal benefit and marginal cost.

7.  You stop into a gas station and buy 15 gallons of $1.39-per-gallon gas that cost the station $1.35 per gallon wholesale. You also buy a 69-cent cup of coffee that cost the station 25 cents to produce. Which product has the higher price-cost margin?

8.  Give three reasons why monopolies may exist, and explain them briefly.

9.  Senior citizens and children often get reduced prices on movie tickets. Are movie theater owners trying to do something nice for people, or can you explain their pricing on the basis of differences in the elasticities of demand for movies?

## WORKING IT OUT

1.  The key difference between a competitive firm and a firm with market power is that the latter faces a downward-sloping demand curve. As a result of this, marginal revenue for a firm with market power (that can't price-discriminate) is less than price. Understanding why this is the case is important to understanding how monopolies work.

2.  The most important thing to learn in this chapter is the monopoly's profit-maximizing output and price decision. Notice that this says "decision," not "decisions," because there is only one choice to make. It can be thought of as either a decision about price or a decision about quantity, but once a choice has been made about one of the variables, that choice determines what the other one will be. The monopoly's decision can be examined by looking at a table of data or by looking at a diagram, and you should be able to do either.

## Worked Problems

The following table gives the demand schedule facing a monopoly; that is, it tells what quantity will be demanded at each price the monopoly might charge.

| Quantity | Price | Revenue | Marginal Revenue |
|---|---|---|---|
| 1 | $11 | | |
| 2 | $9 | | |
| 3 | $7 | | |
| 4 | $5 | | |
| 5 | $3 | | |
| 6 | $1 | | |

1.  Calculate the firm's revenue and marginal revenue at each level of output, and fill in the appropriate entries in the table.

**Answer**

*Multiply the price by the quantity to calculate revenue. Then at each level of output, subtract the revenue received from selling one fewer unit from the revenue received at that level of output to get marginal revenue. You should get the following results:*

| Quantity | Price | Revenue | Marginal Revenue |
|----------|-------|---------|------------------|
| 1 | $11 | $11 | $11 |
| 2 | $9 | $18 | $7 |
| 3 | $7 | $21 | $3 |
| 4 | $5 | $20 | -$1 |
| 5 | $3 | $15 | -$5 |
| 6 | $1 | $6 | -$9 |

2.  At which level of output is the firm's revenue maximized? At which level of output does marginal revenue become negative?

**Answer**

*Revenue is maximized at a quantity of 3 units; the $21 received at that level of output is the highest revenue value. The marginal revenue of the fourth unit (and subsequent units) is negative.*

3.  Plot the demand curve facing this firm. Suppose that the firm sells 2 units this month and is contemplating increasing sales to 3 units next month. Show on your graph how much revenue the firm is earning this month. How much would revenue increase simply from the sale of the third unit? Show this on your graph. How much would revenue decrease as a result of selling the first two units at a lower price? Show this on your graph as well. Verify that the combination of these effects gives the correct marginal revenue.

**Answer**

*Plotting the demand curve facing this firm gives Figure 10.4.*

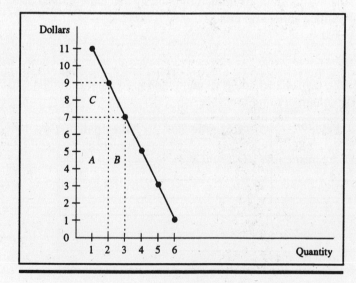

**Figure 10.4**

*If the firm sells 2 units at $9 each, it will earn revenue of $18, which is given by the sum of areas A and C on the figure. This is a rectangle whose base equals the quantity sold and whose height equals the price, and so its area is price times quantity, which equals revenue. In order to increase its sales to 3 units, the firm would have to lower its price to $7. The sale of the third unit itself would add $7 to revenue; this is shown in the figure by area B. Lowering the price of the first two units from $9 to $7 would reduce revenue by $2 × 2 units, or $4; this is shown in the figure as area C. Selling an additional unit causes revenue to change from area A + C to area A + B; area C is lost and area B is gained. Area B is $7 and area C is $4, and so marginal revenue is $3, just as we calculated in question 1.*

4.   Suppose instead that the firm sells 4 units this month and is contemplating increasing sales to 5 units next month. How would your answers to question 3 come out in this case?

**Answer**

*Figure 10.5 plots the same demand curve again.*

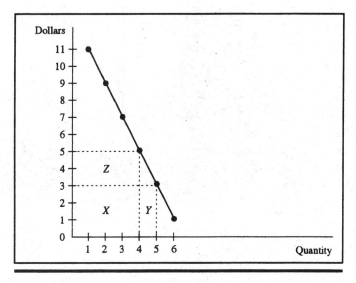

**Figure 10.5**

*If the firm sells 4 units at $5 each, it will earn revenue of $20, which is given by the sum of areas X and Z on the figure. This is a rectangle whose base equals the quantity sold and whose height equals the price, and so its area is price times quantity, which equals revenue. In order to increase its sales to 5 units, the firm would have to lower its price to $3. The sale of the fifth unit itself would add $3 to revenue; this is shown in the figure by area Y. Lowering the price of the first 4 units from $5 to $3 would reduce revenue by $2 × 4 units, or $8; this is shown in the figure as area Z. Selling an additional unit causes revenue to change from area X + Z to area X + Y; area Z is lost and area Y is gained. Area Y is $3 and area Z is $8, and so marginal revenue is –$5, just as we calculated in question 1.*

5.   Now, in addition to the demand schedule, suppose that you also know that the total costs of producing these different levels of output and the marginal cost of producing the first unit are given by the following table. Calculate the marginal cost for the second through sixth units of output and fill in the appropriate entries in the table.

| Quantity | Total Costs | Marginal Cost |
|----------|-------------|---------------|
| 1 | $3 | $1 |
| 2 | $5 | |
| 3 | $8 | |
| 4 | $12 | |
| 5 | $17 | |
| 6 | $23 | |

**Answer**

*By comparing the total costs at each level of output with the total costs of producing one fewer unit, we can determine the firm's marginal cost at each level of output. The results should be as follows:*

| Quantity | Total Costs | Marginal Cost |
|----------|-------------|---------------|
| 1 | $3 | $1 |
| 2 | $5 | $2 |
| 3 | $8 | $3 |
| 4 | $12 | $4 |
| 5 | $17 | $5 |
| 6 | $23 | $6 |

6.    Using the demand and revenue information from question 1 and the cost information from question 5, determine the monopoly's profit-maximizing quantity and price, and calculate how much profit the monopoly will earn at that equilibrium.

**Answer**

*By subtracting the total costs from the total revenue at each level of output, we can find the profit at each output level. You should get the following results:*

| Quantity | Revenue | Total Costs | Profit |
|----------|---------|-------------|--------|
| 1 | $11 | $3 | $8 |
| 2 | $18 | $5 | $13 |
| 3 | $21 | $8 | $13 |
| 4 | $20 | $12 | $8 |
| 5 | $15 | $17 | -$2 |
| 6 | $6 | $23 | -$17 |

*The firm maximizes profit by producing either 2 or 3 units of output; these give the same level of profit. If we assume that the monopoly produces any additional unit that doesn't lower profits (i.e., if there are two output levels that yield the same profit, the firm chooses the higher output), then it will produce 3 units, sell them at a price of $7, and earn $13 in profits.*

7.    Using the demand and marginal revenue information from question 1 and the total and marginal cost information from question 5, graph the monopoly's demand curve, marginal revenue curve, and marginal cost curve. *Hint*: Plot only the *positive* values for marginal revenue, and connect them with a line. Determine the monopoly's profit-maximizing quantity and price from that diagram.

**Answer**

*If you graph the demand curve, the positive points on the marginal revenue curve, and the marginal cost curve, you should get a diagram that looks like Figure 10.6.*

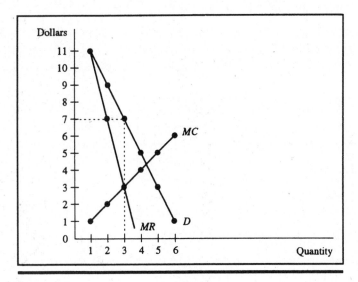

**Figure 10.6**

*Find the point where the marginal cost and marginal revenue curves cross, and draw a line down to the horizontal axis. This shows that the profit-maximizing quantity is 3 units. Extend that line upward to the demand curve and then horizontally to the left to the vertical axis to find the monopoly's price, which is $7 per unit.*

## PRACTICE PROBLEMS

The following table gives the demand schedule facing a monopoly; that is, it tells what quantity will be demanded at each price the monopoly might charge.

| Quantity | Price | Revenue | Marginal Revenue |
|---|---|---|---|
| 1 | $25 | | |
| 2 | $20 | | |
| 3 | $16 | | |
| 4 | $13 | | |
| 5 | $11 | | |
| 6 | $9 | | |

1.   Calculate the firm's revenue and marginal revenue at each level of output, and fill in the appropriate entries in the table.

2.   At which level of output is the firm's revenue maximized? At which level of output does marginal revenue become negative?

3.   Now plot the demand curve facing this firm. Suppose that the firm sells 2 units this month and is contemplating increasing sales to 3 units next month. Show on your graph how much revenue the firm is earning this month. How much would revenue increase simply from the sale of the third unit? Show this on your graph. How much would revenue decrease as a result of selling the first 2

units at a lower price? Show this on your graph as well. Verify that the combination of these effects gives the correct marginal revenue.

4. Suppose instead that the firm sells 4 units this month and is contemplating increasing sales to 5 units next month. How would your answers to question 3 come out in this case?

5. Now, in addition to the demand schedule, suppose that you also know that the additional cost of producing each successive unit of output is $6, no matter how many units are produced. What is the marginal cost facing this monopoly? What are the total costs associated with each level of output?

| Quantity | Marginal Cost | Total Costs |
|----------|---------------|-------------|
| 1        |               | $6          |
| 2        |               |             |
| 3        |               |             |
| 4        |               |             |
| 5        |               |             |
| 6        |               |             |

6. Using the demand and revenue information from question 1 and the cost information from question 5, determine the monopoly's profit-maximizing quantity and price, and calculate how much profit the monopoly will earn at that equilibrium.

7. Using the demand and marginal revenue information from question 1 and the total and marginal cost information from question 5, graph the monopoly's demand curve, marginal revenue curve, and marginal cost curve, and determine the monopoly's profit-maximizing price and quantity from that diagram.

# CHAPTER TEST

1. Which of the following is *not* a characteristic of a monopoly?

   a.  There is only one seller of the good.
   b.  There are no close substitutes for the good.
   c.  Unlike competitive firms, the monopolist is primarily concerned with profits.
   d.  There are significant barriers to entry into the industry.

2. An example of a barrier to entry in the airline industry would be

   a.  the cost of buying a plane to fly between Chicago and Tampa.
   b.  a license for a gate at Chicago's O'Hare International Airport.
   c.  having a trademark on the corporate slogan "Fly Us! We Won't Crash!"
   d.  the need to find customers.

3. Which of the following statements about a monopoly is *true*?

   a.  A monopoly will need to restrict output if it wishes to charge a higher price for the good.
   b.  A monopoly has no need to charge a lower price when it wishes to sell more of the good.
   c.  A monopoly will always make a profit.
   d.  A monopoly can sell any quantity at any price that it wishes to charge.

4. Which of the following statements is *false* for a monopoly equilibrium?

   a.  Marginal revenue is less than or equal to price.
   b.  Economic profits are always greater than zero.
   c.  Price is greater than or equal to both marginal cost and marginal revenue.

    d.    Marginal cost is equal to marginal revenue.

Use the following chart for questions 5 through 9.

| Price | Quantity of Output | Total Cost |
|-------|--------------------|------------|
| 0     | 7                  | 89         |
| 2     | 6                  | 68         |
| 4     | 5                  | 50         |
| 6     | 4                  | 35         |
| 8     | 3                  | 23         |
| 10    | 2                  | 14         |
| 12    | 1                  | 8          |
| 14    | 0                  | 5          |

5.    What is the marginal cost of the third unit of output?

    a.    $6
    b.    $8
    c.    $10
    d.    $12

6.    The marginal revenue associated with the fourth unit of output is

    a.    $10.
    b.    $6.
    c.    $24.
    d.    $0.

7.    Total revenue is maximized at

    a.    2 units.
    b.    4 units.
    c.    5 units.
    d.    both a and b.

8.    The profit-maximizing level of output is

    a.    1 unit.
    b.    2 units.
    c.    3 units.
    d.    5 units.

9.    At the profit-maximizing level of output, total profit is

    a.    $6.
    b.    $14.
    c.    $16.
    d.    $36.

Use Figure 10.7, which shows the demand, marginal revenue, marginal cost, and average total cost curves facing a monopoly, to answer questions 10 through 14.

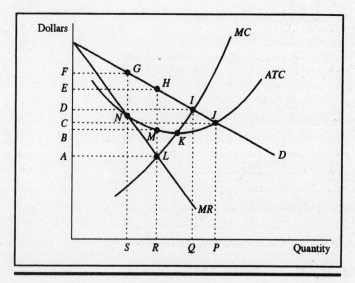

**Figure 10.7**

10. According to the figure, the monopoly's profit-maximizing output level is

    a. *P* units.
    b. *Q* units.
    c. *R* units.
    d. *S* units.

11. According to the figure, the monopoly's profit-maximizing price is

    a. $*A*.
    b. $*B*.
    c. $*D*.
    d. $*E*.

12. According to the figure and assuming no research and development costs or licensing costs, the monopoly's profit is

    a. area *BEHM*.
    b. area *OEHR*.
    c. area *OBMR*.
    d. area *OFGS*.

13. If this monopoly were to be broken up into many small firms, the competitive equilibrium in the market would be

    a. at point *J*, with price = $*C*, quantity = *P* units.
    b. at point *G*, with price = $*F*, quantity = *S* units.
    c. at point *H*, with price = $*E*, quantity = *R* units.
    d. at point *I*, with price = $*D*, quantity = *Q* units.

14. According to the figure, the deadweight loss due to monopoly in this market is

    a. area *HMJ*.
    b. area *LHI*.
    c. area *NGI*.
    d. area *KIJ*.

15. To the economist, monopolies are economically inefficient because of all the following *except*

   a. they charge a higher price than a competitive industry.
   b. they produce less output than a competitive industry.
   c. the price charged for the good is greater than the cost of producing the good.
   d. the marginal benefit of the good is greater than marginal cost.

16. A difference between a firm in a competitive industry and a firm that has monopolized its industry is that

   a. the monopoly can make an economic profit, but a competitive firm will never make a positive economic profit.
   b. the monopoly, through its pricing ability, will never have to shut down in the long run, since it can always increase the price of the good.
   c. the competitive firm always faces a constant marginal revenue curve, whereas the monopoly faces a downward-sloping marginal revenue curve.
   d. the cost curves of the monopoly will always be below those of the competitive firm, since the monopoly has economies of scale.

17. Allocative efficiency is *not* achieved by a monopoly because the

   a. monopoly overproduces, since it can ignore social costs.
   b. monopoly does not produce the good in a technologically efficient manner.
   c. last unit of the good is worth more to society than it is to the monopoly.
   d. marginal revenue of the monopoly is different from the marginal social benefit.

18. Which of the following does *not* contribute to the monopoly power of a firm?

   a. A patent or copyright on a product
   b. Exclusive control over a vital input for the production of a good
   c. A license from the government
   d. Charging a high price for the good in question

19. A natural monopoly can *best* be described as a situation where

   a. greater output would require another production plant.
   b. the government grants a license to only one firm to provide a good in a certain area, and the monopoly buys the license from the government.
   c. one firm can meet the demand of the entire market at the lowest cost.
   d. marginal costs are increasing greatly over average costs.

20. Which of the following would be considered a form of price discrimination?

   a. Selling delivered copies of the *New York Times* to consumers nearer to New York City at a lower price because transportation costs are lower
   b. Setting separate rates for residential and commercial users of electricity
   c. A restaurant offering a kid's menu selling smaller portions at lower prices
   d. An express delivery service charging different prices for overnight and two-day delivery of a package

## ANSWERS TO THE REVIEW QUESTIONS

## Fill-In Questions

1. monopoly; barrier to entry

2. price-makers

3.  Market power; raise price

4.  additional revenue; one additional unit of output

5.  price; less; price; below

6.  revenue; costs; marginal; marginal

7.  profit; marginal revenue; equals; marginal cost

8.  marginal cost; marginal revenue; demand curve

9.  higher; lower

10. producer; consumer; deadweight

11. benefit; marginal cost

12. price; marginal cost; price-cost; zero

13. natural monopoly; minimum efficient scale; one firm

14. license

15. Price discrimination

16. profits; price elasticities

## True-False Questions

1.  **False**.    When there are good substitutes for the product or entry into the industry is easy, a firm that tries to charge a price above what others are charging simply loses its customers.

2.  **False**.    A monopoly's ability to charge different prices is determined by what customers are willing to pay, or in other words, by customer demand.

3.  **True**.    If a competitive firm raises its price above the competitive level, other firms will undercut its price, but there is no one to undercut the monopolist's price.

4.  **False**.    When the monopoly chooses a price, quantity demanded will be determined by the demand curve.

5.  **False**.    *Total* revenue increases with the level of output (at least initially), but marginal revenue declines as more is sold. Marginal revenue is less than price, and price is declining with additional sales.

6.  **False**.    Marginal revenue lies below the demand curve.

7.  **False**.    Any firm, including monopolists, maximizes profits when marginal revenue equals marginal cost. However, for a monopolist, price and marginal revenue are not equal.

8.  **False**.    If marginal revenue is less than marginal cost, selling the last unit doesn't add enough to revenue to pay the additional costs incurred in producing that unit, and so a profit-maximizing firm will want to reduce production at least by that unit.

9.  **False**.    If fixed costs are high enough, average total cost may be greater than price at the monopoly equilibrium. In this case, the monopoly will continue to produce at a loss so long as the price is greater than the average variable cost; otherwise, shutting down the company reduces losses. In the long run, the monopoly will exit the industry if this situation is expected to persist.

10. **False**.    The loss due to monopoly comes from both producer and consumer surplus.

11.  **True**.    At the monopoly's profit-maximizing price and quantity, the price-cost margin is equal to 1 divided by the price elasticity of demand for the good.

12.  **True**.    Patents can produce a monopoly by prohibiting competitors from producing the product.

13.  **True**.    These are examples of firms charging different prices to different people for the same good or service.

14.  **False**.    If consumers can easily resell the good, those who are offered the lowest prices will buy for everyone and resell, and the monopoly will be unable to sell at the higher prices. Similarly, if the monopoly cannot distinguish between high-elasticity and low-elasticity buyers, it cannot charge them different prices.

## Short-Answer Questions

1.  A firm has market power if it faces a downward-sloping demand curve, which means that the firm would not lose all of its customers if it increased its price. This occurs if consumers have only a limited set of substitutes to which to turn when the price increases.

2.  If entry into a monopolist's market is easy, the monopolist's profits will quickly attract other firms who will undercut its price and move the industry back toward the competitive equilibrium.

3.  In order to sell another unit, a monopoly has to charge a lower price, which has two effects on the monopoly's revenue. First, revenue is increased by the sale of the additional unit at the slightly lower price. Second, revenue is decreased because in order to sell the additional unit, the monopoly has to charge a lower price for all its output, not just for the last unit. As a result of these two effects, we know that marginal revenue for a monopoly must be less than the price. That is, if the monopoly is currently selling output for $P$ per unit, then if it lowers the price enough to sell one more unit, its total revenue will increase by less than $P$.

4.  The monopolist should adjust production until its marginal revenue just equals its marginal cost. If marginal revenue is greater than marginal cost, then producing and selling the next unit brings in enough additional revenue to cover the added costs and have something left over that can be added to profits. On the other hand, if marginal revenue is less than marginal cost, then producing and selling the last unit didn't bring in enough additional revenue to cover the additional costs of producing it, and the difference had to be taken from profits. Cutting back production by one unit means that those funds can remain as part of profits, and so profits will be higher. Only when marginal revenue equals marginal cost will it not be possible to increase profits, and therefore profits will be at a maximum.

5.  No, not all monopolies make economic profits. Average total cost may be greater than price at the monopoly equilibrium. In this case, the monopoly will continue to produce at a loss so long as the price is greater than average variable cost or shut down to reduce losses otherwise. In the long run, the monopoly will exit the industry if this situation is expected to persist.

6.  Monopoly is harmful to society because it causes society to miss an opportunity to make someone better off without making anyone else worse off; that is, the monopoly chooses an inefficiently low level of output. At the monopoly equilibrium, the consumer who would purchase the next unit of output if the price were a little bit lower would get a marginal benefit equal to the monopoly price from that unit, and that price is greater than the marginal cost of producing that next unit. Thus, the consumer would be willing to pay enough to cover the additional cost of production and would still be better off after having done so and consumed the additional output, so that both the consumer and the owners of the inputs would be better off. But the monopoly, looking at the effect of lowering the price a little bit, sees that it would have to lower the price to all consumers

and that the addition to total revenue from the sale of another unit would not cover the additional cost, so it is not willing to sell the additional unit.

7. Although the difference between price and marginal cost is higher for the gas (60 cents difference) than for the coffee (44 cents difference), the drink has a higher price-cost margin because 44 cents is 64 percent of 69 cents, whereas 60 cents is only 3 percent of $20.85 (15 gallons × $1.39 per gallon).

8. Any three of the following: (1) economies of scale, which give a single, large firm a cost advantage over any smaller firms, (2) government licenses, which give a particular firm a legal right to be the sole producer of some product or service, (3) a patent or copyright, which gives an inventor, writer, or artist the right to be the exclusive supplier of a product, or (4) a decision by firms to monopolize a market by merging with other firms or undertaking strategies designed to drive their competitors out of business.

9. Children and the elderly may have more elastic demand for things like movies (that is, their demand may be more responsive to price) because they have lower incomes. Remember that people have more elastic demand for goods on which they spend a large portion of their income. A $5 movie ticket may be a large part of the allowance of a child under 12 or of the income of a retired person living on social security. Theater owners may find that they can sell more tickets to those groups by giving them a break on the price, while still charging a higher price to the rest of the customers who have a less elastic demand. If they charged everyone the same price (somewhere between the two prices they currently charge), they would lose more high-elasticity customers than they would gain low-elasticity customers. This price discrimination is made possible in part by the fact that it is generally easy to distinguish children and the elderly from other people, so that only those groups will be able to buy and use the low-price tickets.

## SOLUTIONS TO THE PRACTICE PROBLEMS

1. Multiply the price by the quantity to calculate revenue. Then at each level of output, subtract the revenue received from selling one fewer unit from the revenue received at that level of output to get marginal revenue. You should get the following results:

| Quantity | Price | Revenue | Marginal Revenue |
|---|---|---|---|
| 1 | $25 | $25 | $25 |
| 2 | $20 | $40 | $15 |
| 3 | $16 | $48 | $8 |
| 4 | $13 | $52 | $4 |
| 5 | $11 | $55 | $3 |
| 6 | $9 | $54 | -$1 |

2. Revenue is maximized at a quantity of 5 units; the $55 received at that level of output is the highest revenue value. The marginal revenue of the sixth unit is negative.

3. Plotting the demand curve facing this firm gives Figure 10.8.

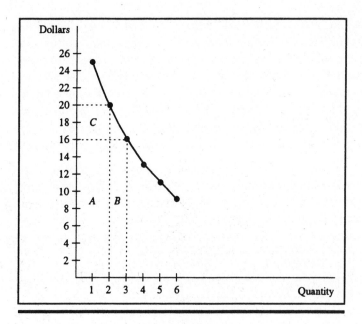

**Figure 10.8**

If the firm sells 2 units at $20 each, it will earn revenue of $40, which is given by the sum of areas *A* and *C* on the figure. This is a rectangle whose base equals the quantity sold and whose height equals the price, and so its area is price times quantity, which equals revenue. In order to increase its sales to 3 units, the firm would have to lower its price to $16. The sale of the third unit itself would add $16 to revenue; this is shown in the figure by area *B*. Lowering the price of the first 2 units from $20 to $16 would reduce revenue by $4 × 2 units, or $8; this is shown in the figure as area *C*. Selling an additional unit causes revenue to change from area *A* + *C* to area *A* + *B*; area *C* is lost and area *B* is gained. Area *B* is $16 and area *C* is $8, and so marginal revenue is $8, just as we calculated in question 1.

4.  Figure 10.9 plots the same demand curve again.

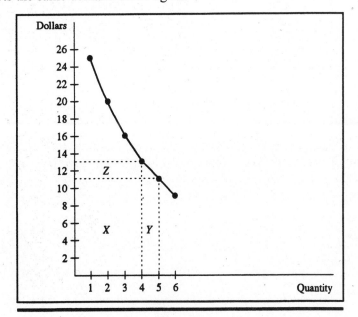

**Figure 10.9**

If the firm sells 4 units at $13 each, it will earn revenue of $52, which is given by the sum of areas $X$ and $Z$ on the figure. This is a rectangle whose base equals the quantity sold and whose height equals the price, and so its area is price times quantity, which equals revenue. In order to increase its sales to 5 units, the firm would have to lower its price to $11. The sale of the fifth unit itself would add $11 to revenue; this is shown in the figure by area $Y$. Lowering the price of the first 4 units from $13 to $11 would reduce revenue by $2 × 4 units, or $8; this is shown in the figure as area $Z$. Selling an additional unit causes revenue to change from area $X + Z$ to area $X + Y$; area $Z$ is lost and area $Y$ is gained. Area $Y$ is $11 and area $Z$ is $8, and so marginal revenue is $3, just as we calculated in question 1.

5.  Since each additional unit adds $6 to total costs regardless of how many units are produced, marginal cost is *constant* at $6 per unit. Note that this doesn't mean that total costs are constant; total costs increase by $6 every time another unit is produced. However, the *rate* at which total costs increase is constant. The table of marginal and total cost information should look like this:

| Quantity | Marginal Cost | Total Costs |
|----------|---------------|-------------|
| 1 | $6 | $6 |
| 2 | $6 | $12 |
| 3 | $6 | $18 |
| 4 | $6 | $24 |
| 5 | $6 | $30 |
| 6 | $6 | $36 |

6.  By subtracting the total costs from the total revenue at each level of output, you can find the profit at each output level. You should get the following results:

| Quantity | Revenue | Total Costs | Profit |
|----------|---------|-------------|--------|
| 1 | $25 | $6 | $19 |
| 2 | $40 | $12 | $28 |
| 3 | $48 | $18 | $30 |
| 4 | $52 | $24 | $28 |
| 5 | $55 | $30 | $25 |
| 6 | $54 | $36 | $18 |

The firm maximizes profit by producing 3 units of output, selling them at a price of $16, and earning $30 in profits.

7.  If you graph the demand curve, the positive points on the marginal revenue curve, and the marginal cost curve, you should get a diagram that looks like Figure 10.10.

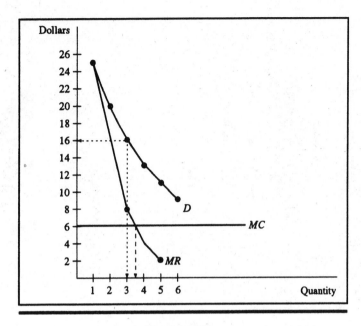

**Figure 10.10**

Find the point where the marginal cost and marginal revenue curves cross, and draw a line down to the horizontal axis. This shows that a profit-maximizing quantity is between 3 and 4 units. What's going on here is pretty simple. The third unit is profitable to produce; the marginal revenue from the third unit ($8) exceeds the marginal cost of the third unit ($6). But the fourth unit is not profitable to produce; its marginal revenue ($4) is less than the marginal cost ($6) of producing it. Since we are allowing this firm to produce only whole units of output, the profit-maximizing quantity is the largest whole number of units for which marginal revenue is still above marginal cost. In this case, that is 3 units. Extend a line upward from that quantity to the demand curve and then horizontally to the left to the vertical axis to find the monopoly's price, which is $16 per unit.

## ANSWERS TO THE CHAPTER TEST

1. c

2. b

3. a

4. b

5. b

6. d

7. b

8. b

9. a

10. c

11. d

12. a

13. d

14. b

15. c

16. c

17. d

18. d

19. c

20. b

# CHAPTER 11

# Product Differentiation, Monopolistic Competition, and Oligopoly

## CHAPTER OVERVIEW

In *competitive industries* where there are many firms selling the same product there is free entry and exit. The previous chapter addressed *monopolies*, where there is only one firm selling a product for which there are no close substitutes and where entry is impossible. In this chapter, we examine two other market structures: *monopolistically competitive* industries, in which there are many firms and free entry and exit as in a competitive industry, but in which each firm produces a product that consumers consider to be somewhat different from the products produced by the other firms, and *oligopolies*, where there are only a few firms in an industry and entry is difficult. We will use many of the same tools that we used in Chapter 10 (and some new ones) to study the decisions of firms in these types of markets, but we will see that the interaction of these firms leads to different outcomes from those that were arrived at in competitive industries or monopolies. As before, we will see how the outcomes in these types of markets measure up in terms of allocative efficiency, and we will look at some ways in which economists measure the market power of real-world firms.

## CHAPTER REVIEW

1.  We start this chapter by looking at monopolistically competitive industries, which like competitive industries have a large number of sellers and easy entry and exit, but which differ from competitive industries because the firms sell differentiated products. Since this is the key difference between competitive and monopolistically competitive industries, we first spend some time understanding what **product differentiation** is, how it comes about, and what its effects are.

2.  When different producers' products are indistinguishable from one another, we refer to the good as *homogenous*. For example, tuna caught by different fishermen are generally indistinguishable; if they were mixed together, no fisherman would be able to identify the ones he or she caught. When different producers' versions of the same product are distinguishable and consumers care about those differences, the product is said to be *differentiated*. For example, there are many different brands of cat food, and cat owners have preferences about which they want to buy for their cats, so the cat food market exhibits product differentiation.

3.  Product differentiation occurs in the markets for many consumer products and also in the markets for producer goods or capital goods. For example, McDonnell-Douglas and Boeing, the two leading U.S. manufacturers of commercial airplanes, produce wide-body jets that are substitutes from the viewpoint of United Airlines, but are not identical aircraft.

4.  Product differentiation sometimes happens naturally (Swiss cheese and cheddar cheese just taste different), but firms often put a lot of effort and resources into deliberately differentiating their products. A firm may be able to earn a profit by making its product distinct in some way from the products of other producers and by showing or convincing consumers that its product is better than those of the other producers.

5.  Product differentiation helps us to understand **intraindustry trade**, which is the term for countries simultaneously importing and exporting the same product. Much of the trade between countries takes the form of one country exporting one good and importing another. This pattern of trade, called **interindustry trade**, is explained by comparative advantage; countries export the goods that they produce most cheaply and import the goods that they can produce only at higher cost. If a country simultaneously imports and exports the same good, however, it can't be producing that good both more cheaply and at higher cost at the same time. The explanation, instead, lies in product differentiation. For example, the United States both imports clothing from France and exports clothing to France. The reason is that French fashions and American fashions are different in the eyes of consumers in both countries, so we are really importing and exporting two different products, French clothing and American clothing.

6.  Product differentiation also helps to explain why there is so much advertising in the economy. Advertising allows a firm both to inform consumers about actual differences between its product and those of its rivals and to get people to think that there are differences between products.

7.  As a result of product differentiation, consumers have many different versions of a product from which to choose. Making a good choice involves knowing about the alternatives, and it would be very costly for consumers to gather all the necessary information themselves by testing the products. As a result, there are consumer information services that do the testing and provide the information to consumers.

8.  Products can be differentiated in several ways. They can be physically different, located in different places, or available at different points in time. For example, high-tops and low-tops, a soft drink in your backpack and a soft drink at the student union, and the 7 o'clock showing and the 9 o'clock showing of a movie are all close substitutes, but are not exactly the same thing to some consumers.

9.  From the viewpoint of the firm, product differentiation may be a profitable strategy. Producing a new version of a product can add to revenues by attracting consumers who prefer your version to those produced by other firms, but it will also add to your costs in the form of research and development costs and marketing and sales costs. We can apply the same sort of marginal revenue and marginal cost analysis that we developed in Chapter 6 to understand the firm's decision about how much product differentiation to undertake. So long as the marginal revenue that results from an additional differentiated product outweighs the marginal cost of achieving it, then the additional differentiated product adds enough to revenue to cover the additional cost and leave something to be added to profits. On the other hand, if the marginal cost of the last differentiated product was greater than the marginal revenue, then the last product didn't bring in enough additional revenue to cover its additional cost, and the difference has to come from profits. Cutting back on product differentiation a bit means that those funds can remain as part of profits, so profits are higher without the last product. When the firm has carried out its product differentiation efforts to the profit-maximizing level, the marginal cost of product differentiation will just equal its marginal revenue.

10. When products are differentiated, the demand curve for each version slopes downward, and the firms have some market power. If any firm chooses to raise its price, it loses some of its customers to the other firms selling different versions of the good, but not all of its customers, because some people prefer this particular version and are willing to pay a bit more for it. In this sense, the producer of a differentiated product is like the monopoly we studied in Chapter 10. However, in **monopolistic competition**, unlike in a monopoly, there are no barriers to entry or exit.

11. Figure 11.1 shows the demand, marginal revenue, marginal cost, and average total cost curves for a monopolistic competitor in the short run. This figure looks just like the monopoly diagram from

Chapter 10. The difference is that the demand curve is for *this* firm's product (e.g., Levi's jeans) and not for the whole market (e.g., jeans). As a result, when new firms enter the industry, the demand curve for each existing firm shifts to the left as some customers buy from the new firms.

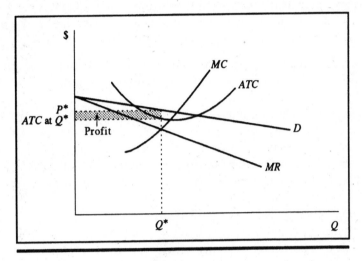

**Figure 11.1**

12.  In the short run, when the number of firms is fixed, the monopolistic competitor's decision about how much to produce to maximize profits is just like the monopolist's. The monopolistic competitor chooses the quantity for which marginal revenue equals marginal cost and charges the price that causes consumers to demand this quantity. The profit-maximizing quantity and price are shown in Figure 11.1 as well. If that price is greater than average cost, the firm makes an economic profit. If the price is less than average cost, the firm takes a loss. In Figure 11.1, the firm is earning an economic profit.

13.  In the long run, profits in a monopolistically competitive industry attract new entrants, just as they do in a competitive industry. Likewise, losses lead some firms to exit. So when equilibrium is reached in the long run and no more firms wish to enter or exit, the firms that are in the market must be earning zero economic profits. This means that the price equals average total cost. Figure 11.2 shows this situation. Notice that entry has caused the demand curve to shift to the left, and that in the long-run equilibrium, the demand curve just touches the average cost curve at the profit-maximizing quantity and price.

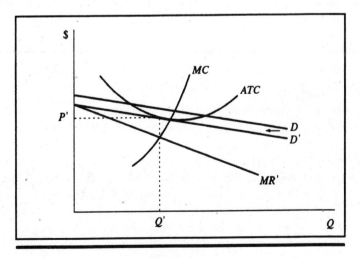

**Figure 11.2**

Thus, when a monopolistically competitive industry reaches long-run equilibrium, two things must be true. First, each firm must be producing the quantity for which marginal revenue equals marginal cost. If a firm isn't producing this level of output, it is not maximizing its profits and will want to change its output level. Second, each firm's price must equal its average total cost. If this isn't the case, firms will be either making a profit or taking a loss, and firms will want to enter or exit.

14. Let's compare the long-run equilibrium of the monopolistically competitive firm with the equilibrium of a firm in a competitive industry. You will see two things. First, since the monopolistic competitor has some market power, the demand curve for its output slopes downward; price is greater than marginal cost. This means that, like a monopoly, the monopolistically competitive firm produces an inefficient level of output. The marginal benefit of another unit of output to whichever consumer would purchase it if the price were slightly lower is greater than the marginal cost of producing that additional unit, but the monopolistic competitor doesn't produce that additional unit because selling it would mean lowering the price to *all* its customers. Second, the monopolistically competitive firm does not choose to produce the quantity that is at the minimum point on the average total cost curve, so that, unlike in the competitive industry, the output is not produced as cheaply as possible. By producing a little more, the firm could take advantage of additional economies of scale and lower its costs, but again, the monopolistic competitor doesn't produce that additional output because selling it would mean lowering the price; thus, the firm operates with **excess capacity** and **excess costs**.

15. When we looked at competitive markets in Chapter 7, we found that the long-run equilibrium of competitive markets had several desirable characteristics. One of the most important of these was that the equilibrium was efficient, in the sense that the sum of producer surplus and consumer surplus was maximized and there was no deadweight loss. We have just seen that the long-run equilibrium of the monopolistically competitive market, on the other hand, does involve some deadweight loss. Does this mean that competition is better than monopolistic competition? Not necessarily. Efficiency is one goal that society has, but it is not the only goal. If people value being able to choose from a variety of differentiated products, the cost of having some deadweight loss may be justified by the benefit of product diversity.

16. Monopolistic competition isn't the only market structure that lies in between competition and monopoly. When there are only a few firms in a market and entry is difficult, the market is an **oligopoly**. The key feature of an oligopoly is that the profitability of any one firm's actions depends on how the other firms respond to those actions. In this situation, a firm must make some prediction of how the other firms will respond to its choices when it decides how much to produce, what price to charge, how much to spend on advertising, and so on. When firms are aware of other firms' expected responses to their choices and take those expected responses into account when making choices, they are said to be engaging in **strategic behavior**. There are two ways to think about strategic behavior, the game theory approach and the conjectural variations approach, and we will look at oligopoly using both of these.

17. **Game theory** is a branch of applied mathematics that studies how people behave in situations that involve conflicts. A typical game of strategy used in such studies is called the **prisoner's dilemma**; the name comes from the scenario that it describes. Two suspected criminals are each offered the following bargain: If you confess and implicate your accomplice, the police will blame the entire crime on your accomplice and let you go. If both confess, they share the blame and will get half the sentence. If both refuse to confess, both will be convicted of a minor offense and get a light sentence. In this example, the best that the two prisoners can do overall is to keep quiet; in that case, they each get a small penalty for the minor offense. But each one has a strong incentive to turn in the other, for two reasons. First, if you turn in your accomplice and your accomplice doesn't confess, you will avoid even the minor penalty. Second, if your accomplice confesses and

you don't, you end up taking all the blame. No matter what your accomplice does, you are better off confessing. So self-interested behavior leads each person to confess and get half the sentence, even though they would both be better off if they both kept quiet.

18. What the prisoner's dilemma highlights is a situation in which the incentives are such that doing what is in their own self-interest doesn't achieve the best overall outcome for the people involved. The best thing the two prisoners could do, if they could make an agreement and stick to it, would be to keep quiet; this is called the **cooperative outcome** of the game because it would involve working together to thwart the police. Self-interested behavior would lead them both to confess, which is called the **noncooperative outcome**, because it results from each person's acting on his or her own. In a Nash equilibrium, players are highly unlikely to deviate from their final chosen strategy.

19. What does all this stuff about the police and accused criminals have to do with oligopoly? The answer is that similar situations, in which incentives arise that prevent self-interested individuals (or firms) from achieving the best outcome for the group, are common in economics. Suppose we change the story, so that instead of two accused criminals, we have two firms in a market for a homogenous product. Such an industry is called a *duopoly*, and it is the simplest type of oligopoly to study. Suppose the two firms' choices are to charge the monopoly price or the competitive price. If they both charge the monopoly price, they each get half of the customers and half of the monopoly profits, and if they each charge the competitive price, they each get the competitive profit, which is zero (the firms are not going broke, but are earning only the normal rate of return on their capital). But if one charges the monopoly price and the other charges the competitive price, the high-price firm gets no customers and takes a loss, whereas the low-price firm gets all the customers and, say, three-quarters of the monopoly profit.

20. This situation has the same structure as the prisoner's dilemma. The cooperative outcome, which is the best that the two firms together can do, is to make the monopoly profit and share it. The monopoly profit is, after all, the most profit that could be earned in this market if it were controlled by a single firm. There are several ways in which the two firms could achieve the cooperative outcome. First, they could engage in **explicit collusion** by making an agreement to charge the monopoly price and sticking to it. A group of producers who make an agreement about prices (or outputs) like this is called a **cartel**; as we will see in Chapter 16, it is illegal in the United States. Second, one firm could decide to match what the other firm did, and if the other firm charged the monopoly price, they would both share the monopoly profit; while there is no actual agreement between the firms and therefore no cartel, the result is the same. This is known as **tacit collusion**. The dominant firm in this case is sometimes called a **price leader**. Finally, the two firms could actually merge and become a monopoly, in which case the new firm will charge the monopoly price and earn the monopoly profit. Again, as we will see in Chapter 16, this merger would probably be illegal in the United States.

21. If the two firms can't achieve the cooperative outcome by a cartel agreement, tacit collusion, or merger, they both have strong incentives to charge the competitive price. First, if the other firm charges the monopoly price and you charge the competitive price, you get all the customers and earn more profit than you would if you charged the monopoly price too. Second, if the other firm charges the competitive price and you don't charge the competitive price as well, the other firm gets all the customers and you take a loss, which can be avoided by charging the competitive price. No matter what the other firm does, you make a larger profit by charging the competitive price than you make by charging the monopoly price.

22. Actually, those incentives to charge the competitive price are still strong even if the firms have entered into a cartel agreement to charge the monopoly price, but in this case lowering the price means cheating on the other members of the cartel. That is why cartels are so unstable; even

though it is profitable for firms to agree to raise their prices together, it is even more profitable to lower *your* price after the other firms raise *theirs*.

23. Although the prisoner's dilemma situation in the duopoly leads to a bad outcome for the two firms (they end up charging the competitive price and earn zero economic profits, when it might be possible for them to act cooperatively and earn the monopoly profits), you need to remember that this is good for society. Consumers benefit from the lower price, and we know that deadweight loss is reduced by competition.

24. If the two firms in the duopoly are going to interact in the market year after year, they may be able to avoid the noncooperative outcome. The reason is that if one firm cooperates now (by charging the monopoly price), the other firm can reward it by cooperating in the future, and if one firm defects now (by charging the competitive price), the other firm can punish it by being noncooperative in the future. A firm that has a reputation for being cooperative has a lot to lose if it stops cooperating, because that reputation is valuable. Thus, the outcome of the prisoner's dilemma game can be quite different depending on whether the game is going to be played once or repeatedly by the two players.

25. The incentive for firms to cheat on a cartel agreement also depends on how difficult it is for the other firms to detect their cheating and punish it. If a firm can lower its price and steal some customers from its fellow cartel members without their knowing it, it is more likely to do so. Cartels often look for methods to make their pricing public, so that it is easier to observe cheating and respond to it. This deters firms from acting noncooperatively and cutting prices.

## ZEROING IN

1. In this chapter, we look at two different industry types: monopolistically competitive industries with many firms producing differentiated products without barriers to entry, and oligopolies, with a few firms producing a single product with barriers to entry. You should realize that in the real world, markets may share features of both of these models. For example, what kind of a market is the market for college education? You might think that it is monopolistically competitive, since there are several hundred colleges and universities offering undergraduate education and each school is unique in its own way. But on the other hand, there are probably barriers to entry into this market, since it is very expensive to acquire the facilities and faculty to start a new college. Similarly, you might think that the market for soft drinks is an oligopoly, with very few firms producing the lion's share of the output, but Coca-Cola and Pepsi go to great lengths to differentiate their products in consumers' eyes. The important thing to remember is that the models in this chapter focus on different issues. The monopolistic competition model focuses on product differentiation, whereas the oligopoly model focuses on strategic behavior. Understanding those issues will help you to see what's going on when you look at things that are happening in real-world markets.

2. Monopolistic competition makes us think about the costs and benefits of product differentiation and diversity. Since we are never going to have perfect competition in every *variety* of every good, monopolistically competitive firms have a little bit of market power and cause some inefficiency in the market. Although inefficiency is a bad thing for society, since it means that there are some opportunities to have benefits that outweigh their costs that are being missed, it isn't the only bad thing a society can face. Eliminating product differentiation so that all markets could be competitive and efficient would not be desirable either. It would be a boring world if all cars looked the same and all ice cream was strawberry. Of course, too much diversity can be too expensive; do we really need 257 models of mountain bikes, particularly if making them in smaller batches adds $50 to the cost and creates a monopoly markup and deadweight loss as well?

The question for policymakers is how much product differentiation is worth the additional cost of production and inefficiency, and unfortunately we don't know the answer.

3.    The key to oligopoly is *recognized interdependence*; all the oligopolists understand that the profitability of their choices depends on the choices of the other firms in the market. So whenever one firm has to make a decision about how much to sell, or what price to charge, or how much to advertise, or whether to introduce a new line of products, it has to gauge what its rivals will do in response. Both game theory and the conjectural variations approach emphasize this. In the prisoner's dilemma and other game theory situations, the players ask themselves, "What is the best choice for me *if my opponent does that*, and what is my best choice *if my opponent does something else?*" In the conjectural variations approach, the particular choice that the oligopolist is considering is the same one that we considered for the competitive firm, monopoly, or monopolistic competitor, "How much do I produce?" (or equivalently, "What price do I charge?"), but again the focus is on taking into account what the firm thinks its rivals will do. So although the two approaches seem very different, they really are looking at the same thing.

4.    In both the monopolistic competition and oligopoly models, the firm's profit-maximizing decision is explained using the same words and diagram used for the monopoly's decision in Chapter 10, except that the demand curve represents the demand for the monopolistically competitive or oligopolistic firm's own output. In fact, we've already seen that even the competitive firm's profit-maximizing decision is a special version of the monopoly story, except that the demand curve for a single competitor's output is horizontal because the competitive firm can't affect the price, and hence marginal revenue equals price for the competitor. This should make it clear to you how important that monopoly diagram and the ideas behind it are. In each case, the firm finds the profit-maximizing output by producing up to the point where marginal cost equals marginal revenue. The differences between the market structures lie in what the demand facing the firm looks like and what it depends on: In competition, demand is perfectly elastic because the firm faces many competitors selling the same good, and it shifts to eliminate profits because there are no barriers to entry; in monopolistic competition, the demand curve slopes down somewhat because the firm's product is differentiated, but it still shifts to eliminate profits because there are no barriers to entry; in oligopoly, the demand curve's slope depends on how the firm expects its rivals to respond to its decisions; and in monopoly, the demand curve slopes down because the firm produces a good with no close substitutes.

## ACTIVE REVIEW

## Fill-In Questions

1.    Stores stock more than 50 brands of breakfast cereal, making this a good example of a(n) _____ product.

2.    In a(n) _____ industry, there are many firms selling a homogenous product, whereas a(n) _____ industry also has many sellers, but the product is differentiated.

3.    Companies selling differentiated products use advertising to _____ and _____ consumers of the differences between their products and their rivals'.

4.    In _____ there is easy entry and exit from the industry and the firm faces a(n) _____ demand curve for its product, unlike that for a firm in perfect competition.

5.    In the short run, a monopolistically competitive firm will maximize profits where _____ equals _____.

6. In the long-run equilibrium of a monopolistically competitive market, economic profits are driven to _____ by the process of _____ and _____ of firms.

7. An oligopoly is a market that is dominated by a(n) _____ firms.

8. In an oligopoly, firms are aware of and take into account the responses of the other firms in the industry in their decision making; this is called _____.

9. The _____ is an example from game theory that captures the idea that the outcome achieved is dependent not only on one's own actions, but also on the other player's actions.

10. In game theory, the best outcome that the players can achieve together is called the _____, whereas the outcome that they reach if both players act in their own self-interest is the _____. In the prisoner's dilemma, the second is _____ for both players.

11. A(n) _____ is a group of producers that coordinates their _____ and _____ decisions; this agreement is called _____ and is illegal in the United States.

12. Firms can sometimes act together as a _____ without actually communicating; this is called _____. For example, if the firms follow the pricing decisions of the largest firm in the industry, a situation called _____ occurs, whereby they can keep the price near the _____ level.

13. As the _____ example shows, firms in an oligopoly may have difficulty keeping their price high because each has an incentive to _____. This occurs because each can increase its _____ by _____ its price.

14. In repeated games, firms may be able to maintain the _____ outcome if they can develop a reputation for not _____.

15. In a _____ players are highly unlikely to deviate from their final strategy.

## True-False Questions

1. T  F    The product in an oligopoly market is always differentiated.

2. T  F    Product differentiation is very common in market economies and is seen in both the consumer goods market and the capital goods market.

3. T  F    Product differentiation helps to explain why countries both import and export the same product.

4. T  F    Despite selling differentiated products, monopolistically competitive firms have no market power because entry is free.

5. T  F    In the long run, the profits of a monopolistically competitive firm are zero, as the average total cost curve is tangent to the demand curve.

6. T  F    Product differentiation is good for society because people prefer a variety of products, but it harms society as well, because monopolistic competition implies some deadweight loss.

7. T  F    If there are positive profits in the short run, firms will not be able to enter a monopolistically competitive industry, because of product differentiation.

8.  T  F     In a perfect competition, there are only a few firms and one firm can control price, regardless of the actions of other firms in the industry.

9.  T  F     In the prisoner's dilemma game, the optimal strategy for Pete is to confess, no matter what Ann decides to do.

10. T  F     A cartel is a group of firms that agree to set the prices of their goods or set the output for the entire industry.

11. T  F     Making bids for public construction projects increases competition, since taxpayers can tell what each firm is bidding.

12. T  F     In a repeated game, the result will still be the noncooperative outcome, since there is still an incentive to deviate from the cooperative outcome.

13. T  F     When firms interact with each other repeatedly, they may be able to develop a reputation for keeping prices high and avoid competing.

14. T  F     Secrecy makes it easier for firms to agree on a price.

15. T  F     In a Nash equilibrium, players are likely to deviate from the final strategy they take.

## Short-Answer Questions

1.  What is product differentiation, where does it come from, and why does it give firms some market power?

2.  How is a monopolistically competitive industry like a monopoly, and how is it like a competitive industry?

3.  If the long-run equilibrium of a monopolistically competitive industry involves firms earning no economic profit, how do the firms stay in business?

4.  What are the advantages and disadvantages of monopolistic competition?

5.  How is an oligopoly like a monopoly, and how is it different?

6.  What do oligopolists have to think about when choosing their profit-maximizing price or quantity that monopolists and competitive firms don't have to worry about?

7.  Explain the difference between explicit collusion and tacit collusion.

8.  What do we learn about duopoly pricing from the prisoner's dilemma?

9.  Explain why collusive agreements often break down into competition and why repeated interaction by the firms may lessen this tendency.

10. What is a Nash equilibrium?

## WORKING IT OUT

1.  In the model of monopolistic competition, even though there are many firms producing close substitutes and entry and exit are easy, firms have some market power. The reason for this is that the different firms' products are not *perfect* substitutes because of product differentiation. Since firms have market power, their demand curves slope downward, and in the short run, their profit-maximizing decision is just like that of a monopolist: equate marginal revenue and marginal cost. In the long run, however, firms can enter and exit, so when equilibrium is finally achieved, no firm can be earning economic profits or losses because those would lead to further changes in the number of firms in the market. The key here is to be able to understand (1) why product

differentiation gives each firm some market power and (2) how long-run equilibrium is determined.

2. Economic games are often depicted in tables like Table 11.6 in the text. One player's choices are given by the columns of the table, and the other player's choices are given by the rows. The choices that the players make determine which cell in the table the players end up in, and each cell contains the winnings or losings of each player if that cell is the final outcome. In game theory, the key is that each player (firm) has control over its own decisions (price, quantity, advertising, or whatever), but the final outcome for the firm depends on *both* firms' choices. So to know what to do, each firm may have to predict what its rivals will do in response to its choices. The prisoner's dilemma situation is actually a bit simpler; the "defect" strategy gives a higher profit for the firm no matter what the other firm does. In game theory, a choice that is the best choice no matter what your opponent does is called a *dominant strategy*; however, game situations often have no dominant strategies, and so understanding one's rivals and predicting their responses become important.

## Worked Problems

1. Most college and university towns of any size have a large number of restaurants catering to students' tastes and budgets. Many of these establishments tend to have their own "niche"; pizza places, sports bars, sub shops are examples. Explain why it is that even though each restaurant has its own menu and clientele, no restaurant owner is likely to make more than the normal market return on his or her investment for long. Explain your reasoning with a diagram.

**Answer**

*Each restaurant offers a differentiated product; if the pizza place raises its prices slightly, some customers will go to the sub shop, but many will be willing to pay a slightly higher price for their food and drinks in order to enjoy pizza. Thus each restaurant has a certain amount of market power. However, if it is easy for people to open new restaurants (and the large number in many towns suggests that it is), and to earn a rate of return on their investment that is greater than the normal return an investor can earn elsewhere, opportunity-minded investors will open new restaurants to take advantage of the situation. This is typical of a monopolistically competitive market.*

*Figure 11.3 shows the demand curve and the marginal revenue curve for the pizza place; the demand curve slopes downward slightly and the marginal revenue curve lies slightly below the demand curve because the restaurant's owners can raise the price a little without losing all of their customers to the sub shop and others, but not too much. In the short run, the owner will want to sell food and drink up to the point where marginal revenue equals marginal cost and raise the price to a level that leads customers to want to buy that quantity. In Figure 11.3, that price is greater than average total cost, and so the restaurant owner earns an economic profit.*

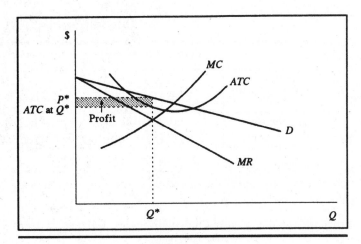

**Figure 11.3**

*In the long run, however, those profits will attract new entrants, and the demand at this pizza place will decrease as some customers switch to the new places. The demand curve will shift to the left until the profits are eliminated and the long-run equilibrium is reached, as shown in Figure 11.4.*

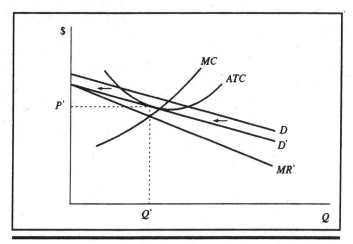

**Figure 11.4**

2.    Consider how AT&T and MCI use advertising to try to attract customers. Since most people in the United States know about telephones, advertising is not likely to get many people to install telephone service for the first time, but each company can try, through advertising, to convince some of the other firm's customers to switch to its services. How successful that strategy is depends, of course, on what the other firm is doing. If AT&T advertises and MCI doesn't, AT&T will be able to attract a lot of MCI's customers, and vice versa, but if both firms advertise, the effects of their ad campaigns may cancel each other out. Advertising is expensive; AT&T spent over half a *billion* dollars on advertising in 1989 alone.

The following table shows some hypothetical profits (in millions of dollars) that result from different choices of the two firms. The profits in the table reflect the fact that AT&T is a bigger company than MCI.

**MCI Strategies**

| AT&T Strategies | | Don't Advertise | Advertise |
|---|---|---|---|
| | Don't Advertise | MCI: $500<br>AT&T: $1,000 | MCI: $700<br>AT&T: $500 |
| | Advertise | MCI: $100<br>AT&T: $1,300 | MCI: $200<br>AT&T: $700 |

a.    If the two companies could agree on a level of advertising and stick to that agreement, what would they choose to do? Explain.

b.    If the two firms are not able to agree, what strategies will they choose? Explain your reasoning.

**Answers**

a.    *The best the two companies could do would be to agree not to advertise. This would give the highest total profit ($500 million + $1,000 million = $1,500 million) of all the possible outcomes. This is the cooperative solution in this example.*

b.    *Each company has strong incentives to advertise. If AT&T doesn't advertise, MCI earns $500 million if it doesn't advertise either (top left cell), but it earns $700 million if it does advertise and steals some of AT&T's customers (top right cell). And if AT&T does advertise, MCI gets $100 million if it doesn't advertise and lets AT&T steal its customers (bottom left cell), but it gets $200 million if it advertises to keep its customers or steal some of AT&T's customers in return (bottom right cell). No matter what AT&T does, MCI is better off if it chooses to advertise. If you check the numbers, you will see that the same thing holds for AT&T's choice. This is the prisoner's dilemma situation again. Both firms spend the money to advertise and end up with about the same number of customers that they would have had without the advertising campaign.*

## PRACTICE PROBLEMS

1.    There are many supermarkets in the San Francisco area. Since people are spread out over the city, each store has a group of local customers who live close to the store's location and shop there rather than incur the higher cost of traveling to a different store to buy groceries. Suppose that people's incomes are falling in California, so that the demand for food has decreased and supermarkets are losing money. Explain, with the use of diagrams, how the supermarket industry will adjust from the short-run equilibrium to a new long-run equilibrium.

2.    School is like an aerobics class. If the aerobics instructor does a bad job, you won't get into shape no matter how hard you exercise; you just waste time and effort, and you may hurt yourself. But if you don't work hard, then no matter how good the instructor is, you don't gain anything and the instructor wastes time and effort. Remember, no pain, no gain. It's only when the instructor and the student *both* put out the effort that the student gets in shape and the instructor enjoys leading the class.

It's the same with school. If your professor doesn't prepare his or her classes well, you won't learn much no matter how hard you study, and you just waste time. But if you don't study, you won't learn anything no matter how well your professor teaches, and your professor wastes time. If you study and your professor prepares well, you are both better off; you learn something, and your professor enjoys teaching the class more.

This situation has the basic structure of a game. Each person (the student and the professor) has to choose a strategy, and the rewards that each receives depend on both his or her own choice and the other's choice of strategy. The payoffs are something like those given in the table below. (It is probably best to think of the payoffs in terms of utility, not dollars.)

|  |  | **Professor's Strategies** | |
|---|---|---|---|
|  |  | **Prepare Well** | **Prepare Poorly** |
| **Student's Strategies** | **Study** | Professor: 10 Student: 10 | Professor: 0 Student: −10 |
|  | **Don't Study** | Professor: −10 Student: 0 | Professor: 0 Student: 0 |

a. What is the cooperative solution of this game (i.e., the one that yields the highest total well-being)?

b. What is the student's best strategy if he thinks the professor is going to prepare well? If he thinks the professor is going to prepare poorly?

c. What is the professor's best strategy if she thinks the student is going to study? If she thinks the student is not going to study?

d. (*Difficult*) In game theory, an equilibrium is a set of choices by the players in which, given what the other players are doing, no player wants to change his or her choice to some other strategy. Each cell in the game table is a set of choices, and to see if that cell is an equilibrium, you need to see whether either player wants to choose the other strategy, assuming that the other player doesn't change. Which cells in this game are equilibria?

# CHAPTER TEST

1. Which of the following goods has the *least* product differentiation?

   a. Ice cream
   b. Wheat
   c. Gasoline
   d. Toilet paper

2. Which of these differences between Bill & Joel's Chocolate Chip Cookie Dough Ice Cream and Dixie King's Cookies'n'Cream Ice Cream is *not* an example of product differentiation?

   a. There are differences in physical characteristics.
   b. Bill & Joel's and Dixie King's are sold in supermarkets and restaurants.
   c. Bill & Joel's is sold on Long Island, whereas Dixie King's is located in Atlanta.
   d. Bill & Joel's is sold only during the summer, whereas Dixie King's is sold all year long.

3. The United States imports motorcycles from Japan and exports motorcycles to Japan because

   a. Harleys and Hondas are not perfect substitutes.
   b. it's cheaper to manufacture motorcycles abroad than to ship them there.
   c. American companies can make a profit by importing Suzukis and selling them back to Japanese consumers.
   d. Kawasakis are cheaper in the United States than in Japan, and Harley Davidsons are cheaper in Japan than in the United States.

4.    The profit-maximizing number of brands of breakfast cereal to offer can be determined by

   a.    the amount of shelf space that a firm can get at a store.
   b.    the firm's tradeoff of the additional cost of a new brand against the additional revenue from product differentiation.
   c.    the number of children watching Saturday morning cartoons.
   d.    new processes for making sugar-filled candy that is "good" for growing kids.

5.    Which of the following industries *best* exhibits the qualities of a monopolistically competitive industry?

   a.    The diamond industry
   b.    The IBM-compatible personal computer industry
   c.    The corn industry
   d.    The steel industry

6.    Which of the following characteristics would be consistent with a monopolistically competitive industry?

   a.    There are strong barriers to entry in the long run.
   b.    There are few sellers in the industry.
   c.    Firms advertise a great deal.
   d.    Consumers view different firms' products as interchangeable.

7.    If the average total cost curve lies above the individual firm's demand curve, we would expect to see firms having a _____ profit and _____ taking place in the industry.

   a.    positive, entry
   b.    positive, exit
   c.    negative, entry
   d.    negative, exit

8.    Bill & Joel's Ice Cream was the first company to make cookie dough ice cream. As more and more firms start making cookie dough ice cream and other flavors, we would expect the demand curve for Bill & Joel's Ice Cream to

   a.    stay the same.
   b.    shift to the right and become steeper.
   c.    shift to the left and become flatter.
   d.    shift to the left and become steeper.

9.    In a monopolistically competitive industry, the short-run profit-maximizing rule is

   a.    marginal revenue equals average cost.
   b.    the same as a monopolist's.
   c.    price equals marginal cost.
   d.    marginal cost equals average cost.

10.    Which of the following is *not* a characteristic of a long-run equilibrium for a firm in a monopolistically competitive industry?

   a.    Profits will be maximized.
   b.    Price will be greater than marginal cost.
   c.    Average total cost will be minimized.
   d.    Price will equal average total cost.

11. Figure 11.5 shows a long-run equilibrium for a firm in a monopolistically competitive industry. In this case, the excess cost due to market structure is _____, and the excess capacity is _____.

    a.    $(P_A - P_B)$, $(Q_B - Q_A)$
    b.    $(P_A - P_C)$, $(Q_B - Q_A)$
    c.    $(P_A - P_B)$, $(Q_C - Q_A)$
    d.    $(P_A - P_C)$, $(Q_C - Q_A)$

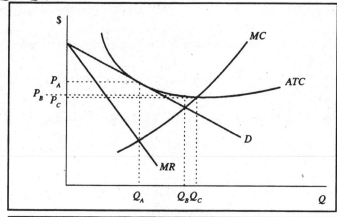

**Figure 11.5**

12. Which of the following characteristics is common to both perfect competition and monopolistic competition?

    a.    Average total cost is minimized in the long run.
    b.    Marginal revenue equals price.
    c.    Economic profits are zero in the long run.
    d.    Price equals marginal cost.

13. The prisoner's dilemma is

    a.    having to choose between pleading guilty and taking a reduced sentence or taking your chances with the jury.
    b.    a way to analyze and understand the interactions between firms in an oligopoly.
    c.    a tactic police use to get information from criminal suspects.
    d.    a game that O. J. Simpson plays with his lawyers.

14. In game theory, the cooperative outcome is

    a.    the result of each firm's acting in its own self-interest.
    b.    likely to be achieved as an equilibrium.
    c.    the outcome that yields the highest payoff to any player.
    d.    the outcome that yields the highest total payoff.

15. An example of an industry in which an agreement to fix price would be difficult to sustain over the long run (i.e., in which the firms will cheat on the agreement) is

    a.    one-price car dealerships.
    b.    retail milk.
    c.    airlines, where ticket agents have access to all prices.
    d.    highway construction, with sealed bids that are opened publicly.

16.   What distinguishes an oligopoly from other industry structures is

a.   strategic behavior.
b.   a downward-sloping demand curve facing the oligopolist.
c.   product differentiation.
d.   the possibility of profits in the long run.

17.   An example of explicit collusion is

a.   Microsoft making Internet Explorer part of Windows 95 to drive Netscape out of the Internet browser market.
b.   Archer Daniels Midland and two Japanese companies meeting in Hawaii to set the price of lysine, a feed additive.
c.   Delta and Southwest airlines matching the price set by United.
d.   Time Warner buying AOL.

18.   Cartel members have an incentive to cheat on the agreed price because

a.   cartels generally choose too low a price.
b.   cartel members are devious criminal types.
c.   they can grab a larger share of the market if they undercut the other members.
d.   they know that if they do, the other firms will match their price next year.

19.   If a final outcome of a strategic game is described as a Nash equilibrium, then

a.   players are unlikely to deviate from their final position.
b.   players are likely to deviate from their final position, suggesting that the game is unstable.
c.   the game is not in equilibrium.
d.   the players are in a prisoner's dilemma.

# ANSWERS TO THE REVIEW QUESTIONS

## Fill-In Questions

1.   differentiated
2.   competitive; homogenous; monopolistically competitive
3.   inform; convince
4.   monopolistic competition; downward-sloping
5.   marginal revenue; marginal cost
6.   zero; entry; exit
7.   few
8.   strategic behavior
9.   prisoner's dilemma
10.   cooperative outcome; noncooperative outcome; worse
11.   cartel; price; output; explicit collusion
12.   tacit collusion; price leadership; monopoly
13.   prisoner's dilemma; defect; profits; lowering
14.   monopoly; defecting

15.   Nash equilibrium

## True-False Questions

1.   **False.**   Although oligopolists can sell differentiated products, there can be oligopolies in markets for homogenous products as well.

2.   **True.**   Product differentiation of both consumer and capital goods is common.

3.   **True.**   If domestic and foreign versions of a product are differentiated, consumers in each country might prefer consuming both versions in order to have some variety.

4.   **False.**   Because consumers value the different characteristics of the products, they are willing to pay some premium to get the version they want. As a result, the firm can raise its price without losing all its sales, even though other firms are free to enter.

5.   **True.**   In the long run, firms are free to enter or exit a monopolistically competitive market and will do so until price equals average total cost and economic profits are zero.

6.   **True.**   The deadweight loss is part of the price society pays for variety.

7.   **False.**   Economic profits will attract new entrants to a monopolistically competitive market.

8.   **True.**   In perfect competition there are many firms, no one of which can affect the price of the product.

9.   **True.**   No matter what strategy one's rival chooses in the prisoner's dilemma situation, playing the "confess" or "defect" strategy always gives you a higher payoff.

10.   **True.**   Firms working together to set price or quantity by agreement is an example of explicit collusion or a cartel.

11.   **False.**   In order to punish a rival for cheating on the cartel agreement, the firm must be able to detect that cheating has occurred. Public announcement of bids makes this easier.

12.   **False.**   In a repeated game, firms have the opportunity to develop reputations for cooperating and to punish cheaters in later plays of the game.

13.   **True.**   This is an example of tacit collusion.

14.   **False.**   Secrecy makes it easier for firms to offer customers discounts without their fellow cartel members finding out.

15.   **False.**   In a Nash equilibrium, players are highly unlikely to deviate from their final strategy.

## Short-Answer Questions

1.   When different firms' versions of a product are distinguishable and consumers care about those differences, the product is said to be differentiated. Some product differentiation arises naturally, but firms also expend resources to deliberately differentiate their products from those of other firms. When products are differentiated, some consumers are willing to pay a slightly higher price to get the version that they prefer, so the firm has some market power. If it raises its price, it doesn't lose all its customers, as it would if the good were homogenous and there were many other firms offering it.

2.   A monopolistically competitive industry is like a monopoly in that firms have some market power, face downward-sloping demand curves, and produce an inefficiently low quantity. It is like a competitive industry in that there are a large number of firms, entry and exit are easy, and in the long run no firm earns an economic profit.

3. In the long-run equilibrium, monopolistically competitive firms earn no *economic* profit. That means they earn the market rate of return on their investment (the opportunity cost of their capital), which is included in economic cost. The firms have no problem attracting investors, since they can offer the same return as other assets.

4. Monopolistic competition differs from perfect competition in that costs are not minimized and not every unit that provides consumer and producer surplus is produced. The monopolistically competitive equilibrium is therefore not efficient. Efficiency (getting the most you can out of society's scarce resources) is a good thing for society to pursue, but it isn't the only goal society has. Having many different versions of goods to choose from is also a good thing, and society has to trade off these and other goals. So incurring a little inefficiency isn't bad if its cost is justified by the benefits of product diversity.

5. An oligopoly is like a monopoly in that firms face downward-sloping demand curves and there are barriers to entry, but it is unlike a monopoly in that there are several firms, and they behave strategically.

6. Oligopolists have to be concerned about how their rivals are going to respond to their decisions. Each oligopolist knows that its choices are going to affect the economic environment of its rivals enough to generate a response. Competitive firms, on the other hand, know that whatever they choose to do has so little effect on the market that their rivals have no need to respond, and monopolists have no rivals to be concerned about.

7. Explicit collusion involves actual communication and agreement amongst the oligopolists on price and quantity; this can involve meetings, phone calls, and so on. Tacit collusion does not involve actual agreement, but simply the recognition that if the firms get too selfish, everyone loses in the end. By following the leader and not trying to undercut him, everyone wins (except the customers!).

8. The prisoner's dilemma shows us how prices in a duopoly can end up at the competitive level, even though both firms would be better off selling at the monopoly price. It shows us how incentives can lead self-interested firms to an outcome that is worse than what they could achieve if they cooperated with each other.

9. Collusive agreements break down because, while they are profitable if everyone sticks to the monopoly price, a single firm can do even better if it sells slightly below the monopoly price while the other cartel members stick to the agreement. Thus everyone has the incentive to cheat. When the firms in the cartel interact with each other repeatedly, they have the chance to punish cheating by responding with a lower price, and they can develop a reputation for sticking to the agreement so other firms will see it's profitable to join them in keeping the price up.

10. A Nash equilibrium represents a set of strategies from which players are highly unlikely to deviate.

## SOLUTIONS TO THE PRACTICE PROBLEMS

1. Because people want to buy groceries nearby and not have to travel all over town, each supermarket has a little bit of market power. Each one can raise its prices a little bit without losing all its customers, but if it raises its prices too much, people will find it worthwhile to shop elsewhere. Each supermarket's output is differentiated by its location. If the demand for food has decreased as a result of lower incomes, and supermarkets are losing money, some supermarkets will shut down and exit the industry. As other supermarkets exit, this supermarket will gain customers who have to find a new place to shop. This is shown in Figure 11.6, where the demand curve facing a supermarket is shifting out to the right. In the long run, profits rise to zero and no more supermarkets close.

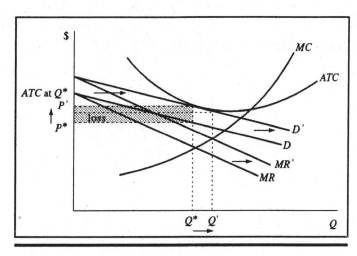

**Figure 11.6**

2.    a.    The cooperative solution of this game is for the student to study and the professor to prepare for class well. This gives a total payoff of 20, which is higher than the total payoff in any other cell.

     b.    If the student thinks the professor is going to prepare well, the student's best choice is to study. This gives the student a payoff of 10 (top left cell), which is better than the payoff of 0 that he would get if he didn't study (bottom left cell). If the student thinks the professor is going to prepare poorly, the student's best choice is not to study; this gives a payoff of 0 (bottom right cell), which is better than the payoff of –10 that he would get if he studied (top right cell). So what's best for the student to do is different depending on what the student thinks the professor is going to do.

     c.    If the professor thinks the student is going to study, the professor's best choice is to prepare well. This gives the professor a payoff of 10 (top left cell), which is better than the payoff of 0 that she would get if she prepared poorly (top right cell). If the professor thinks the student is not going to study, the professor's best choice is to prepare poorly; this gives a payoff of 0 (bottom right cell), which is better than the payoff of –10 that she would get if she prepared well (bottom left cell). So what's best for the professor to do is also different depending on what the professor thinks the student is going to do.

     d.    The top left cell, in which the professor prepares well and the student studies, is an equilibrium. Both players receive a payoff of 10, and if either one were to change this choice while the other didn't, he or she would lose that payoff and get 0. For example, if the student stopped studying while the professor continued to prepare well, the new outcome would be the bottom left cell, where the student gets 0. However, the bottom right cell, in which the professor prepares poorly and the student doesn't study, is also an equilibrium (nobody said there couldn't be more than one equilibrium!). In that case, both players receive a payoff of 0, but if either one were to change this choice while the other didn't, he or she would get a payoff of –10 instead. For example, if the student started studying while the professor continued to prepare poorly, the new outcome would be the top right cell, where the student gets –10. It should be pretty clear that the top right and bottom left cells are *not* equilibria; if we start at the top right cell, the professor can improve her payoff by changing strategy and moving to the top left, and if we start at the bottom left cell, the student can improve his payoff by changing strategy and moving to the top left.

# ANSWERS TO THE CHAPTER TEST

1.  b
2.  b
3.  a
4.  b
5.  b
6.  c
7.  d
8.  c
9.  b
10.  c
11.  d
12.  c
13.  b
14.  d
15.  d
16.  a
17.  b
18.  c
19.  a

# CHAPTER 12

# Antitrust Policy and Regulation

## CHAPTER OVERVIEW

In Chapter 7 we saw that competitive markets produce an allocation of resources that is Pareto efficient. Yet, in Chapters 10 and 11 we saw that noncompetitive markets, such as monopolies and oligopolies, create a deadweight loss for society and are not Pareto efficient. In this chapter, we look at the policies of the U.S. government designed to deal with those market failures. These policies come under two broad headings: antitrust policy and regulatory policy. Both antitrust policy and economic regulation are responses to market power, but they take very different approaches to the problem. In this chapter, we will take a look at how those policies operate, what their costs and benefits are, and how we might evaluate their results to see whether they make things better or worse for society.

## CHAPTER REVIEW

1.  Policies that are aimed at promoting competition among firms in the economy are called **antitrust policies**. These policies can limit the ability of firms to merge, prohibit them from agreeing with one another on price or output, restrict the ways in which they do business, or even break large firms up into smaller ones.

2.  The **Sherman Antitrust Act** of 1890 was the first antitrust law in the United States and continues to be the centerpiece of U.S. antitrust policy. It was passed during a time when mergers in many important industries were producing large firms that dominated their markets, causing concern about market power. These large firms were called *trusts*—hence the name *antitrust* policy.

3.  The Sherman Antitrust Act has two main sections. Section 1 focuses on agreements among firms, and we will get to that shortly. Section 2 makes it illegal for a firm to "monopolize, or attempt to monopolize.. any part of the trade or commerce among the.. states." Since Congress didn't give judges and juries much guidance as to what it meant by "monopolize," the interpretation of the law has evolved through Supreme Court decisions over the last 100 years (with some additions and clarifications from Congress in the form of additional laws).

4.  In 1901, the Roosevelt administration took action against Standard Oil under the Sherman Antitrust Act, claiming that it had violated the law by monopolizing the oil-refining industry. The case went all the way to the Supreme Court, which ruled that in order to monopolize an industry, a firm both had to have a monopoly position (i.e., a dominant share of a market) *and* had to use its monopoly power in some unreasonable way against other firms in order to expand or protect its market position. This approach came to be known as the **rule of reason** in antitrust. Merely having a dominant share and charging a high price was not enough; the alleged monopolist had to do something unreasonable to another firm. However, the Supreme Court was convinced that Standard Oil had done unreasonable things to other oil companies, and it broke Standard Oil up into several smaller firms.

5.  The alternative to the rule of reason is known as the **per se rule**. *Per se* is Latin for "as such," so when something is illegal *per se*, it is illegal "as such." The law has been broken if the forbidden

act takes place, regardless of the circumstances. As we will see, the Supreme Court applied a per se rule to price fixing under Section 1 of the Sherman Act.

6.  The Supreme Court developed the rule of reason in antitrust cases over time, as different cases presented themselves. For instance, it chose in 1920 not to break up United States Steel, despite the fact that United States Steel had a 65 percent share of the steel market, because United States Steel had not used its market power unreasonably against any other steel company. In the Alcoa case in 1945, the Supreme Court refined the rule of reason to include the intent to acquire and protect a monopoly, making it easier for firms to be found guilty of violating the Sherman Act.

7.  The most recent cases under Section 2 of the Sherman Act involving very big firms were those against IBM and AT&T in the 1970s and Microsoft in the late 1990s. After more than 10 years, and having spent millions of dollars on the case, the government decided to drop its suit against IBM, in part because the competitive conditions in the market had changed over that time. The government and AT&T settled their case, with AT&T agreeing to split up its local telephone service into several regional telephone companies (each of which is a local monopoly with regulated prices) in exchange for the ability to enter new markets. AT&T now sells long-distance telephone service, but faces competition from Sprint, MCI, and other rivals.

8.  The Sherman Act makes it illegal for firms to attempt to monopolize a market, and firms often accuse their rivals of trying to drive them out of business in order to monopolize the market. A common allegation is that a firm engaged in **predatory pricing**. This means selling output at a price below its shutdown point, so that other firms are forced to either sell at the same price and lose money (and eventually go broke) or lose all their customers (and eventually go broke).

9.  Other antitrust laws make it illegal for firms to merge if the result is likely to damage competition. The **Clayton Antitrust Act** of 1914 covers mergers, among other things. The Federal Trade Commission Act set up the **Federal Trade Commission (FTC)**, which helps to enforce the antitrust laws. The **Antitrust Division of the Justice Department** also shares responsibility for enforcing the antitrust laws.

10. In deciding whether to challenge a merger or bring an action under the antitrust laws, the FTC and the Antitrust Division of the Justice Department rely on economists for advice about the market power of the firm or firms involved.. One measure of concentration in a market that is used today is the **Herfindahl-Hirschman index (HHI)**, which is named for the two economists who proposed it. The HHI is calculated by taking the market shares of the different firms in the market (the fraction of total market output that each of them sells), squaring them, and adding up the squared shares.

11. In a monopoly, one firm has a 100 percent share of the market, and so the HHI is $(100)^2 = 10,000$. This is the highest value that the HHI can reach, since no firm can control more than 100 percent of the market. In a very competitive industry, in which there are, say, 100 firms, each selling 1 percent of the market output, the HHI would be $100 \times (1)^2 = 100$, indicating very little concentration. In general, the HHI is larger when there are fewer firms in the market and when the firms in the market have more unequal shares, and so the index captures the idea of concentration of sales in the hands of few firms or relatively big firms.

12. When deciding whether to challenge a merger, the FTC and the Antitrust Division compare the HHI in the market before the merger with what it will be after the merger. If the HHI will be high after the merger, almost any merger that significantly raises the HHI is likely to be challenged. If the HHI will be low after the merger, then the merger is likely to be allowed to go unchallenged. If the merger would leave the HHI in an intermediate range, those mergers that increase concentration a lot will be challenged, but those that have only a small effect on concentration will not be. The FTC and the Justice Department also look at other things besides market

concentration, such as ease of entry, when evaluating mergers. Even if a market is concentrated, the ability of new firms to enter easily may force the existing firms to charge a competitive price.

13. The four-firm concentration ratio and the HHI both require information on the shares of the market that the firms control, so it is important to know what goods are included in the market. **Market definition** is a description of the goods and/or services that are included in the market. It has both a product dimension (what goods and/or services are included) and a geographic dimension (where the goods to be included are sold). Getting the market definition right is very important; if too large an area or too many goods are included, the HHI may indicate that the market is very competitive when it really isn't. Conversely, if too small an area or too few goods are included, the HHI will indicate much more concentration and market power than really exists.

14. Merger policy distinguishes between **horizontal mergers**, which are mergers between firms that sell the same product and are competing with each other for customers' business, and **vertical mergers**, which are mergers between a firm and one of its suppliers or customers (many firms' customers are other firms; for example, Coca-Cola sells its products to supermarkets and convenience stores, not directly to people). Economists are much less concerned about vertical mergers leading to market power and inefficiency, so long as there are enough competitors at each stage of production, because vertical mergers do not remove a competitor from the market. There are situations in which vertical mergers can cause problems, however.

15. Section 1 of the Sherman Act makes it illegal for firms to engage in **price fixing**, which occurs when competitors get together and agree on what prices to charge or how much to sell. Price fixing is illegal *per se*; that means that the courts do not investigate whether the firms that were engaged in price fixing had any market power, or agreed to a reasonable price, or failed to stick to their agreement. Price fixing is simply illegal; the only defense is to show that it didn't occur. Both the Justice Department and individual firms or consumers who were harmed by price fixing are able to sue the price-fixers; if they are successful in court, individual firms are entitled to **treble damages**, that is, three times the amount they were overcharged by the conspirators.

16. Price fixing is most harmful when the agreements are made between competing firms. Firms also enter into agreements with their suppliers or customers about how they will sell the product, and these vertical restraints also come under the antitrust laws. For example, a manufacturer may give each of its distributors an **exclusive territory**, in which it and no other distributor is allowed to sell the product. The manufacturer may restrict its distributors to selling only its brand of the product, and not those of other manufacturers; this is called **exclusive dealing**. In **resale price maintenance**, the manufacturer sells the product to its distributors on the condition that they not resell it to customers for less than a certain price. All of these vertical restraints are agreements among firms about price or sales and come under the antitrust laws, but they are not all illegal.

17. Economists believe that vertical restraints only rarely increase firms' market power or lead to inefficiency and may be beneficial to consumers. For example, some argue that firms use vertical restraints to prevent their distributors from free-riding on others' provision of information or services. Suppose customers who want to buy cameras place a value on having a knowledgeable salesperson who can explain the intricacies of different cameras to them. Since the camera store that provides these services can't charge for them directly, it has to include the cost of providing the services in the price of the cameras it sells. It is then possible for other camera dealers to provide no services, offer the cameras at a lower price, and have their customers stop at the full-service dealer to get the explanations before buying from the discount store. If this continues, the full-service store will be unable to survive, and eventually no services will be offered. If the camera manufacturer uses resale price maintenance to prevent discounts, however, all of its distributors will sell the cameras at the same price and customers will go to the stores that offer the best services. This is good for the customers, who pay a higher price but get a service for it

that they value. Others argue that vertical restraints only serve to reduce competition at the retail level. Economists who believe this feel that it is more important to keep up competitive pressure than to avoid the free-rider problem.

18. The goal of antitrust policy is to make markets more competitive and to make firms act more competitively. Under some conditions, however, a single firm can supply the entire market more cheaply than several smaller firms producing the same total output, and in this case, insisting on a competitive market carries a high cost. In Chapter 10, we defined a *natural monopoly* as an industry with such large economies of scale that the average total cost curve is downward sloping (and marginal cost lies below average total cost) to such large levels of output that the minimum efficient scale for a firm is larger than the entire market. That is, any amount of output can be produced at a lower cost per unit by a single firm than by two or more firms, each producing some fraction of the total. In this case, society is in a dilemma. To produce as cheaply as possible means having only one firm, but then that firm will be a monopoly, charge a monopoly price, and cause inefficiency. Insisting on a competitive market, on the other hand, ensures that the price reflects costs, but the costs will be higher because society isn't taking advantage of all the economies of scale available.

19. There are two ways around this problem. One is for there to be only one firm in the industry that is owned and operated by the government and that takes advantage of the economies of scale but sells more output and at a lower price than a monopoly would. The other is to have the firm be privately owned and operated, but for the government to require the firm to sell at a lower price. We will look at the latter alternative, *price regulation*, first.

20. Recall that efficiency requires that every unit that consumers value by an amount that exceeds the marginal cost be produced and consumed. In order to get the regulated natural monopolist to produce the efficient quantity, the government would have to require the firm to sell at a price equal to its marginal cost. This regulatory scheme, called **marginal cost pricing**, suffers from a serious problem. In a natural monopoly, because average total cost is declining at every level of output, marginal cost is always below average total cost. Thus, if a firm is required to charge a price equal to its marginal cost for each unit, it loses money on each unit sold; its total revenue (= Price × Quantity sold = $MC$ × Quantity sold) is less than its total cost (= Average total cost × Quantity sold).

21. In order to solve the problem with marginal cost pricing, the regulator might choose to require the firm to set a price equal to its average total cost. This is called **average total cost pricing**, and it ensures that the firm earns no economic profit. While average total cost pricing leads to more output than the firm would produce if it were an unregulated monopoly, it still falls short of the efficient level of output; price is above marginal cost, so there are still some units for which consumers would get a marginal benefit that exceeded the marginal cost if they were produced, so there is some deadweight loss. Average total cost pricing also has another problem: firms have little incentive to keep their costs down. They know that whatever their costs are, the regulator will set the price to cover them. (Of course, if the regulator knew what the costs should be if the company kept costs down, it could allow the firm to charge only a price that covered those costs, but generally regulators don't have as much information about the firm's costs as the firm has. The firm's lack of incentive to keep costs down comes from the regulator's having imperfect information about the firm's costs.)

22. Some regulators are now using regulatory schemes intended to give firms an incentive to keep costs down. This method of regulation is called **incentive regulation**. In this method, the firm is told the price at which it will be able to sell for some time into the future. If the firm has that price to look forward to no matter what it does, it can earn a profit by keeping its costs below that price, and it will lose money if it allows costs to rise above that price. However, incentive regulation has

its own problems; the regulator needs to predict what average total cost will be in the future if the firm does a good job, and it may not have the information necessary to do this.

23.  Remember that the logic behind *price* regulation is that industries that are natural monopolies are best served by one firm (since that firm can take advantage of economies of scale and keep costs down), but that the single firm needs to be regulated (because otherwise it will act like a monopoly and reduce output, raise price, and cause a deadweight loss). Of the many industries in the United States that have had their prices regulated, some have fit this scenario (water, electricity), but others have not (trucking), and in still other cases it can be hard to tell. In addition, as technologies change, an industry that was once a natural monopoly may become capable of supporting robust competition, and so regulation has to change with the times.

24.  Just because there is the *potential* for government policy to make the allocation of resources more efficient does not necessarily mean that government policy actually will improve things. One example of how policy can fail is called regulatory capture, in which the regulators come to see their role as protecting the regulated firms from competition and allowing them to charge high prices. Regulators may start out with good intentions, but the regulated firms have a strong incentive to influence their decisions, and eventually the regulators start to see things from the firms' perspective. After all, who sends the regulators Christmas cards, takes them out to dinner, offers them a job after their term is up, and so on? Certainly not consumers! One piece of evidence supporting the capture theory is that it is often the regulated firms that are the most vocal opponents of efforts to deregulate an industry.

25.  While price regulation was more common during the 1950s and 1960s, the last 20 years have seen the elimination of much price regulation. This **deregulation movement** was the result, in large part, of the arguments of economists, who pointed out that many of the industries that were regulated were not natural monopolies, and that competition could determine outputs and prices better and would lead to more efficiency. The results of deregulation have been lower prices, greater output, and less deadweight loss in many cases, although there have been some industries (airlines, for instance) in which deregulation has been criticized.

26.  Government regulation is an alternative to the market; when the market fails, government may do better. But government is subject to its own failures, and it may be the case that the market, while not perfect, is better than the alternative. Deciding which way is best depends on a careful weighing of costs and benefits and on trying to improve on both systems by learning their strengths and weaknesses. Economics has a lot to say about how these tradeoffs work out and how the alternative approaches can be improved.

## ZEROING IN

1.  This chapter takes up two different types of government policy, and it is important to keep them separate in your mind. Both antitrust policy and price regulation are concerned with market power, but they take very different approaches to the problem. Antitrust policy attempts to prevent markets from becoming monopolized (by forbidding mergers that create a dominant firm or by forbidding firms from using strategies designed to achieve or protect a dominant position) and to prevent a group of firms from acting like a monopoly (by making price fixing illegal). Economic regulation allows the monopoly to remain (because economies of scale mean that production would be much more costly if it were done by more, but smaller, firms) but limits the ability of the monopoly to raise its price.

2.  One of the biggest problems in antitrust policy is separating monopolistic behavior (which the policy is intended to prevent) from competitive behavior (which we want to encourage). A good example of a situation in which these can be confused involves predatory pricing, which is the

claim that one firm sold goods at a price below the shutdown point in order to drive its rivals out of the market. In a competitive market, we expect firms to try to sell at a price that attracts customers, and if a firm has lower costs than its rivals, those rivals will have a hard time staying in business. A competitive market is a tough place; only those firms that can produce as cheaply as the others survive, and while this may be of little consolation to the firms that can't keep up, it's not a bad thing for society's scarce resources to be in the hands of those firms that can produce the most output from them. But it never seems that way to the firms that can't compete, which are rarely willing to admit that they have higher costs and often bring a lawsuit claiming that something unfair was done to them (i.e., predatory pricing). This is not to say that real predatory pricing never occurs (although it is undoubtedly less common than is claimed). The legal system needs a way to sort these cases out, which is where the *rule of reason* comes in: first, look to see if the defendant has a dominant share of the market. If it does, then perhaps we need to worry about predatory pricing. If not, it's more likely that all you are seeing is competition at work. Price fixing, on the other hand, is rarely if ever a good thing for customers and the economy, and that is why the *per se rule* is applied. Since price fixing is rarely if ever efficient, we have a rule that it is simply illegal.

3.  While you often hear complaints that "there is too much government regulation," you should recognize that there is far less price regulation today than there was even twenty years ago. During the Carter administration, airline fares, air cargo and trucking rates, natural gas prices, oil prices, and cable TV were all deregulated. And while it is tempting to think of price regulation as "big government" getting its hands into the economy, you should be aware that it was largely the regulated firms that opposed deregulation. The airlines argued that deregulating airfares would lead to chaos in the skies. Some Teamsters were even accused of trying to bribe Senator Howard Cannon of Nevada, whose committee was deregulating trucking rates (to his credit, Senator Cannon refused the bribe and blew the whistle). At the same time, however, there has been an explosion of social regulations, some of which may be cost-effective but others of which add far more to costs than their benefits justify.

4.  In evaluating regulation (as with evaluating any other government economic policy), you should always bear in mind that the market and the government are two different ways of arriving at an allocation of resources. Each one can fail to achieve an efficient allocation: markets because of market power and other problems, the government because of rent-seeking special interest groups, and government workers pursuing their own interests. From an economic point of view, the question is always which way of making decisions gives the greatest difference between benefits and costs. There are always tradeoffs and advantages and disadvantages to each way of doing things, and each way can often be improved.

# ACTIVE REVIEW

## Fill-In Questions

1.  The government deals with _____ in two ways: _____ policy, which deals with actions such as price fixing and predatory pricing, and _____ policy, where the government is concerned with natural monopolies.

2.  The _____ Act, passed by Congress in 1890, is the cornerstone of antitrust policy in the United States.

3.  The _____ in antitrust requires that a firm both have market power and use it to _____.

4. If an act is illegal per se under the antitrust laws, it is illegal in and of itself. A good example of something that is illegal *per se* is _____.

5. _____ is an attempt to monopolize a market by selling at a _____ below the shutdown point, in the hopes of driving out the competition and gaining a(n) _____ in that market.

6. Two government agencies are charged with enforcing antitrust policy: the _____ and the _____ of the _____.

7. The four-firm concentration ratio is the sum of the market shares of the top four firms in an industry, whereas the _____ is the sum of the _____ of the market shares of the firms in an industry. These indices are used by the FTC and the Department of Justice to determine whether a(n) _____ should be challenged or not.

8. The Justice Department is more likely to challenge a merger when the postmerger HHI is above _____, and generally won't challenge a merger that leaves the HHI below _____.

9. A merger between Ford and Chrysler would be a(n) _____, while a merger between Ford and Goodyear would be a(n) _____.

10. Examples of vertical restraints are _____, where only one firm is allowed to sell in a particular region; _____, where a retailer may sell only one firm's product and not the competitors' products; and _____, where a manufacturer sets the list price at which the retailer must sell a good.

11. An industry in which one firm can supply the entire market at a lower cost than two or more firms is a(n) _____. It is characterized by _____ and a declining _____ curve.

12. Three methods that governments use to regulate the price that a natural monopolist can charge are _____ pricing, _____ pricing, and _____ regulation.

13. If a firm whose _____ is regulated is allowed to cover its average costs, it has little incentive to _____ its costs. _____ allows firms to keep part of any _____ savings it achieves, thus improving its incentives.

14. In some cases, it is clear that an industry whose price is regulated is not a natural monopoly. This may occur because the industry has _____ the regulators and used them to limit _____.

## True-False Questions

1. T  F  Through its antitrust policy, the government promotes healthy competition among firms by challenging anticompetitive practices like price fixing, collusion, and predatory pricing.

2. T  F  Section 1 of the Sherman Act makes it illegal to have a dominant share of a market, whereas Section 2 makes it illegal to attempt to monopolize a market.

3. T  F  The rule of reason was developed by the Supreme Court in the Standard Oil case, where it held that the government needed to show both that Standard Oil had a large market share and that it had used its market power to restrict competition to prove monopolization.

4.  T   F    The Supreme Court found that Alcoa was guilty of monopolization under the rule of reason by finding that Alcoa did have a monopoly and that it had intended to acquire and maintain that monopoly position.

5.  T   F    The Clayton Antitrust Act was passed to prevent firms from forming monopolies via mergers, since this is not specifically addressed in the Sherman Antitrust Act.

6.  T   F    The FTC and the Justice Department use the Herfindahl-Hirschman index to decide whether or not a firm is using predatory pricing.

7.  T   F    When deciding whether to challenge a merger, the Justice Department looks at the volume of the merging firms' sales and challenges only mergers between large firms.

8.  T   F    When examining a proposed merger, the definition of a market is relatively unimportant, since the main question is the level of the HHI.

9.  T   F    Economists believe that horizontal mergers are healthy for competition, but there is considerable disagreement over the effects of vertical mergers.

10. T   F    Price fixing is illegal *per se*, and treble damages are awarded if a firm is found guilty of price fixing.

11. T   F    When economies of scale extend to all levels of output, a small firm can produce as cheaply as a larger firm.

12. T   F    With marginal cost pricing regulation, the firm earns negative profits and would leave the market. Therefore, the government uses average total cost pricing, since that will allow a firm to earn a normal rate of return and have zero economic profit.

13. T   F    Average total cost pricing forces firms to be as efficient as possible, since they would wish to lower their costs as much as possible.

14. T   F    If a regulatory agency becomes captive to the industry, regulation can be used to thwart competition that would otherwise thrive.

15. T   F    Price regulation has decreased dramatically in the United States over the last twenty years.

## Short-Answer Questions

1.  Name three ways in which the antitrust laws make markets behave more competitively.

2.  What is the difference between Section 1 and Section 2 of the Sherman Antitrust Act?

3.  What is the difference between the rule of reason and the per se rule in antitrust? Explain why price fixing is treated more harshly than dominance of a market by a single firm.

4.  Explain what the Herfindahl-Hirschman index is, and how it is used by the Department of Justice to decide which mergers to challenge.

5.  Compare antitrust and price regulation as alternative ways of dealing with the problem of market power. Under what circumstances is each the best policy?

6.  Explain why insisting on competition in a natural monopoly would be inefficient.

7.  Explain the differences between marginal cost pricing, average total cost pricing, and incentive regulation. What is each trying to accomplish?

8.  What happens when regulators become "captives" of industry?

9.  What have been the trends in regulation over the past twenty years?

# WORKING IT OUT

1.    One of the key issues in antitrust is recognizing market power; after all, if you are going to claim that someone is monopolizing an industry or that some merger is going to create a monopoly, you need to be able to tell when firms have market power and when they don't. In Chapter 10, we learned that market power is the ability to raise price above marginal cost without losing so many customers that you lose money. If we could look at a firm's price and marginal cost, we could measure its price-cost margin and discover its market power directly, but information on marginal costs is often hard to find. If we knew the elasticity of the strategic demand curve facing the firm, we could also calculate the price-cost margin (because price-cost margin = 1/elasticity), and sometimes economists are able to measure this elasticity, but not always.

The way the courts measure market power is by looking at the firm's share of the market and concluding that a firm with a large share has market power. Defining the market in which the firm competes is *critical* in this. Define the market too narrowly, and a firm with no market power at all looks like a monopoly. Define the market too broadly, and a monopoly looks like a competitive firm.

When defining a market, the court looks at what the consequences of a price increase would be. Would customers switch to another product? Would they buy the same product, but from firms located somewhere else? Would firms that produce other products start selling this product? Would firms that sell this product somewhere else start selling it here? If the answer to any of these questions is yes, and the response is big enough, then the group of sales of that product in that location is not a market.

2.    It is also important to be able to understand the rationale for price regulation. If you want to evaluate the efficiency consequences of regulation, you need to start with the question "What problem is this regulation intended to solve?" Is there a natural monopoly? Or would the market probably do an efficient job, in which case the regulation may be the result of special interest rent-seeking? It's not always easy to tell, but the question needs to be addressed up front.

## Worked Problems

1.    McDonald's owns the trademark Big Mac™, meaning that it is the only company with the legal right to sell Big Macs (you know…two all-beef patties, special sauce, lettuce, cheese, etc.). Suppose McDonald's is sued under Section 2 of the Sherman Act for monopolizing the market for Big Macs. How would you analyze the market in this case?

**Answer**

*If you define the market to be Big Macs, then McDonald's is the only producer of Big Macs, and its market share is 100 percent. That certainly looks like a monopoly. But Big Macs is probably too narrow a definition. Suppose McDonald's raised the price of Big Macs while all the other fast-food chains continued to sell their Whoppers and Big Deluxes at $1.89. What would happen to the number of Big Macs sold? Some customers would probably continue to buy Big Macs; after all, these are differentiated products that don't taste exactly the same, and some consumers prefer Big Macs. Some customers would switch to other fast-food burgers, or even to pizza, fried chicken, or tacos. If, as is likely, there are a lot of these, McDonald's will lose money as a result of its price increase. Big Macs would not be a market; you would probably include Wendy's, Burger King, and Hardee's and try the test again. You might conclude that fast-food hamburgers are a market, or that all fast food is a market, or even that all restaurant food is a market. Then again, maybe McDonald's could raise the price of Big Macs profitably, in which case Big Macs would be a market and McDonald's would be a monopoly. That's the way it is with market* *definition; you can't answer the question just by thinking about it. The answer depends on how real consumers behave.*

2.   Consider the following data on the 10 largest U.S. airlines in 1990.

| LEADING PASSENGER AIRLINES IN 1990 | |
| --- | --- |
| **Airline** | **Passengers (in thousands)** |
| American | 73,227 |
| Delta | 65,729 |
| USAir | 60,059 |
| United | 57,550 |
| Northwest | 40,899 |
| Continental | 35,166 |
| Trans World | 24,166 |
| Southwest | 22,064 |
| Eastern | 21,386 |
| Pan American | 17,503 |

Source: Air Transport Assn. of America

How would you analyze market concentration in this industry?

**Answer**

*These data do not suggest a lot of market dominance; the share of American Airlines, the largest airline, is only 17 percent of this group's total (and there are a number of other smaller airlines, so American's share of all passengers is even smaller still). The Herfindahl-Hirschman index for this industry is only 1,223. Of course, this is valid only if all airline travel is a good definition of a market. Remember, you start with a small group of sales, and work up to a market by considering good substitutes. In this case, not all airline travel is perfectly substitutable. If you want to fly from Dallas-Fort Worth to San Francisco, you aren't going to switch to a flight from Minneapolis to Miami in response to a price increase. So start with a pair of cities and ask whether a hypothetical single provider of air travel between those cities could profitably raise its price. This depends on the cities you are talking about. Between Washington and New York, there are buses, trains, and a major highway, and at least some people would switch to other means of transportation. If enough of them would do so, then air travel between these cities would not be a market, and you would have to include other means of transportation in the market and try again. Between Los Angeles and New York, on the other hand, it seems likely that few people would choose to drive or take a train or bus if the price of an airline ticket rose, so air travel between these cities would be a market. If one airline controlled all of the flights between these cities, it could have a monopoly over this market, despite having a relatively small share of all the flights nationally.*

# PRACTICE PROBLEMS

1.   One of the most important antitrust cases in the last twenty years was the Microsoft case. The main allegation was that Microsoft, whose Windows program has a dominant share of the market for personal computer operating systems, attempted to capture a similar position in the market for Internet browser software. It was accused of doing this by making its browser (Internet Explorer) a part of the Windows program, thus making it very difficult for other producers (like Netscape)

to sell their browsers to computer makers for inclusion on their computers. Without getting into the facts of the case, or whether you think Microsoft should have been found guilty or not (they were, but are appealing that verdict), explain the nature of this antitrust case. What law do you think Microsoft was accused of violating? Was the case analyzed under the rule of reason or under the per se rule?

2. Until 1980, the American Telephone and Telegraph Company (AT&T) was the only company that sold long-distance service in the United States, and the prices it charged were regulated by the federal government. Today, there are several long-distance phone companies, and they are free to charge whatever they want. Local phone service prices are still regulated by state governments, but some economists believe that will change soon, too. What caused the change in policy on long distance, and how might the same issue lead to changes in the markets for local phone service?

## CHAPTER TEST

1. Government policy has dealt with market power by

   a. promoting competition using antitrust and regulation.
   b. promoting competition using antitrust and restricting competition using regulation.
   c. restricting competition using antitrust and promoting competition using regulation.
   d. restricting competition using antitrust and regulation.

2. Which of the following statements about antitrust policy is correct?

   a. The primary goal is the creation of perfectly competitive industries.
   b. It is directed only at pure monopoly industries.
   c. It is directed toward direct regulation of monopoly power through government agencies.
   d. It attempts to create and nurture a more competitive environment for firms.

3. Which of the following government agencies has no role in the enforcement of antitrust policy?

   a. The Antitrust Division
   b. The Justice Department
   c. The Federal Reserve Board
   d. The Federal Trade Commission

4. The Sherman Antitrust Act makes it illegal to

   a. engage in a horizontal merger.
   b. have a monopolistic industry.
   c. have vertical restraints.
   d. attempt to acquire and maintain monopoly power in an industry.

5. In the Standard Oil case, the Supreme Court used _____ to find Standard Oil guilty.

   a. the rule of reason
   b. the per se rule
   c. the Herfindahl-Hirschman index
   d. treble damages

6. Which of the following would be a violation of the rule of reason?

   a. A software company is able to drive its competitors out of business because it has developed an application program that is much easier for customers to use.
   b. A refrigerator manufacturer dominates its market because it can produce its refrigerators for substantially less than other producers.
   c. A pharmaceutical firm is able to control the market for a drug because it has a patent.

d. A firm that has a dominant share of the market for X-ray machines is able to extend its dominance to X-ray machine service by refusing to sell parts to independent service companies.

7. The rule of reason requires which of the following things to happen?

   a. Deadweight loss is minimized by taking action against the firm.
   b. A firm is earning excessive profits.
   c. An offense has occurred.
   d. A firm has a dominant share and has tried to acquire or maintain a monopoly position in an industry.

8. In the Alcoa case, the most important precedent set by the Supreme Court was

   a. the use of an analytical economic model to determine the guilt of Alcoa.
   b. the use of the per se rule.
   c. the inclusion of substitutes in the market definition.
   d. expanding the set of acts that were viewed as unreasonable exclusion of competitors.

9. Mergers that may reduce competition are addressed by the

   a. Celler-Kefauver Act of 1950.
   b. Clayton Antitrust Act of 1913.
   c. Robinson-Patman Act of 1936.
   d. Sherman Antitrust Act of 1890.

10. Suppose the only two taxi companies in town agree to avoid price competition by agreeing on a price to charge per mile and by agreeing that each will only service one side of town. This agreement is likely a violation of

    a. Section 1 of the Sherman Act.
    b. Section 2 of the Sherman Act.
    c. the Robinson-Patman Act.
    d. The Celler-Kefauver Act.

11. The per se rule regarding price fixing means that

    a. it must be shown that the firms had large market shares in order for them to be found guilty.
    b. it must be shown that the firms charged an unreasonably high price in order for them to be found guilty.
    c. it must be shown that the firms had the intent to acquire a monopoly position in order for them to be found guilty.
    d. price fixing is a violation of the antitrust law in and of itself, regardless of the reasonableness of its result.

Use the following information for questions 12 and 13.

| Firm | Market Share |
|------|--------------|
| A | 5 |
| B | 10 |
| C | 30 |
| D | 11 |
| E | 1 |
| F | 8 |
| G | 15 |
| H | 20 |

12.  What is the Herfindahl-Hirschman index for this industry?

  a.  100
  b.  1,250
  c.  1,836
  d.  1,984

13.  Which of the following mergers would most likely *not* be challenged by the Justice Department?

  a.  A merger between B and C
  b.  A merger between C and D
  c.  A merger between A and D
  d.  A merger between C and E

14.  An example of a vertical merger is

  a.  IBM buying Compaq.
  b.  Phillip Morris merging with Nabisco.
  c.  the *New York Times* merging with *USA Today*.
  d.  Coca-Cola merging with Burger King.

15.  Which of the following would *not* be considered a vertical restraint?

  a.  Sony setting a retail price at a electronic superstore of $49 for a Walkman
  b.  Ford setting a price of $9,999 for Escorts at Ford-owned dealerships
  c.  Ben & Jerry's Ice Cream allowing Hy-Vee to sell its ice cream in Iowa and Publix to sell its ice cream in Florida
  d.  Pepsi requiring that Wal-Mart sell only Pepsi products at its stores

16.  Under marginal cost pricing regulation, the regulatory agency is trying to

  a.  eliminate barriers to entry into that industry.
  b.  maximize the social benefit and minimize the deadweight loss.
  c.  make sure that a firm has no profit.
  d.  maximize the output to society.

17.  The problem with marginal cost pricing is that

  a.  the firm does not have an incentive to keep costs down.
  b.  the firm earns negative profits and will not enter the industry.
  c.  the firm cannot produce enough output to satisfy the market.
  d.  the price for the good is set too high for consumers to buy the good.

Use Figure 12.1 to answer questions 18 and 19.

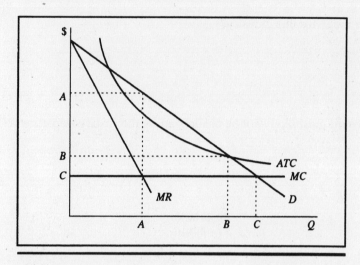

**Figure 12.1**

18. What are the price and output under marginal cost pricing?

    a. *A; A*
    b. *B; B*
    c. *C; C*
    d. Can't tell from the information in this diagram

19. What are the price and output under average cost pricing?

    a. *A; A*
    b. *B; B*
    c. *C; C*
    d. Can't tell from the information in this diagram

20. Which of the following industries was *not* deregulated during the 1970s and 1980s?

    a. The airline industry
    b. The computer industry
    c. The trucking industry
    d. The brokerage industry

# ANSWERS TO THE REVIEW QUESTIONS

## Fill-In Questions

1. market power; antitrust; regulatory

2. Sherman Antitrust

3. rule of reason; restrict competition

4. price fixing

5. Predatory pricing; price; monopoly

6. Federal Trade Commission; Antitrust Division; Justice Department

7. Herfindahl-Hirschman index; squares; merger

8. 1,800; 1,000

9. horizontal merger; vertical merger

10. exclusive territories; exclusive dealing; resale price maintenance

11. natural monopoly; economies of scale; average total cost

12. marginal cost; average total cost; incentive

13. price; reduce; Incentive; cost

14. captured; competition

## True-False Questions

1. **True**.    This is the purpose of the antitrust laws.

2. **False**.    Section 1 of the Sherman Act prohibits agreements among firms on price, quantity, and so on (e.g., price fixing and collusion), whereas Section 2 prohibits monopolization and attempts to monopolize (e.g., predatory pricing by dominant firms, etc.).

3. **True**.    The rule of reason, developed in the Standard Oil case, says that to be convicted of monopolization, a firm must both have a large market share and have taken some action designed to acquire or protect its monopoly position.

4. **True**.    The Supreme Court also expanded the list of things that would count as "acquiring and maintaining that monopoly position" in the Alcoa case.

5. **True**.    Although Section 1 of the Sherman Act covered mergers to some extent, the Clayton Act specifically forbids mergers that are likely to harm competition.

6. **False**.    The HHI is one of the factors that the Justice Department and Federal Trade Commission use when evaluating mergers.

7. **False**.    The Justice Department looks at the shares of the market controlled by the merging firms, not at their volume of business. A large firm in dollar terms (say, Midway Airlines) could still have a very small share of the market.

8. **False**.    If the market is not defined appropriately, the market shares and HHI calculated from it will provide misleading measures of market power.

9. **False**.    Horizontal mergers, in which two or more competitors combine, are likely to lead to more concentration and either oligopoly or monopoly, whereas vertical mergers, in which a firm and one of its suppliers combine, do not reduce the choices available to consumers. While there are some reasons to be concerned about vertical mergers, economists think that most vertical mergers are the result of firms' seeking cost savings.

10. **True**.    Price fixing is illegal per se. The court does not even investigate the market shares of the alleged colluders; if price fixing took place, the firms are guilty.

11. **False**.    Economies of scale mean that a larger firm has a lower average total cost and can produce more cheaply than a smaller firm.

12. **True**.    In a natural monopoly, average total cost is declining, and that means that marginal cost is below average total cost. So if a natural monopolist is required to charge a price equal to its marginal cost, that price will be less than average total cost, and the firm will lose money. Limiting the firm to charging its average total cost solves this problem, although there will be some deadweight loss.

13. **False**.    Since the regulated firm knows that it will be allowed to charge a price that covers its costs, it has little incentive to keep those costs down.

14. **True.**    When an industry captures its regulators, regulation is typically used to suppress competition, to the benefit of the industry and to the detriment of consumers.

15. **True**.    The last two decades have seen a strong deregulation movement, in which much of the price regulation of the 1940s, 1950s, and 1960s was eliminated.

## Short-Answer Questions

1.    Antitrust laws make markets behave more competitively by preventing dominant firms from excluding competitors (monopolization), by preventing firms from merging to form a dominant firm, and by preventing firms from colluding to achieve the monopoly price (price fixing).

2.    Section 1 of the Sherman Act forbids agreements among firms about prices or quantities (e.g., price fixing), and Section 2 of the Sherman Act forbids monopolization (e.g., actions by dominant firms to acquire or protect a monopoly position).

3.    Under the rule of reason, the court examines the market power of the alleged monopolist and decides whether the particular act that the firm is accused of committing is likely to lead to or protect a monopoly position. Under the per se rule, the court only looks to see whether the particular act that the firm is accused of committing actually occurred. Price fixing is treated under the per se rule; the court doesn't inquire into whether the firms that fixed prices had any market power, or whether they actually stuck to their agreed price, or whether the agreed price was higher than the competitive price. Price fixing is almost always harmful, so it is simply illegal. In monopolization cases, on the other hand, we want to be sure that we don't punish firms that simply produce more cheaply, pass those savings on to consumers, and as a result get a large share of the market. That is something to encourage. We *do* want to prevent a firm from unfairly driving rivals out of business and becoming a monopoly, and so the court looks into the circumstances of the case much more closely in order to distinguish the two.

4.    The Herfindahl-Hirschman index (HHI) is a measure of the degree to which the sales in a market are concentrated in the hands of a few firms. The HHI is calculated by taking the market shares of the different firms in the market (the fraction of total market output that each of them sells), squaring them, and adding up the squared shares. The Justice Department uses three different ranges of postmerger HHI to decide whether to challenge a merger. If the postmerger HHI is below 1,000, the merger will probably be unchallenged. If the postmerger HHI is above 1,800, almost any significant merger will be challenged. In between 1,000 and 1,800, the Justice Department is likely to challenge the larger mergers. In all cases, the HHI is not the only thing that the Justice Department looks at; for example, even if the postmerger HHI is above 1,800, the merger may go unchallenged if the Justice Department believes that barriers to entry are low.

5.    Antitrust policy aims to encourage competition, by preventing mergers that lead to dominant firms, preventing dominant firms from driving rivals out of business unfairly, and preventing firms from conspiring to eliminate competition. Regulation allows a single firm to have a monopoly in a market, but restricts its ability to raise the price to a monopoly level. Regulation is preferable when a single large firm can produce more cheaply than many small firms (a natural monopoly) where it would be expensive to have competition. Otherwise, antitrust policy is preferable.

6.    In a natural monopoly, because of economies of scale, average total cost is declining over the entire range of production. Insisting on competition among several small firms would mean sacrificing the cost savings that come from large-scale production in this situation. This would be a waste of resources and inefficient; things would not be produced as cheaply as possible.

7. Under marginal cost pricing, the regulated firm is required to charge a price equal to its marginal cost. This leads the firm to produce the efficient quantity, but leads to losses in a natural monopoly, as marginal cost is below average total cost. Average total cost pricing involves requiring the firm to charge a price equal to its average total cost. This allows the firm to break even and earn no economic profit (it earns the normal rate of return on its investment, which is part of total economic cost), but it gives the firm little incentive to keep costs down. Under incentive regulation, the regulator fixes the price that the firm can charge for the next few years at a price equal to the regulator's best guess of average total cost. This is intended to give the firm an incentive to keep costs down, since any savings are kept by the firm, and any excess costs are losses to the firm.

8. If the regulators have been "captured" by the regulated firms, then they may use regulation to prevent entry into the industry and set the regulated price at a monopoly level. This is like a government-enforced cartel; if you cheat on the price, you are breaking the law, and the government provides the barrier to entry. It would not be surprising for the regulated firms to oppose deregulation in this situation.

9. Over the past twenty years, many industries have had economic (price and entry) regulations lifted. Trucking companies, airlines, and long-distance telephone companies are all free to set whatever price the market will bear. At the same time, there has been a great increase in the amount of social regulation. Firms have to comply with OSHA rules concerning workplace safety, EPA rules concerning water and air pollution, and CPSC rules concerning the safety of the products they sell.

## SOLUTIONS TO THE PRACTICE PROBLEMS

1. The Microsoft case is a dominant firm case; Microsoft was alleged to have market power (in the market for operating systems) and to have used that power to restrict competition (in the browser market). This sort of case comes under Section 2 of the Sherman Act and was evaluated under the rule of reason. The Antitrust Division had to show, using evidence, that Microsoft had market power and that its actions were unreasonable. Microsoft offered its own evidence to show that neither of these things was true.

2. The big change was a change in technology. When phone calls were carried by wire, the industry was a natural monopoly. It would have been more expensive to have two phone companies providing the same calls using two sets of wires. But when technology changed and long-distance calls started to be transmitted by microwave, competition became possible, and the industry was deregulated. Local calls are still carried by wire, however, and are still regulated, but with the invention of cellular phones, e-mail, and so on, the time may soon come when that industry will be deregulated, too. Then you will get to choose your local phone company just the way you choose your long-distance company (and get annoying calls at dinner time asking you to switch companies).

## ANSWERS TO THE CHAPTER TEST

1. b
2. d
3. c
4. d
5. a
6. d

7.   d

8.   d

9.   b

10.   a

11.   d

12.   c

13.   d

14.   d

15.   b

16.   b

17.   b

18.   c

19.   b

20.   b

# PART 3

# Sample Test: (Chapters 8–12) The Economics of the Firm

## SAMPLE TEST QUESTIONS

1. The addition to total cost when one more unit of output is produced is

   a. total cost.
   b. marginal cost.
   c. fixed cost.
   d. average fixed cost.
   e. average variable cost.

2. When marginal costs begin to rise,

   a. variable costs start to rise.
   b. total costs start to rise.
   c. average total cost starts to rise.
   d. average variable cost starts to rise.
   e. marginal product has fallen.

3. The short-run average total cost curve gets its U shape as a result of

   a. economies of scale.
   b. total fixed costs.
   c. diminishing returns to labor.
   d. diseconomies of scale.
   e. constant returns to scale.

4. The breakeven quantity for a firm is where

   a. price equals the minimum of average variable cost.
   b. $P = MC$.
   c. price equals the minimum of average total cost.
   d. price is less than average variable cost.
   e. the firm maximizes profits.

5. If positive economic profit is being earned in a competitive industry,

   a. firms will temporarily shut down.
   b. firms will enter the industry.
   c. firms will leave the industry.
   d. firms will permanently shut down.
   e. no firms will enter or leave the industry.

6. In a competitive market, if short-run economic losses exist, in the long run, they will

   a. continue.
   b. rise.

    c.    disappear because market costs increase.
    d.    disappear because the market supply curve shifts to the left.
    e.    disappear because firms are able to take advantage of economies of scale.

7.    At a competitive firm's long-run equilibrium, price

    a.    exceeds $ATC$.
    b.    equals both $AVC$ and $MC$.
    c.    equals $MC$ at minimum $ATC$.
    d.    exceeds $AFC$.
    e.    equals $TR$.

8.    The rise and fall of industries occurs in response to

    a.    new technology.
    b.    shifts in consumer tastes and preferences.
    c.    new product ideas.
    d.    all of the above reasons.

9.    External economies of scale

    a.    are characterized by an upward-sloping, long-run industry supply curve.
    b.    occur because of some factor within the firm.
    c.    are characterized by a downward-sloping, long-run industry supply curve.
    d.    occur because of diminishing returns.

10.    The rapid growth of the machine tool industry in the United States provides an example of

    a.    fate.
    b.    external economies of scale.
    c.    individual consumer choices.
    d.    government intervention.

11.    The main difference between a competitive firm and a monopoly is that

    a.    the competitive firm cannot affect the price of output, whereas a monopoly cannot affect quantity produced.
    b.    the competitive firm cannot affect market demand, whereas the monopoly can manipulate the demand curve.
    c.    monopolies are numerous in a capitalist system, whereas true competition rarely exists.
    d.    competitive firms produce goods with no substitutes, whereas monopolies produce goods with few substitutes.
    e.    competitive firms have no control over the price of output, whereas monopolies set output price.

12.    The demand curve facing a firm in a competitive market

    a.    is perfectly elastic.
    b.    is equal to its total revenue curve.
    c.    is the market demand curve.
    d.    suggests that the monopoly can sell additional units without lowering price.
    e.    may well bend backward.

13.    A monopoly maximizes profit by

    a.    charging the highest price that anyone will pay for the good.
    b.    producing at the level of output associated with maximum total revenue.
    c.    producing as much as people will buy at $P = AC$.

d.   producing at the level where $MR = MC$.
e.   producing at the level of output associated with unitary price elasticity of demand.

14.  A monopoly

a.   is a price-taker.
b.   is one of many firms in a single industry.
c.   is a price-maker.
d.   generally has a single buyer.

15.  A monopoly

a.   can earn economic profit in the long run.
b.   cannot make a loss.
c.   can be driven out of business or into regulation only if the government regulates it.
d.   produces more than a firm in a competitive industry.

16.  The market power of a firm in a monopolistically competitive industry stems from

a.   product differentiation.
b.   barriers to entry.
c.   patents.
d.   government regulation.
e.   the interdependence of decision making.

17.  Game theory is used to describe the behavior of oligopolists because

a.   they are price-takers.
b.   they are uncertain about internal costs of production.
c.   there is an interdependence in their decision making.
d.   collusion is unlikely.
e.   their strategic demand curve is identical to the market demand curve.

18.  Product differentiation may be manifested in

a.   a product's usefulness for different specialized uses.
b.   the service a producer provides for buyers.
c.   product quality.
d.   all of the above ways.

19.  Advertising may do any of the following *except*

a.   persuade people to try a product.
b.   inform consumers of a product's existence.
c.   inform consumers of how a product is different from others.
d.   mislead consumers into thinking one product is better than another.
e.   persuade individuals to continue buying a product even when they do not need it.

20.  Oligopolists

a.   cannot affect each other.
b.   produce unrelated products.
c.   have no reason to cooperate with each other.
d.   make decisions based on others' actions.

21.  An attempt by a firm to charge a price below its shutdown point in order to drive competitors out of the market is called

a.   effective pricing.

b.    unfair pricing.
c.    predatory pricing.
d.    aggressive pricing.
e.    collusive pricing.

22.  Natural monopolies

a.    can supply the entire market at a lower cost than two firms can.
b.    do not experience economies of scale.
c.    exist only in the presence of a positive externality.
d.    are legal under the Sherman Antitrust Act.
e.    do not create a deadweight loss.

23.  A market in which the threat of potential entry of competitors is enough to encourage firms to act like competitors is called a(n)

a.    competitive market.
b.    horizontal merger.
c.    oligopoly.
d.    contestable market.
e.    vertical merger.

24.  The Justice Department and the Federal Trade Commission use the Herfindahl-Hirschman index because it indicates how likely it is that, after a merger, firms in an industry will

a.    consider setting prices jointly.
b.    increase economic efficiency.
c.    have enough market power to use predatory pricing.
d.    have enough market power to raise prices well above marginal cost.
e.    increase output.

25.  Regulation of a natural monopoly firm would mean society would see

a.    more deadweight loss.
b.    less deadweight loss.
c.    the same deadweight loss.
d.    sometimes more and sometimes less deadweight loss.

# ANSWERS TO THE SAMPLE TEST

1. b
2. e
3. c
4. c
5. c
6. d
7. c
8. d
9. c
10. b
11. e
12. a
13. d
14. c
15. a
16. a
17. c
18. d
19. e
20. d
21. c
22. a
23. d
24. c
25. b

# PART 4

# Markets, Income Distribution, and Public Goods

Chapters 13–16 cover many important areas. In Part 3, the performance of product markets was discussed. Now, input markets are considered, including labor markets and markets for physical and financial capital. These chapters also explore the role of government in our economy. Government redistributes income through the use of various transfers and taxes, it provides public goods, it attempts to redress market failure such as that caused by externalities, and it regulates markets while simultaneously protecting competition. However, government efforts in these areas are neither perfect nor free from controversy. Often, under the guise of government, special interests are promoted or protected. This is an instance of government failure.

Finally, our economy does not exist in a vacuum. We are part of a global community. The economic connection between the United States and the rest of the world can be seen in the trading of goods, services, and capital assets and in the workings of the foreign exchange market. While the flow of trade between countries can be explained, in large part, by Ricardo's theory of comparative advantage, governments also influence trade by using tariffs, quotas, and other trade barriers.

# CHAPTER 13

# Labor Markets

## CHAPTER OVERVIEW

A large number of Americans derive their income solely from selling their labor to businesses. The wages, fringe benefits, and other forms of compensation that they receive are determined in the labor market. This chapter examines the microeconomic foundations of this market. Up to this point in the text, all the markets that we have examined (perfect competition, monopolistic competition, oligopoly, and monopoly) have been output markets. In the present chapter, the focus is on an input market.

As in previous chapters, a vocabulary is introduced and historical trends in data are examined. Pertinent terms include real and nominal wages and fringe benefits. Next, labor demand is derived from the production function, and marginal analysis is employed to determine the number of workers a firm should hire in order to maximize profits. The supply side of the labor market is viewed by economists in an individual's choice among the alternatives of work, leisure, and home work. An issue related to labor supply is that of human capital. This concept recognizes that individuals, by investing in education and training, can increase their productivity and thereby affect their wages. Next, labor demand and supply are combined as we examine the workings of the labor market. The topics discussed include wage differentials, discrimination, and the nature of implicit and explicit labor contracts. The chapter ends with a discussion of current research on the role of unions in the labor market and in the economy.

## CHAPTER REVIEW

1.  A worker's pay can be measured in many different ways. This includes **fringe benefits** as well as the direct payment to a worker. It is important to recognize fringe benefits as a component of compensation because they are an increasingly larger share of total compensation. Economists simply refer to total compensation as the **wage**.

2.  The actual wage paid to a worker is called the *nominal wage*. This can be converted into a measure of purchasing power by dividing it by some measure of prices, such as the consumer price index (CPI). The result is called the **real wage**. Figure 13.2 in the text shows the behavior of real wages over time. It is important to notice that real wages began a significant increase in the mid 1990s after stagnating for several years. Also, the wage gap between skilled and unskilled workers has widened while the male/female wage differential has declined.

3.  The **labor market** is the place where **labor demand** and **labor supply** meet. **Labor market equilibrium** is the point of intersection of demand and supply.

4.  The demand for labor is a **derived demand**. It is derived from the demand for the goods and services that firms produce with the labor they hire. Firms use profit maximization to determine the number of workers they should hire. A firm will hire additional workers if they will increase the firm's profits. To determine the revenue associated with each worker, it is first necessary to determine what each worker produces. This is found by looking at the production function to determine how much output an additional worker adds. This is the marginal product (*MP*) of labor. For a *competitive firm* (one that sells its output in a competitive market), the revenue

produced by each additional worker is equal to the marginal product of labor multiplied by the market price (*P*) of output. This is called the **marginal revenue product (*MRP*) of labor**. For firms that are not price-takers, *MP* is multiplied by marginal revenue (*MR*) to get *MRP*. The additional cost of each worker is given by the market wage (*W*). Thus, a key rule of profit maximization is that firms should hire workers up to the point where *MRP* = *W*. Market demand is simply the horizontal sum of individual firms' demand curves.

5.  It is important to remember that in the short run, the *MRP* = *W* rule leads to exactly the same decision as the *P* = *MC* rule that maximizes profits in terms of output.

6.  Households decide how much labor to supply to firms by making a choice between work and two other alternative uses of time, home work and leisure. In this decision, two factors determine the shape of the supply curve. First, there is the *substitution effect*. Rising wages make time spent working appear relatively more attractive, and people will tend to substitute work time for the other two alternatives. However, the second factor, the *income effect*, acknowledges that rising wages also represent rising income, and this may cause people to want more leisure. Thus, if the income effect plays a larger role in an individual's decision making than does the substitution effect, the result would be a **backward-bending labor supply curve**.

    A concept related to labor supply is that of investment in **human capital**. By investing in education or receiving **on-the-job training**, workers can increase their productivity, and this can affect their wages.

7.  In a perfect world, the labor market would produce efficient outcomes consistent with the discussion in Chapter 7. In fact, real wages seem to track **labor productivity**, the output per hour of work, rather well. This is clearly seen in Figure 13.7 in the text. It is important to see that the change in the trend in real wages seen in the mid 1990s is consistent with a similar change in labor productivity.

    One characteristic of the labor market is **compensating wage differentials**. These are an important reason why workers' wages are not totally based on their marginal products. Hazardous jobs pay more than safer jobs, even for workers with the same skill levels.

    There is also *discrimination* in the labor market. This occurs when workers with identical marginal products are paid different wages. A competitive labor market, however, minimizes discrimination. Government has tried to deal with discrimination in many ways, including *comparable worth proposals*.

    Minimum wage legislation is another way in which government influences the labor market. Currently, there is conflicting evidence over the real-world effects of the minimum wage.

8.  An effect of a long-term employment relationship is to remove, for a time, market oscillations between employee and employer. Thus, a worker's marginal revenue product does not always equal his or her wage. Some contracts have *fixed wages* and others use a **piece-rate** system, under which workers are paid a specific amount depending on how much they produce. Also, **deferred payment contracts**, under which workers are paid less than their marginal revenue product when they are young and more than their marginal revenue product when they are older, as a reward, are widely observed in the labor market.

9.  **Labor unions**, both **craft unions** (those representing workers in a single occupation) and **industrial unions** (those representing most of the workers in an industry, regardless of occupation), are a part of the labor market, although the percentage of workers in unions has declined consistently since the 1950s. Wages of union workers, on average, are approximately 15 percent higher than those earned by similar nonunion workers. There are two explanations for

this. One is that unions raise worker productivity (shifting the labor demand curve to the right), and the other is that unions act like monopolists by restricting supply.

Unions can restrict the supply of their members and may possess market power as a seller of labor. Occasionally, a union may face a single buyer of labor (a **monopsony**). This market is called a **bilateral monopoly**. The outcome of such a market situation is difficult to predict without knowing the bargaining skills and power of the participants.

# ZEROING IN

1.   It is important to understand the use of marginal analysis in the decision to hire workers. Workers are hired as long as they add more to revenue than they add to costs. When this is the case, profits grow (or losses shrink) with the hiring of additional workers. This logic leads to a key rule of profit maximization that firms should hire workers up to the point where $MRP = W$. (For firms with market power, $MRP = MP \times MR$.) So at each wage, a specific number of workers will be hired. The relationship between various wages and the quantity of labor hired is the labor demand curve. The market demand curve for labor is found by adding all the firms' individual demand curves.

2.   The production function shows that a business can increase output when it employs more workers (input). Generally, the production function relates inputs to output. As such, there is an equality between the rules of profit maximization for deciding how many workers to hire ($W = MRP$) and for deciding how much output to produce ($MC = P$). Assume that a firm is competitive in output and input markets; therefore, market price ($P$) and market wages ($W$) are given. The rule of profit maximization identified in this chapter is

$W = MRP$

or

$W = MP \times P$

This can be rewritten with simple algebraic manipulation as

$W/MP = P$

The left-hand side of this equality is defined as the wage per additional unit of output ($MP$) and represents the costs incurred when one more unit of output is produced. This is also a definition of marginal cost ($MC$). A firm maximizing profits when it hires labor ($MRP = W$) is also maximizing profits in terms of output ($MC = P$). The connection is through the production function.

3.   It was shown in Chapter 5 that whenever a price changes, two forces are brought into play: a substitution effect and an income effect. A wage is also a price. Thus, when wages change, there will be substitution and income effects that influence a worker's behavior. For example, if wages increase, the opportunity cost of nonwork uses of time increases. Because of this, wage increases create an incentive for people to work more. At the same time, however, a wage increase also increases a person's income, and this will increase the demand for normal goods. Most people act as if leisure is a normal good. Thus, work time should decrease. In the end, a wage increase causes work time to both increase and decrease! This is the reason why the labor supply curve may have a strange shape. At times the substitution effect is more powerful than the income effect, and the supply curve will have a positive slope. However, if the relative power of the two effects is reversed, the labor supply curve will be backward bending.

# ACTIVE REVIEW

## Fill-In Questions

1. The _____ is defined as all the pay a worker receives, including fringe benefits.

2. Economists adjust _____ for inflation. The resulting measure is called the _____.

3. The demand for labor is a(n) _____.

4. The _____ in quantity produced when _____ labor is employed is called the marginal product of labor.

5. The _____ is defined as the change in total revenue when one additional unit of labor is employed.

6. Competitive firms will hire labor until the point at which the _____ equals the _____.

7. When a firm has market power, the marginal revenue product of labor is derived by multiplying the _____ by _____ and not by _____.

8. The _____ rule leads to the same decision as the $P = MC$ rule.

9. The interaction of the _____ and the _____ can result in a labor supply curve that is backward bending.

10. If the substitution effect dominates the income effect, then the labor supply curve will be _____ sloping.

11. Individuals acquire human capital by investing in things like _____ and by receiving_____ .

12. Often, wages differ for jobs that require similar skills but have different characteristics. This is called a(n) _____.

13. Two workers with identical marginal products and identical jobs may receive different wages as a result of _____ in the labor market.

14. _____ is an example of a government-created wage floor.

15. Long-term labor contracts can be either _____ or _____.

## True-False Questions

1. T   F    Economists treat the labor market the same as other types of markets.

2. T   F    In recent years, fringe benefits have become a smaller share of total compensation.

3. T   F    Real and nominal wages are identical.

4. T   F    The male/female wage differential narrowed during the 1990s.

5. T   F    Marginal product (*MP*) of labor is defined as the change in quantity produced when an additional unit of labor is added to the production process.

6. T   F    The demand for a firm's output is derived from the demand for labor.

7. T   F    The marginal revenue product of labor for a firm with market power is equal to marginal product multiplied by product price.

8.  T  F    The *MRP = W* rule leads to the same decision as the *QD = QS* rule.

9.  T  F    An individual's labor supply curve can be downward sloping if the influence of the substitution effect is greater than that of the income effect.

10. T  F    On-the-job training is a way of increasing human capital.

11. T  F    There is a close empirical relationship between real wages and labor productivity over time, particularly as seen during the 1990s.

12. T  F    Wage differentials never exist in a well-functioning labor market.

13. T  F    A labor contract that pays older workers more than their current marginal revenue product is called a piece-rate system.

14. T  F    A union representing workers with a single skill is a craft union.

15. T  F    A situation in which there is only one buyer is called a monopoly.

## Short-Answer Questions

1.  Distinguish between the real and the nominal wage.

2.  What appears to be happening to the wage gap between men and women?

3.  Why is the demand for labor a derived demand?

4.  Briefly explain the derivation of an individual firm's labor demand curve.

5.  How does the marginal revenue product of labor for a competitive firm differ from that for a firm with market power?

6.  Why do the substitution effect and the income effect work in opposite directions?

7.  Why can a labor supply curve be backward bending?

8.  What are two ways of increasing human capital?

9.  What are compensating wage differences, and why may they exist?

10. Why do some people argue that minimum wage laws contribute to unemployment?

11. Why may a piece-rate pay system be attractive?

12. Why might a firm use a deferred payment contract?

13. Differentiate between a craft union and an industrial union.

14. Differentiate between a monopoly and a monopsony.

15. Generally, economists employed in academia are paid less than economists employed in industry. Why?

## WORKING IT OUT

One of the issues discussed in "Zeroing In" was the use of marginal analysis and profit maximization in employing workers. In this section, we go through the steps required to determine the levels of labor and production a company should achieve in order to maximize profits. Suppose that the market wage is $100 per day and the market price of output is $25 per unit. Also, assume that the marginal product of the very next worker is 10 units per day. The worker's *MRP* is $250 ($25 × 10) per day. Hiring this worker increases total revenue by $250 per day.

This sounds pretty good so far. However, do not forget that people do not work for free. Hiring this worker also adds $100 per day to total costs. Overall, then, this worker makes a contribution to total profit of $150 per day. The next worker also adds $100 per day to total costs, as this is determined by the competitive labor market, not the business. While this worker also adds to total revenue, he or she adds less than $250. Why? Because this worker's marginal product is lower as a result of diminishing returns. Each successive worker's contribution to total profit will be less than that of the previous worker, but total profit will still grow. Marginal analysis (looking at each *additional* worker) is a process or a rule that, in this case, allows the firm to maximize profits.

## Worked Problem

Assume you are given the following information from the production function of your company:

| Workers Employed per Day (L) | Quantity Produced (Q) |
| --- | --- |
| 0 | 0 |
| 1 | 20 |
| 2 | 50 |
| 3 | 60 |
| 4 | 65 |
| 5 | 68 |
| 6 | 70 |

Output can be sold in a competitive market at $10 per unit, and workers can be hired at $50 per day.

a.   How many workers should be hired?

b.   What quantity should the company produce to maximize profits?

c.   How does the analysis in parts (a) and (b) compare?

**Answers**

a.   *The first step is to identify the marginal product (MP) of labor.*

| L | Q | MP |
| --- | --- | --- |
| 0 | 0 | |
| 1 | 20 | 20 |
| 2 | 50 | 30 |
| 3 | 60 | 10 |
| 4 | 65 | 5 |
| 5 | 68 | 3 |
| 6 | 70 | 2 |

Now convert MP into marginal revenue product by multiplying by price (P).

| L | Q | MP | P | MRP |
|---|---|---|---|---|
| 0 | 0 | | | |
| 1 | 20 | 20 | $10 | $200 |
| 2 | 50 | 30 | $10 | $300 |
| 3 | 60 | 10 | $10 | $100 |
| 4 | 65 | 5 | $10 | $50 |
| 5 | 68 | 3 | $10 | $30 |
| 6 | 70 | 2 | $10 | $20 |

Given that W = $50 per day, 4 workers will maximize profits.

b.   First, construct marginal cost. (Hint: remember that MC = W/MP.)

| Q | L | W | MP | MC |
|---|---|---|---|---|
| 0 | 0 | $50 | | |
| 20 | 1 | $50 | 20 | $2.50 |
| 50 | 2 | $50 | 30 | $1.66 |
| 60 | 3 | $50 | 10 | $5.00 |
| 65 | 4 | $50 | 5 | $10.00 |
| 68 | 5 | $50 | 3 | $16.66 |
| 70 | 6 | $50 | 2 | $25.00 |

Next, remember that profit maximization requires that P = MC, so at $10 per unit, the company should make 65 units per day.

c.   In part (a) the firm hired 4 workers. According to the production function, 4 workers will produce 65 units per day. In part (b) the company maximized profits by producing 65 units per day. You end up at the same place—these are two sides of the same coin!

# PRACTICE PROBLEMS

1.   Assume you are given the following information from the production function.

| Workers Employed per Day (L) | Quantity Produced (Q) |
|---|---|
| 0 | 0 |
| 1 | 40 |
| 2 | 100 |
| 3 | 120 |
| 4 | 130 |
| 5 | 136 |
| 6 | 140 |

a.   How many workers should be hired, assuming that the market wage is $200 per day and that output can be sold at $20 per unit?

b.   What quantity of output maximizes profits?

c.   Compare the answers in parts (a) and (b).

2. Assume that you discover that output can be increased by 50 percent by rearranging the factory floor. This requires, however, that you retrain your workers. After the new training, they are worth more to other firms hiring in the labor market, so you must pay them $300 per day. Begin by using the information in the first Practice Problem as your starting point.

   a. What are the new total and marginal products?

   b. What is the new marginal revenue product?

   c. Will you employ a different number of workers after all the changes?

   d. What is total revenue, and what is your total labor expense? (You may assume that the training itself was free.)

# CHAPTER TEST

1. The term *wage* describes a worker's total compensation, which

   a. excludes fringe benefits.
   b. includes fringe benefits.
   c. is always determined by minimum wage legislation.
   d. is totally determined by factors outside of the labor market.

2. Real wages can be calculated by

   a. dividing nominal wages by marginal product.
   b. multiplying nominal wages by the CPI.
   c. dividing nominal wages by the CPI.
   d. multiplying nominal wages by marginal product.

3. Since the 1970s, the wage difference between men and women has

   a. decreased.
   b. increased.
   c. remained the same.
   d. shown no discernible pattern.

4. Marginal product is defined as

   a. the change in revenue when another worker is hired.
   b. the change in output when another worker is hired.
   c. marginal revenue product divided by marginal cost.
   d. the change in cost when another worker is hired.

5. Marginal revenue product is calculated by

   a. dividing marginal cost by the market wage.
   b. multiplying the marginal product of labor by the market wage.
   c. dividing the marginal product of labor by the price of output.
   d. multiplying the marginal product of labor by the price of output.

6. The demand for labor is

   a. derived from the demand for a product.
   b. unrelated to the demand for a product.
   c. proportional to the market supply curve.
   d. always inelastic.

7. The market demand curve for labor is created by _____ individual firms' demand curves.

   a. averaging
   b. vertically summing
   c. horizontally summing
   d. multiplying

8. The *MRP* for firms with market power is equal to

   a. $MP \times W$.
   b. $MP \times MR$.
   c. $MP \times P$.
   d. $MP \times MC$.

9. The rule $MC = P$ (assuming perfect competition) leads to exactly the same decision as

   a. $W = MC$.
   b. $MRP = W$.
   c. $P = ATC$.
   d. $MR = P$.

10. When wages fall,

    a. the labor demand curve shifts to the right.
    b. the labor demand curve shifts to the left.
    c. there is a movement downward along the demand curve.
    d. there is a movement upward along the demand curve.

11. If an individual's labor supply curve has a negative slope,

    a. the income effect is more powerful than the substitution effect.
    b. the income effect is equal to the substitution effect.
    c. the income effect is less powerful than the substitution effect.
    d. the income effect is equal to the wage.

12. According to the substitution effect, a decrease in wages

    a. raises the opportunity cost of leisure, causing work time to increase.
    b. causes real wages to rise.
    c. lowers the opportunity cost of leisure, causing work time to decrease.
    d. has no effect on the quantity of labor supplied.

13. The labor supply curve

    a. is always upward sloping.
    b. can be backward bending.
    c. will never be backward bending.
    d. is always perfectly inelastic.

14. College education

    a. has very little to do with a worker's productivity.
    b. is the only form of human capital worth very much.
    c. no longer pays as an investment.
    d. is one way of increasing human capital.

15. Which of the following closely tracks labor productivity?

    a. Nominal wages

b. The fixed inputs of production
c. Real wages
d. Sunspot activity

16. Often wages of workers with the same skill but employed in different jobs differ because the characteristics of the jobs differ. This is an example of

a. discrimination.
b. market failure.
c. a compensating wage differential.
d. bad managerial practices.

17. A piece-rate wage is

a. based totally on the length of employment.
b. an example of a deferred payment.
c. based on a worker's actual output.
d. observed in situations where workers can be closely monitored.

18. A monopsony is a situation in which there is a(n)

a. single buyer.
b. single seller.
c. oligopoly.
d. competitor with a monopolist.

19. Unions that organize on the basis of worker skills are

a. called industrial unions.
b. nonexistent in the labor market today.
c. not legal under the National Labor Relations Act of 1935.
d. called craft unions.

20. Wages of union workers are generally higher than wages of nonunion workers. Some economists believe that this is due to the relatively higher productivity of union workers. Apparently, these economists believe that unions shift the

a. demand curve for union labor to the left.
b. demand curve for union labor to the right.
c. supply curve of union labor to the right.
d. supply curve of union labor to the left.

# ANSWERS TO THE REVIEW QUESTIONS

## Fill-In Questions

1. wage

2. nominal wage; real wage

3. derived demand

4. change; additional

5. marginal revenue product (*MRP*) of labor

6. marginal revenue product of labor; wage

7. marginal product of labor; marginal revenue; product price

8.  $MRP = W$

9.  income effect; substitution effect

10. upward

11. education: on-the-job training

12. compensating wage differential

13. discrimination

14. Minimum wage legislation

15. implicit; explicit

## True-False Questions

1.  **True.**     The analysis of the labor market follows the common paradigm of supply and demand.

2.  **False.**    Fringe benefits have become more important in recent years.

3.  **False.**    Real wages are nominal wages adjusted for inflation.

4.  **True.**     The male/female wage gap narrowed in the 1990s.

5.  **True.**     This is a standard definition.

6.  **False.**    The opposite is true. The demand for every input a firm uses is derived from the demand for a firm's output.

7.  **False.**    For a firm with market power, marginal product is multiplied by marginal revenue to get marginal revenue product.

8.  **False.**    It should be the P = MC rule.

9.  **False.**    This would give a positive slope.

10. **True.**     On-the-job training raises a worker's productivity.

11. **True.**     Both series track very closely, especially in recent years.

12. **False.**    Compensating wage differentials that are the result of job characteristics can exist.

13. **False.**    It is called a deferred payment contract.

14. **True.**     Craft unions are organized by skill and industrial unions by industry.

15. **False.**    It is called a monopsony.

## Short-Answer Questions

1.  The nominal wage is the actual amount paid to a worker. This may or may not include the dollar value of fringe benefits. The real wage is a measure of the wage that has been adjusted for inflation. This can be done by dividing the nominal wage by the consumer price index.

2.  Data show that it has been narrowing. By the 1990s, women were earning, on average, 70 percent of what men were earning. This is an increase from 50 percent in the 1950s.

3.  The demand for any input is a derived demand because the demand for the input would not exist if consumers were not demanding a firm's product.

4.  You need to determine the number of workers the firm will hire at different wages. This can be done by following the *MRP = W* rule for different wages. The firm's labor demand curve is completely determined by the marginal revenue product of labor curve.

5.  The marginal revenue product of labor for both firms shows the change in total revenue when an additional worker is hired. For a competitive firm, this is determined by multiplying the marginal product of labor by the market price of output. Firms with market power determine *MRP* by multiplying the marginal product of labor by the marginal revenue (not the price) of additional units of output.

6.  When a wage increases, for example, it makes work relatively more rewarding compared to alternative uses of time. This creates an incentive to substitute work for other uses of time. However, a wage increase also increases an individual's income, or alternatively, the individual can earn the same income by working less. Thus, the income effect may reduce the hours worked.

7.  The substitution effect and the income effect may have different magnitudes at different wage levels. At low wages, the substitution effect may dominate the income effect, resulting in an upward-sloping labor supply curve. However, at higher wages, the income effect may be stronger than the substitution effect. This would give the labor supply curve a negative slope.

8.  Attending college and receiving on-the-job training are two ways of increasing human capital. Both increase a worker's productivity.

9.  Often wages differ because jobs have different characteristics. Workers may accept a lower wage because a job is in an air-conditioned, quiet office rather than an office in the middle of a factory floor. Risky jobs pay more than safe jobs. These compensating wage differences are needed to get workers to perform unpleasant and/or risky jobs.

10. A minimum wage law requires employers to pay a wage that is above the market-determined (equilibrium) wage. At the higher wage, the quantity of labor demanded is less than the quantity of labor supplied. There is a surplus of labor, and so there is unemployment.

11. Many times it is necessary to provide incentives to workers, but it is difficult to monitor their activities. A piece-rate system is directly connected to a worker's productivity and minimizes the need for supervision.

12. A deferred payment contract pays an older worker a wage that exceeds his or her marginal revenue product. Such a system may encourage individual loyalty and promote longevity in employment.

13. A craft union organizes workers with a single skill. An industrial union organizes workers according to their place of employment, regardless of occupational skills.

14. A monopoly is a situation in which there is a single seller of a product. A monopsony is a situation in which there is a single buyer. If they face each other in a market, it is called a bilateral monopoly.

15. Academia may be a more attractive place to work. This is an example of a compensating wage differential.

## SOLUTIONS TO THE PRACTICE PROBLEMS

1.  a.   First compute *MP* and convert it into *MRP*.

| L | Q | MP | P | MRP |
|---|---|----|---|-----|
| 0 | 0 |    |   |     |
| 1 | 40 | 40 | $20 | $800 |
| 2 | 100 | 60 | $20 | $1,200 |
| 3 | 120 | 20 | $20 | $400 |
| 4 | 130 | 10 | $20 | $200 |
| 5 | 136 | 6 | $20 | $120 |
| 6 | 140 | 4 | $20 | $80 |

Since $W = \$200$ per day, 4 workers should be hired.

   b.   First construct *MC* (remember that $MC = W/MP$).

| Q | L | W | MP | MC |
|---|---|---|----|----|
| 0 | 0 |   |    |    |
| 40 | 1 | $200 | 40 | $5.00 |
| 100 | 2 | $200 | 60 | $3.33 |
| 120 | 3 | $200 | 20 | $10.00 |
| 130 | 4 | $200 | 10 | $20.00 |
| 136 | 5 | $200 | 6 | $33.37 |
| 140 | 6 | $200 | 4 | $50.00 |

At $20 per unit, 130 units should be produced per day.

   c.   According to the production function, 4 workers produce 130 units. The input answer confirms the output answer.

2.  a.   Take the information from the first Practice Problem and increase the quantity produced by 50 percent.

| L | Q | MP | P | MRP |
|---|---|----|---|-----|
| 0 | 0 |    |   |     |
| 1 | 60 | 60 | $20 | $1,200 |
| 2 | 150 | 90 | $20 | $1,800 |
| 3 | 180 | 30 | $20 | $600 |
| 4 | 195 | 15 | $20 | $300 |
| 5 | 204 | 9 | $20 | $180 |
| 6 | 210 | 6 | $20 | $120 |

The *Q* column is total product and *MP* is marginal product.

   b.   Multiply *MP* by price (*P*) and compute *MRP*.

   c.   Given the new wage of $300 per day, 4 workers should be hired. At this point $MRP = W$ and profits are maximized. This is the same number of workers as in the previous problem.

   d.   Four workers produce 195 units at $20 each for a total revenue of $3,900. Four workers are hired at $300 per day for a total labor expense of $1,200.

# ANSWERS TO THE CHAPTER TEST

1. b
2. c
3. a
4. b
5. d
6. a
7. c
8. b
9. b
10. c
11. a
12. c
13. b
14. d
15. c
16. c
17. c
18. a
19. d
20. b

# CHAPTER 14

# Taxes, Transfers, and Income Distribution

## CHAPTER OVERVIEW

Governments do many things in the economy. In 1996, President Clinton signed an important and controversial piece of legislation that changed the way the federal government assists poor people. As a result, millions of poor people left welfare rolls. This is just one example of the many things the federal government does that affects the incentives that people face when making decisions. The principal mechanisms by which the government affects economic incentives is tax policies and transfer programs. Each of these has stated goals and objectives. Yet, their *actual* effects may be very different from their *intended* effects. The place to begin an analysis of taxes and transfers, and their impact on individual decision making, is at the microeconomic level. Using the tools of supply and demand and marginal analysis, this chapter investigates the impact of taxes and transfers on individual decision making. Besides introducing appropriate terminology, this chapter shows the incentives created by various taxes and by alternative transfer programs. Lastly, the distribution of income is examined using the Lorenz curve and the Gini coefficient. The chapter then identifies the effects that government programs have had on the current distribution of income in the United States.

## CHAPTER REVIEW

1.  Taxes are used by government to pay for transfer payments and government expenditures. There are a number of different types of taxes (**personal income tax**, **payroll tax**, **corporate income tax**, **excise taxes**, *estate* and *gift taxes*, *tariffs*, **sales taxes,** and **property taxes**). Each tax affects economic activity in some manner. A person's **taxable income** is determined by subtracting exemptions and deductions from gross income. A tax bracket is the range of taxable incomes subject to a particular tax rate.

2.  Economists place considerable importance on the **marginal tax rate** as opposed to the **average tax rate**. The marginal rate determines the taxes paid out of additional income. Thus, it determines the net rewards (or the incentives) for additional efforts to earn income. The U.S. personal income tax is a **progressive tax,** meaning that the amount of the tax as a percentage of income rises as income rises. A **flat tax**, with marginal rates held constant at all levels of income, might be an attractive alternative to the current system. The average tax rate declines as income increases under a **regressive tax**, and it remains constant if the tax is **proportional**.

3.  The payroll tax is used to finance social security benefits. Corporate income taxes are taxes on corporations' accounting profits. Excise and sales taxes are taxes on the sale of goods. Local governments depend heavily on property taxes—taxes on residential homes and business real estate—for revenue.

4.  Taxes affect economic activity. These effects can be examined by the use of the supply and demand model. (This is examined in "Zeroing In.") All taxes create, to varying degrees, a deadweight loss. The size of this loss is dependent on the price elasticities of the market demand and supply curves. The deadweight loss is smallest when the price elasticities are very low. Price elasticities also determine the **tax incidence**: who actually bears the burden of a tax. Taxes that

directly affect the labor market (payroll taxes, for example) have both employment-reduction effects and wage-reduction effects.

5.  Not only do taxes affect economic activity by shifting demand and supply curves, they also encourage *tax avoidance* and *tax evasion*. Tax avoidance means finding legal ways to reduce taxes, whereas tax evasion refers to illegal methods. It is possible that raising tax rates above a certain level would actually reduce **tax revenue** because of increased avoidance and evasion. This is illustrated by the Laffer curve.

6.  Because taxes affect economic activity, it is important that tax policy be designed to take into account the *tradeoff between equality and efficiency*. First, in an ideal tax system, the deadweight loss should be minimized by taxing those items that have small elasticities of supply and demand. Second, it is good tax policy to keep marginal rates low and the amount that is subject to tax high. Finally, the ideal tax system should be as simple and as fair as possible. One view of fairness frequently used is the **ability-to-pay principle**, which holds that those with greater income should pay more than those with less income.

7.  **Transfer payments,** which are payments from the government to individuals that are not in exchange for goods or services, can be either **means-tested transfers** (those based on a recipient's income) or **social insurance transfers** (those not based on an individual's income). They can be either in cash or in kind. The major means-tested transfer programs are **family support programs**, which have replaced Aid to Families with Dependent Children (AFDC), **Medicaid, supplemental security income (SSI)**, the **food stamp program, Head Start**, and **housing assistance programs**. A relatively new program is the **earned income tax credit (EITC)**. The EITC is a part of the personal income tax and is a cash payment, in the form of a refundable credit, from the government to people with incomes below a certain level. Also, in 1996 President Clinton signed *welfare reform* legislation that allows states to experiment with new programs.

8.  Transfer programs are often criticized because they contain work disincentives. As program participants earn income at work, their transfer benefits are reduced. In effect, the reduction in the benefit is an increase in the marginal tax rate. Mandated benefits are benefits provided by a firm that have been required by the government.

9.  **Social security, Medicare**, and **unemployment insurance** are also transfer programs. With social security and Medicare, the money paid in by one individual is only loosely related to the funds paid out to that individual. In fact, much of the money paid in each year is paid out to current older people. Thus, income is being redistributed from the young to the old. Also, because these are not means-tested programs, they also transfer income to middle- and high-income individuals.

10. Studies of the distribution of income in the United States use data from the **Current Population Survey**. Typically, they focus on the percentage of total income in population **quintiles** (fifths). This is shown graphically by a **Lorenz curve**. The **Gini coefficient** is a quantitative measure of the area between the Lorenz curve and the 45-degree line depicting perfect income equality. Income mobility, household composition, and the distinction between wealth and income make it difficult to interpret statistics describing the distribution of income.

11. A natural extension of any discussion of income distribution is an examination of the **poverty rate** and the proper setting of the **poverty line**. Data suggest that tax policies and transfer programs have had some success in reducing the poverty rate and reducing income inequality.

## ZEROING IN

1.  A great deal of emphasis is placed on the elasticities of supply and demand when examining the effects of various taxes and mandated benefits. Because of this, a little additional review may prove to be beneficial.

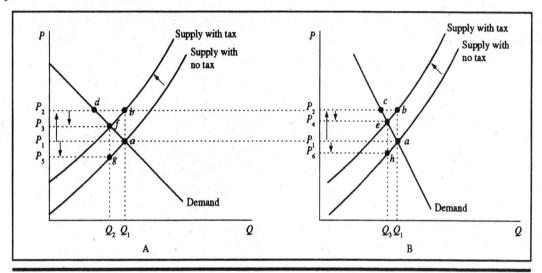

**Figure 14.1**

2.  Figure 14.1 shows two markets, A and B, that are identical except that the demand curve in A is flatter than the demand curve in B; it has a larger demand elasticity. Assume that the initial equilibrium in both markets is at $P_1$ and $Q_1$.

3.  Now suppose a tax is levied on the product, *ceteris paribus*. This causes the supply curve to shift upward by the amount of the tax. The tax is equal to the distance *ab* in both figures. At first, sellers of the product will try to get consumers to pay all the tax. (You would probably do the same thing.) Thus, the price will initially rise to $P_2$ (in both markets), where $P_2 - P_1 = ab =$ the tax. But at $P_2$ there is a surplus of *db* in market A and of *cb* in market B. Notice that the surplus in B is smaller. Why? Because there is a smaller price elasticity of demand in B. As a result of the surpluses, price falls from $P_2$ to $P_3$ in market A and from $P_2$ to $P_4$ in market B. $P_3$ will be less than $P_4$ because of the smaller elasticity of demand in market B.

4.  In each case, the seller must still pay the tax. This is to say, the seller cannot keep $P_3$ or $P_4$ to pay costs and contribute to profits. The tax must first be paid out of these prices. The after-tax price the seller keeps is either $P_5$ or $P_6$ depending on the nature of the market demand the seller faces (distance $fg = ab$ and distance $eh = ab$).

5.  In the end, the difference between $P_3$ and $P_1$ and between $P_4$ and $P_1$ is the part of the tax paid by the consumer. The difference between $P_1$ and $P_5$ and between $P_1$ and $P_6$ is the part paid by the seller. Buyers pay a larger share of the tax when the elasticity of demand is small, as is the case in market B. Not only does it matter that you know that the demand and supply curves are sloped as they are, but it also matters that you think about the *nature* of their slopes.

## ACTIVE REVIEW

### Fill-In Questions

1.  The tax on all income received by an individual is _____.

2.  In computing _____, a(n) _____ may be subtracted for each person in a household. Other items may be subtracted as _____.

3.  The ranges of taxable income listed in the tax tables are referred to as _____.

4.  The _____ in taxes resulting from a change in income is the _____, whereas the percentage of taxable income paid as tax is the _____.

5.  A tax is _____ if the amount of the tax as a percentage of income rises as income increases. If the amount of the tax as a percentage of income falls as income rises, the tax is _____.

6.  A flat tax holds the _____ constant for all levels of income.

7.  The _____ is used to finance _____.

8.  Accounting profits of corporations are subject to the _____. _____ and _____ are taxes that are paid when goods are purchased.

9.  Local governments generally raise revenue through _____.

10. The _____ refers to the one who actually bears the burden of a tax.

11. The burden of a tax is related to the _____ of demand and supply.

12. In designing tax policy, one needs to be aware of the tradeoff between _____ and _____.

13. A payment to an individual from the government that is not in exchange for a good or service is called a(n) _____.

14. Family support programs, Medicaid, SSI, and food stamps are examples of _____ transfer payments.

15. A relatively new means-tested transfer program is the _____.

16. _____ are often criticized because they may create _____ disincentives.

17. Social security and Medicare are examples of transfer programs that are not _____.

18. With _____ a firm is required by law to provide a benefit for its workers.

19. The _____ collects monthly data on people's income in the United States.

20. A graphical depiction of the distribution of income in a given country is the _____. A numerical description of this graph is the _____.

21. The _____ is the percentage of a population with income below the _____.

## True-False Questions

1.  T  F    The payroll tax provides revenue to the federal government.

2.  T  F    Exemptions and deductions are items deducted from personal income prior to the calculation of taxes due.

3.  T  F    The change in taxes resulting from a change in income is the average tax rate.

4.   T   F   The U.S. personal income tax is progressive in nature.

5.   T   F   Under a flat tax, the marginal tax rate is held constant at all levels of income.

6.   T   F   There is a national sales tax.

7.   T   F   The deadweight loss from a sales tax is small if the elasticity of demand is low, *ceteris paribus*.

8.   T   F   The burden of a sales tax falls totally on consumers if demand is perfectly elastic.

9.   T   F   A way to decrease tax avoidance and evasion is to raise the tax rate.

10.  T   F   Means-tested transfer payments are paid regardless of an individual's income.

11.  T   F   Sometimes transfer payments create work disincentives.

12.  T   F   Mandated benefits are the minimum amount of money a person can draw from social security.

13.  T   F   The distribution of income in the United States is considered to be almost exactly equal across quintiles.

14.  T   F   The Gini coefficient is a graphical description of the distribution of income.

15.  T   F   Income and wealth are identical.

16.  T   F   Tax policy and transfer programs in the United States have had no effect on the income distribution or the number of families in poverty.

## Short-Answer Questions

1.   What is the initial effect of an increase in exemptions and deductions?

2.   What is the difference between the marginal tax rate and the average tax rate?

3.   Differentiate between a progressive and a regressive income tax system.

4.   Describe a flat tax.

5.   In terms of demand and supply analysis, what is the *initial* effect of a sales tax?

6.   If the demand curve for a product is perfectly inelastic, how much will the price rise as a result of a sales tax increase?

7.   Is it possible that an increase in tax rates could produce a decrease in tax revenues?

8.   Briefly describe the employment-reduction effect and the wage-reduction effect of the payroll tax.

9.   Why do some transfer programs create work disincentives?

10.  Does the employer actually pay for a government-mandated benefit?

11.  What is a quintile?

12.  Briefly describe the ideal tax system.

13.  How are a Lorenz curve and a Gini coefficient similar, and how are they different?

14.  Differentiate between income and wealth.

15.  Describe the poverty line.

## WORKING IT OUT

The importance of knowing the elasticities of supply and demand in a market-based analysis was stressed in "Zeroing In." Here, we will review the effects of the payroll tax with emphasis on the elasticity of supply.

## Worked Problem

1.  Figure 14.2 depicts two labor markets, A and B, that are identical except for having differing elasticities of supply. Market A has a relatively flat labor supply curve (a higher elasticity), whereas market B has a relatively steep labor supply curve (a relatively low elasticity). What is the effect of a payroll tax? Assume that the employee pays the payroll tax and that the initial equilibrium is at $W_1$ and $H_1$ in both markets.

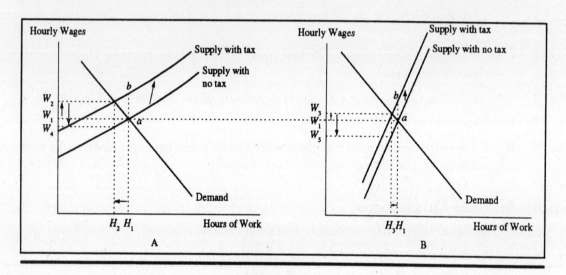

**Figure 14.2**

### Answer

*The supply curve will shift up by the amount of the tax. This is shown by the vertical distance ab in both markets. Holding demand constant, the new before-tax wage is $W_2$ in market A and $W_3$ in market B, and the after-tax wage is $W_4$ and $W_5$, respectively. The wage-reduction effect is the distance $W_1W_4$ in market A and $W_1W_5$ in market B. As shown, this effect is greater in market B because of the lower elasticity of labor supply. The employment-reduction effect is $H_1H_2$ and $H_1H_3$. The employment-reduction effect is greater in market A. This is due to the flatter labor supply curve in this market.*

## PRACTICE PROBLEM

1.  Assume that the government mandates that firms pay for regular back rubs for their employees. It is believed (without supporting evidence) that back rubs make workers happier, and that happier employees work harder! Show the results in two separate labor markets that face similar demand curves but that have supply curves with different elasticities. Identify the wage-reduction effect and the employment-reduction effect, and specify the role of the elasticities. Also, assume that employees value the back rubs less than the costs of providing them.

# CHAPTER TEST

1.  In calculating taxable income, a dollar amount based on the number of qualified people in a household may be subtracted from income. This is called

    a.  an exemption.
    b.  a deduction.
    c.  a capital gain.
    d.  a family allowance.

2.  Under a regressive tax system,

    a.  the marginal tax rate falls as income rises.
    b.  the marginal tax rate rises as income rises.
    c.  the marginal tax rate remains constant as income rises.
    d.  the average tax rate falls as income rises.

3.  The bulk of the payroll tax is used to finance

    a.  national defense.
    b.  transfer payments to college students.
    c.  highway construction.
    d.  social security.

4.  A major source of revenue for many state governments is the

    a.  personal income tax.
    b.  corporate income tax.
    c.  sales tax.
    d.  property tax.

5.  The deadweight loss from a sales tax is high when the

    a.  elasticity of supply is high.
    b.  elasticity of demand is high.
    c.  elasticity of demand is low.
    d.  elasticity of demand is 1.

6.  Graphically, the initial effect of a decrease in the sales tax is to

    a.  increase supply by the amount of the tax.
    b.  increase the quantity supplied.
    c.  decrease supply by the amount of the tax.
    d.  increase the quantity demanded.

7.  The personal income tax

    a.  increases the supply of labor.
    b.  increases the demand for labor.
    c.  decreases the demand for labor.
    d.  decreases the supply of labor.

8.  Assume that the demand for labor is downward-sloping and the supply of labor is upward-sloping. A payroll tax has

    a.  only an employment-reduction effect.
    b.  both an employment-reduction effect and a wage-reduction effect.
    c.  only a wage-reduction effect.
    d.  no effect on wages or employment.

9. If tax avoidance and tax evasion are small enough, an increase in taxes

   a. could increase tax revenues.
   b. will always decrease tax revenues.
   c. will, at the extreme, keep tax revenues constant.
   d. could make supply curves vertical.

10. Characteristics of an ideal tax system include

   a. minimization of the deadweight loss.
   b. low marginal tax rates.
   c. simplicity and fairness.
   d. all of the above.

11. Which of the following transfer programs is *not* means tested?

   a. Food stamps
   b. Social security
   c. Medicaid
   d. Family support programs

12. One of the advantages of the earned income tax credit is that it

   a. has high marginal tax rates.
   b. has a strong work disincentive.
   c. increases the incentive to work.
   d. is not means tested and is a voluntary program.

13. A government health-care program requiring that firms pay a portion of the health insurance costs of workers would be considered

   a. like social security.
   b. purely voluntary.
   c. means tested.
   d. a mandated benefit.

14. If the Lorenz curve is very bowed out (from the 45-degree line), then

   a. the income distribution is very unequal.
   b. the income distribution is about equal.
   c. the Gini coefficient is zero.
   d. all the income quintiles contain the same percentage of households.

15. The value of what you own less what you owe is

   a. your income.
   b. your wealth.
   c. your demand for most products.
   d. your capital gain.

16. One segment of the population that had an increasing poverty rate in the 1970s and 1980s was

   a. college graduates.
   b. the elderly.
   c. children.
   d. professional athletes.

17.  Estimates are that without tax policies and transfers, households in the bottom quintile would have their average income reduced by about

    a.    $1,000.
    b.    50 percent.
    c.    $22,000.
    d.    $9,000.

18.  Estimates indicate that tax policies and transfers make the income distribution _____ unequal and the poverty rate _____ than they otherwise would be.

    a.    less, higher
    b.    more, lower
    c.    more, higher
    d.    less, lower

19.  The federal health-care program for the elderly is called

    a.    Medicare.
    b.    Social Security.
    c.    Medicaid.
    d.    food stamps.

20.  When the marginal tax rate is constant for all taxable levels of income, the tax system is a

    a.    progressive tax.
    b.    regressive tax.
    c.    flat tax.
    d.    proportional tax.

## ANSWERS TO THE REVIEW QUESTIONS

## Fill-In Questions

1.  the personal income tax

2.  taxable income; exemption; deductions

3.  tax brackets

4.  taxes; marginal tax rate; average tax rate

5.  progressive; regressive

6.  marginal tax rate

7.  payroll tax; social security

8.  corporate income tax; Excise taxes; sales taxes

9.  property taxes

10.  tax incidence

11.  elasticities

12.  equality; efficiency

13.  transfer payment

14.  means-tested

15. earned income tax credit
16. Transfer programs; work
17. means tested
18. mandated benefits
19. Current Population Survey
20. Lorenz curve; Gini coefficient
21. poverty rate; poverty line

# True-False Questions

1. **True.**    The payroll tax provides revenue to the federal government in support of social security.

2. **True.**    In general, exemptions are based on the number of qualified people in a household and deductions are other items that can be subtracted.

3. **False.**    It is the marginal tax rate.

4. **True.**    It is progressive. The marginal tax rate rises as income rises.

5. **True.**    Each additional dollar of income is taxed at the same rate.

6. **False.**    Sales taxes are found only at the state and local levels.

7. **True.**    The quantity demanded will not change very much once the tax is instituted.

8. **False.**    Price will rise by the full amount of the tax if demand is perfectly inelastic.

9. **False.**    The higher the tax rate, the greater the incentive to avoid and evade the tax.

10. **False.**    Means-tested transfer payments are inversely related to an individual's income.

11. **True.**    This is one of the major criticisms of these programs. In essence, a transfer that is means tested reduces the amount of additional income a person receives from work.

12. **False.**    Mandated benefits occur when a firm is required by the government to provide a benefit to its workers.

13. **False.**    The bottom 20 percent of families earn only 5 percent of the total income, whereas the top 20 percent of families earn 43 percent of the total income.

14. **False.**    The Lorenz curve is a graphical depiction. The Gini coefficient is a numerical representation of the information shown by the Lorenz curve.

15. **False.**    Income is what an individual earns over a given period of time. Wealth is all that an individual owns less what the individual owes to others.

16. **False.**    Taxes and transfers appear to have lowered the percentage of income received by the top 20 percent of families and increased the percentage of income received by the lower 20 percent. Taxes and transfers have also reduced the number of families below the poverty line.

# Short-Answer Questions

1. Exemptions and deductions are subtracted from household income in order to determine taxable income. Thus, an increase in either exemptions or deductions would lower taxable income and result in a lower tax bill.

2. The marginal tax rate is the change in a person's tax liability resulting from receiving an additional dollar in income. The average tax rate is simply the percentage of a person's income paid in taxes. Economists are interested in the marginal tax rate.

3. Under a progressive tax system, the percentage of income going to income taxes increases as income increases. Under a regressive system, the percentage falls as income rises.

4. The marginal tax rate is the same at all levels of income.

5. Initially, the sales tax shifts the supply curve to the left by the amount of the tax—there is a decrease in supply.

6. From the answer to question 5, the supply curve shifts to the left (or up) by the amount of the tax. If the demand curve is vertical (perfectly inelastic), then the market price will rise by the full amount of the tax.

7. Yes. High taxes create strong incentives for tax avoidance and tax evasion. It is possible that tax revenues will fall as taxes increase if avoidance and evasion are widespread.

8. If the tax is paid by employees, the labor supply curve shifts up by the amount of the tax. If the demand curve for labor has a negative slope, then the quantity of labor demanded will decline, and employment will be reduced. The wage paid to workers will rise, but the after-tax wage will decline. If the tax is paid by employers, then the demand curve for labor shifts down by the amount of the tax. If the supply curve has a positive slope, the quantity of labor employed will decline and wages will fall.

9. Suppose that a person's total income is the sum of labor income and transfer payments, and assume that transfer payments are means tested. If a person decides to work and earn income, transfer payments to that person will be reduced. For example, suppose that a job pays $5 per hour, but transfer payments are reduced by $3 for every hour worked. The net result of an hour of additional work is only $2. This might not be enough incentive to encourage individuals to substitute work for nonwork uses of time.

10. No. In part, a mandated program reduces the demand for labor. There will be a wage-reduction effect and an employment-reduction effect. Employees will end up paying for the benefit through lower wages.

11. A quintile is simply a fifth of something. In studies of the distribution of income, the population is divided into quintiles, or fifths, based on an ordered array of incomes.

12. An ideal tax system minimizes deadweight loss by taxing items with small price elasticities, keeps marginal tax rates low and the amount subject to tax high, and is simple and fair.

13. A Lorenz curve and a Gini coefficient are both tools for describing the distribution of income. The Lorenz curve does this graphically, whereas the Gini coefficient is a numerical representation.

14. Income is the total amount of money an individual earns over a given period of time. Wealth, or net worth, is all an individual owns less what the individual owes others.

15. The poverty line is an estimate of the minimum amount of annual income a family needs in order to avoid severe economic hardship.

## SOLUTION TO THE PRACTICE PROBLEM

1.    Figure 14.3 depicts two labor markets that are similar except for differing labor supply elasticities.

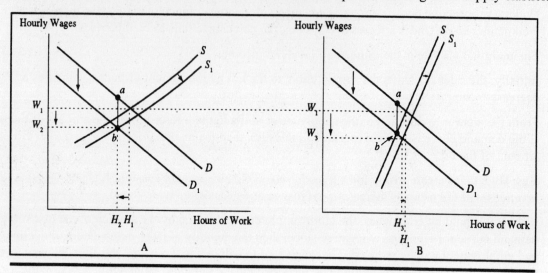

**Figure 14.3**

In both markets, the original equilibrium is given by demand curve $D$, supply curve $S$, wage $W_1$, and hours of work $H_1$. The mandated back rubs shift labor demand down to $D_1$. The vertical distance $ab$ is the cost of providing this service. The supply curve shifts to the right to $S_1$. This shift is only slight because workers do not highly value back rubs. The wage reduction effect is shown by $W_1W_2$ and $W_1W_3$. The employment-reduction effect is shown by $H_1H_2$ and $H_1H_3$. Wage reduction is greater in market B because the supply curve has a lower elasticity, whereas employment reduction is greater in market A because of the higher supply elasticity.

## ANSWERS TO THE CHAPTER TEST

1.    a

2.    a

3.    d

4.    c

5.    b

6.    a

7.    d

8.    b

9.    a

10.    d

11.    b

12.    c

13.    d

14.    a

15.  b
16.  c
17.  d
18.  d
19.  a
20.  c

# CHAPTER 15

# Public Goods, Externalities, and Government Behavior

## CHAPTER OVERVIEW

Chapter 14 examined the tax policies and transfer programs of government and their impact on the economy, including the distribution of income. This chapter investigates two other areas of government involvement in the economy: public goods and externalities. The first area concerns public goods. These products exhibit the characteristics of nonrivalry in consumption and nonexcludability. For these reasons, the private market either will not produce them at all or will not produce the socially desired quantity. This is called market failure. Cost-benefit analysis is presented as a tool for determining the optimum quantity of a public good. The second area concerns externalities. An externality occurs when the costs of producing a good or the benefits from consuming a good spill over to other parties who are not producing or consuming the good. Externalities can be either positive or negative. In the presence of an externality, the market fails to produce the socially desired quantity of the good. Remedies for the problems associated with public goods and externalities are presented. These include user fees, taxes, subsidies, private negotiations, command and control, and tradable permits. All remedies for externalities try to internalize them. Economists also study the behavior of politicians and bureaucrats through public choice models. Related to this is decision making using various types of voting schemes.

## CHAPTER REVIEW

1.  All levels of government participate in the economy in a variety of ways. For example, they produce goods and services, purchase goods and services, and mandate that people buy certain products. Two major ways in which the government affects the economy is by providing **public goods** and by trying to control **externalities**.

2.  Public goods exhibit the characteristics of **nonrivalry** in consumption and **nonexcludability**. Nonrivalry means that more consumption of a good by one person does not mean less consumption of it by another person. Nonexcludability means that one cannot exclude people from consuming a good. Both characteristics create a **free-rider problem**. People can consume the good or service without reducing the enjoyment of others even if they pay nothing. Clean air and national defense are excellent examples of public goods with free-rider problems. If some excludability is possible, then government can address some of the free-rider issues by charging a **user fee**.

3.  **Cost-benefit analysis** may be used to determine whether a public good should be produced and, if so, the amount of the good that the government should produce. Using marginal analysis, the government should expand production of a public good until the marginal benefit from the last unit produced equals the marginal cost of producing it. Measuring the costs is rather straightforward. They should include any deadweight losses from the increased taxes needed to finance the public good. Measuring benefits is more difficult. Often only **contingent valuations**, or estimates of willingness to pay, are available. In addition, many **public infrastructure**

**projects** produce benefits over many years, and these must be discounted. The selection of the appropriate discount rate is difficult.

4. Another rationale for government involvement in the economy is the existence of externalities. An externality occurs when the costs of producing a good or the benefits from consuming a good spill over to individuals who are not producing or consuming the good.

   **Negative externalities** have a negative effect—a cost—on the well-being of others. Often these costs are spread across state and national borders. **Marginal social cost**, or the true marginal cost incurred by society, is the sum of **marginal private cost**, or the marginal cost as perceived by private firms, and marginal external cost. A negative externality exists when marginal external cost is positive. Viewed another way, a negative externality is a cost of production that is not paid by the producer. A classic example is smoke from a smokestack. The firm uses the stack and the prevailing wind to carry away waste. The use of the wind appears free to the firm. However, as the smoke drifts downwind, people are harmed. They bear a cost and the firm does not. In the presence of a negative externality, profit-seeking firms produce too much.

5. **Positive externalities** occur when a positive effect—a benefit—spills over to others. **Marginal social benefit**, or the true benefit to society, is equal to the sum of **marginal private benefit**, or the marginal benefit as perceived by the consumer, and marginal external benefit. A positive externality exists when marginal external benefit is positive. Someone benefits when others consume a product. An example is a flu shot. If you purchase a flu shot, then I will not catch the flu from you. I have benefited from your consumption. However, the producers of flu vaccines do not receive revenue from me, but only from you. Thus, the market will produce less than the socially desired amount of a product that has large positive externalities.

6. Several remedies for externalities are available. All try to **internalize** the externality in some way. First, there are **private remedies**; the affected parties negotiate a solution among themselves. For these remedies to work, *property rights* must be clearly defined, and **transaction costs** must not be too great. Ronald Coase received the Nobel Prize in economics for his work in this area (the **Coase theorem**). When private remedies are too costly or not feasible, government can use **command and control** rules and regulations, or it can use taxes and subsidies, such as research and development tax credits and **emission taxes**. A new approach is the use of **tradable permits**. This is a market-based solution that allows individual firms to trade the rights to pollute. This may encourage firms to make optimum levels of pollution-abatement expenditures.

7. Government intervention is one approach to market failure. However, sometimes government failure occurs: The government fails to improve on the market. When looking at government behavior, a distinction must be made between what the government should do (a normative analysis) and what the government actually does (a positive analysis). **Public choice models** seek to explain government behavior by assigning self-interest motives to politicians and bureaucrats. Government solutions to market failure involve voting schemes. Often there is a **convergence of positions** toward the position desired by the median voter; this is the **median voter theorem**. Kenneth Arrow has argued that voting in a democracy always leads to **voting paradoxes**, or decision-making dilemmas caused by the fact that aggregate voting patterns will not consistently reflect citizens' preferences because of multiple issues on which people vote. The **Arrow impossibility theorem** states that no democratic voting scheme can avoid inefficiency.

8. Government policy is often influenced by special interest groups. These groups arise because the benefits of government programs are concentrated on certain constituencies, whereas the costs of the programs are distributed over all citizens. Lobbying is a form of rent-seeking. Recently, there have been arguments for achieving better government through the use of market-based incentives.

## ZEROING IN

1.  It is important to appreciate why private, profit-seeking businesses will not produce public goods. Recall that public goods have the two characteristics of nonrivalry in consumption and nonexcludability. Although nonrivalry is important, nonexcludability is the key. First, consider a private good. A firm that produces private goods can exclude consumers from benefiting from its products until it is paid (receives revenue). This is always true unless other consumers share their purchase with nonbuyers. With a public good, however, nonbuyers cannot be excluded from benefits. Therefore, firms do not receive revenue from all the consumers. Because of this, if nonexcludability is a large consideration, private profit-seeking firms will not produce public goods unless they are subsidized.

2.  The text discusses the problems of selecting a discount rate to use when discounting future benefits in a cost-benefit analysis. Undoubtedly, political considerations play a role in the selection of the discount rate. President Carter faced such an issue in budget deliberations with Congress. He had campaigned on reducing federal budget outlays. One way he planned to cut spending was to raise the discount rate on water projects, a common variety of public infrastructure expenditures. This would reduce the future benefits from the projects. If the benefits were less than the costs, the projects could be stopped and money saved. Members of Congress simply got mad. If their pet water projects were canceled, they might lose favor with constituents and not be reelected!

3.  The Coase theorem states that no matter who is assigned the property right to pollute, negotiations between the parties will lead to an efficient use of resources if transaction costs are small. Reconsider the example in the text concerning the hospital and the candy factory. Assume that a court rules that the candy factory can pollute the hospital by making machine noise, but that the hospital can negotiate with the owner of the candy factory. Suppose the hospital administrator visits the owner and offers her a payment if she does not run the machines. The money the hospital would pay to the owner would come from the revenue that it would generate by having peace and quiet so that doctors could use their stethoscopes and treat patients. Such an offer changes the costs of making candy! Now the candy company owner must add *the cost of the payments given up* to the marginal cost of candy if it turns down the hospital's offer. Because marginal costs have risen, candy output will be cut back. Silence for the hospital will be produced! Now reverse the court ruling. The hospital can now pollute the candy maker with quiet! But let negotiations begin. The candy factory offers to pay the hospital for the right to make some noise. She will get the money for this payment from being able to make and sell candy for some of the day. For the hospital, this offer raises the marginal cost of treating the next patient, and it will cut back on hours of treatment. Some candy will get produced. In the end, Ronald Coase showed that, with few transaction costs, the same amount of candy and hospital services will be produced regardless of who won in court!

## ACTIVE REVIEW

## Fill-In Questions

1.  _____ is the largest source of total government employment.

2.  A _____ exhibits _____ and nonexcludability.

3.  When _____ is present, more consumption of a good by one person does not mean less consumption of it by another person.

4.  If someone _____ from consuming a good, then nonrivalry in consumption exists.

5.  _____ goods do not exhibit excludability and rivalry.

6.  A(n) _____ is created when a product exhibits nonrivalry in consumption and nonexcludability.

7.  When there is some excludability, consumers of a government-provided service are often charged a(n) _____.

8.  _____ is often used to determine the quantity of a public good that should be produced.

9.  Estimates of _____ that come from public opinion polls are called _____.

10.  Many public infrastructure projects create future benefits. It is often necessary to _____ these benefits to bring them into the present.

11.  As the discount rate falls, the value of the future benefits from a public good _____.

12.  When the costs of producing a good or the benefits from consuming a good spill over to individuals who are not involved in production or consumption, a(n) _____ exists.

13.  Pollution is an example of a(n) _____.

14.  A negative externality causes a divergence between _____ and _____.

15.  To control externalities, economists argue, they must be _____ in some way.

16.  Ronald Coase argued that _____ can solve some externalities.

17.  The use of government regulations to control externalities is an example of _____.

18.  _____ and _____ are common methods used by government to deal with externalities.

19.  By issuing _____, the government is creating a market-based solution to externalities.

20.  It may be the case that the presence of _____ may prevent a private remedy to an externality.

21.  _____ are economic models of government behavior.

22.  The _____ suggests that the middle of political preferences will be reflected in government decisions.

## True-False Questions

1.  T  F    Rivalry is a characteristic of a public good.

2.  T  F    It is virtually impossible to exclude someone from consuming a public good.

3.  T  F    "I don't mow my lawn because my neighbor is a free-rider."

4.  T  F    There are ways to deal with the free-rider problem.

5.  T   F    Changes in technology can transform a public good into a private good.

6.  T   F    Governments provide only private goods.

7.  T   F    It is difficult to measure the benefits of a government-provided service.

8.  T   F    The costs of providing a government service are only the dollar costs of providing it.

9.  T   F    Discounting is used in cost-benefit analysis.

10. T   F    All externalities are only positive.

11. T   F    A negative externality causes a separation between marginal private cost and marginal social cost.

12. T   F    Externalities are always local in extent.

13. T   F    In some instances, externalities can be solved simply by having people talk to one another.

14. T   F    The existence of high transaction costs between private parties may make it necessary for government to deal with an externality.

15. T   F    An emission tax shifts a producer's supply curve to the right.

16. T   F    Democratic voting schemes always lead to efficient outcomes.

## Short-Answer Questions

1.  Differentiate between nonrivalry in consumption and nonexcludability.

2.  How is a public good different from a private good?

3.  Why will profit-seeking companies not produce goods that have free-rider problems?

4.  Most public goods are produced by the government. Why?

5.  What are user fees?

6.  What is the purpose of a contingent valuation?

7.  What is an externality?

8.  What is the difference between a negative and a positive externality?

9.  What is the effect of a negative externality on the costs of production?

10. What does a positive externality do to the valuation of a benefit by private individuals?

11. Name three ways in which government tries to internalize externalities.

12. Why are transaction costs important to private remedies for externalities?

13. How does a tax correct an externality?

14. Why are tradable permits an attractive way of dealing with pollution?

15. What is rent-seeking activity?

## WORKING IT OUT

Supply and demand analysis was used to show the effects of externalities on markets and, therefore, on prices. Assume that the government determines that the firms in a particular competitive market impose a cost on others that are not in the market and levies a per-unit emission charge on these firms. What is the effect of the charge on the market? What does this tax do? Does it create the socially desired level of output?

Figure 15.1 depicts a competitive market with an initial equilibrium of $P_1$ and $Q_1$.

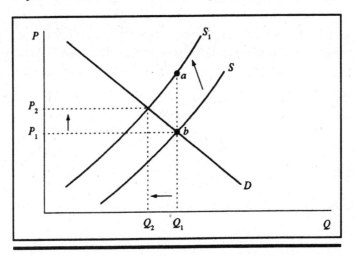

**Figure 15.1**

The problem describes a negative externality. The supply curve $S$ represents the private marginal cost. Accordingly, the emission charge shifts the supply curve to $S_1$; the vertical distance ($ab$) is equal to the emission charge. The equilibrium price rises to $P_2$, and the quantity falls to $Q_2$. The purpose of the tax is to internalize the externality. Whether $Q_2$ is the socially desired quantity cannot be determined without knowing whether the tax ($ab$) is equal to the external cost of the externality.

## Worked Problem

1.    Assume that a government infrastructure project has been proposed by the senators of a small state. They claim that the project will have benefits of $100,000 a year for three years at an initial cost of $250,000. The senators propose a discount rate of 5 percent. However, economists for the president suggest that the appropriate discount rate is 10 percent. Use cost-benefit analysis to determine whether the project should be built. Which discount rate should be used?

**Answer**

*First, calculate the present discounted value of the future benefits, using the formulas in Advanced Topic D. At a discount rate of 5 percent,*

$$PDV = \left[ \$100,00 \big/ (1+0.05) \right] + \left[ \$100,00 \big/ (1+0.05)^2 \right] + \left[ \$100,00 \big/ (1+0.05)^3 \right] = \$272,324.80$$

*At a discount rate of 10 percent,*

$$PDV = \left[ \$100,00 \big/ (1+0.10) \right] + \left[ \$100,00 \big/ (1+0.10)^2 \right] + \left[ \$100,00 \big/ (1+0.10)^3 \right] = \$248,685.19$$

*At a discount rate of 5 percent, the project has positive net benefits of $22,324.80, given the cost of $250,000. However, at a discount rate of 10 percent, there are negative net benefits of – $1,341.84, and the project should not be built.*

*Determining which discount rate to use is difficult and involves a number of considerations. Many times the selection of a discount rate is a political process.*

# PRACTICE PROBLEMS

1.  Assume that the government has determined that the production of a good needs to be subsidized because it has large positive externalities. Show the effect on the market of a per-unit subsidy to producers.

2.  Assume that a government-funded campus improvement project has been proposed for your school. It will cost $530,000 initially and will create benefits of $200,000 a year for three years.

    a.  Use cost-benefit analysis to determine whether or not the project should be built. Use a 6 percent discount rate.

    b.  What happens if the government requires a 7 percent discount rate because budgets are tight?

# CHAPTER TEST

1.  Private goods exhibit

    a.  nonrivalry and nonexcludability.
    b.  rivalry and excludability.
    c.  nonrivalry but never nonexcludability.
    d.  inferior characteristics.

2.  Profit-seeking businesses will not produce products that

    a.  have a free-rider problem.
    b.  are classified as private goods.
    c.  are inferior.
    d.  get subsidies.

3.  Public goods

    a.  do not have free-rider problems.
    b.  exhibit nonrivalry and nonexcludability.
    c.  are identical to private goods.
    d.  exhibit rivalry and excludability.

4.  A technique for determining the benefit of a government-provided service is to

    a.  look at market prices.
    b.  add up the marginal social cost curves.
    c.  conduct a survey and form a contingent valuation.
    d.  divide the cost of the service by the population.

5.  In discounting future benefits from a public infrastructure project, if the discount rate is lowered, then the

    a.  discounted present value rises.
    b.  discounted present value falls.
    c.  future benefit grows.
    d.  discounted present value remains unchanged.

6.  A negative externality occurs when the

    a.  marginal private cost is greater than the marginal social cost.
    b.  marginal private cost is less than the marginal social cost.
    c.  marginal private cost is equal to the marginal social cost.

d.    marginal private benefit is equal to the marginal private cost.

7.    A positive externality occurs when the

a.    marginal social benefit is greater than the marginal private benefit.
b.    marginal social benefit is less than the marginal private benefit.
c.    marginal social benefit is equal to the marginal private benefit.
d.    marginal private benefit equals the marginal social cost.

8.    The issue of global warming

a.    is only a localized externality.
b.    is a problem only within the borders of the United States.
c.    is a global externality.
d.    does not suffer from nonexcludability.

9.    Attempts to remedy an externality involve efforts to _____ it.

a.    externalize
b.    save
c.    invest
d.    internalize

10.    The Coase theorem states that efficient outcomes resulting from private negotiations over externalities

a.    depend on giving property rights to the correct party.
b.    are independent of who is given the property right.
c.    are possible only if transaction costs are very high.
d.    require that everyone be altruistic.

11.    Often, private remedies for externalities are not possible because

a.    all externalities are global in character.
b.    transaction costs are too low.
c.    the law requires the EPA to solve all problems of this sort.
d.    transaction costs are too high.

12.    CAFE standards are one example of

a.    a private remedy for car pollution.
b.    a subsidy.
c.    a user fee.
d.    command and control.

13.    Emission taxes

a.    do not affect the supply of a product.
b.    increase the supply of a product.
c.    decrease the supply of a product.
d.    always make externalities worse.

14.    A new market-based solution for air pollution is found in the use of

a.    command and control methods.
b.    tradable permits.
c.    substance bans.
d.    subsidies.

15. Private firms will produce _____ of a product with positive externalities.

    a.   all that is needed
    b.   the socially correct amount
    c.   too much
    d.   too little

16. Private firms will produce _____ of a product with negative externalities.

    a.   too much
    b.   too little
    c.   all that is needed
    d.   the socially correct amount

17. The optimum amount of a government-provided service is provided when

    a.   marginal cost is less than marginal benefit.
    b.   marginal cost equals marginal benefit.
    c.   marginal cost is greater than marginal benefit.
    d.   marginal social cost equals marginal private benefit.

18. Air pollution is a classic example of a

    a.   positive externality.
    b.   free-rider problem.
    c.   negative externality.
    d.   state of excludability.

19. Which of the following can prevent private negotiations from solving an externality?

    a.   Transaction costs
    b.   Unclear property rights
    c.   Free-rider problems
    d.   All of the above

20. In supporting research, it might be more effective if the government directed money toward projects that have

    a.   small positive externalities.
    b.   large positive externalities.
    c.   small negative externalities.
    d.   no externalities at all.

21. Flu shots create

    a.   a negative externality.
    b.   a positive externality.
    c.   a balance between marginal costs and marginal benefits.
    d.   rivalry in consumption.

22. Often, there appears to be a convergence of positions between political parties. This is an example of the

    a.   problem of rent-seeking.
    b.   problem of market shortages.
    c.   median voter theorem.
    d.   Arrow impossibility theorem.

# ANSWERS TO THE REVIEW QUESTIONS

## Fill-In Questions

1. local government

2. public goods; nonrivalry in consumption

3. nonrivalry in consumption

4. cannot be excluded

5. Public

6. free-rider problem

7. user fee

8. Cost-benefit analysis

9. willingness to pay; contingent valuations

10. discount

11. rises

12. externality

13. negative externality

14. marginal private cost; marginal social cost

15. internalized

16. private negotiations

17. command and control

18. Subsidies; emission taxes

19. tradable permits

20. privatization

21. Public choice models

22. median voter theorem

## True-False Questions

1. **False.**    Public goods exhibit nonrivalry in consumption. The consumption of one person does not reduce the consumption of someone else.

2. **True.**    Nonexcludability is a characteristic of a public good. People cannot be excluded from consuming a public good.

3. **True.**    When I cut my grass, others can enjoy my well-kept lawn and not pay me for the pleasure. (I also might be lazy!)

4. **True.**    If there is some excludability, the government can levy a user fee for a government-provided service. This is one way to address the free-rider problem.

5. **True.**    A good example is cable TV. Before cable, people could not be excluded from receiving a TV signal.

6.  **True**.   Government provides public goods as well. Postal service is an example of a private good government provides.

7.  **True**.   Many times contingent valuations are used. However, public opinion polls are not always very accurate.

8.  **False**.   The deadweight loss should also be included if taxation is used to finance the service.

9.  **True**.   Virtually all government projects involve future benefits and future costs. To make a decision today, these future values must be discounted to the present.

10. **False**.   Negative externalities also exist. These occur when costs spill over to others when a product is consumed or produced.

11. **True**.   This is the essence of a negative externality.

12. **False**.   Pollution can extend for great distances from its source. Acid rain is a global externality.

13. **True**.   Usually, property rights are at the heart of these conversations.

14. **True**.   If transaction costs associated with private negotiations are large enough, government intervention may be necessary to deal with the externality. Intervention can take the form of command and control, taxes or subsidies, or tradable permits.

15. **False**.   It shifts the supply curve to the left. It raises the marginal private cost of the product. This is one way to internalize the externality.

16. **False**.   The Arrow impossibility theorem indicates that no democratic voting scheme involving multiple issues can be efficient.

## Short-Answer Questions

1.  Nonrivalry in consumption means that an increase in consumption by one person does not reduce the consumption of someone else. Nonexcludability means that one cannot exclude others from consuming a product.

2.  Public goods exhibit the characteristics of nonrivalry in consumption and nonexcludability, whereas private goods have rivalry and excludability as characteristics.

3.  A free-rider problem exists when someone can enjoy or consume a product without reducing the enjoyment of others even if he or she does not pay. Profit-seeking firms will not produce goods that have such problems because if they did, they would incur costs, but they would not receive revenues from all the people who benefited from the product.

4.  Through the collective action of government, decisions can be made concerning the level of production of public goods, and tax revenues can be levied in order to pay for them. This is especially appropriate if a public good has large benefits and large free-rider problems.

5.  User fees are charges for the use of government-provided services. They attempt to target payment more closely to the users of the service. A charge to get into a national park is an example.

6.  In doing a cost-benefit calculation for some public good, it is necessary to have estimates of the benefits coming from that public good. Asking people what they would be willing to pay is one method of obtaining such an estimate. This estimate is called a contingent valuation.

7.  An externality occurs when the costs of producing a good or the benefits from consuming a good spill over to others who are not involved in the acts of consuming or producing.

8.  A negative externality is associated with a cost imposed on others, whereas a positive externality is associated with someone's receiving a benefit. In both cases, the costs and benefits spill over to other parties who are not involved in the activity.

9.  In a sense, it lowers production costs because the negative externality represents a cost that is not paid. The marginal private cost, or the marginal cost perceived by the producing firm, is less than the marginal social cost.

10. A positive externality makes marginal private benefit, or the benefit as perceived by the consumer, less than the marginal social benefit, or the true benefit to society.

11. Government tries to internalize externalities through command and control methods, taxes and subsidies, and tradable permits.

12. For private remedies to occur, the affected parties must get together and negotiate a solution. Getting together is not free. People have opportunity costs, and negotiating takes time. Also, there may be many parties involved. This raises the transactions costs and may make negotiating a solution impossible.

13. A tax is levied to raise the cost of the activity so that marginal private cost equals marginal social cost.

14. First, tradable permits assign a property right. Second, a market can develop in which the permits are priced and traded. Third, firms are given an incentive to minimize the costs of pollution control. Fourth, these permits minimize government involvement in the solution. All the government has to do is to determine the overall level of pollution allowed in an area and then *initially* divide (or sell) the permits; after this, the market process takes over.

15. Often, lobbyists try to redistribute government resources or influence legislation to benefit a select, concentrated interest group. These activities use resources that could have been used to produce products that would have benefited the overall economy.

## SOLUTIONS TO THE PRACTICE PROBLEMS

1.  Figure 15.2 shows a competitive market. Price and quantity are initially at $P_1$ and $Q_1$.

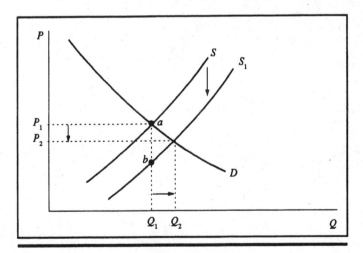

**Figure 15.2**

A per-unit subsidy shifts the supply curve right to $S_1$. The price falls to $P_2$, and quantity rises to $Q_2$.

2.    a.    Calculate the present discounted value at a discount rate of 6 percent.

$$PDV = \left[\$200,00/(1+0.06)\right] + \left[\$200,00/(1+0.06)^2\right] + \left[\$200,00/(1+0.06)^3\right] = \$534,602.39$$

At a discount rate of 6 percent, the project should be built.

     b.    Calculate the present discounted value at a discount rate of 7 percent.

$$PDV = \left[\$200,00/(1+0.07)\right] + \left[\$200,00/(1+0.07)^2\right] + \left[\$200,00/(1+0.07)^3\right] \doteq \$524,863.21$$

As the discount rate rises from 6 to 7 percent, the discounted present benefit falls. At 7 percent, the project should not be built because the net benefits are negative. Maybe your college president could use political pull to change the discount rate back to 6 percent!

## ANSWERS TO THE CHAPTER TEST

1. b
2. a
3. b
4. c
5. a
6. b
7. a
8. c
9. d
10. b
11. d
12. d
13. c
14. b
15. d
16. a
17. b
18. c
19. d
20. b
21. b
22. c

# CHAPTER 16

# Physical Capital and Financial Markets

## CHAPTER OVERVIEW

This chapter examines the microeconomic foundations of three other types of markets, the market for physical capital, the market for financial capital, and the market for foreign exchange. The word *capital* can mean many things. First, there is physical capital. This refers to machines, factories, equipment, computers, and the like. Physical capital will decline in usefulness, or depreciate, over its useful life. Investment is the increase in the stock of physical capital. Next, there is financial capital, mainly stocks, bonds, and other financial assets. Financial markets not only price assets, they also play a central role in the determination of interest rates. An issue related to financial capital is the construction of a financial portfolio. At the heart of portfolio management are the interrelated issues of risk, return, and diversification. The decision to buy capital, both financial and physical, involves the payment and receipt of money at different points of time. Dollars to be received in the future must be converted into present dollars through the process of discounting. Finally, the foreign exchange market is discussed. Purchasing power parity (PPP) is used to show exchange rate determination over the long run.

## CHAPTER REVIEW

1.  It is important to distinguish between *physical capital* and *financial capital*. Physical capital refers to things like machines, factories, computers, and the like, which are combined with labor to produce goods and services. The productive usefulness of physical capital declines over its life through **depreciation**. Residential housing and government capital are included in physical capital. **Financial capital** refers to funds that a business raises. Financial capital can be in the form of a **debt contract** like a bond or loan or in the form of an **equity contract** like a share of stock.

2.  The demand and supply of physical capital can be examined like that of any other input. The **rental price of capital** is the amount a rental firm charges for the use of capital equipment for a specified period of time. This price can be either explicit or **implicit**. Like the demand for any other input, the demand for capital is derived and depends on the **marginal revenue product of capital**. As capital is added to other inputs, output grows. The resulting change in output is the marginal product of capital. If it is assumed that a firm's output is sold on a competitive market, then the marginal product of capital can be converted into revenue by multiplying it by the price of the product ($P$). Thus, the *MRP* of capital equals *MP* x *P*. A firm will add capital until the *MRP* equals the rental price. At this point, profits are maximized.

    The market supply of capital is the sum of the individual supply curves of all the firms renting capital. The interaction of the market demand for capital and the market supply of capital creates the *equilibrium rental price*. If capital is fixed in supply, its price is called **economic rent**.

    With the addition of capital, profit maximization requires that (1) the marginal cost of output equal the marginal revenue of output, (2) the marginal revenue product of labor equal the market wage, and (3) the marginal revenue product of capital equal the rental price.

3.   Discussions of financial capital usually center around stocks and bonds. The **return** from holding a stock is the *dividend*, or the amount the firm pays out to the owners of the stock each year, plus the **capital gain** or **capital loss**, the increase or decrease in the price of the stock during the year. The return and dividend can be expressed as a percent of the stock price. In this form, they are referred to as the **rate of return** and the **dividend yield**. Stocks are often judged, in part, by their **price-earnings ratio**, the price of the stock divided by the annual earnings per share. (**Earnings** is another word for the accounting profits of the firm.)

The issuer of bonds makes periodic payments of a fixed amount (the **coupon**) to the bondholders. At the **maturity date,** the **face value** of the bond is paid. It is important to note that there is an inverse relationship between a bond's price and its **yield**. Assume that you paid $100 for a bond that, after one year, will repay you the $100 plus $5 interest. Now assume that you had to pay only $95 for the same bond. Clearly the yield is greater. Not only do you get $5 interest, but you also earn the $5 difference between the price you paid and the face value of the bond. The price of the bond went down and the yield went up.

Decisions about purchasing either physical capital or financial capital involve comparing payments of money at different points in time. A problem is that future dollars are worth less than current dollars. Ask yourself, would you rather have a dollar today or a dollar next week or next year? Future dollars must be translated into current terms before a decision can be reached. The value of the future in the present is called the present discounted value.

4.   The return on stocks and bonds is also dependent on their riskiness. Most individuals are risk averse. If offered the same return on two alternative investments with different risks, most people would select the less risky of the two. Stated another way, people need greater **expected returns**, or the returns with the different gains or losses weighted according to how probable they are, to take on more risk. This is shown by the **equilibrium risk-return relationship**.

A way of dealing with risk is through **portfolio diversification**. This reduces the risk associated with holding any one specific stock. *Index funds* are an example of extensive diversification. However, diversification does not remove **systematic risk**, which is due to the ups and downs in the economy.

Because stock markets have many participants and ease of entry and exit, many economists argue that stock prices adjust to new information so rapidly that profit opportunities are eliminated. This is the **efficient market hypothesis**.

5.   The **exchange rate** is the price of one currency in terms of another in the **foreign exchange market**. The standard supply and demand model can be used for studying the determination of the exchange rate.

6.   The *law of one price* is a theory that says that exchange rates are determined so that the price for the same good is about the same in different countries. This notion is called **purchasing power parity (PPP)**. PPP works well in the long run, but less so in the short run. Furthermore, it works better for *tradable goods*, where transport costs are low compared to the value of the good, than for nontradable goods, where transport costs are high.

7.   In the short run, exchange rates often differ from what might be expected under purchasing power parity. The primary reason for these deviations is that the rate of return may be expected to be different in other countries. International investors are able to move money between financial assets in different countries.

## ZEROING IN

1.  It is important to recognize that marginal analysis is used in this chapter, as it has been in previous chapters. When employing capital, firms want to maximize profits. To do this, they think about the two effects an additional unit of capital has on a firm. By employing more capital, the firm can produce more products and, thereby, add to revenue. This effect is measured by the marginal revenue product of capital. At the same time, employing more capital adds to costs. This is seen in the (explicit or implicit) rental price of capital. Profits grow (or losses decline) if the added unit of capital has a greater effect on revenue than on costs. Profits continue to grow until the *MRP* of capital equals the rental price. The total is maximized by examining the behavior of marginal units. This is the essence of marginal analysis.

2.  Suppose that the market price of a one-year bond that pays $100 at maturity plus $5 interest is currently $90. The yield is [($105 - $90)/$90]=16.67 percent. Now suppose that the demand for these bonds increases (the demand curve shifts to the right) because the Federal Reserve decided that this would be good for the economy and, as a result of this action, the price rises to $95. The yield from a purchase of a similar bond is now [($105 - 95)]/$95=10.53 percent. Thus, when bond prices rise, the yield falls—an inverse relationship.

3.  Economists generally assume that most people are risk averse. This is to say, if faced with two alternatives that offer the same return but one has more risk than the other, a person will always select the less risky alternative. However, risk-averse persons will take on the risky alternative if they are offered more return. How much more? This is dependent on a person's relative subjective values attached to risk and return. Using the concepts from Chapter 5, risk provides disutility to an investor. Risk by itself makes a person worse off. Return offers positive utility. As such, return is needed to offset the disutility that additional risk would create.

4.  The foreign exchange market is just like any other market that economists might study. There is a demand for a country's currency and there is a supply of a country's currency. The resulting market price is called the exchange rate. This price, or alternatively, the underlying demand and supply relationship, is largely affected by people's expectations concerning the rate of return from holding a country's currency and by the prices of goods and services in the trading countries.

## ACTIVE REVIEW

## Fill-In Questions

1.  _____, _____, and _____ used in production are referred to as physical.

2.  The gradual decline in the _____ of capital is termed depreciation.

3.  _____ may take the form of a debt contract or an_____ .

4.  The _____ is the price of capital in the _____.

5.  The change in total revenue when a firm increases its capital by one unit is the _____.

6.  Even if a business owns the capital it uses, economists still assume that the firm pays a(n) _____.

7.  The sum of the _____ and the _____ is the _____ from holding a share of stock.

8.  The _____ of a company are the same as its accounting profits. Often, stock tables list the _____ as information.

9.  The amount that an issuer of a bond agrees to pay the bondholder each year is the _____. These payments end and the principal is paid back on the _____. The amount of principal paid on this date is the _____.

10. The _____ is defined as the annual rate of return on a bond if the bond were held to maturity. There is a(n) _____ relationship between the yield and the price of a bond.

11. Few people are described as _____ because they like uncertainty.

12. The expected return on an investment weighs the different gains or losses according to their _____ of occurrence.

13. There is a positive relationship between risk and return. This is captured by the _____.

14. Investors use _____ to minimize risk and maximize return. However, _____ cannot be removed by this form of portfolio management.

15. The _____ prices one currency in terms of another.

16. _____ is the theory of exchange rate determination that comes from the *law of one price*.

17. _____ and _____ are two things that often cause PPP to not explain exchange rate determination in the short run.

## True-False Questions

1.  T  F    Physical capital depreciates.

2.  T  F    Shares of stock are a form of equity contract.

3.  T  F    A bond is a form of debt contract.

4.  T  F    The price in the rental market is the marginal revenue product of capital.

5.  T  F    The demand for the final product of a firm is derived from the demand for capital.

6.  T  F    Economic rent is the price of anything that has a fixed supply.

7.  T  F    Even firms that own capital pay a price for using it.

8.  T  F    Stocks experience only capital gains.

9.  T  F    A stock's rate of return and its dividend yield are expressed as percents of the dividends paid.

10. T  F    The coupon and the face value of a bond are the same thing.

11. T  F    There is an inverse relationship between a bond's yield and its price.

12. T  F    Portfolio diversification is a way to get rid of systematic risk.

13. T  F    The return on a portfolio is not always guaranteed.

14. T  F    Some feel that the stock market adjusts to new information so fast that profit opportunities are eliminated.

15. T  F    The theory of purchasing power parity works very well in the short run.

# Short-Answer Questions

1. What are some differences between physical capital and financial capital?

2. How are debt contracts and equity contracts similar, and how are they different?

3. In hiring capital, when does a firm maximize profits?

4. Is the demand for physical capital a derived demand?

5. What is economic rent?

6. With the inclusion of capital, there are now three interrelated rules of profit maximization. What are these three rules?

7. What is the return from holding a stock? Can this be expressed relative to the price of a share?

8. What is the purpose of the maturity date of a bond?

9. Is there a relationship between bond prices and bond yields?

10. What does it mean to be risk averse?

11. Why is expected return important in making investment decisions?

12. What is the purpose of portfolio diversification, and what does it do to systematic risk?

13. Briefly describe the efficient market hypothesis.

14. Explain the *law of one price* and how it relates to the theory of purchasing power parity.

# WORKING IT OUT

This chapter has brought out the role of uncertainty in decision making. Uncertainty is implicit in the idea of an expected return. Many financial choices have uncertain outcomes, and you, as an investor, need to get some handle on the meaning of these possibilities. Also, a better understanding of the underlying determinants of the exchange rate is very useful in understanding the role of the United States economy in a global marketplace.

# Worked Problems

1. Assume that you have $10,000 you want to invest. Suppose your stockbroker tells you of a stock that pays a 20 percent dividend. There is a 40 percent chance that the share price will fall by 50 percent; on the other hand, there is a 60 percent chance that the share price will rise by 50 percent. What is the expected value?

**Answer**

*First, calculate the outcome possibilities. In each case, you will get a 20 percent dividend, so*

$10,000 × 0.20 = $2,000

*But in the first case, you lose half your original investment. Thus,*

$10,000 × 0.50 = -$5,000

*In the second case, however, the opposite will occur:*

$10,000 × 0.50 = -$5,000

*If the first case happens, you will have a net loss of $3,000. However, if the second case occurs, you will have a net gain of $7,000. Over many times, what will the outcome be on average?*

$$(-\$3,000 \times 0.40) + (\$7,000 \times 0.60) = \$3,000$$

*This is the expected value.*

2. Assume that a friend asks you to buy a bond that he or she just purchased. (Your friend just wrecked her car and needs some money fast!) The bond pays $1,000 a year from now with a $100 coupon, for a yield of 10 percent. Your friend is asking $975. What should you do?

**Answer**

*First, calculate the bond price based on the information. (See Table 13.1 in the text for the formula.)*

$$\text{Bond price} = \left[\$100/(1+0.10)\right] + \left[\$1,000/(1+0.10)\right]$$
$$= \$90.90 + \$909.09$$
$$= \$999.99$$

*At a 10 percent rate, the price of receiving $1,100 a year from now is $999.99. Your friend wants only $975. Buy! You can pay less than the calculated bond price, thereby earning a higher yield.*

3. Assume the United States (domestic) has a price level of 1 dollar and Japan (foreign) has a price level of 100 yen.

   a. What is the purchasing power exchange rate?

   b. What is the new purchasing power exchange rate if there is a 20 percent inflation in Japan?

**Answer**

   a. *The purchasing power exchange rate is determined by the formula E x P=P\*, where E is the exchange rate, P is the domestic price level, and P\* is the foreign price level. Substituting for P and P\*, and then solving for E, the purchasing power exchange rate is 100 yen per dollar.*

   b. *If the Japanese inflation rate is 20 percent, then P\* rises to 120. Again, using the formula in answer (a), the new purchasing power exchange rate is 120 yen per dollar.*

## PRACTICE PROBLEMS

1. Assume that you have $5,000 to invest. A good friend tells you of a great investment opportunity in the stock market. The stock pays a 10 percent dividend, and there is a 30 percent chance that it will double in price. However, there is also a 70 percent chance that the stock price will fall by half. What is the expected value of this once-in-a-lifetime opportunity?

2. 
   a. What will be the price of a $6,000 bond that has a coupon of $500 for two years? Assume an interest rate of 6 percent

   b. What happens if the interest rate rises to 10 percent?

3. Assume that the United States (domestic) price level is 100 dollars and the German (foreign) price level is 500 marks.

   a. What is the purchasing power exchange rate?

   b. Assume there is 25 percent inflation in the United States, *ceteris paribus*. What is the new purchasing power exchange rate?

## CHAPTER TEST

1.  A computer used to pace the assembly line in the Saturn factory is an example of

    a.  physical capital.
    b.  financial capital.
    c.  diversification.
    d.  an equity contract.

2.  An example of a debt contract is

    a.  a bond.
    b.  cash.
    c.  the depreciation of physical capital.
    d.  a share of stock.

3.  The marginal revenue product of capital for a business that sells output in a competitive market equals the

    a.  marginal product of labor multiplied by the price of output.
    b.  marginal product of capital multiplied by the price of output.
    c.  marginal product of capital multiplied by the marginal revenue of output.
    d.  marginal product of labor multiplied by the marginal revenue of output.

4.  Profits are maximized by adding units of capital until the

    a.  marginal product of labor equals the wage.
    b.  marginal revenue product of labor equals the wage.
    c.  marginal product of capital equals the rental price.
    d.  marginal revenue product of capital equals the rental price.

5.  In markets where the supply of the product is fixed,

    a.  supply partially determines price.
    b.  demand never determines price.
    c.  demand completely determines price.
    d.  price is always zero.

6.  For competitive firms that purchase inputs in competitive markets, profits are maximized when the *MRP* of labor equals the _____, the *MRP* of capital equals the _____, and the marginal revenue of output equals the _____.

    a.  rental price, marginal cost, wage
    b.  wage, rental price, marginal revenue
    c.  wage, rental price, marginal cost
    d.  marginal cost, wage, rental price

7.  When owners of stock sell it for more than they paid for it, they

    a.  earn a capital gain.
    b.  suffer a capital loss.
    c.  decrease their return.
    d.  will still receive dividends.

8.  The dividend plus the capital gain is the _____ from holding a stock.

    a.  coupon
    b.  return
    c.  price-earnings ratio

    d.    dividend yield

9.    At the maturity date of a bond,

    a.    coupon payments stop and the principal is paid.
    b.    the principal is paid, but coupon payments continue.
    c.    the principal is paid, coupon payments stop, and a stock certificate is issued.
    d.    dividend payments stop and the principal is paid.

10.    There is _____ relationship between bond prices and bond yields.

    a.    an inverse
    b.    a positive
    c.    a proportional
    d.    no

11.    Discounting

    a.    converts present payments into future values.
    b.    converts future payments into present values.
    c.    is never used in investment decisions.
    d.    converts future payments into other future payments.

12.    A bungee jumper who ties two ropes to her legs before jumping off the tower is _____ compared to one who ties only one rope to his leg.

    a.    a risk lover
    b.    thinking less about risk
    c.    risk averse
    d.    discounting

13.    The expected return from an investment

    a.    accounts for the probabilities of alternative outcomes.
    b.    is always equal to an investor's opportunity cost.
    c.    is what an investor must earn to make a profit.
    d.    is an unnecessary calculation because investing is very certain.

14.    In equilibrium, we expect to see a _____ relationship between risk and return.

    a.    negative
    b.    positive
    c.    proportional
    d.    constant

15.    Systematic risk is

    a.    removed through portfolio diversification.
    b.    due to the ups and downs in the economy and affects all stocks to some degree.
    c.    what the first bungee jumper in question 12 is trying to avoid.
    d.    never a factor in investing.

16.    The efficient market hypothesis is

    a.    based on asymmetric information.
    b.    never observed because financial markets are known to work slowly.
    c.    the idea that there is an elimination of profit opportunities in financial markets as prices adjust quickly to new information.
    d.    held to be false by all economists.

17. Exchange rates are determined

    a. in the labor market.
    b. by thelaw of diminishing returns.
    c. in the foreign exchange market.
    d. by government decree.

18. Purchasing power parity suggests that, over the long run,

    a. nontradable goods will have the same price in different countries.
    b. tradable goods will have different prices in different countries.
    c. tradable goods will have the same price in different countries.
    d. nontradable goods eventually become tradable goods.

# ANSWERS TO THE REVIEW QUESTIONS

## Fill-In Questions

1. Machines, factories; computers
2. productive usefulness
3. Financial capital; equity contract
4. rental price of capital; rental market
5. marginal revenue product of capital
6. implicit rental price
7. dividend; capital gain; return
8. earnings; price-earnings ratio
9. coupon; maturity date; face value
10. yield; inverse
11. risk lover
12. probability
13. equilibrium risk-return relationship
14. portfolio diversification; systematic risk
15. foreign exchange market
16. Purchasing power parity (PPP)
17. Inflation rate; differences in rates of return

## True-False Questions

1. **True.** Physical capital depreciates. Its productive usefulness declines over time.
2. **True.** They are a form of equity contract.
3. **True.** A bond is an IOU and, therefore, a form of debt.
4. **False.** It is the rental price of capital.

5.  **False.**  The reverse is true. Capital is an input. The demand for any input is derived from the demand for the output of a firm.

6.  **True.**  With economic rent, changes in price do not result in changes in quantity supplied.

7.  **True.**  This price is called the implicit rental price.

8.  **False.**  Capital losses can also occur.

9.  **False.**  Both are expressed as percents of the price of a stock.

10. **False.**  The coupon is the fixed payment for each period. The face value is the principal amount due at the maturity date.

11. **True.**  When the price of a bond falls, the difference between the price and the face value increases, and so the yield increases.

12. **False.**  Systematic risk is that component of risk that cannot be dealt with through diversification.

13. **True.**  The return is estimated by the uncertain expected value.

14. **True.**  This is a form of the efficient market hypothesis.

15. **False.**  PPP works best in the long run. Inflation rates and differences in rates of return affect the short-run ability of PPP to work very well.

## Short-Answer Questions

1.  Physical capital refers to machines, equipment, factories, and the like, which are combined with labor to produce products. Physical capital depreciates over its life. Financial capital refers to funds raised through the use of debt and equity contracts.

2.  Both debt contracts and equity contracts are tools for raising financial capital. With a debt contract, money is borrowed, interest is paid, and the principal is repaid at some future date. An equity contract is an exchange of ownership for funds. Equity holders receive profits through the payment of dividends.

3.  Profit maximization occurs when the marginal revenue product of the last unit of capital employed equals the rental price (either implicit or explicit) of capital.

4.  Yes. Physical capital is an input, just like labor. There is a demand for capital because there is a demand for the products it produces.

5.  Economic rent is the price of anything that has a fixed supply (perfectly inelastic supply curve).

6.  The rules are that (1) the marginal revenue of output should equal the marginal cost of output, (2) the marginal revenue product of labor should equal the wage, and (3) the marginal revenue product of capital should equal the rental price.

7.  The return from holding a stock is the dividend plus the capital gain or loss. The return is expressed relative to the price, which is the return divided by the price of a share.

8.  The maturity date is the date on which the principal is repaid to the bondholder. The difference between the date of purchase of the bond and the maturity date is the period over which interest payments are received.

9.  Yes. There is an inverse relationship. As bond prices fall, the yields rise.

10. Risk aversion means that people will choose the less risky of two alternatives offering the same return.

11. Often the return from an investment is uncertain. Several outcomes are possible, each with a different probability of occurring. The expected return is created by weighing the different outcomes according to their probabilities.

12. Portfolio diversification reduces the risk associated with holding any one stock. However, it does not remove systematic risk. This is the risk due to the ups and downs in the economy, which affect all stocks to some degree.

13. The efficient market hypothesis states that there is an elimination of profit opportunities in financial markets as prices quickly adjust to new information.

14. The same tradable commodity will sell for about the same price in different countries. PPP is a theory that exchange rates are determined in such a way that the prices of tradable goods in different countries are the same when measured in the same currency.

## SOLUTIONS TO THE PRACTICE PROBLEMS

1. If the first case occurs, you will gain a dividend of

$$\$500 = (\$5,000 \times 0.10)$$

and a capital gain of

$$\$500 = (\$5,000 \times 1.00)$$

for a total of $5,500. If the second case occurs, you still get the dividend of $500, but you will also suffer a loss of

$$-\$2,500 = (\$5,000 \times 0.50)$$

for a total of –$2,000.

The expected value of your opportunity is

$$(\$5,500 \times 0.30) + (\$2,000 \times 0.70) = \$250$$

2. a. Using the formula in Table 13.1 in the text,

$$\text{Bond price} = \left[\$500/(1+0.06)\right] + \left[\$500/(1+0.06)^2\right] + \left[\$6,000/(1+0.06)^2\right]$$
$$= \$471.70 + \$445.00 + \$5,339.98$$
$$= \$6256.68$$

   b. With an interest rate of 10 percent, the bond price will be $5,826.44. The price will fall.

3. a. The exchange rate is 5 marks per dollar.

   b. The new exchange rate is 4 marks per dollar.

## ANSWERS TO THE CHAPTER TEST

1. a
2. a
3. b
4. d
5. c

6. c

7. a

8. b

9. a

10. a

11. b

12. c

13. a

14. b

15. b

16. c

17. c

18. c

# APPENDIX TO CHAPTER 16

# Present Discounted Value

## OVERVIEW

One of the characteristics of investing in financial and physical capital, as well as many other economic decisions, is the fact that there is the anticipation of *future* returns in the form of revenue or benefits. Yet, most of the expenditures for such investments are made up front or at the *present* time. A problem is that individuals prefer dollars received today over dollars that will be received tomorrow. So, how do you know when to invest? The first step is to convert or discount *future dollars* into *present dollars*. The end result of this conversion is called the present discounted value.

## ZEROING IN

1.  The concept of discounting is based on the simple notion that a dollar in the future is worth less than a dollar today. Imagine the following situation. Your economics professor offers you (because you are the best student in the class) $100 today or $100 a year from now. With total honesty, which would you choose? People generally have what economists call a positive time preference—you will pick the $100 now. Instead of waiting, you could purchase things and derive utility from them now or you could invest the money and earn interest. But what if the offer is $100 now or $110 a year from now? Here, waiting provides a benefit of $10. You may still opt for the $100. However, if your professor continued to increase the future payoff, it would eventually reach a point where you would wait.

    This could be described another way. Suppose the offer was $90 now or $100 a year from now? Again there is a benefit from waiting. You may still feel that $90 today is worth more than the future payment of $100. But the present value could be lowered until you did not know which one to take—both would be equally desirable to you.

2.  The formula for finding the present discounted value (*PDV*) of a future amount (*F*) received one year from now is PDV=F/(1+r). This formula can be expanded to determine the present discounted value for future amounts received over many future years as well. Regardless of the length of the chain, it is important to see the role played by the interest rate or the discount rate (*r*) found in the denominator. What rate should you choose? Well, it depends on many things, including what rate you could have made on your next best investment alternative – your opportunity cost. Furthermore, you should note that as the discount rate rises, the discounted present value falls. This is to say, as the interest rate rises, the value of the future falls.

## ACTIVE REVIEW

### Fill-In Questions

1.  The process of converting a future payment into a present amount is called
    _____. The value in the present is called the _____.
    Discounting requires the use of a(n) _____.

2.    As the interest rate rises, the discounted present value _____.

# WORKED PROBLEM

1.

    a.    What is the present value of $5,000 three years from now at a discount rate of 10 percent?

    b.    What would be the present value of $5,000 in each of the next three years?

    c.    What would happen to the present value in (1a) if the interest rate fell to 5 percent?

**Answer**

    a.    *Using the formula in the Appendix to Chapter 16,*

$$\text{PDV} = \left[ \$5,000/(1 + 0.10)^3 \right] = \$5,000/1.331 = \$3,756.57$$

    b.

$$\text{PDV} = \left[ \$5,000/(1 + 0.10) \right] + \left[ \$5,000/(1 + 0.10)^2 \right] + \left[ \$5,000/(1 + 0.10)^3 \right]$$
$$= \$4,545.45 + \$4,132.23 + \$3,756.57$$
$$= \$12,434.25$$

    c.

$$\text{PDV} = \left[ \$5,000/(1+0.05)^3 \right] = \$5,000/1.1576 = \$4,319.28$$

The present value rises as the interest rate falls from 10 percent to 5 percent.

# PRACTICE PROBLEM

1.

    a.    What is the present value of $4,000 to be received two years from now? Assume an interest rate of 4 percent.

    b.    What is the present value of $4,000 to be received in each of the next three years? Again assume an interest rate of 4 percent.

    c.    What happens to the present value in (1a) if the interest rate rises to 8 percent?

# ANSWERS TO THE REVIEW QUESTIONS

## Fill-In Questions

1.    discounting; present discounted; discount rate

2.    falls

# SOLUTIONS TO THE PRACTICE PROBLEM

1.

    a.    Using the general formula in the Appendix to Chapter 16,

$$PDV = \left[\$4,000/(1 + 0.04)^2\right] = \$3,698.22$$

b.

$$PDV = \left[\$4,000/(1 + 0.04)\right] + \left[\$4,000/(1 + 0.04)^2\right] + \left[\$4,000/(1 + 0.04)^3\right]$$
$$= \$3,846.15 + \$3,698.22 + \$3,555.98$$
$$= \$11,100.35$$

c.

$$PDV = \left[\$4,000/(1 + .08)^2\right] = \$3,429.36.$$

The present value falls as the interest rate rises from 4 percent to 8 percent.

# Sample Test: (Chapters 13–16) Markets, Income Distribution, and Public Goods

## SAMPLE TEST QUESTIONS

1. If an individual's labor supply curve is negatively sloped,

    a. the income effect is less powerful than the substitution effect.
    b. the income effect is more powerful than the substitution effect.
    c. the income effect equals the substitution effect.
    d. the substitution effect is not operating.
    e. the income effect is not operating.

2. Competitive firms maximize profits by hiring labor until

    a. the minimum wage equals the *MRP*.
    b. $AVC = P$.
    c. $MC = AVC = MRP$.
    d. $MRP = W$.
    e. $ATC = W$.

3. Supply and demand analysis

    a. has been thoroughly discredited as a basis for analyzing labor.
    b. is used only in relation to commodities, not with services like labor.
    c. is one of the tools economists use to investigate labor markets.
    d. explains all labor market phenomena.
    e. is the only tool of economic reasoning used to analyze labor markets.

4. The wage is the

    a. amount of money directly paid to a worker for hours worked.
    b. amount of labor worked for a specific amount of money.
    c. term used for the price of labor.
    d. amount of total earnings from all income sources over a period of time.

5. In competitive markets, discrimination is

    a. more likely to occur than in other markets.
    b. less likely to occur due to employer profit maximization.
    c. costless.
    d. regulated out of existence.
    e. efficient.

6. If, in equilibrium, no one person can be made better off without making someone else worse off, the economy has reached a point

    a. of Pareto efficiency.
    b. described as Arrow's impossibility theorem.

    c.    where it is in a voting paradox.

    d.    of externality.

    e.    where the median voter decides the distribution of income.

7.    Economic models of government that assume those in government take actions motivated by self-interest (such as getting reelected) are called

    a.    public interest models.

    b.    public choice models.

    c.    median voter models.

    d.    voting paradoxes.

    e.    interest group models.

8.    Business lobbying for legislation or other government actions that will preserve or obtain rights through which above-normal profits can be achieved is a type of

    a.    convergence.

    b.    government failure.

    c.    market failure.

    d.    voting paradox.

    e.    rent seeking.

9.    Market failure is

    a.    always characterized by unequal distribution of resources.

    b.    never caused by externalities.

    c.    any situation in which the market does not achieve economic efficiency for which there is a potential government role.

    d.    any situation in which the market achieves economic efficiency.

10.    The government in a democratic system cannot commit itself to future policies because

    a.    politicians are too easily influenced.

    b.    bureaucrats undermine previous decision.

    c.    voters can always change those policies.

    d.    most politicians cannot make up their minds.

11.    The incidence of a tax is largely determined by the

    a.    length of the demand curve.

    b.    length of the supply curve.

    c.    shape of the Lorenz curve.

    d.    elasticities of demand and supply.

    e.    sign on the Gini coefficient.

12.    A tax is progressive if

    a.    the marginal tax rate falls as income rises.

    b.    the marginal tax rate remains constant as income changes.

    c.    the average tax rate falls as the marginal tax rate rises.

    d.    Republicans oppose it.

    e.    the marginal tax rate rises as income rises.

13.    The amount of income tax that must be paid on an additional dollar of income is determined by the

    a.    payroll tax rate.

    b.    marginal tax rate.

    c.    average tax rate.
    d.    total tax rate.
    e.    highest tax rate.

14.    If a government program successfully reduces income inequality, then

    a.    the Lorenz curve has become more bowed.
    b.    the Lorenz curve has moved closer to the 45-degree line.
    c.    the Gini coefficient will approach 1.
    d.    the tax system will not redistribute income.
    e.    the tax incidence is shifting the demand curve.

15.    The degree of government involvement in redistributing income is ultimately

    a.    a matter for private charity to address.
    b.    a political decision.
    c.    an economic decision.
    d.    something the market can decide.
    e.    a Federal Reserve decision.

16.    A public good exhibits

    a.    rivalry in consumption.
    b.    nonrivalry in consumption and nonexcludability.
    c.    nonrivalry in consumption and excludability.
    d.    a high price and a small quantity.
    e.    rivalry in consumption and nonexcludability.

17.    When the present discounted value of a public infrastructure project exceeds the cost, government should

    a.    reinvest the profits into another public infrastructure project.
    b.    not invest in the project.
    c.    decide that the project is the only one in which to invest.
    d.    ask the private sector to invest in the project.
    e.    consider investing in the project.

18.    If I can enjoy a good without paying and without reducing the enjoyment of others, then

    a.    I am a bum.
    b.    a negative externality exists.
    c.    I am a free-rider.
    d.    I must be taxed so that others can be reimbursed.
    e.    excludability must be present.

19.    A negative externality exists when

    a.    marginal private cost is greater than marginal social cost.
    b.    excludability exceeds rivalry.
    c.    marginal private benefit equals marginal social benefit.
    d.    marginal private benefit equals marginal private cost.
    e.    marginal private cost is less than marginal social cost.

20.    Government regulations and restrictions used to correct market imperfections (such as making it illegal to pollute by more than a specific amount) are called

    a.    taxes.
    b.    subsidies.

    c.    transaction costs.

    d.    command and control remedies.

    e.    private remedies.

21. Depreciation occurs when

    a.    capital is abandoned.

    b.    production lines are shut down.

    c.    machines wear out.

    d.    factories get old.

    e.    capital is sold.

22. Which of the following is an example of financial capital?

    a.    Car

    b.    Vault

    c.    Cash

    d.    Office building

    e.    Computer

23. Systematic risk is

    a.    risk that cannot be avoided by diversifying within the market.

    b.    avoided by diversifying within the market.

    c.    avoided by portfolio rearrangement.

    d.    called market risk.

24. Economists believe that the price of a share of stock contains all the known current information about a firm because

    a.    there are barriers to entry in the stock market.

    b.    stockbrokers have secret information.

    c.    the stock market is an efficient market.

    d.    the costs of entering the marketplace are very high.

    e.    the government regulates the stock market.

25. Discounting is necessary in decisions concerning investing in physical capital because

    a.    future dollars are more valuable than present dollars.

    b.    future dollars are as valuable as present dollars.

    c.    depreciation has tax effects.

    d.    future dollars are worth less than present dollars.

    e.    the increased output will force lower prices on the market.

# ANSWERS TO THE SAMPLE TEST

1. b
2. d
3. c
4. c
5. b
6. a
7. b
8. e
9. c
10. c
11. d
12. e
13. b
14. b
15. b
16. b
17. e
18. c
19. e
20. d
21. c
22. c
23. a
24. c
25. d

# PART 5

# Trade and Global Markets

Chapter 17 demonstrates that international trade between people in different countries is based on the same economic principles as trade between people in the same country. The chapter explores how gains from trade are related to comparative advantage and economies of scale, and how the gains from international trade can be measured.

Chapter 18 covers international trade policy, including the effects of current and historical trade restrictions, the arguments in favor of trade restrictions, and policies meant to reduce trade barriers. Emerging market economies, including centrally planned economies, are the subject of Chapter 19. The discussion focuses on how centrally planned economies operate, how countries can make the transition to a market economy, and how economic reform has actually worked in practice.

# CHAPTER 17

# The Gains from International Trade

## CHAPTER OVERVIEW

It may be an old cliché , but the world does get smaller every day. This author's running shoes were made in Korea; his digital watch was assembled in Malaysia; he is looking forward to French wine with dinner, but not before calling his editor in Boston on a Japanese portable telephone. How international is your world at this moment?

International considerations permeate virtually every nook and cranny of the economy. This chapter begins to explore the role of international trade in the economy by examining the microeconomic foundations of why countries exchange goods and services. The theories of absolute and comparative advantage are presented. While you are just beginning to look at these things, economics has a rich history of interest in international trade, going back to Adam Smith and the *Wealth of Nations* (1776). By comparing and contrasting free trade with mercantilism, Smith showed how countries benefit from trade. The reasons for trade were more formally developed by David Ricardo in his theory of comparative advantage. The theory of comparative advantage stresses the importance of relative opportunity costs in determining what a country exports and what it imports. As a result of trade, the relative prices of products and of factors of production change. In fact, over time they tend to equalize between countries. This is shown using the already familiar production possibilities curve. Next, the Heckscher-Ohlin model is presented. This model addresses the determinants of comparative advantage. At its heart lie the abundance of factors of production and the intensity of their use.

Comparative advantage is not the only reason for trade. Economies of scale are also a reason to gain from trade. Here, complete specialization within a world market permits *ATC* to decline to a lower level than would have prevailed in a smaller market without trade. This is coupled with product differentiation to place the model of monopolistic competition into the world economy. Finally, the movement toward free trade and the costs associated with transition are discussed.

## CHAPTER REVIEW

1.  **International trade** offers many benefits to all countries. These can come in the form of increased specialization, a redistribution of existing supplies of goods, economies of scale in production, and increased competition. The importance of international trade in the world economy can be seen in the recent agreement between Mexico, Canada, and the United States to integrate their economies into a free trade area. In addition, there are many ongoing conversations among countries aimed at developing areas for expanded free trade. The **commerce clause** of the U.S. Constitution prohibits trade restraints between the states.

2.  A basic foundation of international trade is the theory of comparative advantage. A country will export those goods in which it has a comparative advantage. Such an advantage exists when the opportunity cost of producing a good in a country is lower than the opportunity cost of producing the same good in another country. This is to say, a country that is relatively more efficient than another country in producing one good rather than another good has a comparative advantage in the production of that good. This is true even if one country has an **absolute advantage** in the production of both goods. If countries specialize in the goods in which they have a comparative

advantage, the resulting trade flow will equate relative prices in each country. This can be shown with a production possibilities curve. If opportunity costs do not increase, countries will specialize in the production of goods in which they have a comparative advantage, and the total amount of goods available for consumption will increase, leading to **gains from trade**. The relative price after trade, or the quantity of imported goods that a country can obtain in exchange for a unit of exported goods, is called the **terms of trade**.

3.   The Heckscher-Ohlin model attempts to identify the determinants of a country's comparative advantage. According to the model, a country has a comparative advantage in those goods that are intensively produced with its most abundant factor of production—that is, a country that is relatively **capital abundant** has a comparative advantage in goods whose production is relatively **capital intensive**, and a country that is relatively **labor abundant** has a comparative advantage in goods whose production is relatively **labor intensive**. Using the Heckscher-Ohlin framework, it can be argued that **factor-price equalization** will occur.

4.   Gains from trade are also due to economies of scale. By specializing within a larger market brought about by free trade, a firm can take advantage of larger-scale economies. As a result, $ATC$ and price fall as quantity grows. Trade flows founded in economies of scale tend to be intraindustry in character, whereas trade flows based on comparative advantage tend to be interindustry.

5.   As the number of firms in a market of a given size increases, $ATC$ tends to rise, as each firm has a smaller market share. However, as markets grow in size through trade, the $ATC$ of existing firms falls. Also, as new firms enter the market, competition and product variety increase and, as a result, price falls, so that only normal profits are earned over the long run.

# ZEROING IN

1.   One of the most important ideas in economics is that of comparative advantage. A specific example will be explored in "Working It Out." For now, one way to think about comparative advantage is by using opportunity costs, another important economic notion. *Absolute* productivity (or absolute advantage) really does not matter in the determination of what goods are traded. This is hard for many people to accept. If absolute productivity were the determinant of trade, the United States would export nearly everything it produces, since the United States has the most resources, the most physical capital, and many workers with large amounts of human capital. However, in comparative advantage, *relative* efficiency or productivity matters. This can be measured using opportunity cost, or what must be given up to produce another unit of some product. Given the fundamental problem of scarcity, the maximization of net benefits also includes the minimization of costs. Comparing opportunity costs across countries focuses trade on the most efficient producer. So absolute advantage does not necessarily matter.

2.   The Heckscher-Ohlin model is one of the better-known theories that attempt to identify the determinants of comparative advantage. This explanation is based on two things. First, comparative advantage depends on the relative abundance of inputs within a country. For a given demand, inputs that are relatively abundant have lower prices than they would if they were less plentiful. The second consideration is the way resources are used within the production process— the intensity of their use. Therefore, goods that are produced with a lot (intensity) of the most plentiful (abundant) resource are goods that can be produced by giving up the least amount of other things. Stated another way, the Heckscher-Ohlin model also identifies the determinants of opportunity costs.

## ACTIVE REVIEW

### Fill-In Questions

1.    The movement of goods and services between countries is called _____.

2.    Although sovereign governments often restrict trade with other countries, the _____ of the U.S. Constitution prevents such restraint between states.

3.    Quotas and _____ are forms of _____ .

4.    _____ are taxes on imports.

5.    In the *Wealth of Nations*, _____ argued that _____ would create benefits for trading partners.

6.    Adam Smith argued that international trade increases the size of the market, which allows for a(n) _____.

7.    The theory of comparative advantage was initially developed by _____.

8.    _____ can also be expressed in terms of opportunity costs.

9.    A person with a lower opportunity cost of producing a good than another person has a(n) _____ in that good.

10.   _____ efficiency is synonymous with comparative advantage.

11.   The price of one good in terms of another is called its _____.

12.   With trade, the _____ of a good in different countries will converge to the same value.

13.   The after-trade relative price is called the _____.

14.   A straight-line production possibilities curve will result in _____ within an economy after trade.

15.   _____ describes changes in comparative advantage over time.

16.   The _____ is used to describe an exception to the Heckscher-Ohlin model.

17.   One implication of the Heckscher-Ohlin model is that trade will bring about factor-price _____ in different countries.

18.   Not all gains from trade are based on _____; there are also gains based on _____.

19.   The gains from trade that result from economies of scale are the _____.

20.   Trade due to comparative advantage tends to be _____, whereas trade due to economies of scale tends to be _____.

21.   There is a(n) _____ relationship between the number of firms and the *ATC* of each firm.

### True-False Questions

1.    T    F    International trade creates gains only by exploiting a country's comparative advantage.

2.    T    F    Trade within the United States can be subject to tariffs levied by individual states.

3.    T   F      International trade has been growing rapidly as a result of declining costs of transportation and communication and the removal of restrictions on trade between countries.

4.    T   F      David Ricardo argued that trade was based on comparative advantage.

5.    T   F      International trade makes home markets more competitive.

6.    T   F      David Ricardo's concept of comparative advantage shows how a country can improve the incomes of its citizens by allowing them to trade with others.

7.    T   F      Absolute advantage can be expressed in terms of opportunity costs.

8.    T   F      Trade has very little effect on the prices of goods within a country.

9.    T   F      International trade allows countries to consume beyond their domestic (before trade) production possibilities curves.

10.   T   F      Increasing opportunity costs produce complete specialization within a country in a free trade environment.

11.   T   F      A straight-line production possibilities curve reflects constant opportunity costs.

12.   T   F      A country's comparative advantage remains constant over time.

13.   T   F      The Heckscher-Ohlin model is based, in part, on a country's factor supplies.

14.   T   F      The Heckscher-Ohlin model implies factor-price equalization.

15.   T   F      Trade that is a result of economies of scale tends to be interindustry in nature.

16.   T   F      As the number of firms in a market of a given size grows, the *ATC* falls.

17.   T   F      The movement toward free trade has no costs.

## Short-Answer Questions

1.     Give two reasons why international trade is beneficial.

2.     How did mercantilism promote the wealth of nations?

3.     "The tailor does not attempt to make his own shoes, but buys them from the shoemaker." Explain.

4.     Briefly explain David Ricardo's theory of comparative advantage.

5.     Why do prices change with trade?

6.     What are the terms of trade?

7.     What does trade do to a country's production possibilities curve?

8.     Is comparative advantage dynamic?

9.     What is the purpose of the Heckscher-Ohlin model?

10.    Is the Heckscher-Ohlin model always correct in predicting the nature of trade?

11.    What is factor-price equalization?

12.    Why does *ATC* tend to fall for a given number of firms as the market grows?

# WORKING IT OUT

Because of the importance of the theory of comparative advantage, it is worthwhile to try to identify the comparative advantage in a specific example. There are several ways to determine comparative advantage. One way is to look at the relative productivity per worker in each country. Another way is to look at the opportunity cost of moving workers from one type of production to another.

Suppose that both wool yarn and beef are produced in both Australia and Argentina. Assume that both goods are made with only labor, and that the following relationships hold:

- In Australia, 3 units of labor produce 105 pounds of beef, and 1 unit of labor produces 40 spools of wool yarn.

- In Argentina, 2 units of labor produce 60 pounds of beef, and 2 units of labor produce 30 spools of wool yarn.

Furthermore, Australia has 600 units of labor and Argentina has 200 units of labor.

1.  Figure 17.1 shows the production possibilities curves for Australia and Argentina. The production information may be used to determine the end points for each curve. For example, Australia can produce 21,000 pounds of beef [(600/3) × 105] or 24,000 spools of wool yarn [(600/1) × 40].

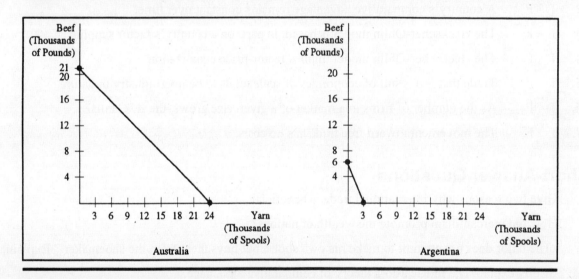

**Figure 17.1**

2.  First, look at the absolute advantage in each good. Australia has an absolute advantage in the production of both beef and wool yarn. One Australian worker can produce more of both yarn and beef.

3.  To describe the comparative advantage, let's look first at the relative productivity per worker in each country. In Australia, 1 worker produces 35 pounds of beef (105/3) or 40 spools of yarn (40/1). In Argentina, 1 worker produces 30 pounds of beef (60/2) or 15 spools of yarn (30/2). Thus, workers are relatively more productive in beef production in Argentina and in yarn production in Australia. Alternatively, to produce an additional 1,000 pounds of beef, it takes 28.6 workers in Australia (1,000/35), whereas it takes 33.33 workers (1,000/30) in Argentina. If those workers were moved into beef production from yarn production, Australia would lose 1,144 spools of yarn (28.6 × 40) and Argentina would lose approximately 500 spools of yarn. Obviously, beef is more expensive in terms of yarn in Australia than it is in Argentina. Thus, Australia has a comparative advantage in wool production and Argentina has a comparative advantage in the production of beef.

4.  What happens to the price of the imported good in each country? Australia imports beef from Argentina. The supply curve for beef in Australia shifts to the right as a result of the imports. Assuming that demand is constant, the price of beef in Australia will fall. Argentina imports yarn from Australia. The supply curve of yarn shifts to the right, and the price of yarn in Argentina falls, *ceteris paribus*.

## Worked Problems

1.  Assume that both Japan and France produce both cloth and computers. Assume that they are produced with only labor according to the following schedule:

    *   In France, 5 units of labor produce 100 bolts of cloth, and 2 units of labor produce 50 computers.

    *   In Japan, 6 units of labor produce 132 bolts of cloth, and 3 units of labor produce 45 computers.

    France has 1,000 units of labor, and Japan has 1,200 units of labor.

    a.  Construct the production possibilities curves.

    b.  Which country has an absolute advantage?

    c.  Identify the comparative advantage.

    d.  How does trade flow?

**Answers**

a.  *First, determine the end points of the production possibilities curves. France can produce 20,000 bolts of cloth [(1,000/5) × 100] or 25,000 computers [(1,000/2) × 50]. Japan can produce 26,400 bolts of cloth or 18,000 computers. Figure 17.2 shows the production possibilities curves for Japan and France.*

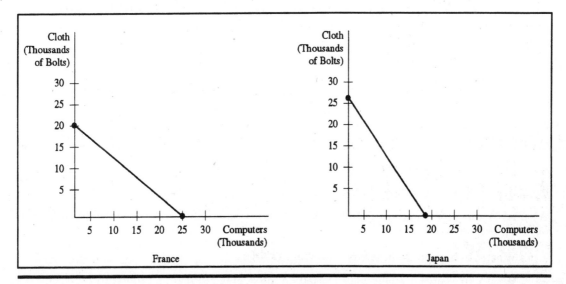

**Figure 17.2**

b.  *France has an absolute advantage in the production of computers, and Japan has an absolute advantage in the production of cloth.*

c.  *In France, 1 worker can produce 20 bolts of cloth or 25 computers. In Japan, 1 worker can produce 22 bolts of cloth or 15 computers. Thus, workers in Japan are relatively more efficient in cloth production than are French workers. Alternatively, to produce 100 additional bolts of cloth, France must give up 125 computers [(100/20 × 25], and Japan must give up 68 computers [(100/22) × 15]. Thus, the opportunity cost of cloth in terms of computers is lower in Japan. Japan has a comparative advantage in cloth production, whereas France has a comparative advantage in the production of computers.*

d.  *Computers flow from France to Japan, and cloth flows from Japan to France. The price of computers will fall in Japan, and the price of cloth will fall in France.*

2.  Whenever possible, it is helpful to present a new concept using the familiar tool of supply and demand analysis. Here we will look at the Heckscher-Ohlin model from a market perspective.

It was shown in "Working It Out" that Australia has a comparative advantage in wool production and Argentina has a comparative advantage in beef production. Assume that two kinds of labor, skilled and unskilled, are used to produce both wool and beef in both countries. Furthermore, assume that Argentina's comparative advantage is based on the fact that it has a very large number of unskilled workers and that they are employed intensively in beef production. Will the wage level of unskilled workers in Australia fall to that of unskilled workers in Argentina? Use the Heckscher-Ohlin model to support your answer.

**Answer**

*Trade causes a reallocation of existing supplies of beef and wool between Argentina and Australia. It also causes a movement in each country toward specialization in the good in which that country has a comparative advantage. This movement causes shifts in the demand for skilled and unskilled workers. Assume that the supply curve of unskilled workers is upward sloping (and not backward bending). With trade, beef production in Australia falls. This results in a decline in the demand for unskilled workers in Australia, and their wages will fall. At the same time, the demand for unskilled workers in Argentina rises as the production of beef increases. As a result, their wages rise. In a perfect Heckscher-Ohlin model, factor prices will tend to equalize between the two beginning wages, not necessarily at the lowest one.*

## PRACTICE PROBLEMS

1.  Assume that Japan and France initially trade cloth and computers as described in Worked Problem 1. However, assume that the Japanese government subsidizes computer research so that 3 units of labor now produce 90 computers. Also, because of a unique environmental problem, Japanese cloth producers have had to cut back to 120 bolts per 6 workers.

    a.  Identify the comparative advantage.

    b.  Briefly discuss the trade flows.

2.  Assume that the comparative advantage for Japan in Worked Problem 1 was due to an intensive use of abundant unskilled workers.

    a.  What will happen to these workers' wages?

    b.  What will happen to their wages based on the events in Practice Problem 1?

3.  Using Figure 17.2, what happened to price, *ATC*, and the number of firms when trade is allowed?

4.  What happens to Figure 17.2 when a new technological discovery lowers the *ATC* for all firms?

5.  Compare your answers in problems 3 and 4.

# CHAPTER TEST

1.  David Ricardo based his ideas concerning international trade on

    a.   comparative advantage.
    b.   absolute advantage.
    c.   the commerce clause of the Constitution.
    d.   the use of effective tariffs.

2.  Individual states in the United States are prohibited from restricting the free flow of goods by the

    a.   Federal Reserve Act of 1914.
    b.   Fair Labor Standards Act.
    c.   Declaration of Independence.
    d.   commerce clause of the U.S. Constitution.

3.  Constant opportunity costs lead to

    a.   absolute advantage.
    b.   total specialization.
    c.   no trade at all.
    d.   incomplete specialization.

4.  Factor-price equalization

    a.   is a foundation of absolute advantage.
    b.   tends to promote intraindustry trade.
    c.   suggests that the price of inputs in different countries will tend to equalize with trade.
    d.   will prevent trade from occurring.

5.  The benefits of free trade come from

    a.   a redistribution of existing supplies of goods.
    b.   a movement toward specialization.
    c.   increased competition.
    d.   all of the above.

6.  Free trade increases the size of markets. As a result, firms

    a.   can take advantage of economies of scale.
    b.   can strengthen their monopoly positions.
    c.   can maximize *ATC*.
    d.   are guaranteed profits.

7.  David Ricardo's theory of _____ advantage shows how a country benefits from trading with others.

    a.   absolute
    b.   constant
    c.   comparative
    d.   proportio

8.  Economists often use the concept of opportunity costs to explain

    a.   demand.
    b.   comparative advantage.
    c.   monopoly.
    d.   gravity.

9. With trade, relative prices within a country

   a. only rise.
   b. change.
   c. only fall.
   d. are unaffected.

10. Trade causes a country's production possibilities curve to

    a. change slope.
    b. shift inward in a parallel manner.
    c. shift outward in a parallel manner.
    d. remain constant.

11. If there are increasing opportunity costs, trade results in

    a. complete specialization.
    b. constant specialization.
    c. partial specialization.
    d. no specialization.

12. A major attempt at explaining the determinants of comparative advantage is found in

    a. the model of consumer behavior.
    b. diminishing returns to variable factors of production.
    c. the Taylor model.
    d. the Heckscher-Ohlin model.

13. According to the Heckscher-Ohlin model, a country will export goods

    a. produced intensively with its least abundant resource.
    b. not produced with its most abundant resource.
    c. produced intensively with no more than 10 percent of its most abundant resource.
    d. produced intensively with its most abundant resource.

14. If Sri Lanka exports products produced intensively with labor, its most abundant resource, then

    a. wages will fall relative to the prices of other resources.
    b. wages will remain unchanged.
    c. there is a Leontief paradox present.
    d. wages will rise relative to the prices of other resources.

15. Intraindustry trade refers to

    a. trade between different industries.
    b. trade within the same industry.
    c. trade within a country's own borders.
    d. trade determined by tariffs.

16. Interindustry trade refers to

    a. trade between different industries.
    b. trade within the same industry.
    c. trade within a country's own borders.
    d. trade determined by tariffs.

17. In a given market, as the number of firms increases,

    a. *ATC* falls.
    b. *MC* falls.

    c.   *ATC* rises.

    d.   *ATC* remains constant.

18.   For a given number of firms, as the market grows,

    a.   *ATC* rises.

    b.   *AFC* rises.

    c.   *ATC* remains unchanged.

    d.   *ATC* falls.

19.   When free trade occurs between countries,

    a.   the number that benefit is equal to the number that do not benefit.

    b.   there will be no impact on the price of factors of production in the countries involved.

    c.   quotas and tariffs will be used to enhance the benefits for every country.

    d.   all parties involved will benefit.

# ANSWERS TO THE REVIEW QUESTIONS

## Fill-In Questions

1.   international trade

2.   commerce clause

3.   quotas, trade restrictions

4.   Tariffs

5.   Adam Smith; free trade

6.   greater division of labor

7.   David Ricardo

8.   Comparative advantage

9.   comparative advantage

10.   Relative

11.   relative price

12.   relative price; converge

13.   terms of trade

14.   complete specialization

15.   Dynamic comparative advantage

16.   Leontief paradox

17.   equalization

18.   comparative advantage; economies of scale

19.   reduction in costs per unit

20.   interindustry; intraindustry

21.   positive

## True-False Questions

1.   **False**.   Gains from trade also result from economies of scale.

2.   **False**.   The commerce clause of the U.S. Constitution prohibits the restriction of trade between the states.

3.   **True**.   Recently, the United States, Canada, and Mexico formed a free trade area.

4.   **True**.   Ricardo's ideas of free trade were based on absolute advantage.

5.   **True**.   International trade increases the number of suppliers in a country. When there are more sellers, the market power of each is reduced.

6.   **True**.   Ricardo used the theory of comparative advantage and not absolute advantage. The benefits from trade between countries are based on the relative advantage of each country.

7.   **False**.   Opportunity costs are a way to define comparative advantage and not absolute advantage.

8.   **False**.   International trade is the movement of supplies of goods between countries. By changing the location of supplies, international trade does affect the prices of goods. In fact, trade flows will quickly eliminate price differences.

9.   **True**.   This is one way to show the gains from trade.

10.   **False**.   Under increasing opportunity costs, as more and more of a good is produced, the opportunity cost changes. These changes can reduce the gains from trade to the point where further specialization is no longer beneficial.

11.   **True**.   The tradeoff between the goods remains the same over the entire curve. Increasing opportunity costs are reflected by a production possibilities curve that bows outward.

12.   **False**.   Comparative advantage is a dynamic concept, especially if a country invests in human and physical capital and in technology.

13.   **True**.   According to the Heckscher-Ohlin model, a country will export those goods that are produced intensively with the country's most abundant resource.

14.   **True**.   Not only does trade change the location of the supplies of products, it also changes the demand for factors of production. Over time, shifts in demand and supply in product and input markets (in trading countries) will tend to equalize prices.

15.   **False**.   It tends to be intraindustry. Trade based on comparative advantage tends to be interindustry.

16.   **False**.   As the number of firms in a market of a given size rises, the market share of each falls. Thus, ATC will rise.

17.   **False**.   Often trade barriers need to be phased out over an extended period of time. Trade adjustment assistance programs may be necessary to help workers who are adversely affected by the movement toward free trade.

## Short-Answer Questions

1.   First, firms are able to reduce costs through economies of scale because trade makes markets larger. Second, trade allows countries to specialize in producing those goods in which they are relatively efficient.

2. According to mercantilist theory, a country would become wealthy through the accumulation of gold and silver. This was accomplished by maximizing exports while minimizing imports, or maximizing net exports. Government regulation of trade through tariffs and quotas is required for this to happen.

3. This is from the *Wealth of Nations*. In this passage, Adam Smith is arguing that trade is based on absolute advantage.

4. The theory of comparative advantage explains how a country can gain from trading with others. A country exports those products in which it has a comparative advantage. Simply stated, country A has a comparative advantage in a good relative to country B if the opportunity cost of producing that good in country A is less than it is in country B.

5. Trade reallocates the supplies of products. Assuming competition and negligible transportation costs, trade moves goods to the place (country) where they command the highest price. As a result, the price falls in one country and rises in the other.

6. Simply stated, the terms of trade for a country are given by the quantity of imported goods that it can obtain per unit of exported goods.

7. Trade causes the production possibilities curve to rotate out along the axis of the good that is imported. The change in the slope of the curve reflects the change in relative prices caused by trade.

8. Yes, comparative advantage can change. This can occur through investment in physical and human capital and in technology.

9. The Heckscher-Ohlin model attempts to explain the determinants of comparative advantage. The model argues that comparative advantage is based on the relative abundance of resource supplies and the relative intensity with which those supplies are used in production.

10. Not necessarily. The Leontief paradox describes a situation in which trade does not clearly reflect relative factor intensities.

11. Factor-price equalization is the tendency of the prices of factors of production to equalize across countries. As countries trade and specialize in production, the demand for inputs also changes. This causes the prices of factors of production to change. The wages of unskilled labor will fall in countries that import goods made with unskilled labor, whereas the wages of unskilled workers in countries that export these goods will rise as production expands.

12. As markets grow, the amount produced by each firm increases. This allows firms to take advantage of economies of scale, and, as a result, *ATC* falls.

## SOLUTIONS TO THE PRACTICE PROBLEMS

1.
   a. In France, 1 worker still produces 20 bolts of cloth or 25 computers. In Japan, however, 1 worker now produces 20 bolts of cloth or 30 computers. Therefore, as a result of the research, Japan is now (relative to France) more productive in computer production than in cloth production—to get 100 more computers, Japan must give up 67 bolts of cloth $[(100/30) \times 20]$, whereas France must give up 80 $[(100/25) \times 20]$.

   b. Comparative advantage has shifted, and the flow of trade reverses.

2.
   a. As cloth production increases, the demand for unskilled workers in Japan will rise. This will cause the wages of the unskilled workers to rise, *ceteris paribus*.

b.    Comparative advantage has shifted. The demand for unskilled workers in Japan will fall, and their wages will fall.

3.    NAFTA made the area of free trade larger. Thus, each firm had a larger market. As a result, firms should have become larger, and $ATC$ should have fallen. This results in a rightward shift in $F$ to $F_1$.

4.    This will shift $F$ to the right, indicating a lower $ATC$ for a given number of firms in a market of a given size.

5.    The results are essentially the same. Expanding free trade is like discovering a new technique of production.

# ANSWERS TO THE CHAPTER TEST

1.    a
2.    d
3.    b
4.    c
5.    d
6.    a
7.    c
8.    b
9.    b
10.   a
11.   c
12.   d
13.   d
14.   d
15.   b
16.   a
17.   c
18.   d
19.   d

# CHAPTER 18

# International Trade Policy

## CHAPTER OVERVIEW

In the previous chapter, we explored the case for free trade. By exploiting comparative advantage and economies of scale, the citizens of a country (large or small) benefit from the free exchange of goods with other countries. However, free trade is not widely observed. For many reasons, governments restrict trade through tariffs, quotas, and other barriers. This chapter examines the consequences of these actions, looks at reasons supporting the use of trade restrictions, and presents ways of moving toward an environment of free trade. First, tariffs, quotas, and various nontariff trade barriers are examined, using the supply and demand model. Then a history of trade restrictions in the United States is presented. The discussion ranges from the tariff of abominations and Smoot-Hawley to GATT, the Uruguay Round, and the WTO. Next, many arguments supporting the use of trade barriers are discussed. These include strategic trade policy, infant industries, national security, and simple retaliation. Finally, the chapter ends with an examination of alternative policies to reduce trade barriers, including unilateral disarmament, bilateral and multilateral negotiations, customs unions, and free trade areas.

## CHAPTER REVIEW

1.  The United States is a relatively open economy. But this is a minority position in the world. Virtually all countries have protectionist policies; they impose **tariffs** (**ad valorem** and **specific**) and **quotas** on imported goods. Tariffs shift the **export supply curve** up by the dollar amount of the tariff, so that it intersects the **import demand curve** at a lower quantity. Tariffs generate duties or revenues for the government. Quotas can be analyzed in a similar fashion. Quotas, however, generate revenues for the individuals who hold the quota—those having the right to import the specific good.

2.  In recent years, new alternatives to tariffs and quotas have been observed. One of these is the **voluntary restraint agreement (VRA)**. Under a VRA, a government asks another country to "voluntarily" reduce its exports. This has market effects similar to those of a quota, except that the revenues go to the foreign producer. Other trade barriers include quality and performance standards, labor and environmental standards, and national defense.

3.  The U.S. economy has not always been a relatively free trade environment. The use of **revenue tariffs** can be traced back to before 1800. Some of the more infamous and disruptive tariffs include the "tariff of abominations" of 1828 and the **Smoot-Hawley tariff** of 1930, which led to a **trade war** as each country tried to beat the others with higher tariffs. In 1934 the **Reciprocal Trade Agreement Act** was passed, allowing President Roosevelt to reduce tariffs if other countries reciprocated. This process was made permanent in 1947 with the passage of the **General Agreement on Trade and Tariffs (GATT)**. Another form of trade restriction is **antidumping duties**, which address the problem of a foreign firm selling below its average cost or below the price in the home country (**dumping**). Other **nontariff barriers** to trade include the Multifiber Agreement (MFA).

4.  Even though estimates suggest that removing trade restrictions from the economy would produce an annual gain of as much as $60 billion, arguments for the continuation of trade restrictions are many. One such argument is that trade restrictions create benefits if the output of a monopoly can be reduced. Another argument suggests that tariffs and the like should be used to protect industries that are necessary for the national defense. Then there is the **infant industry argument**—trade restrictions should be imposed to give firms time to get established and become competitive. Finally, it is argued, if others restrict trade, why should we not also restrict trade? All of these arguments have weak points and disadvantages. It is also the case that there are alternatives to trade restrictions that are less harmful to the economy but that achieve the same ends.

5.  There is a growing movement toward expanding free trade. There are five approaches to doing this. One approach is simply unilateral disarmament; this is difficult to achieve today. An alternative is **multilateral negotiation**, which allows opposing political interests to cancel each other out. An example is the recent **Uruguay Round** of GATT negotiations and the creation of the **World Trade Organization (WTO)**. Multilateral negotiations are almost always conducted on a **most-favored nation (MFN)** basis. Creating regional trading areas is another approach. With this approach, it is hoped that the increase in trade that results, or **trade creation**, will outweigh the replacement of low-cost firms from outside the area with high-cost firms within it, or **trade diversion**. There are two types of regional trading areas: **free trade areas** and **customs unions**. NAFTA is a recent example of a free trade area (FTA) involving the United States, Mexico, and Canada. With a free trade area, **domestic content restrictions** are needed to prevent external tariff avoidance.

## ZEROING IN

The model of supply and demand was used to examine the effects of tariffs and quotas. Practicing with supply and demand will reaffirm your developing knowledge of this essential economic paradigm.

1.  Figure 18.1 shows the market for some imported good. $D_1$ is the import demand curve, and $S_1$ is the export supply curve before any trade restrictions are instituted. Thus, $P_1$ and $Q_1$ are the equilibrium price and quantity.

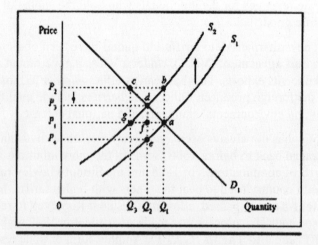

**Figure 18.1**

Assume that a tariff of amount $ab$ is levied. As described in the text, this shifts the export supply curve up to $S_2$, where the vertical distance between $S_1$ and $S_2$ is equal to $ab$. Consumers must now pay $P_1$ plus the tariff, or $P_2$ ($P_2 = P_1 + ab$). At this point, however, there is a surplus on the market of *cb*. As a result, the price falls to $P_3$ with equilibrium quantity $Q_2$. Consumers now pay $P_3$ instead of $P_1$, and consumer surplus has fallen by the area $P_1P_3da$. However, although buyers pay $P_3$, foreign sellers get only $P_4$, where the difference *de* is the tariff collected by the government. Like consumer surplus, producer surplus has declined by the area $P_1P_4ea$. The tariff has made both domestic consumers and foreign producers worse off. The government, however, collects tariff revenue equal to the tariff per unit multiplied by the number of units subject to the tariff. In Figure 18.1 this is shown by the area $P_3P_4ed$. As you can see, the government is capturing some of the surplus lost by consumers and producers. The triangle *dea* is that part of the reduction in consumer and producer surplus that no one gets; this is the deadweight loss. So, a tariff is like a black hole in space—it makes some consumer and producer surplus disappear!

2.  Figure 18.1 may also be used to review the effects of a quota. Assume that the free trade equilibrium is shown by $P_1$ and $Q_1$. One way a quota works is for the government to give someone an importing license. This allows this person to be the only importer of a product, making it easy for the government to keep track of imports to be sure the quota limit is not being violated. In terms of Figure 18.1, suppose that the license agreement says that no more than $Q_2$ may be imported. The quota holder now buys this amount from foreign suppliers for $P_4$ and sells it to domestic buyers for $P_3$. The area $P_3P_4ed$ is the revenue earned by the quota holder. Also, there is still the deadweight loss of *dea*.

3.  A VRA works like a quota, but we do away with the quota holder. The government sends an official representative to the foreign country and asks that country to export only $Q_2$. Alternatively, the official asks the country to hold $Q_1Q_2$ off the market. The foreign supplier now sells $Q_2$ at price $P_3$, and the area $P_3P_4ed$ comes to the foreign firm as extra revenue. Also, like a tariff or quota, the VRA results in a deadweight loss of *dea*.

# ACTIVE REVIEW

## Fill-In Questions

1.  A(n) _____ is a tax equal to a certain percentage of the value of an imported good.

2.  A specific tax is a tax on the quantity sold of an _____.

3.  When the United States government imposes a tariff, the _____ shifts by the dollar amount of the tariff.

4.  _____ set a maximum amount of a good that can be imported.

5.  _____ generate tax revenue for the government.

6.  A(n) _____ or _____ is similar to a quota, but it is imposed by a foreign government before goods are shipped to the United States.

7.  Foreign firms have located factories in the United States to avoid _____.

8.  _____ and _____ are examples of trade barriers related to domestic issues. These are often referred to as _____.

9.  In general, over time, tariffs in the United States have _____.

10. The _____ was levied during the Depression of the 1930s and may have, in fact, increased its duration and depth.

11. The _____ allowed President Roosevelt to lower tariffs if certain conditions were met in other countries. This approach was made permanent in 1947 with the creation of the _____.

12. Dumping occurs when a foreign firm sells a product at a price below _____ or the price in the home country. This has promoted the creation of _____.

13. Trade restrictions designed to permit firms to achieve economies of scale are referred to as _____.

14. Alexander Hamilton favored tariffs based on a(n) _____ argument.

15. The repeal of the Corn Laws in England is an example of the _____ approach to reducing trade barriers.

16. If a country is not granted _____, _____ are imposed on the imports of that country.

## True-False Questions

1. T  F   A tariff shifts the export demand curve upward.
2. T  F   Tariffs create revenue for the government.
3. T  F   A VRA and a quota are both imposed by the importing country.
4. T  F   Fuel economy standards for cars sold in the United States are a form of trade restriction.
5. T  F   Tariffs are a new and growing method used by the U.S. government to raise revenues for domestic transfer payments.
6. T  F   The Smoot-Hawley tariffs of 1930 helped create a worldwide trade war.
7. T  F   Dumping is not permitted in the United States.
8. T  F   Tariffs are mutually beneficial.
9. T  F   National security has been used as a rationale for trade restrictions.
10. T  F   Unilateral disarmament is a more popular way of reducing trade barriers than multilateral negotiations.
11. T  F   A VRA is a way to manage trade.
12. T  F   NAFTA created a common currency in Canada, Mexico, and the United States.

## Short-Answer Questions

1. What are some differences between a tariff and a quota?
2. Is the effect of a VRA similar to that of a quota?
3. What is a transplant?
4. What is a nontariff trade barrier?
5. What is the Reciprocal Trade Agreement Act, and how is it related to GATT?
6. Why is it difficult to identify dumping?
7. What is the infant industry argument?

8.   Describe the Uruguay Round.

9.   Differentiate between free trade areas (FTAs) and customs unions.

10.  What is MFN?

# WORKING IT OUT

International trade has linked markets in different countries and, as a result, has changed the prices of products and of factors of production. These linkages created net benefits for all the economies involved. In this chapter, we have examined the impact of blockages or restrictions to these connections. It is always useful to practice analysis with the supply and demand model. Let us look once again at the similar effects of tariffs, quotas, and VRAs on supply and demand.

In the competitive supply and demand model, tariffs, quotas, and VRAs are best modeled by shifting the supply of the imported product. Please refer to Figure 18.1. Assume that the beginning equilibrium price is $P_1$ and the equilibrium quantity is $Q_1$. In the case of tariffs, the supply curve shifts back by the amount $ab$. Under a quota, the domestic government limits imports to quantity $0Q_3$. This has the effect of shifting the supply curve back as well. Under a VRA, the foreign government tells its producers to only export the quantity $0Q_3$ to the importing country, and the effect is the same as the quota. The source of the limitation is different. In each instance, however, the final equilibrium price is $P_3$. In the case of the tariff, this price was reached from the excess supply of $cd$. The quota and the VRA initially created excess demand of $ga$. All three policies have a deadweight loss of $dea$.

## Worked Problems

1.   Show the effects of a tariff on a market, assuming that demand is perfectly inelastic. How does your answer change if demand is less than perfectly inelastic?

**Answer**

*Figure 18.2 shows the effects of a tariff and the role of differing elasticities.*

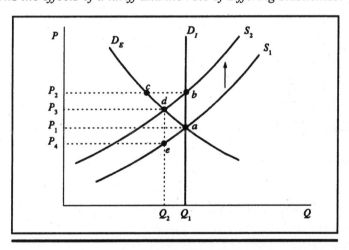

**Figure 18.2**

*Assume that the pretariff supply curve is $S_1$. Two demand curves are indicated, $D_I$ and $D_E$. For convenience, they both cross the supply curve at point a, making $P_1$ the pretariff equilibrium market price. As in previous examples, a tariff shifts the export supply curve up to $S_2$, where the distance ab is the amount of the tariff. If demand is perfectly inelastic ($D_I$), the effect of the tariff is* to raise the market price to $P_2$. Here, quantity demanded is unaffected. Tariff revenue is shown by the area $P_2P_1ab$. Also, there is no deadweight loss. However, if the demand is relatively more elastic ($D_E$), the tariff raises the price only to $P_3$—because demand has a negative slope (not vertical), at $P_2$ there is a surplus of $cb$, and quantity falls to $Q_2$. Tariff revenue is now $P_3P_4ed$, which is less than the revenue generated when demand was vertical. Also, a deadweight loss exists equal to the area $dea$. When demand is perfectly inelastic, more revenue is generated and the deadweight loss is minimized.

2.    Using Figure 18.2, tell who bears the burden of the tariff.

**Answer**

When demand is $D_I$, price increases by the full amount of the tariff ($P_2P_1 = ba$); therefore, domestic consumers bear the burden. However, if demand is $D_E$, the price increases only to $P_3$. Thus, domestic consumers pay $P_3P_1$ of the tariff, while foreign producers pay the portion $P_1P_4$. From this it appears that consumers bear more of the burden the greater the inelasticity of demand.

# PRACTICE PROBLEMS

1.

   a.    Draw a market in such a way as to make foreign sellers pay all of a tariff.

   b.    From whom does the government collect revenue?

2.    Would a quota holder rather have a license for an imported product that had a relatively inelastic (not perfectly inelastic) demand or a relatively elastic demand? Draw a market diagram to support your answer.

# CHAPTER TEST

1.    Policies that restrict trade are called

   a.    protectionist policies.
   b.    GATT agreements.
   c.    reciprocal trade agreements.
   d.    free trade zones.

2.    A tax equal to a certain percentage of the value of an imported good is a(n)

   a.    specific tariff.
   b.    ad valorem tariff.
   c.    quota.
   d.    nontariff trade.

3.    Tariffs

   a.    move the export supply curve right.
   b.    move the import demand curve left.
   c.    move the export supply curve left.
   d.    do not generate revenue for the government.

4.    The increased revenues that result from a quota are collected by

   a.    the government.
   b.    consumers through enhanced consumer surplus.

c.   foreign monopolies.
d.   the quota holder.

5.   Protectionist policies include the use of

a.   VRAs.
b.   quotas.
c.   tariffs.
d.   any of the above; they are all tools of managed trade.

6.   The revenue collected under a VRA goes to

a.   the government.
b.   the quota holder.
c.   the foreign producer.
d.   consumers as part of reduced consumer surplus.

7.   Fuel economy standards for all cars (foreign and domestic) sold in the United States may be considered a form of

a.   nontariff trade barrier.
b.   quota.
c.   tariff.
d.   government labor standards.

8.   Possibly the worst U.S. tariff policy

a.   was that under Smoot-Hawley.
b.   came from GATT.
c.   was started under the Reciprocal Trade Agreement Act of 1934.
d.   was passed in 1826 and was called the tariff of abominations.

9.   Dumping is the selling of a product by a foreign company at a price below

a.   the level of a tariff.
b.   average costs.
c.   average fixed costs.
d.   marginal cost.

10.   The deadweight loss from a VRA is

a.   equal to the revenue collected by the government.
b.   equal to the revenue collected by the quota holder.
c.   the difference between the reduction in consumer surplus and the increase in producer surplus.
d.   the extra taxes paid by firms as a result of their higher profits.

11.   Arguments in favor of trade restrictions include

a.   strategic trade policies.
b.   national defense considerations.
c.   infant industry arguments.
d.   all of the above.

12.   To encourage the development of new firms in a particular country is an example of the

a.   infant industry argument.
b.   retaliation argument.
c.   environmental standards argument.

    d.    labor standards argument.

13.  The stockpiling of strategic materials is an alternative to

    a.    tariffs.
    b.    antidumping rules.
    c.    infant industry arguments for restricting trade.
    d.    national security arguments for restricting trade.

14.  According to a story written by Frédéric Bastiat,

    a.    French candle makers wanted trade protection from the sun.
    b.    infant industries need protection.
    c.    quotas are better than tariffs in generating revenue for the government.
    d.    it rains in Spain, but mainly on the plain.

15.  GATT is an example of

    a.    how nontariff trade barriers are formed.
    b.    unilateral disarmament.
    c.    multilateral negotiations.
    d.    a customs union.

16.  Recently, China

    a.    signed VRA agreements with the United States.
    b.    increased its quotas.
    c.    was granted MFN status.
    d.    was fined under its GATT status.

17.  A disadvantage of a regional trading area is

    a.    the lack of a common currency.
    b.    trade diversion.
    c.    the tendency to have trade wars within the area.
    d.    that there are fewer countries involved than in multilateral negotiations.

18.  If tariffs are increased, the export supply curve

    a.    does not shift.
    b.    decreases (shifts upward).
    c.    increases (shifts downward).
    d.    becomes perfectly inelastic.

19.  Quotas

    a.    cause the price of imports to fall.
    b.    reduce the quantity of imports.
    c.    raise revenue for the government.
    d.    cause all of the above to happen.

20.  If import demand is perfectly inelastic and a tariff is levied,

    a.    foreign suppliers will pay all of the tariff.
    b.    the government will collect no revenue.
    c.    quotas are needed to shift export supply downward.
    d.    consumers will pay all of the tariff.

# ANSWERS TO THE REVIEW QUESTIONS

## Fill-in Questions

1.   ad valorem tariff

2.   imported good

3.   export supply curve

4.   Quotas

5.   Tariffs

6.   voluntary restraint agreement (VRA); voluntary export restraint (VER)

7.   voluntary restraint agreements (VRAs)

8.   Environmental; labor standards; nontariff trade barriers

9.   fallen

10.   Smoot-Hawley tariff

11.   Reciprocal Trade Agreement Act of 1934; General Agreement on Trade and Tariffs (GATT)

12.   average costs; antidumping duties

13.   strategic trade policy

14.   infant industry

15.   unilateral disarmament

16.   most-favored nation status (MFN); Smoot-Hawley tariffs

## True-False Questions

1.   **False**.    It shifts the export supply curve upward.

2.   **True**.    Tariffs create revenues for the government and are called duties.

3.   **False**.    A quota is imposed by the importing country. With a VRA, the foreign government (in the exporting country) agrees to limit exports. Quotas and VRAs have similar market effects.

4.   **True**.    This is an example of a nontariff trade barrier.

5.   **False**.    Tariffs have a long history in the United States. However, tariffs are a declining source of revenue for the government. This has been especially true since 1910.

6.   **True**.    In fact, the Smoot-Hawley tariffs have been cited as one reason for the length and depth of the Great Depression of the 1930s.

7.   **True**.    Dumping occurs when a foreign producer sells in a foreign country at a price below average cost or below the price in the home country. There is antidumping legislation in the United States.

8.   **False**.    Tariffs possibly benefit one country at the expense of another. Thus, such actions cannot be mutually beneficial.

9.   **True**.    This argument claims that certain things need to be produced during times of war. Depending on foreign suppliers might be dangerous. Thus, domestic producers need to exist.

10.    **False.**    Some areas of the economy are hurt by unilateral disarmament. With multilateral negotiations, there is a simultaneous tariff reduction among many countries.

11.    **True.**    A VRA is a voluntary restraint agreement. It is one method that governments use to manage trade.

12.    **False.**    NAFTA only removed tariffs and quotas that existed between the three countries.

## Short-Answer Questions

1.    Tariffs are essentially taxes that are levied on an imported product. They generate duties, or tax revenue, for the government. Quotas simply limit the amount of a product that can be imported. Quotas generate revenue for the quota holder.

2.    Yes. A VRA is a voluntary restraint agreement—for example, the U.S. government asks another government to voluntarily restrict exports to the United States. Thus, VRAs act like quotas. Foreign suppliers experience increases in profits.

3.    Often, foreign companies try to avoid VRAs by building factories in the restricted country. The products of these factories are called transplants.

4.    A nontariff trade barrier is anything that limits trade that is not a tariff or a quota. Examples include quality and performance standards, government procurement rules, regulatory rules and standards, and minimum content or fiber requirements.

5.    The Reciprocal Trade Agreement Act of 1934 gave President Roosevelt the authority to cut tariffs if other countries cut their own tariffs. This legislation successfully reduced tariffs from the levels imposed under Smoot-Hawley. This process of tariff reduction was so successful that it was made permanent by GATT in 1947.

6.    Dumping is a form of predatory pricing, and it is difficult to differentiate between predatory pricing (discussed in Chapter 16) and aggressive pricing that results from active competition.

7.    This is an argument used in favor of tariffs to protect an industry that is just getting started. Once the industry is established, the tariff on imports can be removed and competition proceeds. A problem with this argument is that infant industries never seem to grow up.

8.    The Uruguay Round is the latest round of multilateral trade negotiations under GATT. This was a meeting (a round) of countries that tried to come to an agreement on a list of tariff reductions and the removal of other trade restrictions. The Uruguay Round included a reform of GATT. It created the World Trade Organization (WTO) to deal with trade disputes between countries.

9.    Both are special trading areas within which barriers to trade between countries in the area are removed. However, external tariffs are the same for all countries in a customs union but may differ in a free trade area. Both forms may result in trade diversion.

10.    MFN stands for most-favored nation status. When tariffs are reduced under GATT, they are reduced for all countries with MFN status.

# SOLUTIONS TO THE PRACTICE PROBLEMS

1.

a.    Figure 18.3 shows a tariff that is paid completely by foreign suppliers.

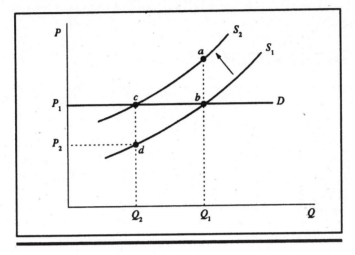

**Figure 18.3**

Assume that the pretariff export supply curve is $S_1$ and the pretariff demand curve is $D$. Note that demand is perfectly elastic at the free trade equilibrium price $P_1$. A tariff of amount $ab$ shifts the export supply curve up to $S_2$. Given the perfectly elastic demand curve, the market price remains at $P_1$ even though the quantity supplied falls from $Q_1$ to $Q_2$. Domestic consumers pay the same price as before the tariff. However, foreign producers get only $P_2$. The distance $P_1P_4$ is equal to the tariff $ab$. Thus foreign producers pay all of the tariff.

b.    Because of the perfect elasticity of the demand curve, the domestic price stays at $P_1$. The before and after tariff price is the same. However, after the tariff, foreign producers get only $P_2$ for their production. Thus, the government collects tariff revenue from foreign producers.

2.    Figure 18.4 can be used to communicate the value of a quota based on differing elasticities.

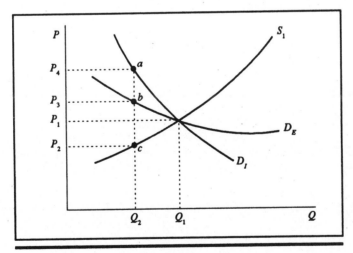

**Figure 18.4**

Assume that the export supply curve is $S_1$. Import demand curve $D_E$ is relatively more elastic than import demand curve $D_I$. Further, assume that free trade equilibrium is at $P_1$ and $Q_1$. If the quota allows imports of only $Q_2$, the quota holder will purchase this quantity from foreign suppliers for $P_2$. The price at which the quota holder sells the imports to domestic consumers depends on the slope of the demand curve. Clearly, the quota holder can get a higher price if market demand is $D_I$. The revenue earned by the quota in this case is shown by area $P_4P_2ca$, as opposed to $P_3P_2cb$, when demand is based on $D_E$. Thus, quota holders would like to face relatively inelastic import demand functions.

# ANSWERS TO THE CHAPTER TEST

1.  a
2.  b
3.  c
4.  d
5.  d
6.  c
7.  a
8.  d
9.  b
10. c
11. d
12. a
13. d
14. a
15. c
16. c
17. b
18. b
19. b
20. d

# CHAPTER 19

# Emerging Market Economies

## CHAPTER OVERVIEW

The demise of communism, exemplified by the tearing down of the Berlin Wall, the reunification of Germany, and the breakup of the Soviet Union, is one of the major events of the twentieth century. The emergence of market economies in China, Eastern Europe, and the former Soviet Union is of similar importance. In this chapter, we study these countries, called emerging market economies. We first learn about how centrally planned economies operate. We then study different paths that countries can follow as they make the transition to a market economy and see how economic reform has actually worked in practice. The success of these emerging market economies is perhaps the most important economic issue facing the world today, not only for themselves but also for the United States, Europe, and Japan. We all have a lot to gain if these countries can make a successful transition to market economies, and a lot to lose if they cannot.

## CHAPTER REVIEW

1.  *Emerging market economies* are those countries that are making the transition from central planning or tight government control to an economy based much more on markets and freely determined prices. These include China, Eastern Europe, and the republics of the former Soviet Union.

2.  In a market economy, also called **capitalism**, individuals own the capital—factories, farms, and machines—and decisions about production and employment are decentralized. In contrast, **socialism** is an economic system in which the government owns the capital and decisions regarding the economy are made by those who run the government as part of a central plan. **Communism** is a situation in which all the people of the country *collectively* own the capital without direct government ownership. While the former Soviet Union was called a communist country, its economic system was socialism.

3.  The former Soviet Union operated under a system of central planning, through which government commands determined what was produced. Private firms were taken over by the government, in a process called **nationalization**. The state planning commission, called **Gosplan**, established **five-year plans** that stipulated **production targets** for the economy. Production of most industrial and agricultural goods took place at **state enterprises** and **collectivized farms**, business firms and farms that were owned and controlled by the government. Prices for individual goods were also controlled by the government. These were rarely set at levels that would equate the quantity supplied with the quantity demanded, with resultant shortages and surpluses. Central planning in China followed a similar pattern.

4.  Reform of the central planning system in the Soviet Union began in 1985, when Mikhail Gorbachev became the leader of the Communist party. The process of reform began with **perestroika**, which translates as "restructuring." For example, enterprise managers were to be more accountable for their actions through worker and public criticism. Following the resignation of Gorbachev and the breakup of the Soviet Union in 1991, Boris Yeltsin, the president of Russia, disbanded central planning and began to enact more comprehensive reforms.

5. The goals of economic reform are simply the essential ingredients of a market economy. Prices must be freed and determined by competitive markets. A legal system must be established to specify property rights and enforce contracts. Freedom to trade at home and abroad is needed to realize economic efficiencies. A monetary system and a system of tax collections must be put into place.

6. How a centrally planned economy should make the transition to a market economy is more controversial than the ultimate goals of economic reform. A major question is how fast the transition should be. The alternatives are **shock therapy**, in which all the elements of the market economy are put in place at once, and **gradualism**, in which the reforms are phased in slowly.

7. **Privatization** is the process by which existing state enterprises are sold by the government, or privatized, and new private firms are allowed to start up. This process is necessary in order for a market economy to succeed.

## ZEROING IN

1. How has economic reform worked in practice? For the countries of Eastern Europe and the republics of the former Soviet Union, the transition has been difficult. Most countries have deep recession, and for some the decline in real GDP has been comparable to that of the United States during the Great Depression.

2. While the transitions of all of the countries of Eastern Europe and the former Soviet Union have been difficult, their experiences have not been monolithic. While there are significant signs of improvement in most of the countries of Eastern and central Europe, Russia and the central Asian countries continue to suffer transition problems.

3. Poland was the first country in Eastern Europe to attempt a transition to a market economy, putting a reform program under way at the beginning of 1990. It is interesting to look at the Polish experience in more detail, for it may serve as a guide to the future prospects of other countries.

   a. The Polish stabilization program has several aspects. The government budget deficit was reduced sharply and most prices were deregulated. These reforms were instituted quickly, making Poland an example of the shock therapy approach to economic reform. Another important aspect of the Polish stabilization program involves the privatization of state enterprises. This part of the Polish reform program was instituted gradually.

   b. The most dramatic effect of the stabilization program was on inflation, which declined from an average of 420 percent in 1989 and 1990 to 25 percent in 1992. The cost of bringing down inflation can be seen by the decline in real GDP, which fell by 12 percent in 1990 and 7 percent in 1991. By 1992, however, real GDP had stopped falling and, by 1994, economic growth was 6 percent.

4. Market reform in China began in 1978, much earlier than in the former Soviet Union. In the agricultural sector, where the reforms occurred first, the growth rate of production has doubled since 1978. In the mid-1980s, reform spread to the industrial sector, and GDP growth increased rapidly. China has also reduced restrictions on foreign trade. Economic growth has remained strong throughout the 1990s.

# ACTIVE REVIEW

## Fill-In Questions

1. _____ are those countries that are making the transition from central planning or tight government control to a market-based economy.

2. A market economy is also called _____.

3. _____ is an economic system in which the government owns the capital.

4. _____ is an economic system in which all the people of the country own the capital.

5. Under a system of _____, the government determines what is produced.

6. The state planning commission of the former Soviet Union was called _____.

7. In the former Soviet Union, Gosplan established _____.

8. Five-year plans in the former Soviet Union stipulated _____ for the economy.

9. Production of most industrial goods in the former Soviet Union took place at _____.

10. Production of most agricultural goods in the former Soviet Union took place at _____.

11. The process of reform in the former Soviet Union began with _____, which translates as "restructuring."

12. The goals of economic reform are to establish the essential ingredients of a(n) _____ economy.

13. Two alternative paths for making the transition to a market economy are _____ and _____.

14. _____ is the process by which existing state enterprises are sold by the government.

15. _____ was the first country in Eastern Europe to attempt a transition to a market economy.

## True-False Questions

1. T   F   Emerging market economies are those countries that are adopting central planning.

2. T   F   Russia is an example of an emerging market economy.

3. T   F   Poland is an example of an emerging market economy.

4. T   F   Socialism is an economic system in which the government owns the capital.

5. T   F   Capitalism is an economic system in which the government owns the capital.

6. T   F   The economic system of the former Soviet Union was communism.

7. T   F   In the former Soviet Union, government commands determined what was produced.

8. T   F   Central planning in the Soviet Union was disbanded in 1985.

9. T   F   The ultimate goals of economic reform are not a matter of much controversy.

10. T  F    In order for a centrally planned economy to make the transition to a market economy, the reforms need to be phased in slowly.

11. T  F    Economic reform can succeed without privatization.

12. T  F    Economic reform in the countries of Eastern Europe and the former Soviet Union has been relatively painless.

13. T  F    The countries of Eastern and central Europe have had fewer transition problems than Russia and the central Asian countries.

14. T  F    Market reform in China began later than in the former Soviet Union.

15. T  F    Market reform in China has been a failure.

## Short-Answer Questions

1. What are emerging market economies?

2. Which countries are classified as emerging market economies?

3. What is socialism?

4. Where did production of most goods in the former Soviet Union take place?

5. Why were there often shortages and surpluses of goods in the former Soviet Union?

6. How were production targets set for the economy in the former Soviet Union?

7. What was perestroika?

8. What are the goals of economic reform?

9. What are the alternative paths that a centrally planned economy can follow in order to make the transition to a market economy?

10. What is privatization?

11. What aspects of the Polish stabilization program were instituted quickly?

12. What aspect of the Polish stabilization program was instituted more gradually?

13. What happened to inflation during the Polish stabilization program?

14. What happened to real GDP during the Polish stabilization program?

15. What happened to economic growth in China following market reform?

## WORKING IT OUT

1. Analyzing economic performance during a transition from central planning is in some ways different from and in some ways the same as evaluating the performance of a market economy.

   a. A key element in macroeconomic analysis for the United States is the monetary policy rule that the Fed increases the interest rate when inflation rises. For the countries of Eastern Europe and the former Soviet Union, the policy rule is very different. During the past few years, government budget deficits have been very large. These deficits have been too large to finance through borrowing, and central banks have been forced to accelerate money growth in order to finance the deficits. With prices freed from central control, inflation has skyrocketed. The link between government budget deficits and inflation is much tighter for these countries than for the United States.

b. The magnitude of the inflation and recession experienced by the countries of Eastern Europe and the former Soviet Union dwarfs the problems faced by the United States. When we discussed the rise of inflation in the United States in the 1970s and its fall in the 1980s, we were talking about an increase from 3 percent to 10 percent, with a subsequent fall back to 3 percent. For Russia and Ukraine, the two largest former republics of the Soviet Union, inflation was over 1,000 percent in 1992. In addition, the decline in real GDP in some of these countries has been nearly as large as the decline in real GDP in the United States during the Great Depression.

2. The issue of credibility, which we have discussed in the context of the cost of lowering government budget deficits and reducing inflation for the United States, is even more important for countries making a transition from central planning to a market economy.

a. An important element in our macroeconomic analysis has been the assumption that prices are sticky. For the countries of Eastern Europe and the former Soviet Union, prices, which were suddenly freed from decades of government control, have fluctuated dramatically. If the government's anti-inflation policy is credible, it is possible, at least in theory, for inflation to be brought down at relatively low cost. This appears to be what has occurred in Poland. If the anti-inflation policy is not credible, a large recession will be needed to reduce inflation. While it is too early to evaluate most of the reform programs, this may characterize most of the countries of the former Soviet Union.

b. Achieving credibility is one argument for a shock therapy program. When all of the elements of a market economy are put in place at once, there is no doubt about the government's commitment to reform. With a gradualist approach, where the reforms are phased in slowly, you are never sure if the next step toward reform will actually occur.

## Worked Problems

1. Consider two emerging market economies characterized by the following data:

| Year | Country A | | Country B | |
|------|-----------|-----------|-----------|-----------|
| | **Real GDP Growth** | **Inflation** | **Real GDP Growth** | **Inflation** |
| 2001 | 0 | 100 | 0 | 100 |
| 2002 | −20 | 90 | −5 | 95 |
| 2003 | −15 | 20 | −7 | 90 |
| 2004 | −1 | 10 | −9 | 85 |
| 2005 | 1 | 10 | −7 | 80 |

Both real GDP growth and inflation are measured in percent per year. Which of these countries is characterized by a policy of shock therapy, and which is an example of a policy of gradualism?

**Answer**

*Country A is characterized by a policy of shock therapy. There is a very large recession, but inflation is brought down relatively quickly. Country B is an example of a policy of gradualism. The recession is smaller, but inflation is brought down only very slowly.*

2.    Consider two emerging market economies characterized by the following data:

| Year | Country A | | Country B | |
|---|---|---|---|---|
| | **Real GDP Growth** | **Inflation** | **Real GDP Growth** | **Inflation** |
| 2001 | 0 | 100 | 0 | 100 |
| 2002 | −30 | 90 | −15 | 90 |
| 2003 | −25 | 20 | −10 | 20 |
| 2004 | −5 | 10 | 0 | 10 |
| 2005 | 0 | 10 | 1 | 10 |

Both real GDP growth and inflation are measured in percent per year. Both countries have instituted shock therapy reform programs. Which government has greater credibility?

**Answer**

*With credibility, inflation can be brought down at lower cost. Inflation falls at the same rate in the two countries, but the recession is more severe in country A than in country B. Therefore, the government of country B has greater credibility.*

# PRACTICE PROBLEMS

1.    Consider two emerging market economies characterized by the following data:

| Year | Country A | | Country B | |
|---|---|---|---|---|
| | **Real GDP Growth** | **Inflation** | **Real GDP Growth** | **Inflation** |
| 2001 | 0 | 100 | 0 | 100 |
| 2002 | −10 | 90 | −25 | 95 |
| 2003 | −15 | 87 | −30 | 90 |
| 2004 | −15 | 83 | −9 | 20 |
| 2005 | −12 | 80 | −2 | 10 |

Both real GDP growth and inflation are measured in percent per year. Which of these countries is characterized by a policy of shock therapy, and which is an example of a policy of gradualism?

2.    Consider two emerging market economies characterized by the following data:

| Year | Country A | | Country B | |
|---|---|---|---|---|
| | **Real GDP Growth** | **Inflation** | **Real GDP Growth** | **Inflation** |
| 2001 | 0 | 100 | 0 | 100 |
| 2002 | −40 | 90 | −35 | 95 |
| 2003 | −10 | 15 | −30 | 90 |
| 2004 | 0 | 5 | −5 | 15 |
| 2005 | 2 | 5 | −1 | 15 |

Both real GDP growth and inflation are measured in percent per year. Are these two countries characterized by policies of shock therapy or by policies of gradualism?

3.　Consider two emerging market economies characterized by the following data:

| Year | Country A | | Country B | |
|------|-----------|---|-----------|---|
| | **Real GDP Growth** | **Inflation** | **Real GDP Growth** | **Inflation** |
| 2001 | 0 | 100 | 0 | 100 |
| 2002 | −20 | 95 | −35 | 95 |
| 2003 | −15 | 30 | −30 | 30 |
| 2004 | −2 | 10 | −20 | 10 |
| 2005 | −1 | 10 | −10 | 10 |

Both real GDP growth and inflation are measured in percent per year. Both countries have instituted shock therapy reform programs. Which government has greater credibility?

4.　Consider two emerging market economies characterized by the following data:

| Year | Country A | | Country B | |
|------|-----------|---|-----------|---|
| | **Real GDP Growth** | **Inflation** | **Real GDP Growth** | **Inflation** |
| 2001 | 0 | 100 | 0 | 100 |
| 2002 | −4 | 95 | −6 | 95 |
| 2003 | −6 | 90 | −8 | 90 |
| 2004 | −4 | 85 | −6 | 85 |
| 2005 | −3 | 80 | −5 | 80 |

Both real GDP growth and inflation are measured in percent per year. Both countries have instituted gradualist reform programs. Which government has greater credibility?

# CHAPTER TEST

1.　A market economy in which decisions about production and employment are decentralized and individuals own the factories, farms, and machines is called

　　a.　socialism.
　　b.　capitalism.
　　c.　communism.
　　d.　central planning.

2.　Which of the following countries is *not* classified as an emerging market economy?

　　a.　Hungary
　　b.　Romania
　　c.　Germany
　　d.　Bulgaria

3.　An economic system in which the government owns the capital and decisions regarding the economy are made as part of a central plan is called

　　a.　socialism.
　　b.　capitalism.
　　c.　communism.
　　d.　a market economy.

4.    An economic system in which all the people of the country own the capital is called

    a.    socialism.
    b.    capitalism.
    c.    communism.
    d.    a market economy.

5.    Which of the following is *not* one of the essential ingredients of a market economy?

    a.    Prices must be freed and determined by competitive markets.
    b.    A legal system must be established to specify property rights and enforce contracts.
    c.    A monetary system and a system of tax collections must be put in place.
    d.    Protectionist trade policies should be followed.

6.    The state planning commission of the former Soviet Union was called

    a.    Gosplan.
    b.    central planning.
    c.    perestroika.
    d.    Gorbachev.

7.    The process by which existing state enterprises are sold by the government and new private firms are allowed to start up is called

    a.    gradualism.
    b.    shock therapy.
    c.    privatization.
    d.    restructuring.

8.    The process of reform in the former Soviet Union began with

    a.    Gosplan.
    b.    central planning.
    c.    privatization.
    d.    perestroika.

9.    A transition to a market economy, when the reforms are phased in slowly, is called

    a.    gradualism.
    b.    shock therapy.
    c.    Gosplan.
    d.    perestroika.

10.    Which of the following countries was the first in Eastern Europe to attempt a transition to a market economy?

    a.    Hungary
    b.    Poland
    c.    Romania
    d.    Bulgaria

11.    What happened to real GDP during the Polish stabilization program in 1994?

    a.    Real GDP rose by 6 percent.
    b.    Real GDP rose by 12 percent.
    c.    Real GDP declined by 7 percent.
    d.    Real GDP did not change.

12. What happened to inflation in Poland between 1990 and 1992?

    a. Inflation declined from 42 percent to 25 percent.
    b. Inflation rose from 25 percent to 42 percent.
    c. Inflation declined from 420 percent to 25 percent.
    d. Inflation was unchanged.

13. Which of the following was *not* one of the aspects of the Polish stabilization program?

    a. The government budget deficit was reduced sharply.
    b. State enterprises were privatized.
    c. The government budget deficit was financed through borrowing.
    d. Most prices were deregulated.

14. Which of the following does *not* characterize market reform in China?

    a. Reform in China first occurred in the agricultural sector.
    b. Reform in China began after reform in the former Soviet Union.
    c. Restrictions on foreign trade have been reduced.
    d. Inflation has been a problem.

15. Following market reform in China, GDP growth

    a. increased rapidly.
    b. increased slowly.
    c. decreased rapidly.
    d. decreased slowly.

16. Which of the following was *not* one of the difficulties that the countries of Eastern Europe and the republics of the former Soviet Union experienced during the transition?

    a. High inflation
    b. Deep recession
    c. Rising government budget deficits
    d. Deflation

17. For the countries of Eastern Europe and the former Soviet Union, central banks have financed government budget deficits by

    a. borrowing.
    b. accelerating money growth.
    c. increasing the interest rate.
    d. spending more.

18. In Russia, in 1992, inflation was over

    a. 5 percent.
    b. 50 percent.
    c. 1,000 percent.
    d. 500 percent.

Use the following table for questions 19 and 20.

| Year | Country A | | Country B | |
|------|-----------------|-----------|-----------------|-----------|
|      | **Real GDP Growth** | **Inflation** | **Real GDP Growth** | **Inflation** |
| 2001 | 0   | 100 | 0  | 100 |
| 2002 | −25 | 95  | −6 | 95  |
| 2003 | −20 | 25  | −8 | 90  |
| 2004 | −4  | 8   | −6 | 85  |
| 2005 | 2   | 8   | −5 | 80  |

19. Which of these countries is (are) characterized by a policy of gradualism?

    a. Country A
    b. Country B
    c. Neither country A nor country B
    d. Both country A and country B

20. Which of these countries experienced the largest recession?

    a. Country A
    b. Country B
    c. The recessions were equally severe.
    d. Not enough information to tell

# ANSWERS TO THE REVIEW QUESTIONS

## Fill-In Questions

1. Emerging market economies
2. capitalism
3. Socialism
4. Communism
5. central planning
6. Gosplan
7. five-year plans
8. production targets
9. state enterprises
10. collectivized farms
11. perestroika
12. market
13. shock therapy; gradualism
14. Privatization
15. Poland

# True-False Questions

1.  **False.**    Emerging market economies are those countries that are making the transition from central planning to an economy based much more on markets.

2.  **True.**    Russia is one of the republics of the former Soviet Union.

3.  **True.**    Poland is a formally centrally planned economy in Eastern Europe.

4.  **True.**    Under socialism, the government owns the capital and decisions regarding the economy are made by those who run the government as part of a central plan.

5.  **False.**    Under capitalism, individuals own the capital.

6.  **False.**    Although the former Soviet Union was called a communist country, its economic system was socialism.

7.  **True.**    The former Soviet Union operated under a system of central planning.

8.  **False.**    Although economic reform began in 1985, central planning was not disbanded until after the breakup of the Soviet Union in 1991.

9.  **True.**    The goals of economic reform, the essential ingredients of a market economy, are widely agreed upon.

10. **False.**    An alternative is to put all of the elements of a market economy in place at once.

11. **False.**    Privatization is necessary if a market economy is to succeed.

12. **False.**    The transition has been difficult. Most countries have experienced high inflation and deep recession.

13. **True.**    While there are significant signs of improvement in most of the countries of Eastern and central Europe, Russia and the central Asian countries continue to suffer transition problems.

14. **False.**    Market reform in China began in 1978, much earlier than in the former Soviet Union.

15. **False.**    Economic growth in China has been very rapid since market reform.

# Short-Answer Questions

1.  Emerging market economies are those countries that are making the transition from central planning or tight government control to an economy based much more on markets and freely determined prices.

2.  Emerging market economies include China, Eastern Europe, and the republics of the former Soviet Union.

3.  Socialism is an economic system in which the government owns the capital and decisions regarding the economy are made as part of a central plan.

4.  Production of most goods took place at state enterprises and collectivized farms.

5.  Prices for individual goods, which were controlled by the government, were rarely set at levels that would equate the quantity supplied with the quantity demanded.

6.  Gosplan, the state planning commission, established five-year plans that stipulated production targets for the economy.

7.  Perestroika, which translates as "restructuring," was the beginning of the process of reform in the former Soviet Union.

8.  The goals of economic reform are freely determined prices, property rights and incentives, competitive markets, freedom to trade at home and abroad, a role for government in establishing monetary and fiscal policy, and a role for nongovernment organizations.

9.  The alternative paths are shock therapy, in which all the elements of the market economy are put in place at once, and gradualism, in which the reforms are phased in slowly.

10. Privatization is the process by which existing state enterprises are sold by the government and new private firms are allowed to start up.

11. The government budget deficit was reduced sharply and most prices were deregulated quickly.

12. Privatization of state enterprises is the aspect of the Polish stabilization program that was instituted more slowly.

13. Inflation fell dramatically in Poland between 1990 and 1992.

14. Real GDP in Poland declined sharply in 1990 and 1991, but rose significantly by 1994.

15. Economic growth in China has been very rapid.

## SOLUTIONS TO THE PRACTICE PROBLEMS

1.  Country A is an example of gradualism, whereas country B is characterized by shock therapy.

2.  Both country A and country B are examples of shock therapy.

3.  The government of country A has greater credibility.

4.  The government of country A has greater credibility.

## ANSWERS TO THE CHAPTER TEST

1. b
2. c
3. a
4. c
5. d
6. a
7. c
8. d
9. a
10. b
11. a
12. c
13. c
14. b
15. a
16. d

17. b
18. c
19. b
20. a

# PART 5

# Sample Test: (Chapters 17–19) Trade and Global Markets

## SAMPLE TEST QUESTIONS

1.  Adam Smith explained trade between countries by

    a.  absolute advantage.
    b.  the Heckscher-Ohlin model.
    c.  Arrow's impossibility theorem.
    d.  comparative advantage.
    e.  tides.

2.  According to the Heckscher-Ohlin model, a country will export those goods that are

    a.  produced most intensively with its least abundant resource.
    b.  produced most intensively with its most abundant resource.
    c.  capital-intensive.
    d.  produced the least intensively with its most abundant resource.
    e.  produced the least intensively with its least abundant resource.

3.  Intraindustry trade is defined as trade

    a.  limited to a small group of trading partners.
    b.  without any trade restrictions.
    c.  between countries in goods from different industries.
    d.  between countries in goods from the same or similar industries.
    e.  primarily due to economies of scale.

4.  International trade based on comparative advantage achieved through differences in capital per worker will tend to

    a.  equalize wages in different countries.
    b.  widen the wage gap in different countries.
    c.  lower wages for technological jobs in high-productivity countries.
    d.  cancel out any equalizing trends in different countries.

5.  Even though transition to free trade is beneficial in the long run, it can cause problems in the short run, unless phaseout of restrictions is

    a.  immediate.
    b.  tempered by the placement of new restrictions.
    c.  slow.
    d.  limited to nonmanufacturing industries.

6.  The use of quotas to give domestic industries time to develop is

    a.  the national security argument for trade barriers.
    b.  the infant industry argument for trade barriers.

   c.    required for product differentiation to occur.

   d.    supported under the Heckscher-Ohlin model.

   e.    strategic trade policy.

7.   Governments attempt to influence trade with

   a.    tariffs.

   b.    quotas.

   c.    procurement regulations.

   d.    VRAs.

   e.    all of the above.

8.   We can measure the impact of trade restrictions on an economy by the deadweight

   a.    loss caused by the increase in quantity.

   b.    gain caused by the reduction in quantity.

   c.    loss caused by the reduction in quantity.

   d.    gain caused by the increase in quantity.

9.   Those who benefit from protection

   a.    lobby their governmental representatives heavily.

   b.    do not lobby their governmental representatives.

   c.    are indifferent toward their governmental representatives.

   d.    are more diffuse and have less power.

10.   A possible reason for a government to deviate from free trade is

   a.    to promote a strategic trade policy when domestic firms have a monopoly or considerable market power.

   b.    to retaliate against another countrys trade restrictions.

   c.    to encourage development of an infant industry by protecting it from imports.

   d.    national security.

   e.    all of the above.

11.   Emerging market economies are countries making the transition from

   a.    central planning or tight government control to an economy based much more on markets and freely determined prices.

   b.    markets and freely determined prices to an economy based much more on central planning or tight government control.

   c.    free trade to managed trade.

   d.    managed trade to free trade.

12.   Which of the following is *not* one of the goals of economic reform?

   a.    Prices must be freed and determined by competitive markets.

   b.    A legal system must be established to specify property rights and enforce contracts.

   c.    Decisions about production and employment must be centralized.

   d.    A monetary system and a system of tax collections must be put into place.

13.   An economic system in which the government owns the capital and decisions regarding the economy are made as part of a central plan is called

   a.    socialism.

   b.    capitalism.

   c.    communism.

   d.    a market economy.

14.   A communist system is *best* described as an economic system where

    a.   the government owns the land and the capital and makes decisions about production and employment.

    b.   the government is involved in the economy because of market failures.

    c.   the people of a country collectively own the land and capital and make decisions about production and employment.

    d.   prices are determined in a decentralized fashion.

15.   Perestroika was

    a.   an attempt by the Soviet Union to free trade.

    b.   an attempt by the Soviet Union to reform centralized planning.

    c.   an attempt by the Soviet Union to make its economic system more centralized.

    d.   a plan for dismembering the Soviet Union.

## ANSWERS TO THE SAMPLE TEST

1.  a
2.  b
3.  d
4.  a
5.  c
6.  b
7.  e
8.  c
9.  a
10. e
11. a
12. c
13. a
14. c
15. b